AL SIEBER

Chief of Scouts

BY DAN L. THRAPP

Foreword by Donald E. Worcester

UNIVERSITY OF OKLAHOMA PRESS
NORMAN AND LONDON

To Grace and Frank Thrapp,
my parents, who bestowed upon me a
love for frontier history, a recognition
of bravery, integrity, and devotion to
duty, and an appreciation for the
unappreciated.

Library of Congress Cataloging-in-Publication Data

Thrapp, Dan L.
    Al Sieber : chief of scouts / by Dan L. Thrapp ; foreword by
Donald E. Worcester.
        p.   cm.
    Includes bibliographical references and index.
    ISBN 0–8061–2770–8 (alk. paper)
    1. Sieber,   Al.   2. Scouts   and   scouting—Arizona—Biography.
3. Apache Indians—Wars. 4. Indians of North America—Wars—
1866–1895.   5. Frontier and pioneer life—Arizona.   6. Arizona—
History—To 1912. I. Title.
F811.T5S5   1995
979.1'04'092—dc20
[B]   95-8305
                                                                        CIP

The paper in this book meets the guidelines for permanence and durability of the Committee on Production Guidelines for Book Longevity of the Council on Library Resources, Inc. ∞

2   3   4   5   6   7   8   9   10   11

Foreword

THE LATE NINETEENTH-CENTURY Apache wars in Arizona undoubtedly involved some of the most strenuous campaigning ever
undertaken by American soldiers. Apache hideouts were in extremely rugged mountains, and many of the expeditions against them took
place during midwinter. Deep snow, freezing temperatures, and icy
gales made life miserable for the troopers, who were often out in the
field a month at a time. Under such conditions they experienced
great difficulty in locating the elusive Apaches in their native terrain.
To ensure more successful expeditions, the troops turned to scouts,
both white and Indian, to track down and locate the Apaches.

General George Crook, who was Commander of the Department of Arizona from 1871 to 1875 and again in the 1880s,
discovered by experimenting what none of his predecessors had
learned—only Apaches could catch Apaches. Thereafter, he relied
heavily on Apaches both as scouts and as fighting men under
civilian scouts, a practice General Philip Sheridan frowned on
because it reflected poorly on the fighting ability of the cavalry.

The detachments sent after hostile Apaches typically were a
combination of Apache scouts and U.S. troops. Crook advised
recruiting the "wildest" Apaches as scouts, for they enjoyed
battle and knew of their kindred's hiding places as well. Such
Apaches, often enemies one day and scouts for the cavalry the
next, required unusual men to control them and ensure their
loyalty. Crook was fortunate in being able to hire some excellent
white scouts to manage the Apaches, of which the very best was
German-born Albert Sieber.

Sieber's ability to control the fiercest Apaches and to use them effectively against renegades was indeed extraordinary. When asked to explain the secret of his success in managing the Apache scouts, he replied, "I do not deceive them but always tell them the truth. When I tell them I am going to kill them, I do it, and when I tell them I am their friend, they know it."

In 1866, after serving in the Civil War with the First Minnesota Volunteers and being wounded at Gettysburg, Sieber headed west and eventually reached California. From there he helped drive a herd of horses to Arizona Territory, and then he turned to managing a ranch near Prescott for a few years while doing some prospecting. Pursuits of Apache raiders were frequent around Prescott, and soon he began learning the rudiments of scouting from Dan O'Leary, one of the best scouts.

When General Crook launched his campaign against the Apaches in 1872, Sieber signed on as a scout. This was to be his calling for the next two decades, and his successes made him well known and respected throughout the territory. Most of the punitive operations he accompanied against the Apaches were highly successful, and those operations from which he was absent met with few triumphs. Perhaps the greatest tribute to his abilities was paid by a San Carlos Apache who, although strongly contemplating it, decided against bolting the reservation, no matter how miserable life might become, because, he said, Sieber would find him even if he left no tracks.

According to the author, Dan L. Thrapp, Sieber was involved in more Indian fights than Daniel Boone, Jim Bridger, and Kit Carson combined. He took part in scores of Apache hunts because it was difficult for the nomadic Apaches to give up their freedom—some never were reconciled to reservation life. The deadly raids and killings by these renegade Apaches made it necessary for U.S. troops to hunt them down and eliminate them. Later, cheating contractors and dishonest agents forced some starving Apaches to make a break out of desperation. The main reason the Apache wars were prolonged for a decade, however, was because of the government's ill-advised concentration policy, which motivated

iv

the Army to reassign Crook to Arizona in an effort to force the Apaches into the reservation system.

This book is not a full-fledged biography of Sieber. At times he will be absent from the narrative of a particular segment of the Apache wars, for his name does not appear in every historical record. More importantly, he is part of a larger story of a scout's involvement in the Apache wars. If more records existed on Sieber, I am confident the author would have found them, for he was a peerless researcher. One of the great values of this book, in addition to relating the feats of one of Arizona's most respected pioneers, is that almost every reference to an individual or a place, however obscure, is identified in a footnote. These notes, together with the excellent bibliography, make the book invaluable for anyone researching Arizona in the territorial era.

Dan L. Thrapp (1913–1994) was the author of six books on the Apache wars and a leading authority on the subject, with two of his most highly praised works being the present volume (1964) and *The Conquest of Apacheria* (1967). His final work was the monumental three-volume *Encyclopedia of Frontier Biography* (1988), with a supplemental volume completed not long before his death. All Western historians are in his debt, as are all who care deeply about our heritage.

DONALD E. WORCESTER

Fort Worth, Texas
December, 1994

Preface

AL SIEBER took part in more Indian fights than Daniel Boone, Jim Bridger, and Kit Carson together. He shot more red adversaries than all of them combined. Yet he was as well loved and respected by the Indians he fought as were any of the great scouts of American history.

It has been said that in the course of slaying half a hundred or more hostiles Al was wounded twenty-nine times by Indian arrow, knife, or bullet. This may possibly be true, for it was said and printed during his lifetime, and he never denied it—and Al Sieber was a blunt and honest man—although his recoverable record reveals but five wounds. He began his fighting career as a Civil War soldier and ended it, thirty years later, old and crippled and discredited in central Arizona. But those who sought to cast a shadow on his final days of service were not themselves without fault, and there is reason to believe that ulterior motives may have been responsible for their charges against him.

No one individual's life can fully illustrate those tumultuous years which decided the question of supremacy in the Southwest. The final great collision between two diverse races was not simple of solution, and many had a hand in resolving it. When Sieber's era began, the odds were with the red man—on the surface. When it ended, the Indian as a force to be reckoned with had ceased to exist. To a large extent, Al Sieber and men like him had brought this about. They were a unique breed, a type that never was before and never would be again, men of bravery, devotion, integrity, of lawfulness and lawlessness, kindliness and extreme callousness, men who could be deadly serious yet were full of lighthearted joy.

vii

I do not seek to glorify Al Sieber unduly, for to do so would be unhistorical. Sieber was a rough man, one who could be callous, although he was never cruel as that word is generally understood. My purpose is to show him for what he was: a man who operated at the focal point of events of moment and who had a real, sometimes decisive part in them. It would be an exaggeration to say that he made history, with the exception of a very few instances, in which he was sometimes acting in error; but he *helped* to make a lot of it, and the development of a vast region of America would have been quite different without him. For this reason alone he deserves a place, as those army officers who knew and worked with him often ranked him, alongside Kit Carson, Joe Walker, and the other great scouts and guides of the frontier West, for he is a part of the American saga.

The Indians Sieber fought are also part of that story. They were personified by such warriors as Big Rump, Eschetlepan, Delshay, Chan-deisi, and others whose names are lost to us now and whose deeds have perished with their people's memories. But the natives had still greater leaders—Victorio, Mangas Coloradas, Cochise, Juh, Nana, Chato—men so outstanding that not even their enemies could forget them. And what we know of them, for the most part, was written by their enemies.

So this is more than a biography. It is also a part of the story of that long and varied southwestern war, written as fairly as may be done from the evidence and records now available.

No book like this can be written alone. Acknowledgments will be found elsewhere, but here I would like to pay a tribute, however inadequate, to my long-suffering wife and family, who accompanied me on many of my field trips and who patiently bore with me during the preparation of the manuscript. Without their support and help, this volume could not have been completed.

DAN L. THRAPP

Whittier, California
January, 1964

Acknowledgments

IT SHOULD BE APPARENT that no book such as this can be written without help, and I would like to pay tribute here to the hundreds of people who have generously given of their time, their memories, and their talents in the preparation of *Al Sieber, Chief of Scouts*. For reasons of space, most of them must remain anonymous but there are some whose special contributions should be acknowledged.

Of particular help at every stage in assembling this book was Mrs. Clara T. Woody of Miami, Arizona, historian unrivaled of central Arizona, whose gracious generosity is equaled only by her knowledge of all phases of her chosen subject. Also of pre-eminent value to any writer on latter-day Apache Indian troubles is Thaddeus "Bud" Ming, who will never forgive me for here revealing his true first name. Bud, who lives in Ray, Arizona, was born during the turbulent days of San Carlos and is the son of Dan Ming, noted stockman and Indian fighter. His memory of various phases of the old days is exact and vivid. A special word should also be devoted to Mrs. Lillian T. Bennett of Minneapolis, who generously placed family recollections, Sieber letters and photographs, and other items at my disposal and answered my many questions as fully as possible. Mrs. J. F. Connor of Englewood, New Jersey, kindly permitted me to use her collection of the correspondence of Britton Davis and answered a large number of questions about it.

Mr. Watt P. Marchman of the Rutherford B. Hayes Memorial Library at Fremont, Ohio, lent me copies of that institution's vast collection of Crook documents.

Thanks and appreciation should also go to Walter A. Richards,

Burbank, California, without whose hospitality and generosity this project would have had a much slower start; Leroy Middleton of Phoenix, who pleasantly shared his recollections of Sieber and the Apache Kid story; Thad Frazier, Roosevelt, Arizona, who did the same with reference to Al's last weeks; Mrs. Gertrude Ellison Hill of Phoenix, who contributed photographs as well as Tonto Basin memories; San Carlos Superintendent Thomas H. Dodge; and L. Burr Belden, San Bernardino, California, whose knowledge of pioneer routes through his county is unsurpassed.

Air Force Sergeant John A. Perez, Everett Helm, and Mrs. Helen Martell are acknowledged for help in tracking down records of Sieber's birth in Germany. Mrs. Alta Brannan, Whittier, California, gave me the story of her ancestor, William H. Hardy. Also of appreciated assistance were Donald McIntosh, San Carlos, son of Archie McIntosh; Mrs. Margaret E. McNelly, Redwood City, California, who contributed photographs and recollections of Sieber and Bill McNelly at Globe; Mrs. Suzanne R. Snyder, Oatman, Arizona, the late Charles Battye of San Bernardino, and Paul Booth of Needles, California, who helped with the Dan O'Leary story; and Albert Francis French of Los Angeles and Mrs. Ora Townsend French of Prescott, who helped me with information regarding John Townsend. Much generous aid also was given by District Forest Ranger Perl Charles of Phoenix in exploring the Turret Mountain country.

Among Al Sieber's relatives and friends and the descendants of others who figured in Al's story, the following gave me assistance in a notable manner: William T. Corbusier of Long Beach, California; the late Mrs. John P. Clum of Los Angeles; Mrs. Sydney K. Davis, Atlanta; Mrs. Maggie Armer, Phoenix; Austin H. Oswald, Palo Alto, California; W. C. "Pecos" McFadden, Phoenix; Chet Wyant and Robert Riell, Globe; Mrs. Charles Crawford McLaughlin and Mrs. Nona Crawford Johnson, also of Globe; Mrs. Paul Stone, Cascade, Montana; Dr. C. S. Greusel, Houston; George S. Schaeffer, New York City; Louis Menager, Tucson; Frank T. Elsesser and Amy M. Vannet, Barnesville, Minnesota; and Mrs. Emmet Crawford Morton, Tumacacori, Arizona.

Special thanks are also due the late Jason Betzinez, an Apache who was once a hostile, and Colonel W. S. Nye, the editor who brought him to public attention; Mrs. Bertha Sieber of Lancaster, Pennsylvania; the Right Reverend Joseph J. Schweich, V.G., of St. Joseph's Catholic Church and the Reverend Mercurio A. Fragapane of St. Mary of the Assumption Catholic Church, both in Lancaster; Mrs. Alice Jack Shipman, Marfa, Texas, and City Editor Tom McGowan of the San Antonio *Express*, who helped me with the Bullis story; and Minneapolis Police Captain Donald W. Johnson.

Scholarly research depends upon assistance from the staffs of libraries and other repositories, and to the personnel of all of those I used go my deep thanks.

Particular mention should be made of Professor Martin F. Schmitt, University of Oregon Library, Eugene; the Arizona Pioneers' Historical Museum Library and its staff, including Historical Secretary Emeritus Mrs. George F. Kitt, Historical Secretaries Mrs. Eleanor B. Sloan and Mrs. Yndia S. Moore, Mrs. Sadie S. Schmidt, and Historian Ray Brandes; Mrs. Elsie M. Knight and Mrs. Lorine W. Garrett of the Sharlot Hall Historical Museum at Prescott; the late Mrs. Alice B. Good and Mrs. Marguerite B. Cooley of the Arizona State Library and Archives at Phoenix; Miss Haydée Noya of the Department of Manuscripts and Mrs. Frances King, both of the Huntington Library; John Barr Tompkins of the Bancroft Library; Mrs. Ella Robinson of the Southwest Museum Library at Los Angeles; Ruth Rambo of the Museum of New Mexico Library at Santa Fe; Mrs. Minnette Martin, Los Angeles County Library; and Mrs. Lucile B. German of the Fort Verde Museum at Camp Verde, Arizona.

At the National Archives in Washington, D.C., Archivist Josephine Cobb of the Still Pictures Branch, Jane F. Smith of Interior Department Records, and Victor Gondos, Jr., of the Old Army Branch, as well as David C. Mearns, chief of the Manuscript Division of the Library of Congress, were infinitely and skillfully helpful, and my deep appreciation goes to each and all of them.

The writings and firsthand accounts given me by the late Mrs. Emma Marble Muir of Lordsburg, New Mexico, proved to be quite useful, and so was the knowledge of George Kerr of that community.

Special help at various stages of preparing this book was given by

Mrs. Agnes Wright Spring of Denver; author Weldon Heald, Tucson; the late Milo M. Quaife of Detroit; authors J. Frank Dobie, Don Russell, Jay Monaghan, Ross Santee, Paul I. Wellman, Bert Fireman, and Roscoe Willson; historian W. W. Robinson of Los Angeles; historical writer Bill Murphy, also of Los Angeles; and librarians Romeo O. Carraro and E. Kenneth Hayes of the *Los Angeles Times*.

Needless to say, although the help of these people and many others was significant and vastly useful, any errors in this book—and there no doubt are some—are mine alone.

Contents

Illustrations

MAP

AL SIEBER

Chief of Scouts

I. The Immigrant

SPRING COMES EARLY to the valley of the Kraich River, sometimes even by late February, for the winters are mild and short along this chaste tributary of the Upper Rhine. But the February of 1844 was an exception, a wild and stormy month with snow and winds whipping the undistinguished hamlet of Mingolsheim.[1] It was a fitting time for the arrival of Albert Sieber, whose career was to prove as turbulent as the current weather, although his birth in the month of February came only by grace of leap year; he was born on the twenty-ninth.

Albert's father, Johann Sieber, "citizen, miller and farmer," as the dim old parish records put it (since the "miller" is sometimes omitted, one may conclude that he was more a farmer than anything else), and his mother, Katherina,[2] already had eight children, seven of whom still lived. There was Johann, the third generation to bear that name,[3]

[1] Mingolsheim, with a population today of some 3,200, is on the railroad midway between Heidelberg and Karlsruhe. Farming is the chief occupation of its people, and potatoes, wheat, corn, and other vegetables and grains are commonly raised, although tobacco (for the local cigar industry) and grapes (for wine) are the principal money crops. The Deutscher Wetterdienst Zentralamt confirms that in February, 1844, in this vicinity, "storms with rain and snow were quite frequent, which led to floods on February 26," and that the month was colder than normal. Correspondence with the author, February 27, 1959.

[2] In later life she was usually called Margaret, sometimes Barbara, but on legal documents she signed her name Katherina or Katherine, and the name so appears on parish records at Mingolsheim, where eight of her nine children were born.

[3] Young Johann's grandfather, Johann Sieber, the son of Maria Sibella and Friedrich Valetin Sieber, was born August 3, 1772, married Franziska Gorner, and died September 2, 1842. Their eldest son, Johann, was born May 19, 1799, presumably at Mingolsheim, one of six children. He married Katherina Fischer of Rothenburg; it is not known where the wedding took place, but it was neither at Rothenburg nor at Mingolsheim.

born at Rothenburg[4] on February 14, 1823, and, though still single, by this time a young adult with his mind full of strange political notions. And Barbara, first to be born at Mingolsheim, she and her twin sister, who had died at birth, arriving August 25, 1824; and Margarete, also called Gretchen, born October 1, 1829; and Peter, December 9, 1832; and Theresia, sometimes called Theresa, born November 13, 1834. The year 1838 had been full, with the arrival of Rudolph on January 27 and his sister Magdalena, nicknamed Lena, on November 5.

Albert Sieber was born into a land of almost idyllic beauty and gentleness, although vagrant whisps of unrest had already appeared on the political horizon. As yet, however, they had done little to dilute the sturdy Rhineland customs which grew from that region's rich traditions and lent it strength. Such a tradition, for example, was that of fine marksmanship, tested each Whitmonday at the *Schützenfest*, when the villages' expert shots fired at a wooden bird until they had destroyed it, the winner being he who blasted down the final bit of wood.[5] Albert, by the time he left the country, was far too young ever to have taken part in such a contest, but the tradition of the worth of shooting skill must have been imparted to him—and absorbed.

In 1845, the year after Albert was born, his father died. The impact of that tragedy was mitigated, however, by the sturdy qualities of his mother, who must have been a remarkable woman. She saw her large brood through vicissitudes scarcely imaginable to our generation. No doubt she received assistance from relatives and the older children, but the problems she faced must often have seemed virtually insurmountable to her, and yet she triumphed over them all.

Almost everyone in the Rhineland knew people who had emigrated abroad, and many had relatives who had done so; the Siebers prob-

---

[4] So says a parish record at Mingolsheim. However, an obituary of John Sieber, appearing in the Barnesville, Minnesota, *Record-Review* of August 19, 1909, states that he was born at Waldstetten, Baden, and gives the year as 1822. The source of this information is not known.

· [5] Carl Schurz, *The Reminiscences of Carl Schurz* (cited hereafter as Schurz, *Reminiscences*), I, 45–48. Schurz, whose account details the *Schützenfest* as he recalled it from his boyhood at Liblar, near Cologne, explains that similar events were held annually throughout Germany.

ably were no exception. They must have read and reread the occasional letters they received from those who had settled in unpronounceable Pennsylvania, telling of that far-off country, its beauties, its opportunities, its freedom. Why, some letters said, *you didn't even have to pay taxes in America!*

The urge for freedom, the notion that something better than the paternalistic feudalism of the Rhineland could be forged, was beginning in these years to take hold in Baden, the Palatinate, and other parts of Germany and Austria. Students and intellectuals became restless and talked of liberty; from them the feeling spread to the smallest hamlets. Among those deeply affected was Johann, Albert's oldest brother, who marked his twenty-fifth birthday early in 1848. He joined the burgeoning movement.

Toward the end of February, the French deposed Louis Philippe, proclaiming the Second Republic, and the fiery young men of the Rhine guessed, rightly, that the fever of republicanism would burn eastward. The *Marseillaise* became the hymn of liberty for much of Europe. There was ferment at Cologne, demonstrations at Coblenz, Düsseldorf, Aachen, and other Rhine towns. In Baden, Württemberg, Bavaria, and elsewhere the revolutionary spirit "burst forth like a prairie fire." At Vienna, blood flowed in the streets. Commotions occurred in Prussia. Fighting broke out, the most severe of it occurring in Baden and culminating at Rastatt Fortress, where the Forty-eighters made their last stand and were beaten.[6]

Yet their campaign was not entirely futile. "Years of political reaction and national humiliation followed in which all that the men of 1848 had stood for seemed utterly lost," wrote Carl Schurz, but eventually Bismarck became prime minister and through him there came about German unity and a national parliament. "Thus . . . a great and important part of the objects struggled for by the German revolutionists of 1848 was, after all, accomplished—much later, indeed, and less peaceably and less completely than they had wished,"

[6] Schurz, who was a prime mover, analyzes the causes and origin of the revolutionary movement of 1848 in *Reminiscences*, I, 102–109 and 262–69. Oddly, the revolutions of 1848–49 had no single leader or cabal at their head, although much inspiration came from philosopher Ludwig Andreas Feuerbach. He lacked the qualities of a popular leader, however.

but without the "national awakening" of 1848 they might have been impossible of accomplishment at all.[7] Albert Sieber could therefore take pride in the things his brother had fought for and, in the end, helped to win. There is evidence that he did so; many of his friends in later life were made very much aware that he was the brother of a Forty-eighter.

The exiles from Germany—and thousands of hotheaded young student-warriors did become such—filled the refugee centers of Europe. Sooner or later, many came to America, where large numbers of them assumed prominent roles in civil, political, and even military life. Schurz and scores of others, a young composer named Richard Wagner among them, escaped to Switzerland. Still others fled to Paris or Antwerp or London. Johann Sieber found his way to Le Havre. From there, about the middle of 1849, he wrote his mother at Mingolsheim and urged her to bring the family to Le Havre so that all might go to America and create a new and perhaps a better life.[8] She probably had little choice. Johann, the eldest son, was now nominal head of the family, and besides, the prospects of going to the United States must have seemed more alluring than those of remaining in strife-torn Baden.

So this unusual woman made her decision, bundled up the family equipage, sold her home or turned it over to relatives, loaded her brood and their belongings into a conveyance, and drove off. She must have realized, and her older children knew, that it was unlikely any of them would ever again return to this lovely land. What courage it must have required for this resolute mother to exchange the well-worn world she knew for something half-known and half-conceivable! What thoughts must have passed through her mind as she set out to guide her captainless expedition to the other side of the moon!

The Siebers reached Le Havre with no incident worth recording and found that Johann had already booked passage for New York.

[7] Schurz, *Reminiscences*, I, 404–405.

[8] Phoenix, Arizona, *Arizona Republican*, February 20, 1907 (cited hereafter as *Republican* obituary). This biography, which appeared the day after Al Sieber's death, was based on material previously supplied by the scout himself and is a prime source for information on his career.

He had written a brother-in-law[9] to meet them there, so when they embarked, they were spared the nagging worry of how to become introduced to their new homeland.

The covey of Siebers probably saw little of New York,[10] tidy community that it was, and soon no doubt were aboard a train, riding happily through a gritty cloud of cinders and acrid smoke toward Pennsylvania. Railroad fever had struck hard at the eastern United States by this time. Already nine thousand miles of lines had been sent sprawling along every conceivable route and in all directions from the seaboard. Some reached well toward the Middle West, although none had yet linked with the scattered rail patterns in Ohio, Indiana, Michigan, or Illinois. Even now the railroad was a *fait accompli* from New York to Philadelphia and well across Pennsylvania, which had more trackage than any other state. The future was plain to see. No wonder financiers, engineers, and dreamers were gripped by the craze to build a railroad. Any railroad. To anywhere. Albert, in the autumn of his life, would have a minor role in charting the course for one of the last lines to be built, but that was far off, in time and miles, in the still almost unknown Southwest.

The Siebers were carried westward by this reeking marvel to an inland town called Lancaster, in a county of the same name, one of the border counties of southern Pennsylvania. It was a booming com-

[9] *Republican* obituary. This may well have been Henry Rosenfeld, husband of Barbara, Al's oldest sister, who then was twenty-five; if so, it would mean that she had married and emigrated to America in advance of the rest of the family. Unfortunately, the newspaper account does not state of whom the individual was a brother-in-law. If of Mrs. Sieber, he would have been someone who married another Fischer girl, one of her sisters, but it seems likely that Al would have referred to this man, not as a brother-in-law, but, rather, as an uncle. Johann, Al's father, had four brothers but only one sister, Magdalena, who died at birth or shortly thereafter, so the brother-in-law could not have come from that side of the family. He must therefore have been a husband of Barbara or Gretchen, then twenty, and since the latter is believed to have married in this country, Barbara remains the most likely mate for this individual.

[10] The Barnesville *Record-Review* obituary states that John, his mother, "and other members of the family" emigrated to this country, "settled first in New York state, and two years later removed to Lancaster County, Pennsylvania." It is possible that John remained in New York, but every other account I have seen says the Siebers went directly to Lancaster from New York. Of possible significance is the fact that John first appears on parish records at Lancaster two years after the move from Europe.

munity, for those times. The county, which had reported only about 3,500 people in 1729, now had nearly 100,000 people; the town had grown from 15 souls to 12,369 in the same period. It was proud of its charcoal and anthracite furnaces, its glass works and foundries, which broke their backers as often as they enriched them. Lancaster was a suitable place for a family of immigrants to be introduced to America and her strange, bumbling, exuberant ways.

The countryside duplicated the Rhineland about as exactly as could be expected on another continent. The climate was a bit sharper, and perhaps the society more crude, but the Siebers could feel at home among descendants of the honest burghers who had migrated here from the banks of the Neckar and the Rhine. Much of the population was German or of German descent; religious conviction brought most of them. About 1711 the Mennonites from Zürich and Bern had come, then the Ephrata community of German mystics, and the Reformeds and Lutherans and Dunkers, and finally the self-reliant Moravians.[11] The Siebers were Catholic, and they soon found that others of their faith had preceded them. They became part of the parish of the Assumption of the Blessed Virgin Mary Church, established in 1742, but they arrived just as a petition was being sent to the Bishop, pointing out that there were too many parishioners now for the church and not saying what the Bishop already knew: that most of the petitioners were Germans and there were too many Irish in the parish to suit them. The good Bishop chuckled to himself and readily acceded to their request, appointing the Reverend Bernard Bayer, a Redemptorist, to organize another parish, called St. Joseph's, only a block and a half distant from St. Mary's. Twenty-five families, among them probably some of the Siebers, withdrew from St. Mary's in 1850 to found it.[12] Here and there they appear in the old parish records, or at least some of them do. It may be that the family was forced to split up and that some joined another parish. It appears that Barbara and her husband, Henry Rosenfeld, remained at St. Mary's, for their son, William, born in 1852, was baptized there on July 17, 1853.[13] At any

[11] H. M. J. Klein (ed.), *Lancaster County, Pennsylvania: A History*, I, 360.
[12] *Ibid.*, II, 1112.
[13] Sponsors of William were recorded as Charles and Catherina Seiber. The latter is

rate, the Siebers settled down for six or seven years—long enough so that Albert could say he was raised in Pennsylvania and some could get the impression that he was born there.[14]

Only John (as Johann henceforth called himself), the revolutionist, figures prominently in St. Joseph's records.[15] Two years after his arrival, he and an Elizabeth Hartmann, also from Germany, were married,[16] a union blessed with many children, none named for Albert, although most of his brothers and sisters were so honored. Maybe there just weren't enough babies to go around.

For any growing boy, Lancaster must have seemed a city of delights. The surrounding countryside was a wonderland of fields and woods and marshes and hills, heavily farmed in places but wild enough in others. The country roads, especially the Philadelphia pike, throbbed with traffic that featured the huge Conestoga wagons (named for Conestoga Creek, which wound through Lancaster) for which the region was famous. Originating among the thrifty German farmers, Conestogas had been built for almost a century and were

probably Katherina Sieber, but I don't know who Charles Seiber may have been. For this record I am indebted to the Reverend Mercurio A. Fregapane, assistant pastor of St. Mary of the Assumption Church.

[14] Britton Davis, *The Truth About Geronimo* (cited hereafter as Britton Davis, *Geronimo*), 35. When he voted in Arizona elections during the early 1880's, Sieber stated that he was a native of Pennsylvania. Jess G. Hayes, *Apache Vengeance* (cited hereafter as Hayes), 67n. Al was naturalized on October 30, 1889. Minutes of the Second Judicial District Court, Globe, Arizona, Book 2, 1889, p. 39.

[15] For copies of these I am indebted to the Right Reverend Monsignor Joseph J. Schweich, pastor of St. Joseph in 1960.

[16] The wedding took place on October 30, 1851, a Thursday. Elizabeth was recorded as the daughter of John Hartman and Catherine Mueller. John's first child, a daughter, was named Catherine Barbara, perhaps after Elizabeth's mother and John's mother and sister; this baby arrived June 12, 1852. Emma Theresa was born February 9, 1854; Mary Magdalene on June 13, 1856; Thecla on October 27, 1858 (she died the following March 3). John H. Sieber, who appears briefly later in this narrative, was born June 12, 1860, and lived the last forty-seven years of his life at Houston, Texas, where, through investments in real estate, he became a man of some means. He died there on November 30, 1947. Francis Rudolph Sieber was born February 22, 1862. He, too, died at Houston, on October 17, 1921; his occupation was listed as "hotel manager." Andrew William Sieber, the last child of this union of whom I have found record, was born on May 11, 1870, at Pittsburgh. A carpenter by trade, he eventually made his way west and lived for sixty years or more at Cascade, Montana, where he died on December 23, 1954.

9

usually drawn by four, five, or six horses of a distinctive breed that was also called Conestoga. In the fall it was not unusual to see fifty to one hundred such wagons each day, en route to Philadelphia, hauling the fresh produce for which Lancaster was renowned. Although built by a variety of craftsmen, the wagons were nearly uniform: top sheets of white canvas, blue bodies, red wheels and running gear, and black ironwork. Often the teams were of a single hue—all whites, or grays, or blacks, or bays, or even roans or sorrels. It was a matter of pride among good wagonmen to match their teams in color and conformation, and so well trained were the best of them that they could be driven by word of mouth alone, although the single rein pioneered by these Conestoga teamsters was used for emergencies.

Conestoga Creek was humming, too, with arks, flatboats, and rafts bringing coal, lumber, and ore from the Susquehanna River, a major waterway bordering the county, seventeen miles and seventeen chains, by meandering tributary, west of the city. Upstream traffic on the creek was now at a peak, but the stream's days were numbered: sometime during the Civil War the last vessel would traverse it and the picturesque route would fall into disuse.

Lancaster County, low and undulating, was well settled. The Indians had left the area long before, and with them went most of its combative spirit. It had sent a few men to the recent war with Mexico, and these had returned with improbable yarns about that remote country which no white man was apt to see again, but they found few listeners. The buffalo had vanished with the Indian. The beaver was no more, nor the elk. No wolf had been seen in the county since 1834, nor a panther, but small game was common, especially birds, for Lancaster was on a major migratory route. Overpowering by sheer weight of numbers and the mighty spectacle of their migrations were the passenger pigeons. People still talked about the last great flight of these birds the country would ever see. It had occurred in March, 1846, in the southern part of the county. Abraham R. Beck, then twelve, remembered it this way in later years:

> It was about 12:30 o'clock of a dull, cloudy day when the cry came, "The pigeons are flying!" I ran out to see a vast flight passing northward.

The western edge of the flock was approximately overhead. It extended eastward to the horizon. There were four or five pigeons to the square yard of sky—enough to cast a distinct shadow had there been sunshine. They flew in approximately this formation continuously until about 4:30. A mighty detachment left the main flock to settle for the night in a nearby woodland where the mass of their piling numbers broke branches from the trees. The birds were low enough to be within range of the crude shotguns of the village and a number were shot.[17]

If Albert Sieber was like other boys, he prowled the woods of oaks, shellbark hickories, and hemlocks whenever he could escape household chores, and he must have found it a good life. But like all things, it had to end. Theresia, by now almost twenty-two, had caught the eye of one Henry Oswald, an enterprising young man with a talent for business and a yearning for far places. Henry and Theresia were married, apparently in 1856, for in that year they moved to Minneapolis,[18] and once more Katherina Sieber gathered up her belongings —and Albert. Where this daughter went, she would go. Albert, of course, could scarcely have been reluctant.

It would be another two years before the Pennsylvania Railroad could complete its line to Pittsburgh, but a consolidation of haphazard short lines, known collectively as the Pittsburgh, Fort Wayne & Chicago, provided service of a sort from there to the spongy metropolis at the southern tip of Lake Michigan. Already there was a line from Chicago northwestward to Galena, tapping the rich lead mines and heading out at one of the busiest steamboat ports of the northern river country. From it each year hundreds of emigrants boarded packets which bore "Saint Paul" destination signs and churned up the Father of Waters to the head of navigation at the Falls of St. Anthony. St. Paul had five thousand or more settlers and was growing at the rate of a thousand a year. It had forgotten its days as Pig's Eye, so called for a one-eyed French-Canadian whiskey seller, and had far outstripped Minneapolis, across the river.[19]

[17] Klein, *op. cit.*, II, 1112.

[18] *Republican* obituary.

[19] Edward Duffield Neill. *The History of Minnesota from the Earliest French Explorations to the Present Time*, 475–79. For the description of early-day Minneapolis

Some of the newcomers were men of vision and latent power. Among them, arriving this very year, was a single-eyed, furiously energetic one-man legend named James Jerome Hill. Only eighteen, he was anxious to become a mountain man but unsure of how to go about it. While he hesitated, he could not help but see the gaping opportunities at St. Paul. He availed himself of them, and Minnesota was glad, sorry, and glad again that he did. J. C. Oswald, Henry's brother, who either made the trip to Minnesota with Henry or went there shortly afterward, ran a saloon and liquor store at the Falls. Later he associated with Jim Hill and "became very rich,"[20] although none of it rubbed off on the Siebers.

The city of Minneapolis—if it could be called such in 1856—was a buckshot scattering of log cabins and rude shanties when Henry and Theresia decided to settle there, but it had a tradition even then. Ever since the establishment of Fort Snelling in 1819 (on the Minnesota River near its junction with the Mississippi) there had been a few squatters here and there through the wilderness about the Falls. Most were graying *voyageurs*, French-Canadian or mixed French and Indian, with a leetle preponderance of the latter. Some stayed on to become men of affluence and influence in the growing communities, but most simply disappeared.

Logging seemed to hold the future for Minneapolis at first. Lumber mills comprised the fastest-growing industry. A steam sawmill was built in 1856 at the mouth of Bassett's Creek, above the Falls, and another would soon go into operation. One of Albert's first jobs was that of teamster, hauling saw logs to the mills and lumber from them to the docks.

But if he continued the outdoor schooling begun at Lancaster, he found more than that to interest him. A wolf track in the mud, a buckskin-clad Indian, a woods runner pacing the stump-obstructed Minneapolis "streets," could all attract his attention. Old-timers

and its neighboring communities, I have depended principally upon Neill's *History* and his "St. Paul and Its Environs," *Graham's Magazine*, Vol. XLVI (January, 1855), 3–17, reprinted in *Minnesota History*, Vol. XXX, No. 3 (September, 1949), 202–19.

[20] Austin H. Oswald, Palo Alto, California, in correspondence with the author, July 5, 1960.

recollected skirmishing with red men.[21] They even bandied rumors of possible trouble to come with the Mdewakantons (a subtribe of the Sioux), who were called Santees by most frontiersmen.

The frontier was "just over yonder" in geography, but Albert Sieber would find that it was also a state of mind. There wasn't a fence or a trace beyond which you could say the wilderness began. From the heart of the village, on a still night, while the snow lay firm and luminous under a star-powdered sky, one could hear the rising, dismal wail of a timber wolf. It was no uncommon thing to jump a white-tailed deer, or even an elk, within hiking distance of Minneapolis. There was still plenty of wilderness for those who could see it.

Many boys ran winter trap lines, catching muskrats, mink, raccoons, skunks, and even weasels and selling the skins to neighborhood women, who used them as powder puffs for their babies. Al recalled his Minnesota youth as a time of happiness and hard work, but the thing he remembered most distinctly, judging from his rare letters, was the cold of wintertime, although he was to engage in many an Indian campaign in the supposedly benign climate of Arizona and find himself more miserable from snow and chill temperatures than he had ever been in the north country, and in this respect he did not differ from other men. Deep snow seems colder than light snow, forty below zero more uncomfortable than twenty above, even though one dressed properly for northern winters, while barely freezing temperatures of southwestern mountains often caught desert dwellers unawares. It is likely that more people of early times suffered illness and death from exposure in Arizona and California than in Minnesota and Michigan. Al, too, probably suffered more from the climate in the Southwest than in the North, but he would never have admitted it.

Among the settlers there was a lively and growing interest in the involved politics back east as the years passed. Anyone could see that the nation was heading for a showdown on the issue of slavery. The main question never meant much in Minnesota, where there were few slaves, but, having become a state in 1858, she knew there would be a role for her to play.

[21] Neill, *op. cit.*, 464–70, describes in detail one of these intertribal fights and its consequences.

Governor Alexander Ramsey[22] was in Washington on Saturday night, April 13, 1861, when news of the surrender of Fort Sumter was received. Early the next morning, he hurried over to the War Department, only to find Secretary Simon Cameron, with a fistful of papers, heading for the White House. Lincoln had already asked for 75,000 volunteers, and Ramsey told Cameron it was his business to offer a thousand. "Sit down," said the Secretary, "and write the tender out." Ramsey did so. Thus the very first pledge of troops for Union armies came from Minnesota. On Monday, Ramsey telegraphed St. Paul of his offer, and that same evening, at the Pioneer Guards meeting at St. Paul Armory, several men volunteered. First was Josias H. King, who thereby became the senior volunteer in the Federal service during the Civil War. From her scant population, Minnesota sent 25,072 volunteers into uniform.

The First Minnesota Volunteers, destined to become one of the famous Union Army contingents, were swiftly recruited. Farm boys were issued a few Springfields and a lot of Mississippi rifles with sword bayonets, one blanket, an extra pair of socks, and one flannel shirt apiece and sent to Fort Snelling to become soldiers. Within a month the state furnished its troops black felt hats and black pantaloons to go with their red shirts (except Company K, from Winona, whose townspeople bought them neat gray uniforms). Willis A. Gorman,[23] veteran of the Battle of Buena Vista in the Mexican War, was named colonel, and in a short time the regiment was ready for service. On June 22 it embarked on the steamers *War Eagle* and *Northern Belle* and was huffed away to battle.

Albert was too young to go as yet, and he restlessly filled in the

22 Ramsey, first governor of the Territory of Minnesota and later a United States senator, was born at Harrisburg, Pennsylvania, on September 8, 1815. Although a man "of glaring faults," as Neill puts it, he was a giant of the Northwest, possessing intellect, industry, good humor, and caution to the point of tardiness. He died April 22, 1903. W. H. C. Folsom, *Fifty Years in the Northwest*, 760, describes his offer of troops.

23 Gorman was born in Fleming County, Kentucky, on January 12, 1816, but moved with his parents to Indiana, where he eventually became an able attorney and a politician. He enlisted in the Third Indiana Volunteers in the Mexican War, was promptly appointed major, "won the reputation of a gallant, dashing officer," and emerged a colonel. He became the second governor of Minnesota Territory and died at St. Paul on May 20, 1876. Folsom, *op. cit.*, 581–82.

time doing this and that. It is reported that he became the first volunteer policeman in Minneapolis,[24] and if this information is correct, he may have served during this period. When he reached enlistment age, however, he lost no time. Early on March 3, 1862 (since 1862 was not a leap year, his eighteenth birthday had come on Saturday, March 1, and he had to wait until Monday for the enlistment office to open), he marched his mother to the place of recruitment and she gave her written consent, whether reluctantly or not the record doesn't state, but she gave it. He was enrolled as "Albert Sebers"[25] in Company B, First Minnesota, and formally mustered in at Fort Snelling. He had enlisted at Minneapolis, but he gave his residence as Stillwater, where he may have been employed.

Approaching manhood, Albert was an ax-toughened farm hand, an expert rifle shot, a good companion, a prankster, filled with zest for life—and war. An entry in the Muster and Descriptive Roll lists him as nineteen, which he wasn't, gave his occupation as "teamster," and

[24] Minneapolis, Minnesota, *Tribune* obituary of uncertain date, but probably late February, 1907, according to Austin H. Oswald, in whose collection is a clipping. Written in ink beside the statement that Sieber had been a policeman is the date 1868, but by 1868 he was in Arizona. The data from which the obituary was written came from Al's niece, Louise Wall Taylor, with whom he maintained a desultory correspondence during the later years of his life and of whom he was apparently quite fond. Despite her close study of her uncle's career, the obituary contains some curious errors. For instance, it says that Sieber came to this country when he was seventeen (seven would be more like it), an error which has been repeated, with embellishments, by several writers. It also says he left Minnesota for the West in 1870, but the actual date of his departure was four years earlier. However, the item does contain information not found elsewhere and confirms that Louise had a solid impression that Al "was one of the first police officers" of Minneapolis, a belief shared by other descendants of Sieber's brothers and sisters. Mrs. Taylor repeated the statement, in substance, to Frank C. Lockwood in a letter dated September 3, 1933, now in the Lockwood Collection of the Arizona Pioneers' Historical Society (APHS), Tucson (cited hereafter as Lockwood APHS). At my request, Minneapolis Police Captain Donald W. Johnson kindly examined the early records of his department but could find no confirmation of Al's service, although he added that "my search does not preclude the possibility of him working in that capacity because records were very poor in those days." Johnson to author, December 18, 1958.

[25] Although Al signed his enlistment paper "Albert Sebers," his mother's consent to it bore the signature "Katherina Sieber." Letter from the Adjutant General's Office (AGO) to Frank C. Lockwood, October 19, 1933, Lockwood APHS. This and subsequent information on Sieber's army service is taken from a photostat of his service record, now in the National Archives.

described him as of fair complexion, five feet, ten and one-half inches tall, with dark eyes (recorded in later documents as "hazel") and dark hair (which was later often called "sandy").

The party of recruits which included Sieber was given very little time for drill, then shipped east to join the regiment in the siege of the redoubtable fortress at Yorktown. I have found very little direct information about Sieber for the next year and a half, but in that time he was absent from his company just one day, and its history is his history. An excellent regimental narrative follows closely the adventures and misadventures of the First Minnesota Volunteers, of which he was an active member, and describes quite well the incidents in which he took part.

It was a well-blooded outfit that Albert joined, and it matured in other soldierly qualities, as when the men stole the sutler's whiskey, rolling the barrel (under cover of night) out into a field, filling a dozen canteens and a couple of camp kettles, and burying the remainder. When the alarm was sounded, a lieutenant came by, stopping before tent after tent to sniff all the canteens, but by a ruse the culprits made three clean canteens do for fifteen and thus escaped punishment. Months later the regiment chanced to camp during a cold, damp night on that very field. Someone remembered the buried whiskey; it was dug up, and "its contents, fairly distributed, were probably beneficial in countering the effects of the exposure."[26]

When Sieber joined it, the regiment was bivouacked in bottomless mud about two miles from Yorktown. It seemed to rain all the time. The boys dubbed the place "Camp Misery" and were glad for the ax-swinging, muscle-heating work of building corduroy roads, which they could do better than anyone. A bit of excitement occurred on April 11 when a balloon, ascending to their right near the York River, broke away from its mooring, sailed over the Confederate works with its desperate crew, then caught a fortunate air current and settled softly in division headquarters. The Minnesotans didn't have much time to study the aeronautical monster, however, for they were ordered to move a mile nearer the fortress, given newfangled pup tents, and assigned a more pleasant camp on higher ground. Much of the

26 *Minnesota in the Civil and Indian Wars 1861–1865*, I, 7–8.

time the rains continued, and often the men were wet to the skin. No one knew when Yorktown would fall, or if it would. No one seemed to have any idea of how to take it. Where was all the glory to this kind of war?

The First realized, though, that Yorktown was a key to the great Union offensive toward Richmond, a major obstacle to the success of the Peninsular Campaign, into which Lincoln had finally pried General George B. McClellan. The Peninsula, a finger of land between the York and James rivers, seemed an ideal avenue to Richmond. Union forces there could be supported by warships and supplied by water almost to within a cannon shot of their goal, and one of the keys to it was Yorktown, on the Peninsula's northern side. And before Yorktown the army sat and waited while the Confederates reinforced Richmond. The fortress was McClellan's fixation. He was a good soldier and an able commander; he lacked only the ferocity that keeps a top field general stubbornly battering at an opponent until a weakness appears, then smashing with such fury and single-mindedness that he sweeps everything before him. It is thus, and thus only, that grimly contested campaigns are won. On a much smaller scale and in a far different theater, in distant Arizona, another able officer would hammer this lesson home anew, as Sieber would learn. Meanwhile, McClellan's army waited.

Brilliant Stonewall Jackson was dispatched on a wildly successful diversion up the Shenandoah Valley, which forced the Union chiefs to detach a strong element to safeguard Washington, thereby diminishing McClellan's force; the latter was always one to see how much had been taken away, rather than what he had left. Nor was his intelligence system of the best; he constantly overestimated Confederate strength and miscalculated that which he would have at his own disposal. Terrain and geographical features of the Peninsula held endless surprises for him, and although he handled the massive expedition with his customary administrative skill, it was to no ultimate purpose.

The infantrymen of the First Minnesota were as little concerned with grand strategy as any other soldiers. The things that did matter to them were salt beef and hardtack, foraging (against orders) for an occasional chicken, picket duty, manual labor, and the everlasting rain and mud.

Before daylight on May 4 the First filed into Yorktown; the Confederates had abandoned it during the night. The fortress had served their purpose: it had occupied McClellan for as long as was necessary —and longer than the Rebels thought it could. Quietly and safely, they walked out during the night and early morning, with scarcely a shot fired, withdrawing toward Richmond.

The First Minnesota was glad to see them go. Inside the fortress the men found provisions and camp equipage everywhere, breakfasts still cooking over fires—"not very tempting messes," but it beat salt beef! A plantation smokehouse near by was well filled, and the Minnesotans stuffed the wrinkles out of their bellies with ham and bacon.

The army floundered up muddy roads toward Williamsburg, advancing for three hours during the night. Then the First was about-faced and marched back to Yorktown again. On the afternoon of the seventh, it boarded the steamer *Long Branch* and puffed up the river through the darkness, landing under artillery fire at West Point, where the Pamunkey and Mattaponi join to form the York. The First moved on to Eltham, on the Pamunkey, slopped on to New Kent Court House, and, in short marches, reached the Chickahominy on May 23. The regiment was ordered to construct a bridge over that important stream, and in a single day whacked down enough trees, binding them with vines, to give the structure its nickname of "Grapevine Bridge." They had it ready for the big show, opening May 31, called the Battle of Fair Oaks.

About 1:00 P.M. enemy artillery roared out over the roll of musketry off to the south of the Chickahominy, which was so swollen from the constant rains that only Grapevine Bridge was serviceable, and even it seemed risky. Judging from the fire, the corps south of the river was having a bad time. The division to which Gorman's brigade belonged got under arms, crossing the river at 2:30, the First in the lead. The Minnesotans soon ran into "fleeing stragglers and cowards, who reported utter and irretrievable defeat."[27] The North Woods soldiers paid no attention and hurried on, reaching Courtney

[27] *Ibid.*

House just as a crowded column in gray moved out of a woods close in front. The enemy recoiled for a moment, then moved on toward its target, past the Minnesotans, who got in a flanking fire and took many prisoners, including a North Carolina colonel and other officers. McClellan himself congratulated the brigade for its part in defeating the Rebels within five miles of Richmond, but the victory meant little. Rains continued and rations failed; supplies could not be moved up in quantity. During all of June the two armies remained in position and glared at each other, neither moving so much as a mile and nothing spent but time, which the Federals could ill afford to waste and the Confederates desperately needed.

Pickets were attacked or shelled nearly every day; scarcely a night passed that the men weren't on the line because of some alarm. They were forced to keep their arms by them, and they never had time to wash their clothing. The weather turned hot. The only drinking water available was surface water. Malaria and diarrhea were rife. To while away the time, and for military reasons, too, the First erected a breastwork to protect the men from small-arms fire. Sieber had become a sharpshooter, testifying to his aptitude for such work and his backwoods training; he counted it lucky, no doubt, that sharpshooters were usually busy when everyone else was engaged with spade, mattock, and ax. Al never cottoned much to that sort of work. Although there was nothing really lazy about him, he, like any other soldier, dodged such details when he could.

McClellan was waiting for the army of 35,000 which had been assigned the defense of Washington at the time of Stonewall Jackson's Shenandoah raid. While 60,000 Union troops were hunting him, Jackson deftly disengaged and hastened to Richmond, where he joined Robert E. Lee in preparations to lift the threat to the Confederate capital.

The great assault came north of the Chickahominy. The Minnesotans could hear it and all but taste the gunsmoke drifting their way. In the dampness of early morning it lay like a blue fog over the meadows and woods. The fighting was murderous north of the river, and eventually the Confederates caved in the Union right flank. On June 28 the Minnesotans were told to pack everything. Wagon trains had been going south all day; at dark the sick and disabled also were sent back, and at dawn on the twenty-ninth the First swung into file at the rear of the army. By one o'clock the Minnesotans had reached Savage Station, where they had to destroy much equipment abandoned by their army. They loaded a railroad bridge with locomotives and stores and blew it up, not taking time to appreciate the spectacle. The First was called to beat off a Rebel attack. The Confederate infantry appeared farther to the left, and again the First was sent to meet the threat. At dark they withdrew across White Oak Swamp. Rebels were everywhere.

The Minnesotans were sent to fight for a stream crossing, then back to another troubled spot, and after that to a third front to help salvage a badly used-up Union regiment. General Edwin V. Sumner personally ordered them to this last sector, saying sadly, "Boys, I shall not see many of you again, but I know you will hold that line!" Dog tired as they were, the men rose with a cheer and competently did the job. By July 1 they had reached Malvern Hill, on the James River, where concentrated Union forces beat off a terrific Confederate assault, then fell back to Harrison's Landing. The Peninsular Campaign was over.

On into the summer, on one front or another, skirmishing and fighting continued. What worried the Minnesota soldiers most, however, was not the problem at hand; dire news from back home had reached them. Amid the sensuous beauty of the Minnesota Valley there was suddenly unleashed the most savage and bloodiest Indian war in middle western history, and for all the men of the First knew, it would carry right to the Mississippi.

Demoniacal in its fury was the outbreak led by Little Crow of the Kapozha band of the Mdewakanton Sioux, who not only attacked defenseless settlers but fought vigorous pitched battles with troops, causing 358 casualties among them, 126 soldiers being killed. To this day no one knows how many men, women, and children died before the bows, rifles, and tomahawks of the Indians. Estimates run from the 360 whose names are known to the more than 1,000 some sources give.[28] Split the difference for a likely total.

[28] Frederick Webb Hodge, *Handbook of American Indians North of Mexico* (cited

The reasons for the outbreak were many, but the immediate causes were probably these: Indian resentment of the pre-emption of Indian lands by whites, delays in the issue of provisions and promised cash at the agencies, and a belief among the Sioux that the state's manpower was so committed to the Civil War that few would be spared to put down an outbreak.[29] Battles took place at Birch Coulee, Fort Ridgely, and Fort Abercrombie, and such towns as New Ulm were assaulted. The whole valley was ravaged.

How much Sieber learned of the uprising is not precisely known. Henry Oswald enlisted in Captain Louis Buggert's company of Brown County militia in time for the Second Battle of New Ulm, fought on August 23, 1862. "We sure gave those Indians a bad time," Henry boasted later. The Sioux gave the defenders a bad time, too: 26 whites were killed, more than 50 were wounded, and a good part of the town was burned.[30] The Oswalds and the Siebers no doubt kept Al informed as fully as the irregular mails allowed. He and his comrades must have been relieved when the danger passed, and even more so when, on the cold and wet day after Christmas, 38 of the Sioux ring-leaders were executed in a mass hanging at Mankato. Originally, 309 Indians were sentenced to death, but President Lincoln disallowed all but 39, one of whom was reprieved. This was the first Indian war of which Sieber had personal knowledge, and the effect on his curiosity and imagination is problematical.

The First gave a good account of itself at Antietam and at Fredericksburg. In the latter engagement, it stood firm while green regiments to the right and left were crumbling under assault. General Oliver O. Howard, whom Sieber would have reason to recall years later in the Southwest, noted approvingly that the northerners were

hereafter as Hodge, *Handbook*), II, 770; Louis H. Roddis, *The Indian Wars of Minnesota*, 298–99.

[29] In addition to the general histories of Folsom and Neill, the account here depends upon Roddis, *op. cit.*; Hodge, *Handbook*; and *Minnesota in the Civil and Indian Wars 1861–1865*, I and II.

[30] New Ulm, the county seat of Brown County, is about seventy-five miles southwest of Minneapolis. Buggert's company of fifty-five men, organized August 19, served only until August 25, just long enough to take part in the one battle. No member of the company was either killed or wounded. *Minnesota in the Civil and Indian Wars 1861–1865*, I, 760.

holding their own and said to their commander, "Your First Minnesota doesn't run!" The officer proudly replied, "General, the First Minnesota never runs," and he was being strictly accurate. It had never lost a color or a gun. The following spring, at Chancellorsville, the First again performed creditably.

By early summer of 1863 the regiment was toughened, hardened, and tempered in blood, with veterans predominating in each of its units. There were undoubtedly other regiments in the Army of the Potomac which were just as good, but few could have been better. To the magnificent physiques and arrogant individualism of the men from the North Woods had been added the training, discipline, experience, and battle wisdom which alone can forge a superb fighting organization.

Sieber was one of these veterans, no better and no worse than scores of them. His company muster record shows that in the year and a half of his service up to Gettysburg, he had been ill only on August 29, 1862, when the First was about to join in the Second Battle of Bull Run. He was still a private. In later years he confessed to an acquaintance that he had been "too full of the devil—played too many pranks" ever to get promoted to anything,[31] but then to be a member of the First Minnesota was to be an elite soldier. Major General Winfield Scott Hancock was now commander of the corps to which the First Minnesota was assigned, and the northerners were proud to serve under so distinguished and able an officer.

It was mid-June, 1863. The still heat of early Virginia summer flowed with whispered rumors that the Rebs were up to something big. The whispers became louder: Lee was pushing large bodies of troops toward the upper Potomac; General Joseph Hooker wanted to strike the enemy's extended supply and communications lines, but Washington, fearful of its safety, wouldn't let him. The rumors hardened into fact. The First, along with the rest of the army, prepared to move out, not on the trail of Lee, but parallel to it, shielding Washington as the

[31] A penciled note in Lockwood's hand credits former Arizona State Historian Dan Williamson (of whom more later), a long-time friend of Al Sieber, with this explanation (direct from Sieber) of Al's low rank during his Civil War service. Lockwood APHS.

Confederates moved northwest of it. Again the First undertook a long and tedious march, which was enlivened by a near-riot. Somebody, from some regiment, got into a feud with the sutler of the Ninth Massachusetts Artillery, and soon there was a gleeful mob of soldiers, including some Minnesotans, bearing down upon that hapless individual, intent on "a general confiscation of his effects." A couple of artillery pieces were rolled out to quell the uproar, but these were instantly "captured," run down a hill, and overturned. The rioters melted away to their regiments, and officers decided there was no time for an inquiry.

In due course the column arrived in southern Pennsylvania and reached Gettysburg, about fifty miles west of Lancaster, on July 2, the second day of the battle. The Minnesotans were placed on the line to the left of Cemetery Ridge and joined on their left by the Third Corps, commanded by Major General Daniel Edgar Sickles. Shortly after noon, Sickles advanced his corps half a mile, and most of the First Minnesota, about 262 men, was sent to the position Sickles had vacated in order to support Battery C of the Fourth U.S. Artillery. Not far distant was Battery A of the same regiment, including among its officers a Cushing of that gallant family of whom one member was to write a stirring page in the history of Apachería in Sieber's time.

From its new position, the men of the First could look down upon the battlefield as if it were a map. Sickles' men were having a rough go, with the full weight of General James Longstreet's and General Ambrose P. Hill's forces falling upon them. The Union men fell back, at first slowly, then, under extreme pressure, they broke and rushed back in wild disorder toward the ridge. The veteran Minnesotans braced for the impact that was sure to come:

> Just then Hancock, with a single aide, rode up at full speed and for a moment vainly endeavored to rally Sickles' retreating forces. Reserves had been sent for, but were too far away to hope to reach the critical position until it would be occupied by the enemy, unless that enemy were stopped. Quickly leaving the fugitives, Hancock spurred to where we stood, calling out, as he reached us, "What regiment is this?" "First Minnesota," replied the colonel. "Charge those lines!" commanded Hancock.

Every man realized in an instant what that order meant,—death or wounds to us all; the sacrifice of the regiment to gain a few minutes' time and save the position, and probably the battlefield,—and every man saw and accepted the necessity for the sacrifice.[32]

In perfect line, the regiment, with arms at right shoulder, swept down the slope toward the overwhelming forces charging toward it. Directly upon the Confederates' center drove the Minnesotans. No hesitation, no stopping to fire, heedless of the men dropping to right and left, each soldier ran gallantly on, without further orders. Then they leveled their bayonets.

The First rushed the Rebels' first line, which was slightly disordered after crossing a brook at the foot of the slope. "The men were never made who will stand against leveled bayonets coming with such momentum and evident desperation. The first line broke in our front as we reached it, and rushed back through the second line, stopping the whole advance. We then poured in our first fire."[33]

The Confederate charge had been stemmed. The enemy milled until Union reserves flowed down from the ridge and pushed on past the mangled remnants of the Minnesotans to press the withdrawing Confederates. The First had stopped the enemy, but with what a sacrifice! Of the 262 men who had begun the charge, 215 were casualties, 47 still in line, and not a man was missing. One historian of the war said that this percentage of loss was "without equal in the records of modern warfare." Another wrote: "This is said to be the heaviest sacrifice made by any single unit in one fight, during the entire war. But it saved the situation."[34] And General Hancock, who fell wounded on the same field the next day, said: "There is no more gallant deed recorded in history."

Among the casualties lay Albert Sieber, unconscious on that bloody field. A shell fragment had fractured his skull, and as he toppled, a rifle bullet struck his right ankle, plowed up through his leg, and emerged at the knee. The wounded were gathered in darkness by their

[32] *Minnesota in the Civil and Indian Wars 1861–1865*, I, 35.
[33] *Ibid.*
[34] *Ibid.*, 36. See also General Edward J. Stackpole and Colonel Wilbur S. Nye, *The Battle of Gettysburg: A Guided Tour*, 63.

surviving comrades and sent to field hospitals, such as they were. Carl Schurz, by now a major general with a command at Gettysburg, visited one of these stations following the bloody battle, and his eloquent pen has left a vivid picture of the sort of place to which Sieber and thousands of other wounded men were consigned:

> The wounded were carried to the farmyards behind our lines. The houses, the barns, the sheds, and the open barnyards were crowded with moaning and wailing human beings, and still an unceasing procession of stretchers and ambulances was coming in from all sides to augment the number of sufferers. A heavy rain set in during the day . . . and large numbers had to remain unprotected in the open, there being no room left under roof. I saw long rows of men lying under the eaves of the buildings, the water pouring down on their bodies in streams. Most of the operating tables were placed in the open where the light was best, some of them partially protected against the rain by tarpaulins or blankets stretched upon poles. There stood the surgeons, their sleeves rolled up to the elbows, their bare arms as well as their linen aprons smeared with blood, their knives not seldom held between their teeth, while they were helping a patient on or off the table, or had their hands otherwise occupied; around them pools of blood and amputated arms or legs in heaps, sometimes more than man-high. . . . As a wounded man was lifted on the table, often shrieking with pain as the attendants handled him, the surgeon quickly examined the wound and resolved upon cutting off the injured limb. Some ether was administered and the body put in position in a moment. The surgeon snatched his knife from between his teeth . . . wiped it rapidly once or twice across his blood-stained apron, and the cutting began. The operation accomplished, the surgeon would look around with a deep sigh, and then —"NEXT!"[35]

For five months, until December, Sieber was in the hospital. Upon his release on December 8, he was mustered into the First Company, First Battalion, Invalid Corps, at York, Pennsylvania, apparently a convalescent camp. By March 1, 1864, this unit had become Company K, First Regiment, Veteran Reserve Corps, an outfit composed of wounded men who had proved their courage and value; the regiment was accredited to Waltham, Massachusetts.[36] By way of variety,

35 Schurz, *Reminiscences*, III, 39–40.
36 The records here become complicated. Apparently, Sieber was carried as "Absent"

Al signed his re-enlistment papers that spring as Albert Seabers, listing his occupation as "Farmer" in one place and "Soldier" in another, had his hair described variously as "Dark," "Brown," or "Fair," his eyes as "Dark" or "Hazel." The description depended pretty much, it would seem, on who looked at him and wrote it down.

During his convalescence he no doubt visited any relatives still living at Lancaster. Some of his brothers may have joined the army. There is a report that a Peter Sieber from Lancaster, possibly Al's brother, was a Civil War veteran and had a finger shot off; later he ran a railroad-station restaurant at Mount Pleasant, Pennsylvania.[37] One report says that John, at the outset of the war, "organized a company of volunteers . . . of which he was captain," but no official record of such service now exists.[38] Albert's sister, Magdalena, had married a John Wall at Lancaster, and he served with the Seventy-seventh Pennsylvania, organized at Pittsburgh on October 15, 1861. It fought mostly with the Army of the Ohio, ending up in Texas in the summer of 1865.[39]

On February 19, 1864, Al made corporal, a rating he held during the remainder of the war, but he was not to see combat again. He did provost duty until fall, then was sent to Albany briefly and at length to Elmira, New York, where he served as guard over Rebel prisoners until the summer of 1865.

About twelve thousand Confederates were confined at this camp. Lack of discipline had grown to serious proportions under careless supervision by the regiments of short-term men whom the veterans replaced. The prisoners were sullen, unruly, turbulent. One day this was to change abruptly. Sieber may have noticed, or at least should

on the muster roll of the First Minnesota for the remainder of the war. When Company B was mustered out on July 14, 1865, the roll states specifically that Sieber received no discharge. This is because he was formally discharged on May 1, 1864, and re-enlisted on May 4 of that year at Washington, D.C., in Company K, First Regiment, Veteran Reserve Corps, the unit to which he already belonged and from which he would be discharged after the war.

[37] Miss Bertha Sieber, Lancaster, Pennsylvania, in correspondence with the author, May 20 and June 7, 1958.

[38] Barnesville *Record-Review* obituary of John Sieber.

[39] Mrs. Lillian T. Bennett, Minneapolis, in correspondence with the author, September 17, 1958.

have, the slight, sandy-haired, blue-eyed artillery lieutenant who arrived at the camp one day with his kepi at a rakish angle and a slight swagger in his walk. Howard Bass Cushing was twenty-seven, an older brother of the Cushing who was killed on Cemetery Ridge. With his battery, Cushing had been sent to restore order at Elmira, and he made his first inspection with Lieutenant Frank Wilkeson. The officers were greeted with jeers. Cushing halted, coldly surveyed the prisoners, and when they quieted, said:

See here, you —, —, —! I am just up from the front, where I have been killing such infernal wretches as you are. I have met you in twenty battles. I never lost a gun to you. You never drove a battery I served with from its position. You are a crowd of insolent, cowardly scoundrels and if I had command of this prison I would discipline you, or kill you, and I should much prefer to kill you. I have brought a battery of United States artillery to this pen, and if you give me occasion I will be glad to dam that river [pointing to the near-by Chemung] with your worthless carcasses, and silence your insolent tongues forever. I fully understand that you are presuming on your position as prisoners of war when you talk to me as you have; but you have reached the end of your rope with me. I will kill the first man of you who again speaks insultingly to me while I am in this pen, and I shall be here daily. Now, go to your quarters![40]

No one reported trouble with Elmira captives after that speech.

All prisoners of war were released in the summer of 1865. Sieber received three hundred dollars in bounty money from Massachusetts and returned to Minneapolis.[41] He had left home a boy so young that his mother had to sign a waiver so that he might enlist. He returned a man, toughened and restless.

[40] Theron Wilber Haight, *Three Wisconsin Cushings* (cited hereafter as Haight), 92–93, quoting Frank Wilkeson, *Recollections of a Private Soldier in the Army of the Potomac* (New York 1887), 223–24.

[41] Most accounts of Sieber say he was discharged in mid-July, 1865, and this may be true, for that is when Company B, First Minnesota Infantry, was mustered out. Sieber himself, in a statement dictated in 1903 for Colonel James H. McClintock, said that he was mustered out on July 15, 1865. McClintock Collection, Phoenix Public Library. However, the records of Company K, Veteran Reserve Corps, show that it was mustered out on November 14, 1865, and that Sieber was mustered out under *General Orders 155*, AGO, October 26, 1865.

II. The Way West

THE MINNESOTA to which Albert Sieber returned, with a three-hundred-dollar stake in his pocket, was different from the place he had left almost four years before. There had been material changes. The country had tamed down. The railroads had arrived, or, rather, had thrown out spurs from the large centers of population. These often linked with spurs from other cities. The lumber and shingle mills had devoured great stands of hardwood and pine, and the country had a different look. One could no longer stand on a snowy street corner and hear a wolf splitting a winter's night with his lonesome cry.

Most war veterans feel an inexplicable restlessness when they suddenly leave the service, and it might be assumed that Al Sieber shared this feeling. He must have heard a great deal of talk about the West, especially California. The flood to that state, at high tide the year the Siebers came to the United States, had ebbed a bit, but there was still a surge of travel across the plains each year. The trend of American settlement had been westward; it always would be. These factors, and perhaps others, combined to influence Al, and before very long, he, too, determined to go west. His mother would be taken care of. Not only were Theresia and Henry Oswald well established, but Lena and John Wall came from Lancaster in 1866; soon John and Elizabeth Sieber and Al's older brother, Rudolph, would try their fortunes in that northern state.[1] There appeared to be nothing in Minnesota

[1] Mrs. Lillian T. Bennett to author, September 17 and November 19, 1958. (Mrs. Bennett is the oldest of four children of Louise Wall Taylor, who, in turn, was born to Lena and John Wall at Minneapolis on February 27, 1870.) Magdalena's death certificate, dated February 5, 1891, says she came to Minneapolis twenty-five years earlier, i.e., in 1866. The Barnesville *Record-Review* notes that John and Elizabeth came to

to keep Al home, so, sometime early in 1866,[2] he packed what he wanted to take and struck out on his long, long journey.

I have found no record to show how he crossed the continent, save that he went overland[3] and arrived at San Francisco within a short time. Perhaps he made the trip by stagecoach, possibly from Omaha or Fort Kearny.[4] If so, he would have ended the wearying journey at Sacramento, then taken a river boat to San Francisco, where, it is said, he remained several months. But the city proved too tame—and too expensive, no doubt—and we next hear of him in the vast forests of northern California, getting out ties for the Central Pacific, at that time rapidly constructing its line eastward.[5] The labor of sawing and shaping the wooden sleepers, Al must soon have decided, was nothing on which to build a career, but he would have had to admit that it was exciting to be a part of the construction of this vast, unprecedented railroad. The project was easily among the greatest peacetime efforts America had undertaken up to that time.

Coming across the Sierra Nevada, anyone would notice the anthill bustle marking construction of the Central Pacific, now struggling toward the 7,017-foot crest of Donner Pass. Camp upon camp in the rugged mountains and narrow gorges teemed with pig-tailed Chinese, oxen and mules, powdermen and engineers. Much of the work was in hard rock, where tunnels and shelves had to be blasted with black powder or nitroglycerin. Fifteen tunnels were being driven to enable the roadbed to cross the Sierras. In the summer of 1866, work continued around the clock, and all through the savage winter of 1866–67 it went on by candlelight in the fearsome depths of the mountain where workmen ground away on the 1,659-foot summit tunnel. Forty-

Minneapolis about 1869, moving to Barnesville a decade later, but the Cascade County, Montana, death certificate of Andrew William Sieber, John's youngest son, shows him to have been born at Pittsburgh, Pennsylvania, on May 11, 1870, and it is unlikely that the family would have reached Minnesota before that year. I have not found a date for Rudolph's arrival in Minnesota, but since he joined John at Barnesville, it seems probable that he would have gone there shortly after the Civil War. A Minneapolis city directory for 1870–71 lists Rudolph Sieber as a "tanner."

2 *Republican* obituary.

3 *Ibid.*

4 Captain William Banning and George Hugh Banning, *Six Horses*, 343.

5 Which, in due course, became the Southern Pacific.

four snowstorms were counted that awful winter, with drifts sometimes forty feet deep; in one particularly bad stretch of winter weather, ten feet of snow fell in a single storm and caverns had to be dug through the drifts to get crews to the rock tunnels they were hewing. There had never been an engineering feat like it.[6]

But all that was way up in the mountains and Sieber was working in the lowlands, where the activity was considerably less. Before long, getting out ties palled on him. He never pointedly shunned hard work, although he had no relish for it. Throughout his life he readily performed prodigious feats of endurance and strength, but when it came to drudgery, he was a quick man to find a Mexican, Indian, or Chinese to work while he undertook the supervision. Yet the sawing and ax-swinging must have broadened his shoulders still more and toughened his arms and body, reinforcing a remarkable constitution until he was strong as a mule. Within a few months he quit tie-cutting and headed back over the Sierras for the mining camps of Nevada. Here there were attractions and prices that would quickly eat up a man's money. There was no help for it; back to work again. He secured some sort of job on a road-grading operation near Virginia City, at that time the mining and population capital of the state.

Nevada, he found, was wild as they came, ranking with Arizona in the sheer abandon of her ways. Bad men were of infinite variety and a dime a dozen, even in that frontier of inflated prices. Law enforcement was often whimsical. For example, Storey County Sheriff Howard had original concepts about juries. He summoned one consisting entirely of squint-eyed men; the lawyers, it is written, nearly went crazy trying to get their attention. Howard rounded up a jury of fat men for the next trial. They overflowed the box. Then he scored with a jury of thin men, one of tall men, and so on, but the judge drew the line when Howard sought to enlist a jury of the ugliest men in Storey County. "Making a circus out of the court," scowled His Honor.[7]

Stage holdups were commonplace. Most folks were not upset, hating the express company and figuring robberies signified a more

[6] Neill C. Wilson and Frank J. Taylor, *Southern Pacific: The Roaring Story of a Fighting Railroad*, 18–21, 23–27.

[7] Myron Angel (ed.), *History of Nevada*, 577.

judicious division among thieves. Homicides, however, were all too frequent. One historian lists 402 known killings in Nevada between 1846 and 1881. As a result, only 8 men were hanged, 23 sent to prison, 29 reached court but were acquitted, one jury was hung (if the killer was not), and one individual was fined. Vigilantes eliminated 13 supposed slayers, and 3 murderers committed suicide after their crimes.[8]

Some notorious killers ran a town to suit themselves. There was Farmer Peel, with ten known slayings to his credit, who terrorized a court and banged up a judge who had the temerity to fine him for a minor offense.

Another outlaw, if a man could be called that in a place where the law barely existed, was incredible Sam Brown, a soiled individual whose beard was so long that he tied it in a bow under his chin. Back in 1860 he carved a man to pieces in a saloon, wrapped the remains in a blanket, and fell asleep on the floor beside the corpse. He had committed at least half a dozen wanton murders. One day he invaded a courtroom to free an acquaintance, but the prosecutor, later senator, William M. Stewart, got the drop on him and made him a witness for the prosecution. Leaving the court in a foul mood, Brown took a shot at one he supposed to be an inoffensive farmer, but he misjudged. This man, Henry Van Sickles, secured a shotgun, chased Brown all over the neighborhood, and finally blew his head off. A hastily assembled coroner's jury promptly brought in the verdict that Sam Brown had come to his sudden and violent death from "a just dispensation of an all-wise Providence."[9]

If Al tangled with the likes of Brown or Peel, he never said anything about it, but he did have at least one brush with an outlaw, while working on the Virginia City road crew. A bandit held him up, taking all he had, which was fifty cents. Nobody could frighten Sieber, and he teased the gunman so much for robbing a workingman of a few pennies that he was almost killed. Or so Al later told it.[10]

8 *Ibid.*, 341–56.

9 Samuel Post Davis (ed.), *The History of Nevada*, I, 245–47 and 247–49.

10 Dan R. Williamson, "Al Sieber, Famous Scout of the Southwest," *Arizona Historical Review*, Vol. III, No. 4 (January, 1931), 60 (cited hereafter as Williamson, "Sieber") ; "Al Sieber, Man of Blood and Iron," in Frank C. Lockwood, *More Arizona*

In those years there was not much doing around Virginia City for a single man with no capital. Most of the major strikes had been made, and mining was a big business controlled by the "ins"; to buck it, the "outs" needed strong determination and outstanding qualifications. There is nothing in Sieber's record to indicate that he had either, or desired them. About this time, however, a fresh rush began toward White Pine, three hundred miles distant and clear across the state. With thousands of others, Sieber plunged into the wasteland toward it—and toward his first real boom.

White Pine County, covering 8,200 square miles, is one of the most spectacular parts of the Silver State, corrugated as it is with numerous ranges of bony mountains trending generally north and south. The White Pine Range, dominated by 10,741-foot Mount Hamilton, is almost in the center of the county. One of the range's east-jutting spurs was early named Treasure Hill, and for good reason.

About 1865 a prospector from Austin, midway across the state, made a strike on the slopes of the White Pines, but it didn't arouse much interest. There were boomlets all over Nevada at the time, many seemingly more promising than this one. Since prospectors were a gregarious lot, they went where there was the most noise. White Pine was not such a place.

One night a couple of years after that first strike, Al Leathers, a blacksmith by trade, was awakened by a cascade of tin pans in his kitchen. He leaped from his bed in time to catch an Indian named Napias Jim (*napias* being an Indian word for silver, it is said) dipping into the bean pot. He ousted the intruder and went back to bed. There is probably more to the story than this, but all that is recorded is that a few days later Jim came around with a heavy rock in his hand as a peace offering. The rock was almost pure silver. Jim agreed to show the whites where he got it. Leathers, Tom Murphy, Ed Marchand, and others followed him to the top of Treasure Hill, where, on January 4, 1868, they staked out a rich claim on the bleak slopes above nine thousand feet. A short time later, J. E. Eberhardt made another strike in the vicinity.

Characters, 19 (cited hereafter as Lockwood, "Sieber"). Williamson, a solid friend of Sieber during Al's later years, no doubt got this tale firsthand.

There was noise enough now. "Population gathered in, like the waters of a cloudburst,"[11] and among the newcomers was Al Sieber. This is what he must have seen:

> Within the first season some 10,000 or 12,000 men had established themselves in huts and caves 9,000 feet above the sea. All locomotives were in requisition, from Shank's mare to the dashing coach, and teams groaned under the burden of subsistence for the pilgrim army. In the midst of the small-pox, with the thermometer at zero, a carnival of riot and speculation were [*sic*] inaugurated. Mines, land, wood and water were claimed; towns were built; lots rose to the thousands; and mining claims, good, bad, or indifferent, were bought and sold at unconscionable prices.[12]

The communities of Treasure City, Hamilton, and Shermantown sprang up as this first big boom in eastern Nevada stormed financial circles. White Pine stocks with a total list value of $70,000,000 were on the exchange. Water in the towns sold at a quarter a bucket. Miners digging an artesian well struck ore and quit their jobs to file a claim. Two prospectors building a rock hut found the walls worth $75,000 and forgot about the weather. No bandit or sharpie could resist the White Pine lure. Bullion-laden stagecoaches were held up at the rate of two a week over a period of two years.

Newspapers eagerly reported every scrap of news from the bonanza. On November 21, 1868, the Prescott (Arizona) *Miner* enthused: "There is no getting around it, the White Pine mines are rich—wonderfully rich. . . . Wm. Woodburn, of this city, who spent some days in the mines, believes there is enough silver in the one small range . . . to pay off the national debt—large as it is." The strike was not all fake, by any means. Leathers and Murphy sold their Hidden Treasure for $250,000. The Eberhardt included one pocket worth $3,200,000, taken from a deposit seventy feet long, forty wide, and in no place more than twenty-eight feet deep. Men thought White Pine would never wear out.

But she did. Fire, the nemesis of every mining camp, swept its towns again and again. Before dawn one summer morning in 1873,

11 Angel, *op. cit.*, 649.
12 *Ibid.*, 650.

33

Hamilton was burned to the ground by one Alexander Cohn, who set fire to the rear of his cigar store to collect insurance—after first thoughtfully cutting off the town's water supply. Other camps burned. Silver became a dead issue, and attention turned to lead, then copper, and the county's population dwindled to the point where a few stockmen could take over.[13] But that, of course, was long after Sieber had shaken its dust from his boots.

While in White Pine, Al no doubt became acquainted with men who would play important roles in his life. The first of these was a lively Irishman named Dan O'Leary, who had the makings of one of the greatest scouts of the Southwest. There is no proof that the two met at Treasure City or Hamilton, but both were there at the same time and in view of their close association later, it seems probable that they did.[14]

Sieber may also have run across a singular figure, one he would meet and journey with again, the mysterious Thomas Miner, who had been following the rushes since 1861, had not yet amassed his fortune,

[13] Unfortunately, none of the mining records of White Pine County during the rush years have survived, again because of fire. On January 1, 1885, the county courthouse, which until then was at Hamilton (since vanished), burned to the ground, the records with it. "The story is that the Deputy Clerk and Treasurer [of the county] could have been short in his funds and started the fire to cover up. He later killed himself. . . . [Thus] our records only go back to 1885." Boyd K. Smith, county clerk of White Pine County, in correspondence with author, May 26, 1960.

[14] That Dan O'Leary at least visited the White Pine silver camps during the rush is established, I think, by several references to him in the Treasure City, Nevada, *White Pine News*. Thus it lists a letter awaiting him at the Hamilton post office on February 16, 1869, and another on February 20 (lists of letters arrived were carried by most pioneer newspapers as a courtesy to their readers and to the postmaster as well; they are a good source for names of persons residing in such communities or expected to arrive there). The *News* of April 20, 1869, reports that D. O'Leary arrived in town. On June 4, 1869, it reported that a Daniel O'Leary was registered to vote in the Treasure City municipal election. A standing advertisement in the newspaper is for a King & O'Leary's Saloon at Austin, but I have seen no reference to indicate the first name of that O'Leary, and there were others of that surname—for instance, in the *News* issue of May 10, 1869, a Fergus O'Leary is mentioned, and a John O'Leary was said to have been injured in a mining accident. Because of the small number of O'Learys to be found in the pages of early southwestern history, one is tempted to speculate on a possible relationship among them, but I have uncovered no evidence to substantiate such a theory.

but thought he knew where to get it. The *White Pine News* announced his coming:

PARTY FOR THE COLORADO.—We understand that there is a man in Hamilton endeavoring to organize a prospecting expedition to prospect the mountains beyond the Colorado River, and east of San Francisco mountains. He claims to have been there, and run out by Indians, and says that he discovered placer diggings in that section which are good for one hundred dollars a day to the hand. He wants a party of one hundred men to return with him.[15]

It would be almost two years before Thomas Miner could actually embark on his expedition, but he would do it. Adventurer, visionary, man of undetermined background, promoter—Miner was all of these and more. He would make half of Arizona swallow his yarn before he was through.

Al may have prospected over into Utah briefly,[16] but if he did, he found nothing and soon was in southern California, again broke and looking for something to do. This time, horses were the answer.

Everybody in Arizona, or almost everyone, got horses from California in one way or another. There was a steady demand, because those the Indians didn't steal and eat were worn out by settlers chasing Indians who did steal and eat them. Driving livestock from southern California became quite a business, albeit for only the hardiest of men, and as long as the Indians ruled the territory, which in 1868 looked as though it might be forever, the market would continue. San Bernardino was the port of embarkation.[17] Horses from the ranches

15 *White Pine News*, May 10, 1869.

16 On May 12, 1892, the Florence-Tucson, Arizona, *Enterprise* reprinted an article (cited hereafter as *Enterprise*, "Sieber") from the Solomonville, Arizona, *Graham County Bulletin* which quoted Sieber as saying he came to Arizona in 1867, prospecting through the southern part of Utah and landing in Mohave. But the paper is in error on the date, since the White Pine rush didn't get under way until the following year, and other writers who mention the subject at all say that Sieber came to Arizona from southern California, which is undoubtedly correct, even if he did make some sort of prospecting junket across the border into Utah. Even Tom Horn, who is always interesting, if usually unreliable, wrote that "no one knew where he came from originally [which is nonsense]. A few people in Arizona had known him in California." Tom Horn, *Life of Tom Horn: A Vindication* (cited hereafter as Horn), 168.

17 San Bernardino was founded on the site of an Indian rancheria in 1852 by a

of the vast interior valleys were brought there and sold to men who would take them across the deserts, beyond the Colorado, to the half-known land beyond. And, one must point out, many a herd was moved from California to Arizona without benefit of bill of sale. Daniel Conner tells of stumbling across two fresh graves of horse thieves on the Bill Williams River a hundred miles from Prescott. They had brought the herd that far, he later learned, when, convinced they were close to their destination, one killed the other—so that he would not have to divide the anticipated spoils—and was then slain himself while "resisting arrest," as people said in those days.[18]

Hubert Howe Bancroft says that as late as 1880, Californians were driving thousands of cattle to Arizona and that the movement remained an important one for many years.[19] Horses and mules for the U.S. Army also arrived by this route. Tom Horn, writing of 1875, recalled that "the cavalry horses for the Department of Arizona all came overland from California . . . in big bunches of about 400 each."[20] This may have been an exaggeration because there was neither water nor grass enough across the desert to support herds of that size; smaller bunches must have been the rule. That the people of Arizona wanted horses is shown by this not unique item:

> HORSES WANTED.—The attention of the people of southern California is called to the fact that the proposed exploring expedition of Jack Swilling, and other enterprises in Arizona, will require a new supply of serviceable horses. The Los Angeles and Wilmington papers will please make a note of this.[21]

It was not a simple thing to move horses, often wild and unbroken,

---

colony of five hundred Mormons who settled on a section of the San Bernardino Rancho known as Agua Caliente. Brigham Young, who had given permission for the migration, became alarmed at the tendency toward apostasy and recalled some of his people, but the community flourished anyway and became the commercial and transportation hub for Arizona travel. W. W. Robinson, *The Story of San Bernardino County*, 27–47.

[18] Daniel Ellis Conner, *Joseph Reddeford Walker and the Arizona Adventure*, ed. by Donald J. Berthrong and Odessa Davenport (cited hereafter as Conner), 273.

[19] Hubert Howe Bancroft, *History of California*, VII, 55n.

[20] Horn, 27. His statement has been accepted uncritically by various writers, e.g., Gene Fowler, *Timberline*, 169, and others.

[21] Prescott, Arizona, *Arizona Miner*, April 11, 1866.

on so long a drive, as Charley Genung[22] discovered. He and a companion had contracted with settled Indians along the Colorado to bring them horses—at a good profit if they succeeded. Unfortunately, however, early in the drive the animals stampeded and there went the dividends.[23]

Others had better luck. The *Miner*, on October 17, 1868, reported that "Messrs. Roddick[24] and Feland have returned from Los Angeles, California. They brought with them a small band of very fine horses, which they did *not* steal, although Tom, who is a jokist of no mean calibre, says that in San Bernardino, the natives thought he was a horse thief!" Sieber may have come to Arizona with these men or some similar group following the same trail.

The desert limited routes from the comparatively lush valleys of the Los Angeles Basin to the Colorado Valley, for where there was no water, animals could not go. Thus it was water, more than terrain, that proscribed certain areas to travel and blocked out the courses trails (and, later, roads) had to follow. Most famous of these was the old Butterfield Stage route. It went east from Los Angeles to Chino and Sierra Rancho, then dropped down to Temecula, where the wind blew so regularly that when it failed, superstitious natives remained indoors to avoid the evil spirits who had stilled it. Beyond Temecula, Butterfield's coaches progressed to Warner's Ranch,[25] to Vallecito and the old Carrizo stage station, and through the stifling valley now

22 Charles B. Genung, born in Yates County, New York, on July 22, 1839, moved to California when only sixteen, then went to Arizona for his health in 1863. Despite his arrival as a near-invalid, he strengthened under the strong sun and bracing climate and became a noted prospector, miner, pioneer, and Indian fighter, settling in his old age in the Kirkland Valley, not far from his first mining ventures. Thomas Edwin Farish, *History of Arizona* (cited hereafter as Farish), IV, 27. Genung died August 16, 1916, "and was buried at Prescott with great honor." Roscoe G. Willson, *Pioneer and Well Known Cattlemen of Arizona* (cited hereafter as Willson, *Cattlemen*), II, 63.

23 Farish, II, 324–25.

24 This was Thomas G. Roddick, a noted Arizona figure who was, among many things, a hard drinker, a fortunate Indian fighter, and a successful miner. Born in Ohio about 1837, he reached Arizona in 1864, when he was twenty-seven, and died at Tucson in the late spring of 1879 at the age of forty-two. *Arizona Miner*, June 13, 1879.

25 It was three and one-half miles southeast of Warner's Hot Springs in San Diego County. The ranch was established by Jonathan Trumbull Warner, who had acquired a land grant from Mexico in 1844.

called Imperial, crossing the New River near present-day Calexico and dipping into Old Mexico to avoid the awful sea of sand dunes before touching the Colorado at Yuma, or, as it was then called, Arizona City. A slight variation went east to Beaumont, then curved south to Warner's Ranch.

A second and much newer route was the Bradshaw road, named for William Bradshaw, who charted it more or less by accident in the spring of 1862 while making his way to the Arizona mining camps near La Paz.[26] Bill followed the usual freighters' route east to San Bernardino, continued through San Gorgonio Pass, went by way of Agua Caliente (later Palm Springs) to what is now the northern edge of the Salton Sea, then swung almost due east, via Tabaseco Tank, Chucowalla Well, and Mule Springs (probably the present-day Wileys Well), to the Colorado just south of the modern town of Blythe. There he established ferry service to Olivia, or Olive, named for Olive Oatman, whose survival of a massacre, captivity, and ultimate release by the Indians comprised a thrilling early Arizona adventure.[27] Bradshaw operated his ferry for two years before slicing his throat in a fit of delirium tremens, but not before he had made at least one important prospecting trip into the interior, bequeathing his name to an imposing mountain range that bulked historically in the conquest of Apachería.

In the spring of 1868 the Post Office Department adopted the Bradshaw Road as the official route from Los Angeles to Prescott, by way of Wickenburg, and it was never completely abandoned until the Southern Pacific bridged the Colorado at Yuma in 1877. As a matter of fact, it is still used by a few desert travelers and prospectors. Nevertheless, stock could employ it only with difficulty because of the scarcity of water and forage, so horse herders, including the party with which Sieber traveled, took a third way to Arizona. They followed what was called the Old Government Road,[28] the most crooked

[26] See Franklyn Hoyt, "The Bradshaw Road," *Pacific Historical Review*, Vol. XXI, No. 3 (August, 1952), 243–54, and Genung's description in Farish, IV, 28–34.

[27] For a contemporary account of the captivity of Olive Oatman, see William B. Rice, *The Los Angeles Star 1851–1864*, 272–84, which reprints a long account that appeared in the *Star* on April 19, 1856, and was widely copied.

[28] For details of this route, now totally abandoned except where modern roads chance

but by all odds the most comfortable way to Arizona, if that be the right word to describe two hundred miles of burning desert, white flats, stony mountains, little vegetation, and almost no water.

From San Bernardino, horses were driven north up Brown's Toll Road, via broad Cajon Canyon, to Summit Valley, emerging into what is today, as it was a century ago, the blue world of the Mojave Desert: blue ranges, blue sky, blue distance. The animals were pushed along the present route of the Santa Fe Railroad to the Verde Ranch, known then as the "Upper Crossing," and down the Mojave River to the "Lower Crossing" at Lane's, a station where a Captain Lane kept a stock of whiskey and tobacco for travelers.[29] Now fifty miles from San Bernardino, cavalcades would follow the valley of the dwindling Mojave another twenty-two miles to Old Grocery, just beyond the present-day Helendale. From here the trail bore east, past the Fish Ponds, still following the Mojave as the surest source of water and cottonwood shade and fuel. At Forks in the Road,[30] a branch trail split off toward the north. Called variously the Spanish Trail or Salt Lake Trail, it meandered its way east of Death Valley and into Deseret.

The Mojave was often dry east of Forks in the Road, although there was usually water at Camp Cady, five miles east of the Forks and situated on the white stone benches north of the river bed.[31] Built to afford travelers nominal protection from wandering bands of the miserable Indians who infested the Mojave, it found most of them only a nuisance, although a couple of years earlier the Ninth Infantry had had a scrap with them in which it lost three men killed and a

to touch or follow its course for a few miles, I am indebted to L. Burr Belden of the *San Bernardino Sun*, the best authority on the desert regions of San Bernardino County. He has personally traversed most of the old road, and his knowledge and guidance have enabled me to visit portions of it.

[29] This is the present-day Oro Grande, northwest of Victorville.

[30] Five or six miles east of Barstow, today the site of a Marine Corps supply depot.

[31] Camp Cady, established in April, 1860, was named for Lieutenant Colonel Albemarle Cady, and in this year, 1868, it was moved from its original location to a site half a mile west, where buildings of stone and adobe were being built. It was abandoned in 1871. Aurora Hunt, *The Army of the Pacific*, 263–64; see also Phil Townsend Hanna, *The Dictionary of California Land Names*, 42.

guide wounded.[32] These may have been Paiutes, but more likely they were fierce Chemehuevis, a people whom Sieber, it is said, once listed among the Indians he had fought.[33]

Bands of horses moved past The Caves (in Afton Gap) and on to Fort Soda (erected at what is now Zzyzx Springs), on the eastern edge of Soda Dry Lake, a blinding sheet of white which looks today as it did a hundred years ago. Only a few stone walls mark the site of this outpost, some forty-five miles from Camp Cady. It surely must have been the least desirable of all military stations.

From Fort Soda the herds were driven into the rolling country between Old Dad and Club mountains, thence down Willow Wash to Camp Marl Springs, where was to be seen the novelty of a log stockade in the desert—built of timber cut in Cedar Canyon, through which the Old Government Road threaded the Mid Hills beyond in order to reach Fort Rock Springs.[34] About a year earlier, a seventeen-year-old mail rider named Higgins had had a lively brush with hostiles in the vicinity of Marl Springs, killing two Indians and wounding a third. "When asked what kind of shots he made," reported the Prescott *Miner*, "he replied that he was in and about the center every time. He has, within two years past, killed more Pah-Ute Indians than all the troops combined."[35]

After Fort Rock Springs came Lanfair Valley, then Fort Piute (at Piute Springs), the ruins of whose stone structures today command a view of three states.[36] From here the trail swung north a bit, then offered a choice of divergent routes. Military traffic bore south across the Dead Mountains toward Fort Mohave, which lay east of

---

[32] *Chronological List of Actions, &c., with Indians, from January 1, 1866, to January, 1891* (cited hereafter as *Chronological List*), 3, states that the action, on July 29, 1866, involved a detachment of D Company, Ninth Infantry, commanded by Lieutenant J. R. Hardenbergh. The account does not claim that any Indians were hit, nor does it identify the enemy by tribe.

[33] Lockwood, "Sieber," 20, says Al campaigned against "Hualpais, the Chemehuevis, the Mohaves, and the White Mountain, San Carlos, and Chiricahua Apaches."

[34] There is still a settlement named Rock Springs at this place, which was also called Camp Rock Springs, thirteen miles south of Ivanpah. Few ruins remain of the military establishment.

[35] *Arizona Miner*, July 27, 1867.

[36] Hunt, *op. cit.*, 264–65 .

the river. Most civilians followed a more northerly course, passed Firpo's Well, crossed the Eldorado Mountains, and descended into the wide, welcome river valley within sight of Hardyville, 260 or 275 miles from San Bernardino, depending on which particular course was followed. This, of course, was the route that Sieber's party took.

From Eldorado Gap, travelers of today can see, as could those of yesterday, the great barrier range of the Black Mountains beyond the river—black on top, presumably to give them their name, but splotched and banded and marked with a multitude of colors on their lower reaches. Beyond them, and barely discernible over them, lie the Cerbats, topped by Mount Scherum on the left and the high Hualpais on the right. It seems to the viewer as if the earth continues endlessly like this: range after broken range, dusty, brushy valleys between, and the monotonous succession continuing forever. But this world is cut off from California by the Colorado, bent and roily in that day before dams were built, emerging from an unnamed gorge to the left and fading into the remote distance on the right. On the far bank of the river lay Hardyville, toward which the trail of the 1860's made its way.

III. The Road to Prescott

AL SIEBER's horse herd had reached a semblance of civilization once more. Tied to a makeshift dock on the east bank of the Colorado was a "large ferryboat capable of crossing, entire, a ten mule team."[1] On that bank, too, lay Hardyville,[2] a cluster of buildings of the type common to the southwestern frontier, a few topped with shingles but most with the brush-and-earth roofs more generally used. It boasted twenty permanent residents and often scores of transients, for, 337 miles upstream from Yuma, it was for nine months of the year the head of navigation, as well as the point where the San Bernardino–Prescott freight road crossed the river. Here, seven miles above Fort

[1] *Arizona Miner*, August 29, 1868.

[2] The editor of the *Miner* wrote of a visit to the place about this time: "Hardyville, a cluster of large, fine adobe buildings which Wm. H. Hardy has erected, at great expense. The main building is the largest seen by us in the Territory, and very cool and handsome. A portion is occupied by S[amuel] Todd, who has the largest and best stock of goods seen by us on the trip, and who, all Arizonans know, is a large-hearted, liberal trader. Another portion of the Building is occupied by H[enry] F. Hardy [a nephew], who runs a saloon and hotel, where creature comforts are very liberally dispensed. The town is, of course, on the east bank of the Colorado, about 200 feet above the ocean level, and about 450 miles from the mouth of the river." *Arizona Miner*, September 30, 1871. The site is at the head of a big bend of the river, which here narrows, shortening the ferry distance. Hardyville was built on a point of rocks between Silver Creek and Montana Wash about two miles below the present Bullhead City, which is an equal distance below Davis Dam. Only the outlines of foundations and a few tipsy markers in a dreary little cemetery are left of this once most promising village. Failing mines and construction of a railroad crossing at Needles, farther south, doomed it, but fires also proved disastrous. Up Silver Creek Wash a short distance lies a rusting boiler and stone foundations of a once busy mill, and rubbish from former structures and homes suggests the promise of the camp a century ago.

Mohave, stern-wheeled river boats, drawing no more than twenty-five inches of water, or an occasional schooner met wagon trains.

The boats brought and took away high-priced cargo, although costs were not exorbitant when all factors were considered. Freight was eighty dollars a ton from San Francisco to Hardyville and ore from twenty to twenty-five dollars a ton to Selby Smelter at San Francisco, or other Pacific ports, or even Swansea, Wales.[3] Hardyville was a busy place, and by rights it should have become the first commercial metropolis of northwestern Arizona, but it didn't make it and by now has totally disappeared.

In 1868, however, Hardyville was the pride of its founder, Captain William Harrison Hardy,[4] one of the wealthiest men in Arizona Terri-

[3] Farish, IV, 14; Richard G. Hinton, *The Handbook to Arizona,* 66.

[4] The census of 1864 showed William Harrison Hardy, with a reported personal fortune of $40,000 (which he had brought from California), the second richest man in the Territory; Mark Aldrich of Tucson, with $52,000, ranked first. Low man on this scale of measurement was Thomas J. Gooman, who reported his assets at twenty-five cents. Rufus Kay Wyllys, *Arizona, the History of a Frontier State,* 172. Hardy was born in Allegheny County, New York, on April 25, 1823, of sturdy New England stock. The family was descended from a Thomas Hardy, born in England in 1605, who came to America with Governor John Winthrop in 1630. Thomas was one of a dozen men picked to start a new settlement at Ipswich, where a well he dug is still in use. His descendants included Francis Hardy, who fought in the French and Indian War under Captain Edmund Moore, taking part in the 1759 invasion of Canada; Samuel Hardy, a Minuteman, who marched at the Lexington alarm, September 19, 1775; and Sam Hardy, William's father, a War of 1812 soldier who fought at Lundy's Lane, Chippewa, and Black Rock. William was one of nine children. With an older brother, John Nelson Hardy, he settled for a time in Wisconsin, expecting to marry a certain girl, but she died before the wedding; heartbroken, he never married thereafter. In 1849 he joined a wagon train of about one hundred persons bound for California. He was elected captain of the company and thereafter was known as Captain Hardy, although he never saw military service. Until 1864 he was a merchant at Forest Hill, Placer County, California, where he became a personal friend of such empire builders as Collis Potter Huntington, Leland Stanford, and Mark Hopkins, with whom he had frequent dealings. No doubt he worked up a desire to emulate them, or at least duplicate their phenomenal successes. At any rate, having amassed a respectable fortune, he went to Arizona and built his toll road, through Indian country, from the Colorado to Prescott. In 1866 he was elected a member of the Territorial Council from Mohave County, along with Captain A. E. Davis. He and Davis had a three-day running fight with Indians on their return to the Colorado. Several members of their party were wounded, no doubt adding fuel to Hardy's enthusiastic and abiding hatred of all Indians. "Uncle Harrison had the frontiersman's dislike of Indians," confided a niece. "Once, I remember, he told how coyotes

tory. With his development and maintenance of a 165-mile toll road to Prescott and his business interests there and at San Bernardino, the thin, bearded frontiersman was not only one of the most colorful Arizona pioneers but also one of the most influential. He was an odd mixture of business acumen, relentless drive, fatherly advice to anyone who would listen, and a robust hatred for Indians if they were hostile, which, unfortunately for them, they generally were. "When I had the advantage," he boasted, "I cared but little for an Indian. I looked upon them as upon wild animals. They are wild human beings, and when hostile are but little better than a wolf or a bear. Killing makes good Indians of them."[5]

His prices were high, as they were all over northern Arizona, and no wonder, the circuitous route by which supplies arrived. "Hardy's stock consisted of flour, $20 a hundredweight; bacon, 50¢ per pound; coffee, 50¢ per pound; sugar, three pounds for a dollar; soldier's boots, $10 per pair; overalls, $3 per pair, cash down and no kicking," grumbled one former customer, adding, somewhat more charitably, that "his ferry was also a paying business, but if you had no money, he would give you what you wanted out of the store, and cross you over the river for nothing."[6]

Hardy possessed a mine in the shaft-pitted mountains about nine miles from Hardyville, and he also owned the mill at the town. Al Sieber allowed he'd stick around awhile, and Hardy probably gave him a job of some sort, although there is no surviving record to show what it was. Al later said that he stayed at the place "a few weeks."

Here he no doubt heard firsthand of Indian escapades in the vicinity. Most of them referred to the Walapais, who gave the Apaches

---

had eaten poison put out for them, and died. Indians then ate the coyotes, and died, too. He seemed pretty pleased about it." Nevertheless, Hardy was an empire builder and while he had it, he distributed his wealth generously and was well liked and respected among a courageous, self-reliant, and robust people. He died of cancer June 23, 1906, at the home of his sister at Whittier, California, and is buried there. Time, or vandals, or both, have toppled the tombstone over his grave in a forlorn cemetery there. Information from Mrs. Alta Brannan, Hardy's niece; from Emma Freeland Shay, *Mariet Hardy Freeland: A Faithful Witness*; and from the *Los Angeles Times*, June 26, 1906.

[5] Farish, IV, 87.

[6] *Ibid.*, 74.

nothing when it came to ambushes and sudden slaughter. Only a couple of years earlier they had come upon Ira Woodworth, first recorder of Mohave County (Hardyville had been the county seat), and a man named Nathaniel Benjamin sinking a shaft and fired on them. Both were wounded. Woodworth ran about forty yards and tumbled down an arroyo bank, where he was found with four bullets in him and his skull crushed to a jelly. Two miners, Andrew Judson and Metcalf Baker, were working in a 130-foot shaft near by. They probably heard the shooting, and while trying to climb out were met by a shower of rocks with which the Indians smashed them back to the bottom, killing both. Sam Knodles and a companion, James L. Conover, tried to fight off the Walapais but found the odds too great and escaped, somehow reaching the river, eight miles distant. A search party found Benjamin's body six miles from the scene, where he had wandered, mortally wounded.[7]

All over northern Arizona at this time the story was the same. That same year, Hardy had taken a gaggle of miners on a wild-goose chase after a "silver mountain" somewhere on the Little Colorado, and on the way back they had been jumped by hostiles near Cataract Creek.[8] They fought off the Indians, but their mules got away and the prospectors had to hoof it back to Hardyville. Less than a year before Sieber arrived there occurred a fabulous battle which pitted a lone white man against almost overwhelming numbers of Indians. It was on March 21, 1868, that angular Charley Spencer, in the rocks above the Hardyville-Prescott road, held off seventy-five Indians after his two companions had been slain and he himself seriously wounded.

Periodically, Hardy secured contracts to haul government freight from Fort Mohave to Fort Whipple, just outside Prescott, and made up trains to haul it, with ten-mule teams or a dozen yoke of oxen to a wagon, manned by hired teamsters or, quite often, "men who were

---

[7] *Arizona Miner*, October 13, 1866.

[8] A beautiful creek, also called Havasu, north of Williams. John D. Lee hid out in its canyon for several years after the Mountain Meadows Massacre. Will Croft Barnes, *Arizona Place Names* (cited hereafter as Barnes, *Place Names*), 1935 edition. A second edition, "revised and enlarged by Byrd H. Granger," was published by the University of Arizona Press in 1960. Unless otherwise indicated, the first—and superior—edition is meant in citations of this immensely valuable work.

travelling through from California and would volunteer for protection." Thus when Sieber worked up a desire to go to Prescott after three or four weeks, he may have accompanied such a caravan over the road, such as it was.[9] One freighter grumbled—and he no doubt spoke for many—that just about all repairs on the road were made by "Hardy walking along and leading his horse and kicking out such rocks as he could with a pair of number eleven boots."[10] A small part of the route laid out by Hardy is still in use, but most of it has been sacrificed to the sudden storms, the leaching of the sun, and the whirling desert winds of nearly a century.

Upon leaving Hardyville, wagon trains climbed to an elevation of nearly four thousand feet to cross Union Pass[11] through the Black Range, or Blue Ridge, as the southern part of the chain was often called at that time. The trail continued due east past Coyote Holes to Beale's Springs, at the southern toe of the Cerbats a little north of present-day Kingman. In December, 1867, the Walapais had raided the mail station there, killing all the stock just for mischief, and one never knew when they would sweep down like wolves again.

Working almost due east, freighters cursed their way across an interminable stretch of team-whipping, wagon-wrenching arroyos and sandy creek beds—almost always dry. About thirty-five or forty miles east of Union Pass, after threading the saddle between the high Hualpais and the Peacocks, they camped at a welcome tank. On the road again, they entered Cactus Pass.[12] They could sight eastward as

[9] This may have been early in 1869, putting his arrival at Hardyville in the fall of 1868. An unlabeled note in the APHS files says simply that Sieber came to Arizona, "stopping first at Hardeyville [sic] near Old Fort Mojave, continuing to Prescott," while the *Republican* obituary says that he stopped at Hardyville and "in 1869 he continued his journey to Prescott." The Florence-Tucson *Enterprise* reports Sieber's "landing in [Fort] Mohave, where he remained only three or four weeks and proceeded to Prescott."

[10] Farish, IV, 73–74.

[11] Used in 1857 by Lieutenant Edward F. Beale, who named it John Howell's Pass in honor of one of his men, and traversed even earlier, in 1851, by Captain Lorenzo Sitgreaves, for whom it was named Sitgreaves Pass by Lieutenant J. C. Ives, who crossed it in 1858. Barnes, *Place Names*, 465.

[12] Cactus Pass was so named by Lieutenant Amiel W. Whipple in 1854 because of "the peculiar vegetation" which abounded there. "The pass," he said, "is a deep gorge in a high range of granite mountains," now called Cottonwood Cliffs. Barnes, *Place Names*, 2nd ed., 204.

down a gun barrel, through this canyon at bulky Cross Mountain, a noted landmark.

Hardy's road curved over to The Willows, or Willow Grove, a beautiful spot that became a noted station and was once a short-lived army base.[13] Then it worked up Lookout Wash and southeastward to Fort Rock, where a youngster's playhouse had saved the lives of a party of whites.[14] Fort Rock was just five miles west of Cross Mountain, at the head of Fort Rock Creek. Hardy liked to reminisce about an incident which could have occurred in this vicinity; it involved a German known as Dutch Jake, who was accompanying a train to Prescott. The teamsters urged Jake to throw his pet white horse in with the herd for the night, but instead he tied the animal to a tree and went to sleep beside it. During the night, the horse was stolen, and in the morning, there it was, in a small clearing high on the mountainside. "There is my horse, mein Gott!" Jake cried, starting up the slope toward it, despite the efforts of Hardy and his teamsters to dissuade him. "We all saw the trap, and I watched the poor fellow climbing to be shot," Hardy recalled. "The Dutchman reached a little open space near his horse, when he suddenly stopped, fired his rifle, and gave a peculiar moan and yell. I well remember the different expressions made by the boys. One said, 'The Dutchman has got his horse.' Another remarked: 'We will have Jake for breakfast. We will mix a little Indian with Dutch.' After dropping his gun the poor fellow made fast time for camp. One of the boys said, 'He doesn't want his horse.' Another said, 'He'll have no further use for a horse, he won't get back.' The poor Dutchman got within thirty yards of camp and fell. I got hold of a canteen of water and ran to assist him, but he was dead. I pulled six arrows out of his back and sides."

One might well think the teamsters were callous, but they had been seasoned by years of freighting and Indian fighting and it wasn't that they wouldn't lay down their lives for Dutch Jake. It was just that he was so stubborn. They quickly mounted the horses and team mules

[13] Barnes, *Place Names*, 489, says that Willow Grove was at the south end of the Cottonwood Cliffs on a White Cliff Creek, which may be the Cottonwood or Willow Creek of today. The camp was established in the summer of 1867 and abandoned two years later.

[14] Farish, IV, 133–34.

and sped after the Indians, killing and scalping a couple and wounding others. When they returned, they buried Dutch Jake, whose proper name no one knew, in a shallow grave, ate breakfast, and continued their journey.[15]

From Fort Rock the road circled the southern flank of Cross Mountain, then bore southeast down Muddy Creek to Muddy Station, about twenty miles southeast of Willow Grove. The canyon which the road followed was usually a quagmire in winter. Freighters dreaded it. But they pushed on, passing Anvil Rock, to the famous Oaks and Willows, where they would be within seventy miles of Prescott. The road went through Aztec Pass between the Santa Maria and Juniper mountains, gaining on the eastern side Big Chino Valley by way of Walnut Creek and Old Camp Hualpai. About the time Sieber came through, Hardy established a tollgate at this point and changed its name to Camp Tollgate.[16] His rates were not published, but probably did not differ much from those established for the later toll road to the mouth of Bill Williams River on the Colorado: "For two-horse wagons, horse, mule or oxen, four cents a mile; one-horse wagon, three and one-half cents a mile; horse and rider, two and one-half cents a mile. No charge for footmen."[17] Once a traveler was beyond Camp Tollgate and well into Chino Valley, it was a more or less straight shot to Prescott, entering from the northwest.[18]

Trail time varied widely, depending mostly on the means of conveyance. In 1868, the *Miner* told of one California train that "was over 30 days making the trip. On the road, Indian fires were frequently seen, and it is very evident that the savages were anxious to capture the train, but they did not attempt it."[19] Two years earlier, Hardy, on horseback, made it in four days from San Bernardino to Hardyville

---

[15] *Ibid.*, 77–84.

[16] It was also called Defiance and Hualpais, at various times.

[17] Barnes, *Place Names*, 472.

[18] Aside from references already cited, I have depended upon Hinton's 1878 map and much interpolation for the route of the Hardyville-Prescott Road, tracing it out on topographical maps of the Geological Survey. There were undoubtedly many modifications and variations in the route from month to month and year to year, as weather, experience, and exigencies dictated, but in general it followed the course given.

[19] *Arizona Miner*, June 27, 1868.

The skills, abilities, and deeds of Chief of Scouts Al Sieber helped win the war against the Apaches.

General George Crook planned and organized the long but successful Apache campaign. The theory behind it was uniquely simple: Use Indians to catch Indians.

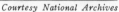

August V. Kautz commanded the Department of Arizona from 1875 to 1878. Sieber served him as guide in central and northern Arizona in 1877.

General Orlando B. Willcox, commander of the Department of Arizona from 1878 to 1882.

and four days more to Prescott—good time, even though he knew the road and had good luck.[20]

No matter how you reached it, Prescott was a pretty sight. It was as different from the adobe communities of southern Arizona as Minneapolis from Mexico City. Situated in a pine forest at an elevation of 5,355 feet, it was built almost entirely of wood; there was scarcely an adobe brick in town. It never had the "man for breakfast" gunfighting bad temper of many southwestern cities, but that is not to say it wasn't tough, well blooded by Indians, and full of weird characters. But it had an aura of permanence, the seeds of an established settlement, and was the logical place for the first territorial capital.

Prescott had rapidly outgrown and absorbed its short-lived rival, Gimletville, best noted for a restaurant run by a woman known as "Virgin Mary" (no one knew her real name). It was politely suggested that she was so called "because of her charity and benevolence," though one is tempted to suspect it was for the same reason that westerners tab bald men "Curly." Anyway, her fame was swallowed up in the growth of the area, and she died about 1888 on Lynx Creek and was buried in a grave unmarked and forgotten.[21]

Founded in 1864, the city had grown apace. George W. Barnard opened the Juniper House, its first hotel, on July 4 of that year, advertising the opening-day menu as follows: "Breakfast: Fried Venison and chili; Dinner: Roast Venison and chili; Supper: Chili." The first "well-regulated saloon" was established by Tom Hodges.[22] He was adept with any type of weapon, so when it came time to organize Indian fighters, he was voted captain. Thus "well-regulated" was no doubt an accurate description of his place of business.

The Indian menace grew along with the town. Conflict between the whites and the red men was inevitable. White men began to steal what the Indians had, to drive them from their ranges, to shoot out their game and destroy their means of livelihood. The Indians, who at first welcomed them, came to covet the goods the whites brought—

[20] *Arizona Miner*, March 28, 1866.

[21] Farish, III, 212.

[22] From a February 27, 1877, lecture before the Prescott Library Association by Judge Edmund W. Wells, as quoted in Farish, III, 190–99.

their horses and mules, their firearms, and, as native foods diminished, the foodstuffs the whites raised or imported. Both races were wild and violent by inheritance, training, and inclination. Whoever was to blame for starting the carnage, from the moment it began, Arizona's soil was repeatedly drenched with blood as thousands of men, women, and children, both white and red, were slain and many thousands more inflicted with grievous wounds in wanton sacrifices to the gods of misunderstanding and cruelty.

By the time Al Sieber arrived, there were more than two thousand placer miners working the gulches around Prescott, which had been established as a gold camp, and the community itself had a population of four or five hundred.[23] There were ten saloons, and no bank; many mercantile establishments, but not a school, church, or missionary. Gambling halls were open day and night, seven days a week. Prices were high, since most supplies had to be brought in by pack animal or freighted over the long San Bernardino Road. Potatoes sold for up to a dollar a pound, and a sack of flour cost one hundred dollars, payable in greenbacks, worth seventy-five cents for a dollar in Prescott gold.[24]

The best account of Prescott's growth is contained in the files of the *Miner*, its early newspaper and one of the best journals in the Southwest. The reason for this is not hard to find, for the record actually began with the issue of September 21, 1867, when the *Miner* was taken over by a different editor and came to life. The new proprietor, a diminutive and cocky fellow named John H. Marion, took over about the time Sieber arrived at Prescott, and, judging by the newspaper's frequent references to Al and his campaigns against Indians, the two became friends and no doubt admired each other.

Born at New Orleans in 1835, John Marion came to Arizona in 1864 with a party headed by Theodore W. Boggs and Will Short. He was attracted to the mines and also owned a Chino Valley ranch, but

[23] An 1867 census showed Arizona's population that year to be 7,136, up from 5,524 the previous year and 4,187 in 1864. Of the total, Yavapai County, of which Prescott is the county seat, had a population of 2,327; Pima County, with Tucson the county seat, 2,776; Yuma County, 1,156; Mohave, 336; and Pah-Ute, 541. *Arizona Miner*, May 4, 1867.

[24] Farish, III, 190–216, presents many details on the growth of Prescott.

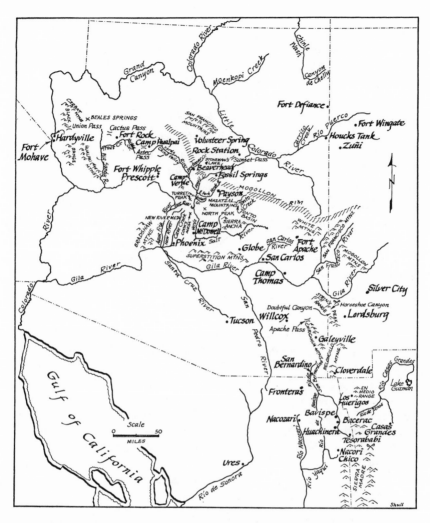

Al Sieber's Theater of Operations, 1869–1907

he was a newspaperman at heart and either owned or edited sheets at Prescott most of the time until his death in 1891. He liked pioneers and they liked him. Marion got on well with army officers and soldiers. He took them to task occasionally, but there was mutual respect. General George Crook, the greatest Indian fighter Arizona ever knew, often quoted from the *Miner*, which he seemed to accept as a responsible sheet—a novel attitude for a Department of Arizona commander to have toward any newspaper! And Marion named his first son after the General, whom he admired immensely. Wise, witty, honest, pugnacious, devoted to Prescott and its people, John Marion was a great frontier editor and "his newspapers formed an inseparable part of the pioneer days of Arizona."[25]

Editing a mining-camp newspaper was not without its tribulations. One Christmas Eve, John was working late when some shooting started, and it seemed to be directed at him. He told his readers about it:

> As we were meditating silently, solemnly, and alone, in the office, some valiant heroes from the Post, filled with vim and lager beer, jerked their six-shooters and opened fire upon our den. Imagining we heard a bullet whiz through our roof, over our head, we quickly changed our base and entrenched ourself behind the stovepipe, but the firing ceased, and the enemy passed on. We thought no more of the matter, and, indeed, had forgotten all about it, until [William] Felt, the gentlemanly baker across the street from the MINER office, mentioned the subject, and said the soldiers thought that someone shot at them out of the office and, of course, they felt duty bound to return the fire. Well, that's all right, boys, but be a little more careful and sober next time.[26]

There were, nevertheless, compensations to running your own print shop. On the morning after a political campaign in 1868, Marion was disturbed at his office by "the welcome footsteps of Sol and Joe, two of the tastiest got up men in town," representing the liquor firm of Cal. Jackson & Co.:

> In a moment they entered our sanctum and presented us with two boxes filled with bottles containing champagne, brandy, whiskey, etc., and van-

[25] Estelle Lutrell, *Newspapers and Periodicals of Arizona 1859–1911*, 90–91.
[26] *Arizona Miner*, December 28, 1867.

ished before we had time to say Governor, His Excellency, Captain, Pard or anything else. We opened bottle after bottle, sampled contents, thought each and every brand first-rate, asked our friends to partake, which they did. Kept on so all day, and about sundown felt like writing a patriotic article, and did so. Next morning we awoke, looked over said article, and found it composed of such sentences as the following: The starspeckled bottle; long may it let down. Jackson & Co.—long may they w-a-v-e! Hurrah for Rush! We've met the enemy and they are ourn! "Everything is lovely, and the goose hangs high!"—our goose, not the Governor's goose —for it, we think, is cooked forevermore.[27]

Now twenty-four, Al Sieber was probably as broke as usual when he reached Prescott. It is said he had but fifty cents in his pocket, which appears to have been, up to this point, his normal capitalization. A meal, such as it was, went for a dollar—a slab of venison, heavy biscuits, gravy, and maybe a wedge of pie if the cook had opened a can of peaches—but there was no reason for Sieber to go hungry because "the custom in this country then was that no one should be barred from the bean pot," broke or not. He wandered down to John Rush's corral and went to work for five dollars a day, a job that lasted five days. After that he drove a team and acted as guard for Dan Hazzard, a bold and resolute guard being as important as a competent teamster in the central Arizona of that day.[28]

A man never knew when he was going to be ambushed; if not by Apaches or Mohaves or Yavapais, then by some white ruffians. But the Indians were the worst and most likely. So daring had they become that they even ran off horses from within the town itself—in broad daylight. "On Thursday at noon," wrote John Marion, "a band of Indians jumped the herd kept by Mr. A. G. Dunn,[29] and at the time grazing within half a mile east of the center of the town. An alarm

<hr/>

[27] *Ibid.*, June 6, 1868. "Hurrah for Rush!" refers to John A. Rush, who operated one of Prescott's two livery stables and corrals.

[28] Florence-Tucson *Enterprise*, May 12, 1892.

[29] Dunn, also the town butcher, was called (by A. F. Banta) "the most dangerous man in Prescott" at this time, having come from Oregon, where he had just been released from a penitentiary after doing time for a killing. At Prescott he was badly shot up by Sheriff Jerome B. Calkins and Deputy Sheriff John P. Bourke in an affair over a woman, but recovered from both the bullet wounds and his infatuation. Farish, III, 36–38.

was immediately given, and our citizens turned out in force, but being mostly on foot they soon gave up the chase. In an hour Lieut. [Samuel] Purdy [Jr.], and 25 cavalrymen from Whipple were on the track, with several citizens well mounted, but after an absence of 24 hours they returned, having been unable to follow the trail. In the herd were five horses belonging to O. Allen, one to Sheriff [John P.] Bourke, one to Ben Block, and one to the Governor making some five or six valuable saddle animals the Indians have taken from him within three years. This is a great country."[30] Even a year later, Marion admitted, the Indians were swarming like bees around Prescott: "Just now, our red brethren are awful thick hereabouts. They are seen in the woods, close to town, in the rocks below town, on Granite Creek, in fact, everywhere."[31] He urged his readers to "keep your powder dry and whenever you see an Indian that says 'Americano mucho bueno . . .' kill him; he don't mean it."

It was a busy town, Sieber found. Freight wagons rumbled in from the Colorado and pack strings from the mines. Carters hauled towering loads of lumber through the pitted streets, and once in a while there was even a fiercely screeching train of *carretas* up from Sonora, drawn by miserable oxen yoked in the "good old Mexican style," that is, by the horns instead of the neck.[32]

Perhaps most interesting to a young war veteran new to the country were the Indian fighters from the remote canyons and deserts, men who made the hunting of Indians an avocation, men like John Townsend, Tom Hodges, Tom Roddick, Willard Rice, Ed Clark, Gus Spear, Joe Felman, Lew Ellit, and a dozen more. Pre-eminent among them were two men almost unknown today, or remembered only through some isolated peak or pass named for them. More than to any others the successful opening and pacification of central Arizona could be credited to these two—to Dan O'Leary and Ed Peck. In personality they were far apart, but they were akin in courage and frontier skills.

[30] *Arizona Miner*, July 27, 1867.
[31] *Ibid.*, November 7, 1868.
[32] *Ibid.*, May 30, 1868.

Edmond George Peck,[33] as handsome as a matinee idol, was a dark-haired, dark-eyed man with a neatly trimmed dark beard. Everything he did, he did well. He went about the perilous business of scouting and Indian hunting so sagely that, as far as I know, he was never even wounded, yet he penetrated areas until then never explored by white men and studied the country until his knowledge of it was unequaled. He was the most sought-after guide in the Territory and served for a long time as general scout at Fort Whipple. He was an expert rifle shot, and his toll of Indians and game must have been extremely high, although he never boasted of it and tempered the anti-Indian philosophy of his times with a measure of kindliness and humanity which alone would set him apart from his rude companions.

Daniel Conner describes an occasion when, roaming the mountains alone, he was overcome with "mountain sickness" and barely reached a deserted cabin. He stumbled inside, faintness and fever draining his strength and will, and collapsed on its earthen floor. During the following days and weeks, he was delirious much of the time and for the remainder scarcely had the strength to mix *pinole* and creek water into a form of gruel, which alone kept him alive. Early in his ordeal he had the presence of mind to turn his mule loose; it was picked up some twenty miles distant and readily identified, but the finders concluded that Conner had fallen prey to wild Indians or some other wilderness hazard, and he was mourned as lost.

For somewhere between thirty-five and forty days—he lost count —Conner wasted from fever, his sickness, and starvation. Fortunately, the Indians didn't find him, but he began to think no one else would, either. Then, when hope was all but gone, a mule with a slain deer across its back passed the open door of the cabin. Behind it was an acquaintance, who abruptly paused with one foot on the doorsill.

[33] He was usually called "Ed. Peck," or "Ed. G. Peck," and often referred to as "Edward Peck." He was born in Canada on December 28, 1834. In 1858 he joined a party of emigrants, probably the George Banghart party, for he became a brother-in-law to Banghart en route to California. On reaching the vicinity of Bear Springs, not far from present-day Flagstaff, the party gave in to the Indians and returned to the Zuñi villages. It was not until 1863 that Peck, by now an experienced frontiersman, returned to Arizona for good.

He stared at Conner for a moment, and Conner, lying on the floor, stared back out of his feverish, sunken eyes.

"The Lord—Jesus—Christ," Ed Peck drawled slowly, carefully enunciating each syllable. "Have you been alone here all this time?" Conner groaned that he had. Peck threw the deer off the mule's back, hurriedly roasted some meat and left it for Conner, mounted the mule, and hastened to Prescott, returning at once with help. Within a few days Conner had regained enough strength to ride a mule, and they took him to town. It was such deeds as this that made Ed Peck beloved by half the Territory.[34]

The Canadian-born Peck later turned to mining and helped to develop a million-dollar silver mine named for him, but he lost out on it through litigation. He died December 14, 1910, at Nogales, a poor and forgotten man. In 1868, however, he was in his prime, thirty-three years of age and among the most popular men of Arizona.

Dan O'Leary was probably the most famous of all Arizona's scouts and guides by 1868, largely because his operations centered in the country of the Walapais, into which tribe he eventually married and whose language he spoke; the Walapais and Apache Mohaves were the prime devils of the period from 1864 to 1870. Dan was born in Ireland about 1834,[35] was of medium height, wiry as a tomcat, and must have had red hair.[36] One newspaper, in a comment typical of the good-natured banter editors liked to indulge in when speaking of O'Leary, observed:

> We may as well say, for it is the truth, that Dan, as his name indicates, is an Italian, born somewhere on the green banks of the Shannon, and

[34] Conner, 237–41.

[35] According to an unidentified statement in the APHS files. His death certificate, however, the statistics of which seem to be largely guesswork, would indicate that he was born about 1820, and one acquaintance seems to recall that when he knew Dan in the 1880's or 1890's, Dan was "an old man." Charles Battye, correspondence with the author, November 28 and December 2, 1958.

[36] In a sense, Dan merely continued, rather than originated, Irish participation in the affairs of Arizona. Hubert Howe Bancroft, *History of Arizona and New Mexico*, (cited hereafter as Bancroft), 378, says that a Hugo Oconor, who must have been an Irishman or descended from one, came in 1774 as inspector (in the service of Spain) to oversee reforms in military discipline at establishments below the Gila, where the Apaches were giving serious trouble.

as we have broken bread with him often in the mountains, we are prepared to say that he is as brave as he is warm-hearted. He has always lived somewhere from the Colorado river along up to Prescott, and is especially proud of the valley and the people about Hualpai. The citizens swear by him, mothers name their children after him, and somehow we thought nearly all the little ones looked like him, and if the future Arizonans are as good and true as he we shall be satisfied.[37]

Dan had been hired as guide for General William Jackson Palmer's hurried survey for a railroad route across northern Arizona and probably in late 1867 led the surveyors and engineers back across the desert (which they named "Dismal Plain") from Hardyville to Albuquerque. Dan enjoyed himself thoroughly, since the party was willing to undertake innumerable side trips to waterfalls, parks, and prehistoric ruins.[38] It was the sort of trip any scout dreamed of: plenty of rations, plenty of transportation, slow moving, no important fighting, freedom for the guides to do as they pleased, and a pack of educated greenhorns to bedevil.

The day after Christmas, 1868, the *Miner* noted that Dan O'Leary, "one of the best guides in Northern Arizona," had paid a visit to Prescott and Fort Whipple. He and Ed Peck were often in the news in those years. These two great scouts, the taciturn, thoughtful, wise Ed Peck and the "irrepressible" Dan O'Leary, as one editor liked to describe him, each pre-eminent in his own area, were in and out of Prescott constantly at the time Al Sieber arrived. Impressionable, good natured, eager to learn, and willing to tackle anything that looked interesting, Al, in due time, became associated with each of them and absorbed what they had to teach. They proved able instructors, and Al Sieber an apt pupil.

Between trips as a rifleman-guard for Dan Hazzard, Al may have wandered about Prescott, sampling the wares in its many saloons, playing a little poker, and taking in an occasional hop or other amusement offered in a typical frontier town. But some had noted its lamentable moral tone. No minister of the Gospel, except perhaps an itinerant preacher now and then, had held services, and something ought

[37] Tucson, Arizona, *Arizona Citizen*, June 22, 1872.
[38] Newspaper clipping, Los Angeles Public Library.

to be done about it. The *Miner* at length printed, probably for free, an item: "It has been suggested that, in the absence of regular preaching, it would be well to have a sermon read every Sabbath, after the Sabbath school exercises are closed, and a number of gentlemen of Prescott have agreed to read, in turn, a sermon or moral essay."[39]

Four gentlemen of substance were among those who responded to this clear civic duty: William H. Hardy, who occasionally visited Prescott; "fat and jolly" Judge William H. Berry; William F. Turner, first chief justice of Arizona Territory; and C. C. Bean, rancher, political figure, businessman, and prospector. For his part, John Marion plugged the meetings with moderate enthusiasm:

> RELIGIOUS SERVICES.—Our worthy friend, Judge Wm. H. Berry has agreed to give some good advice to sinners, next Sunday evening at the Court House at 3 p.m. We do not wish to be understood as capping for the Judge, when we advise sinful mortals to go and hear him explain his process for working one's way into the Heavenly District, where there are no Apaches and where gold is found free in the rock.[40]

The first lecture of the series was read by Curtis Coe Bean, "a good reader and talented gentleman," as the *Miner* put it. Bean spoke at many subsequent meetings, and it is likely that Al Sieber attended some of them. Born a Catholic and presumably reared as one, he, like anyone else who went to them, would have looked upon these services as the best way to pass a hot and otherwise idle Sunday afternoon, and in so doing, he would have come to the attention of Bean.[41] The

---

[39] *Arizona Miner*, September 12, 1868.

[40] *Ibid.*, November 14, 1868.

[41] Bean, who may have come from New York City, was born about 1828 and arrived in Arizona "in the early sixties." He lived in the vicinity of Prescott until the late eighties. He contracted with the army, established a ranch or two in the Williamson Valley, and was associated with Peck and others in the discovery and development of Peck's fabulous silver mine. Later he became interested in copper properties and made a good thing of it, confining his mining activities to southern Arizona. He served a term as delegate to Congress from Arizona. Bean was a "man of wonderful vitality and energy, optimistic to the greatest degree, and a man beloved by all who knew him." He died at New York City on February 3, 1904, at the age of seventy-six. *Prescott Weekly Journal-Miner*, February 3, 1904.

upshot was that Bean hired Sieber as foreman for one or two ranches he had established in the Williamson Valley northwest of Prescott, where, by reason of hostile Indians and the normal exigencies of frontier ranching, Al would be called upon for his utmost reserves of resourcefulness and courage.

IV. The Williamson Valley

WHEN AL SIEBER left Prescott for the Williamson Valley, he must have expected trouble. Hostile Indians seemed to be lurking everywhere that season; occasionally, stock was run off or someone killed within sight of the governor's "mansion" itself.[1] Bean's ranch, little more than twenty miles northwest of Prescott, was at the mouth of Mint Creek Wash,[2] and there Indian activity was at its worst.

Bean enjoyed the good life too much to live in such a remote place himself. He had opened an office on the east side of Prescott Plaza, and such items as this in the *Miner* suggest how he spent his leisure: "Col. E. D. Baker and wife, Mr. C. C. Bean and wife, have been rusticating on Dickason's ranch, Lower Agua Frio, and had a right nice time of it. The Colonel and Mr. Bean killed ever so many quail."[3] He preferred to send a good man to work his Williamson Valley ranch while he played the gentleman of leisure, and in Sieber he got one of the best.

Eighteen men had been killed by Indians between Williamson Valley and Prescott in 1868 alone,[4] and hostile attacks had been increas-

---

[1] Conner, 271.

[2] Near the place now called Simmons, which is at the site of a ranch started by either a John A. or William J. Simmons, depending upon which edition of Barnes's *Place Names* you read. The second edition says that Simmons was established at a former stage station, which probably is true, since it was on the Hardyville Road.

[3] *Arizona Miner*, October 10, 1868. Colonel Baker was a friend of Ed Peck and an avid hunter; I. Q. Dickason was at this time a noted Indian slayer in those parts, possibly because his ranch was continually harassed by raiders. He was U. S. marshal for Arizona in September, 1872, and died or was killed at Deadwood, South Dakota, on July 1, 1878.

[4] Farish, IV, 250.

ing regularly in frequency and brutality. They were about the only feature to plague the area, for Williamson Valley,[5] as the settlers used to say, stood "in the front rank of beautiful valleys." It had deep lakes, where fish a foot long were taken by the barrelful. Deer and antelope abounded, and there were fat bears in the woods that bordered its broad and rolling basin. The valley was easy of access, since the Hardyville Road threaded a portion of it and its mouth was at Chino Valley, about where Paulden is shown on modern maps. Despite its presently bloody reputation, it was among the first valleys settled north of Prescott. There may have been temporary camps there by 1865, but James Fine and his partner, J. W. Jenkins, an Ohioan, established the first permanent farm there in 1866,[6] and by 1870 at least twenty-seven ranches lay in its graceful folds.

Fine and Jenkins put in a corn crop in the spring of 1867 and it was ready for picking in the fall. On a brisk October day, Fine was shucking corn in the field near the house when he spotted Indians prowling around the corral and yelled at Jenkins, still in the house. His partner grabbed a double-barrel rifle loaded with buckshot and chased the intruders to a knoll about two hundred yards from the house. There five Indians ambushed him. The antagonists fired at each other simultaneously from a distance of only a few paces. Jenkins apparently wounded some of the hostiles but collapsed with three arrows through his neck, his jugular vein severed. Fine gathered him in his arms and had started back to the house when Jenkins murmured, "I'm dying, Jim," and expired. Nothing could have saved him. The neighbors gave Jenkins as proper a burial as they could, and the matter would have been forgotten save that Charley Spencer brought Prescott word a month later that the Indians had returned, opened the grave, "took out the body, cut the heart and lights out, and mutilated the body and limbs in a shocking manner." Charley believed that the hostiles had thrown pieces of Jenkins down the well

---

[5] Named for Lieutenant Robert Stockton Williamson, a topographical engineer with the Lieutenant Joseph C. Ives exploration party of 1854. Williamson is said to have surveyed the valley first. Barnes, *Place Names*, 2nd ed., 363.

[6] Farish, IV, 250.

to pollute it. Muttered the *Arizona Miner*: "What horrible brutes these Indians are!"[7]

The Williamson Valley was an avenue for Indian aggression across northern Arizona. Walapais, Apache Mohaves, Moquis, Paiutes, Yavapais, Navahos, and Tonto Apaches were all, at times, reported to have ravaged it,[8] and one was rarely sure which people he was fighting. But nothing could discourage the whites for long. The Indians learned that where a white man sank the toe of his plow, there he would remain, come flood or fire, murder or pillage, havoc or hell, and if he were killed, others would come in his stead. The settlers soon regarded ambush and silent murder "as the natural features of the country" and "rather expected them as a matter of course."[9]

As elsewhere in Arizona, everyone in Williamson Valley worked with firearms within easy reach. A plume of smoke in the distance might mean that someone was burning brush—or again, it might signify that the Indians were burning someone out. Lives and livestock were equally hard to keep.

In mid-April of 1870 the Indians launched a typical raid up the valley and gave Sieber what was probably his first real fight with the hostiles. Either by design or chance, they picked Saturday afternoon for it, when most of the ranchers would be at home or working near their houses, in anticipation of the evening's recreation. The foray was called "about the boldest of the season" by the *Miner*. The enemy descended first upon the ranch of Eli Puntney and "gobbled 'Bourbon,' a fine blooded horse," whose value they appreciated, suggesting that the raiders were neither Yavapais nor Apaches, since those Indians ate first and evaluated later with respect to horseflesh. On this occasion the raiders busily swept on. They drove off another valuable horse from the Davis place.[10] From elsewhere they got a fine mare

---

[7] *Arizona Miner*, October 19, 1867; November 23, 1867.

[8] The reports may have been inaccurate, of course, but settlers who should have been able to recognize these various tribesmen claimed that each, at one time or another, raided into the valley—the Paiutes very rarely, and then as what the settlers called "renegades," since this was far from their normal range; the Moquis only to steal; the Navahos only to raid stock; and the others to kill and rob as opportunity arose.

[9] John G. Bourke, *On the Border with Crook* (cited hereafter as Bourke, *Border*), 37.

[10] This was probably one C. Davis, who must have been a Southern sympathizer,

but for some reason let her go. And so they came to Bean's ranch, where Sieber and his men were in the house cleaning up.[11]

Racing to the stable, the hostiles tried to loot it but were driven off by Sieber's men, who used almost all of their ammunition and then, having forced the Indians to cover, rounded up what stock was loose and drove it swiftly to the Simmons ranch near by, where there was enough ammunition and manpower that the Indians didn't try to follow. Instead they entered the Bean house and rummaged through it, "robbed it, and played smash with things generally," said the *Miner*.

"Their last visit was paid to West's ranch," wrote Marion, "but the men on the place, having heard the shooting, and howling of dogs up the valley, imagined all was not right, and were watching for the moccasined thieves and murderers, who presently made their appearance. Fire was opened upon them, and John Martin . . . had the very good fortune to put a bullet through the carcass of one of the scoundrels. This 'slight incident' caused the remaining reds to take to their heels. . . . The settlers in the valley are willing to swear that the Indian killed was either a Moquis or a Navajo, and we are inclined in the opinion that the wretch was a Navajo."[12] Substance was lent to this suspicion when, some weeks later, Puntney's fine stallion was seen in the possession of the Zuñis, who claimed they got him from the Navahos.[13]

Al had other opportunities to sharpen his shooting eye during his year or more in the valley. In midsummer, for instance, Bean's ranch got it again. On August 21 the Indians "gobbled up fourteen head of horses and mules" belonging to Bean, Puntney, and other ranchers, and the following night they swooped down on a government train about a mile east of Camp Hualpai and ran off six government mules and two of Dan O'Leary's horses. A hastily organized expedition, including, no doubt, O'Leary as well as Sieber, tracked the raiders to

since he was nicknamed "Jeff." *Arizona Highways*, Vol. XIII, No. 3 (March, 1937), 24 *et seq.*

[11] I cannot prove that Sieber was at the ranch at this time, but the fight sounds as if he were in on it; he was foreman at the ranch from sometime in 1869 to sometime in 1870.

[12] *Arizona Miner*, April 22, 1870.

[13] *Ibid.*, August 27, 1870.

Hell Canyon but lost them. They returned convinced they had been chasing Navahos.[14]

Most of the many white expeditions against the Indians were spur-of-the-moment affairs, hastily organized after the hostiles raided some cabin or ran off livestock. Leaders of these counterraiders, if they proved adept or had good luck, might become quite famous locally. Sieber no doubt was influenced by them and developed a desire to emulate them. The population of central Arizona was so small, and the Indian fighters so few, that he doubtless knew all of them, or at least all who had made any sort of reputation.

Among the better known of these partisan leaders and professional Indian killers, who matured with Sieber's arrival in the Prescott area, was John Benjamin Townsend, himself said to be one-half Cherokee, but an implacable foe of the entire red race. This, according to legend, was because Comanches killed his parents, and perhaps other relatives, in Texas.[15] He was one of that breed of men, wrote John G. Bourke, "whose lives were a romance of adventure and danger" but the details of which are largely unwritten.[16]

Townsend was a Tennessean, although he was raised in Burnet County, Texas. He was born July 24, 1833, and his parents must have moved to Texas soon afterward, settling north of Austin in country disputed by Comanches and whites. Townsend signed up for service in Bernard Timmons' Company, Nichols' Regiment of Confederate

14 *Ibid.*

15 Farish, II, 249; James H. McClintock, *Arizona: Prehistoric, Aboriginal, Pioneer, Modern* (cited hereafter as McClintock), I, 191; Patrick Hamilton, *The Resources of Arizona*, 397 *et passim.*

16 Bourke, *Border*, 26. Most historians call him a Texan and his Confederate discharge states that he came from Fayette County, Texas, but his daughter, Ora Townsend French, who at this writing is still living, says that he came from Tennessee and there also is a Fayette County in that state. I have accepted her statement. Ora, or "Ory," as she is universally called, was the fourth of Townsend's six children and was born April 19, 1870. The others were Clara, December 18, 1863, and a son, Dee, October 24, 1864, both born in Texas; Lou, November 2, 1867; Ora; Chancy, born July 27, 1872; and John Benjamin "Ben" Townsend, Jr., born March 9, 1874, after his father's death. Chancy died in childhood, Dee never married, and Ben left no male children, so the family name died with these sons.

Infantry, on December 10, 1861, but served only six months and was discharged a private. He married Elizabeth R. Vickers[17] some time after his discharge and they migrated to Arizona in 1865, settling for a time in Prescott and then acquiring a ranch on the Lower Agua Fria southeast of the present town of Mayer. At this time John Townsend was of medium height, hardy, and dark complexioned, with eyes of a shade to match his jet-black hair and curly whiskers.[18] He took to Indian hunting as naturally as to ranching, and his reputation spread. By 1873 he could truthfully say, "I am well known here. . . . There is not a man in Prescott but what is acquainted with me."[19] By that time, anyone who read the *Miner*, at least, would know of John Townsend. He was first mentioned on February 29, 1868: "Theodore W. Boggs has sold his ranch on the lower Agua Frio to a Mr. Townsend. . . . We believe Mrs. Townsend is the first white woman who has settled upon the lower Agua Frio." By late 1869 it referred to him in connection with the return of a scout[20] headed by Lieutenant Thomas Ware Gibson[21] and guided by Ed Peck and Townsend, who was described as a "man who knows no fear, and is thoroughly skilled in Indian warfare." The expedition pursued Indians who had killed two men on the Lower Agua Fria ranch of I. Q.

---

[17] A Texan, born March 15, 1844.

[18] Information from his Confederate discharge, now in the possession of his grandson, Albert Francis French of Los Angeles, who generously supplied much of the information on John Townsend given here.

[19] In a letter dated July 16, 1873, to the Waltham Watch Company, from which he ordered a timepiece, which, unfortunately, failed to arrive before his death.

[20] The use of the word "scout" as a noun to indicate the reconnoitering of a party of soldiers or enlisted Indians—as "we made this scout," or "we returned from a scout" —is very ancient, although not clearly understood by philologists. I don't know its ultimate origin, but it appears, for example, during the French and Indian Wars. See Robert Rogers, *Journals of Major Robert Rogers*, 4 *et passim*. Rogers handles the word as if it were in common usage at that date in this connection.

[21] Gibson, an Indianan, served in the ranks throughout the Civil War, was commissioned after the war, and was mustered out as a first lieutenant on January 1, 1871. Francis Bernard Heitman, *Historical Register and Dictionary of the United States Army, from its Organization, September 29, 1789, to March 2, 1903* (cited hereafter as Heitman).

Dickason,[22] located a rancheria about thirty miles east of Camp Mc-Dowell, and reported eighteen Indians killed.[23]

On his next recorded adventure, Jack and a party of citizens chased a score of hostiles who had stolen corn during a midnight visit to Dan Hatz's place, neighboring the Townsend ranch. The trail was followed twenty miles, an Indian camp attacked, and three Indians felled, each by Townsend, "the first man to discover and attack the rancheria." The raiders found four babies, too, this news story said, but "did not injure them."[24] By the following summer, Townsend was deemed worthy of special mention by the *Miner*:

> CITIZENS WHO HAVE DISTINGUISHED THEMSELVES.—There are in the Territory many, very many, citizens who have distinguished themselves and rendered the country good service by "reconstructing" copper-colored rascals, among whom there are none more worthy than I. Q. Dickason and John Townsend. . . . The former gentleman has killed thirteen Indians; the latter, some seven or eight. Dickason's bravery is of the cool, calculating kind; while Townsend's is rash and impulsive. Both are "dead" shots, and the savage who comes within range of their rifles or revolvers had better never been born.[25]

Until this time Townsend had been like many an Arizona frontier Indian hunter, indulging in the "sport" for its own thrills, but now he began to change, and, judging by his record, the killing of Indians became almost an obsession with him. He hunted them because he wanted to kill them more than he wanted to do anything else. When others would go along, a grand expedition could result; when they didn't, he went alone.

"At the time of the new moon, when Apache hunting parties usually started, Townsend would leave his home and make a stealthy and wide circuit in the mountains to cut the trail of possible Apache raid-

22 Not to be confused with John H. Dickson, or Dixon, who was a member of the original party that settled in Skull Valley and who married Mary J. Ehle November 17, 1864, in Prescott's first wedding. Conner, 183n.

23 *Arizona Miner*, October 2, 1869.

24 This story, passed on by Ory French to Roscoe Willson of the Phoenix *Arizona Republic*, is reprinted in his *No Room for Angels* as a singular instance of pioneer mercy toward the Indians, who were cordially hated. In the story, however, the number of infants spared is given as seven.

ers. If he did find a trail he would secrete himself at night in the rocks above his cabin and wait in ambush for the expected raid."[26] He became the Lewis Wetzel of the Arizona frontier, the greatest of its Indian slayers, although his total never approached that of Al Sieber, according to the best published figures. Yet Sieber never became, as Jack Townsend did, simply an Indian killer, and he rarely slew unless he felt at the time that it was the thing to do. The more Townsend killed, the more popular he became with his fellow settlers. They wanted the Indians killed as badly as he wanted to do away with them. "His law was the law of reprisal, an eye for an eye and a tooth for a tooth, and the violent loss of every white man and white woman and white child coming to his knowledge, a living Apache, man, woman and child paid the penalty in kind, and the checked up dead list registered on his rifle stock was a long one," wrote Judge Edmund Wells.[27] But with Al Sieber, Dan O'Leary, and others, killing Indians was the dirty climax of the exciting sport of hunting them, and it remained just that.

When he left the Williamson Valley after a year or so of working for Bean, Sieber joined O'Leary and murderous-tempered George Thrasher at their ranch on Walnut Creek, somewhat farther to the west.[28] Adjoining it was a place claimed by Andrew Stainbrook. Sieber, who could get along with almost anyone, found his new companions congenial and, best of all, ready at any time for a joke.

One day Dan was down on the Walnut Creek bottom, no doubt reflecting on some skirmish with Indians, or at least wary of another, for if you weren't alert in that country, you soon ceased to be anything. For some reason, O'Leary had not brought a gun with him. Now it so happened that Andy Stainbrook was hunting that day. He saw something move in the brush along the bottom, and, not knowing whether it was deer, steer, or red-skinned prowler, he flung a shot in

25 *Arizona Miner*, July 16, 1870.

26 McClintock, I, 191.

27 Edmund Wells, *Argonaut Tales*, 464.

28 Thrasher's name is spelled "Thasher" in the Florence-Tucson *Enterprise* story from which this is taken. A Canadian like Peck, Thrasher was born at Belleville, Ontario, and arrived in Arizona in 1864. *Arizona Miner*, October 18, 1873; APHS in correspondence with the author, July 5, 1960.

its direction. The bullet clipped twigs above Dan's head, and he "put on a big head of steam and, with all his might, ran towards the house," from the door of which George and Al urged him on as if a whole passel of Indians were right at his heels. Unluckily, Dan's course led over a freshly plowed field, which, in his haste, he crossed by cartwheel after somersault, to the delight of his tormentors and his own Irish "disgust and mortification" when he learned that no Indians were in pursuit after all.[29]

From these men, and particularly from O'Leary, Al learned the rudiments of scouting. He thought he had learned a great deal on the Bean place, and indeed he had, but now he was a student of the greatest scout of the Southwest, and he made the most of his opportunity. Becoming a superlative scout, he found, required the application of a high order of intelligence to the products of acute perception: to vision, scent, and sound. Not all men of fabulous vision became good scouts and good trackers, nor did all of even intelligent men possess the requisites of the profession. It was, first, the ability to see, hear, and smell—to accumulate the evidence—then rapidly analyze and evaluate it, calculating what was happening, what would probably happen, and why it all happened, sometimes at a very rapid pace. These things Al Sieber learned, and learned well, at the hands of masters of the trade.

"From O'Leary he learned much concerning the habits and country of the Indians, and from there he went on two scouts after the thieving and murdering devils, they being numerous and hostile at that time in every portion of the territory, the Wallapais, Yuma Apaches and Mohave tribes being the most dangerous."[30] Many years later, in a dictated statement, Sieber said that he had "done some scouting under Gen. [George] Stoneman . . . in 1871," most likely meaning military expeditions rather than private hunts. Stoneman was department commander at that time.

One of the military excursions probably began in late 1870 when

---

[29] *Arizona Miner*, March 2, 1872. Sieber is not mentioned by name, but George "and other tormentors" assuredly includes him, since he was probably at the ranch at the time.

[30] Florence-Tucson *Enterprise*.

mounted Indians raided Willow Grove and in a sudden rush made off with thirty-two horses and fifteen head of cattle. The Walapai herder brought in the word, so experienced Indian men thought the raiders were probably Apaches or Yavapais. Notice was sent to Camp Hualpai, whereupon Captain Fred Van Vliet sent Lieutenant Oscar Elting[31] and twenty-five men of the Third Cavalry after the marauders, with Dan O'Leary as guide and a Walapai, whom O'Leary selected, as tracker. The trail was easily struck and was followed past Mount Hope into Williamson Valley, where the Indians had picked up eighteen more head of horses and mules and eleven more cattle. The command quickened its pace, augmented now by Thomas Stonehouse and some other citizens, who were also trailing the Indians. They followed the sign in the direction of Black Mountain. In Chino Valley the trail became confused with that of other stock and was lost. Two of the civilians volunteered to go in search of it if they could borrow the Walapai. The Lieutenant consented.

Some time later the two whites reined up at the Chino Valley settlement, threw down a scalp, and reported that they had run into four Indians and killed one. The thing looked sour, and under questioning, one finally admitted that they couldn't discover the hostiles' trail, so they had killed and scalped the Walapai tracker. What the hell, he was only an Indian. Dan O'Leary was furious, and the *Miner* agreed with Dan. "We pronounce the act one of the most uncalled-for, dastardly affairs we have ever heard of," it stormed, "and eminently calculated to make hostile every Wallapais, as well as furnish a weapon for [the Indian 'lovers'] who charge all blame for Indian wars upon the whites."[32] But of course nothing was ever done to the whites. There was no law against killing an Indian any time you could.

Al's stay with Dan and George didn't last long, for there were big things brewing in Arizona, and he was to have a part in them. O'Leary, too. Poor George, however, was not to see them concluded. In the autumn of 1873, he and Andy Stainbrook took to arguing about their

---

[31] A New Yorker, Elting served in the ranks throughout the Civil War and was appointed a second lieutenant of cavalry in 1867. He made captain by 1881, retired in 1895, and died November 6, 1902.

[32] *Arizona Miner*, December 3, 1870.

stock trespassing on each other's ranches and damaging crops. A few words led to a full-fledged feud, in spite of all their neighbors could do to quell it. It finally ended, as feuds often did in those days, with a shoot-out—and mutually destructive results: their bodies were found within three feet of each other. A double murder, said the law.[33]

[33] APHS in correspondence with the author, July 5, 1960.

V. Retaliation

THERE IS NO PROOF that Al Sieber accompanied John Townsend's great campaign against the hostiles, but there is no proof that he didn't either. Although it is somewhat unlikely that Al did go, the foray itself was such a rousing success and is so well described in accounts handed down to us that it seems worth while to recount it here, particularly since it is illustrative of the generally civilian operations against the Indians which for many years seemed the only answer to persistent hostility. I say "generally civilian" because even though a party of soldiers joined Jack on this trip, they behaved more like civilians than troopers and the whole undertaking had a distinctly nonmilitary aura about it.

Townsend's expedition was perhaps the most famous citizens' operation against the hostiles and was remembered vividly and proudly by Prescott pioneers for a long time. It began one month after the slaying of Lieutenant Howard Bass Cushing, the former artillery officer who had upbraided the Confederate prisoners at Elmira, as Sieber would have remembered. He was killed in a sharp fight with Apaches in the Whetstone Mountains down in southeastern Arizona.

Indians drove off stock from the ranch of Herbert and Nathan Bowers, about twenty miles from Prescott, in early June of 1871. Word of it first reached the capital with a messenger who dashed up Montezuma Street shouting that John Gantt,[1] a herder, had been killed, another wounded, and 137 head of stock seized. A second courier had been sent to Camp Verde, about forty miles east of Prescott, asking military help.

[1] Gantt, from Allegheny County, Pennsylvania, was a Civil War veteran.

Charley Genung came out of the Diana Saloon and met Herbert Bowers, who still suffered from the ravages of yellow jaundice, standing as if in a trance, for much of his wealth had disappeared in a cloud of dust. From him Genung learned that no help was to be expected from Whipple, since its troops were on a scout. He told Bowers to get what animals he could from a livery stable and turned back to the saloon to seek a war party. He found Tom Roddick and Jeff Davis eager for the expedition, and some others as well. By eleven o'clock, ten or eleven men started for Bowers' ranch, where they were joined by John Townsend and others, sixteen in all. At dawn they took up the trail.

Tom Roddick was suffering. He had been on a several days' drunk and badly needed a drink. As the group jogged along, Tom felt worse and worse. No one admitted having a bottle. At last he called to Townsend: "Captain, if I can't get a drink I'll die, sure." "Oh! not so bad as that, Tom," laughed Townsend. "I bet you two hundred dollars I'll die in fifteen minutes if I don't get a drink!" Roddick retorted. But he didn't.

The hunters camped on a hill where there was good grass the first night. With sunup they were in the saddle again, but scarcely started before they ran into an army scout from Camp Verde. It included twenty-nine enlisted men, a doctor, and, in command, Lieutenant Charles Morton, fresh out of West Point and sent on this scout to see whether he had the right stuff in him.[2] The officer called Jack aside

[2] He had, and he had already demonstrated it, but unbeknown to the frontiersmen. Born at Chagrin, Ohio, on March 18, 1846, he was raised in Missouri and volunteered in a home-guard outfit in April, 1861. This unit ultimately became the First Missouri Volunteer Engineers, and with it Morton took part in the Battle of Shiloh, the sieges of Corinth and Atlanta, and a number of other actions and distinguished himself for bravery. He entered West Point on July 1, 1865, and upon graduation joined the Third Cavalry as a second lieutenant; that was June 15, 1869. He was assigned frontier duty at Fort Union, New Mexico, until December of that year, then marched with his company to short-lived Camp Rawlins in the Williamson Valley, and at this time was stationed at Camp Verde. He later took part in the Big Horn and Black Hills expeditions but returned to Apacheria in time to get in the Battle of Big Dry Wash. By 1903 he was a full colonel and by 1907 a brigadier general. He had been brevetted first lieutenant, incidentally, for gallant service in action against Indians on this Townsend expedition. He died December 20, 1914. George W. Cullum, *Biographical Register of the Officers and Graduates of the U.S. Military Academy at West Point, N.Y.* (cited hereafter as Cullum).

and said, "Mr. Townsend . . . I suppose we are all out on the same business and I would like to accompany you." "All right," said Townsend, "come ahead." He tried not to show it, but, possessing the arrogance toward the army that was typical of frontiersmen, he was upset about the intrusion, as he considered it, of the Lieutenant and his men. Before the trip was over, however, even crusty old Jeff Davis had ceased calling Morton "Corporal," in fact was addressing him, respectfully, as "Mr. Morton." In addition, the military party had with it José de Ruiz (or José de León), who had been captured and raised by the Apaches and knew the trace over which the stolen livestock would likely be driven.[3]

Horses and men scrambled over a terrible trail all morning, the brush so thick that sometimes two horses couldn't pass on the trail. At the top of a hill they found some yokes Indians had stripped from stolen cattle and the whites named this Ox Yoke Mountain, although no one now knows where it was.[4] The riders crashed down the mountainside at breakneck speed, for their guide had warned them that the Indians might fire the brush ahead; the searing flames would sweep like a hurricane up the slope. Finally the searchers reached the cool waters of the Verde, which they crossed at the East Fork's mouth, camping there. Townsend and Morton conferred, the Lieutenant asserting he would continue on the trail for two days more and Jack allowing he would like to, as well, but had only enough rations to return home. Morton laughed and said he would divide food with them, as long as the civilians would stay, to which Townsend agreed.

At dawn the hunters were doggedly following sign up a trail, still in existence, along the East Fork. After a dozen miles they turned

See also Heitman and *Who Was Who.* This account of the Townsend expedition is based in part on Genung's recollections, printed in the Los Angeles *Mining Review* of May 13, 1911, as quoted in Farish, VIII, 170–95; James M. Barney, "The Townsend Expedition," *Arizona Highways,* Vol. XIII, No. 3 (March, 1937), 12 *et seq.*; and Lieutenant Morton's report of the scout dated Camp Verde, June 20, 1871, Record Group 94, National Archives.

3 This man was considered by many to be the "best guide in Arizona." He came to a tragic end on a scout which he and Sieber guided a couple of years later.

4 Barnes identifies it as Oxbow Hill, but that is much farther along on their trail and cannot be right.

up and over Polles Mesa,[5] not then called anything, although it later became well known to Indian fighters. Townsend could recall one occasion when hostiles had sent boulders from its summit down on an army column, forcing the troops to withdraw.

Hiking along single file, the expedition hugged the cliff for several miles until the trail turned north, up toward the rim of the mesa. Some started to climb. Townsend remained at the base, however, and at length called the men back. The party returned to the campground at the mouth of East Fork, and Townsend asked the Lieutenant to have some of his men shoot at a mark. He "wanted the shots fired," wrote Genung, so that any listening Indians might be misled, but he "did not want the citizens to waste their ammunition. He thought it did not make so much difference whether the soldiers had ammunition or not."

The men built huge fires, made a lot of noise, then bedded down—until 2:00 A.M., when they silently mounted and struck back up the trail, noiselessly climbing the face of the mountain. By daylight they were hurrying along the length of the mesa toward the east. Just at six o'clock, León spotted an Indian on a horse ahead. Townsend saw a track leading to the right and led his party on a dead run down a steep slope, across the dry bed of the East Fork, and into a well-concealed Indian camp. Everyone shot at anything that moved. Genung killed two Indians and was almost shot by soldiers who mistook him for another. Meanwhile, the Lieutenant had found another trail leading to a smaller rancheria, charged it, and killed an Indian with his revolver. "Altogether we had killed about thirty-five Indians that we knew were dead," Genung wrote. The boys plundered the camp and then took the trail again, but within a mile and a half they went into camp at the mouth of the northern tributary of the East Fork.

On the fourth morning the party traveled at a trot or lope up the East Fork about one and one-half miles, then turned southwest up a wash coming down from the Mazatzal Mountains and gradually veered south, traversing cedar-covered foothills for three or four miles

[5] Barnes said it was so named for an old-timer named Polle Chilson. His real name, however, was Napoleon Chilson, and he was nicknamed "Poly." Barnes, *Place Names*, 342; interview with Mrs. Maggie Armer, herself a Chilson.

before breaking out into open country in the valley of Tonto Creek. At about 11:30 A.M., José informed Morton that they were approaching another ranchería; the command closed up and moved on cautiously until the camp was sighted. Again it was every man for himself, with the Indians scurrying into the brush and the hunters close on their heels.

In this fight Townsend had a narrow escape when he plunged into some brush within a few feet of a wounded Indian who was lying in ambush for him. Jeff Davis called a warning to Townsend, shot the Indian, and gave Jack the enemy's rifle. Twenty-three Indians were said to have been slain, and two others, at least, were wounded but escaped.

The trail now led southeast through low hills and long mesas and again the Mexican trailer, in the lead, threw up his hand. He had seen what he thought were two Indians on horses across a canyon nearly two miles ahead. Townsend and Genung began a careful stalk, coming to within forty yards of their prey before leaping off their horses and firing. They killed one Indian and soon wounded another, discovering that they had three to deal with, two being mounted on a single horse. The two survivors, one with a broken arm, took to the brush and Townsend and Genung ran to get their horses, but the latter couldn't catch his and it was Townsend who killed the unwounded one. The other got away.

Both Genung and Townsend had inflicted mortal wounds on the first Indian; there was doubt as to who should count him. "Townsend said to me, 'How many have you killed?'" Genung wrote. "I said, 'Two yesterday and two this morning.' 'Well,' he replied, 'you count this one.' 'How many have you got?' I asked. 'Eight,' was the answer, 'and one gone with his right arm all shot to pieces. We will track him up in the morning and that will be nine for me.'" But the wounded Indian was never scored.

About eight miles to the southwest a soldier spotted a dim wagon trace and recognized it as one that had run from Old Camp Reno, on Reno Creek three miles west of Tonto Creek, to Green Valley. The weary men, partially in rags now, with many of their horses shoeless and lame and everyone hungry, out of grub, and exhausted, made for that abandoned post. There they found enough horseshoes and old nails to reshoe their mounts; a patch of blackberries, providing a real treat; and a troop of cavalry on a scout from Fort McDowell, thirty miles away over the Mazatzals. The cavalrymen were guided by Hi Jolly,[6] one of the most widely known characters of the West. Cavalry rations tasted mighty good, and the party, refreshed now and in fine fettle, made its way to McDowell and from there to the Verde and Prescott with 150 head of recaptured stock. It was the first time hostiles had been pursued with such success. No wonder Prescott was fit to be tied! The "grand jollification" that followed lasted the rest of the day, June 18, and almost all night and became known locally as the "Prescott Jubilee."

The saloons were crowded of course, and at 8:00 P.M. the doors of the Niles and Griffin Restaurant were thrown open, disclosing groaning tables the full length of the building: they were laden with every delicacy the season and locale had to offer. The place soon was jammed. Judge Berry, by acclamation, was named president for the occasion and decided that the first order of business was "destruction of the fluids and solids." The festivities continued as long as anyone could keep on his feet, and the heroes staggered home full of wine, whiskey, meat, and other good things and the warm recollection of fifty-six Indians fully reconstructed and no one could guess how many others wounded mortally but escaping to a lingering death in the wilderness. Some calculated Townsend's personal total this trip at fifteen,[7] but at any rate his lifetime total was now twenty-six he was

[6] He was a Greek named Philip Tedro who was converted to Islam and took the name Hadj Ali. He came to the United States in 1857 with a shipment of camels for use in the Southwest, and border men promptly corrupted his adopted name to Hi Jolly. The camel experiment was soon abandoned, and Hi Jolly became a good guide and scout and a well-known character. He died at Quartzsite, Arizona, where there is a monument to him.

[7] This figure may be the basis for a statement in McClintock, I, 191, in regard to Townsend: "Fifteen scalps were taken by him single-handed while he was accompanying as scout one of General Crook's commands, sent out from Whipple. When he displayed the scalps to testify to the truth of his modest tale, Crook is said to have discharged him at once from the service." McClintock based his statement on the account in Orick Jackson, *The White Conquest of Arizona*, 20. Jackson said that while Townsend killed fifteen Indians, the soldiers hadn't killed any, which "incensed General

sure of, although one account estimated his actual toll at his death to be sixty-five.[8]

The citizens of Prescott were not yet done with Townsend, Genung, Roddick, Jeff Davis, and Lieutenant Morton. On June 22, Townsend was presented with the finest Henry rifle money could buy. On its polished stock was a 2x3-inch engraved silver plate:

> Presented to
> J. B. Townsend
> By the citizens of Prescott
> June, 1871.
> HONOR TO THE BRAVE![9]

He was also given a thousand rounds of ammunition to shoot at Indians. Charles Genung received a Winchester, Tom Roddick and Jeff Davis a pistol each, and Lieutenant Morton a brace of gold-mounted pistols. Genung said that John Dunn personally purchased the Winchester given him.[10]

Impressive in results though it was, this expedition had no lasting effect in curbing Indian depredations, and by midsummer of 1871 the hostiles were more active than ever, with stock thefts, ambushes, and the usual outrageous conduct reported regularly in the press. But in the Arizona of that day there were other things to do besides fight Indians. Almost everyone turned his hand now and then to mining, or

Crook," and he fired Jack. The incident was no doubt based by Jackson on a Townsend legend current in his day at Prescott. Whether true or not, it is in keeping with the apparent characters of both Townsend and Crook. Townsend served as one of several scouts for General Crook's great offensive, being employed in that capacity from December, 1872, through February, 1873, when he was dropped for no stated reason. Yet Crook, with typical thoughtfulness, did what he could to ease the way for the widowed Mrs. Townsend after Jack's death.

[8] McClintock, I, 191.

[9] *Arizona Miner*, June 24, 1871. At his death the rifle was presented to the Masonic Lodge at Prescott and was hung in a prominent place on its walls. From there it disappeared some years ago.

[10] This scout, with its fortunate outcome, led directly into a high-level squabble at Washington over whether Medals of Honor should be given to soldiers engaged in Indian fighting or restricted to Civil War actions. Secretary of War William Worth Belknap, General W. T. Sherman, and others engaged in the controversy, which first ruled against, then for, granting the medals. Ultimately they were authorized for Indian and subsequent wars. Record Group 94, National Archives.

at least to prospecting, and Al Sieber was no exception. All his life, or at any rate until the last few months of it, he maintained an interest in prospecting and mining, although never with very tangible results. Now, for the first time in Arizona, he found himself swept up in something big, and it had to do with mining on a vast scale.

In the mid-nineteenth century everyone was strike crazy. The West was crisscrossed by rushes to here, to there, to anywhere. A few struck it rich, but by far the greater number barely made wages and many didn't even do that, eking out a miserable existence as best they could. Nothing but an actual Indian attack could excite westerners as much as rumors of a rich strike, or strike-to-be, so it is not surprising that interest quickened when the *Miner* reported the arrival of a large party of men from White Pine. It was led by the mysterious Thomas Miner and was well provided with animals, wagons, and so on, determined to prospect the remote White Mountains or the Pinals. To make final preparations—and collect more recruits—the newcomers established temporary headquarters at Bradshaw.[11] Sieber was as interested in them and their tale as anyone.

Word swept the camps, from Rich Hill to Tubac, that Miner had a secret clue, that this expedition could lead to another Antelope Hill, so far Arizona's richest camp. Miner claimed to have seen seventeen ounces of gold panned from one shovelful, did he?[12] California couldn't beat that, now could she? This sounded as good as Doc Thorn's find! Maybe it was the same one. Maybe Miner could find it again . . . .

It was the same one, all right. The conclusion is inescapable.

Everyone in the Southwest had heard of Doc Thorn (or Thorne), and half of them believed his yarn, believed it because they wanted to, although logic told them it was unlikely to be true. But since when

[11] *Arizona Miner*, June 2, 1871. The Bradshaw Mountains lie southeast of Prescott on the west side of Black Canyon, Lower Agua Fria. They were named for Bill Bradshaw and bear important silver deposits, which Bill didn't find. The townsite of Bradshaw had been established just under Mount Wasson, and by 1871 it had a dozen log houses and a store. It eventually boasted some five thousand inhabitants, although it is now nearly gone. Barnes, *Place Names*, 60; 2nd ed., 335.

[12] Williamson, "Sieber," 60–61.

did logic have any hold on a prospector? If it had, half of our richest mines would never have been discovered.

Thorn had said in substance that he had been held captive by the Apaches about 1859 or 1860 somewhere on the Upper Salt River. In return for medical assistance, he was permitted to prospect and, eventually, to return to the settlements. He came out of the wilderness with a tale about huge gold and silver nuggets lying on the ground in a mountainous area near a distinctive, hat-shaped butte.

His yarn reached Corydon Eliphalet Cooley, who was to become one of the greats of the Arizona frontier.[13] Cooley wanted to believe Doc's story and easily succeeded. He questioned Thorn closely about landmarks, route, and general direction and in July, 1869, went off into the wilds to hunt up the strike. With him went Henry Wood Dodd, who cared little about the possible returns but wanted to leave town long enough to sober up, and Albert Franklin Banta,[14] a journey-

[13] Cooley, who was born in Loudoun County, Virginia, on April 2, 1836, came to Santa Fe in 1856, then spent two years in Colorado. He served two years (1861–63) with the Second New Mexico Infantry, attaining the rank of first lieutenant. He was said to have been at Fort McLane when Mangas Coloradas was killed in January, 1863. Cooley came to Arizona as a prospector. He married two Indian girls simultaneously, it is said, the daughters of Chief Pedro of the White Mountain Apaches, but one soon died, leaving him a monogamist. C. E. and Mollie Cooley established a ranch at the forks in the road from Fort Apache to what became Holbrook and Springerville. This ranch, at the town now called McNary, was one of the most noted stopping places in eastern Arizona and is mentioned in many of the early journals, the praise being unanimous for Mollie as a tidy and gracious housewife and Cooley as a generous and notable host. About 1875, Cooley moved to another location and established a ranch—and later a sawmill, trading post, and so on—at a site he named "Show Low" after he won the exclusive rights to the area in a card game. This, too, became a well-known oasis for travelers. When, about 1890, he and a partner had a falling out, Cooley moved back to his original place on Fort Apache Reservation. Cooley was a scout and guide for Crook off and on during 1871–75 and for other officers later; he was probably one of the top two or three scouts in the business. There was much mutual respect between Cooley and Crook, and Bourke notes that Cooley's influence was always on the side of peace and understanding between red and white. He died March 18, 1917, according to Barnes, *Place Names*, 2nd ed., or March 19, 1915, according to Barnes, *Place Names*, 1st ed., and the files of APHS.

[14] Banta, who came to Arizona in 1863 with Governor John N. Goodwin's party, was a man of no consequence on the southwestern frontier, except in his own estimation. But in this his importance grew and grew as the old-timers died off and personal

man printer and teller of tales who went along just for the adventure. If you believe Banta, they had a fine time but located no riches.

Cooley held to his stubborn faith in Doc Thorn's strike, however, and a party of twenty-eight men was organized at Prescott to try again. Led by Calvin Jackson, it included such well-known frontiersmen as Adna French, Rodney McKinnon, and Solomon Shoup. Others, including Jacob Snively, who figures in the later Miner expedition, were recruited near Wickenburg and in the Salt River Valley. When the party reached the mouth of Canyon Creek, on the Salt, they met Cooley and his men, who, while awaiting them, had scouted Sombrero Butte, which some supposed to be Doc Thorn's hat-shaped promontory, and had a brush with the Apaches, having a man wounded and a horse killed. Cooley and Jackson led their combined party about thirty miles up the Salt, prospecting as they went, and then into the Pinals and on to the mouth of the river. If they found anything, it was not reported.[15]

This was not the end of Doc Thorn's fable, however, not by a long shot. Apparently, the story had also reached the ears of the individual who called himself Thomas Miner, and it captivated him as it had Cooley, Cal Jackson, and a good many others.

Miner himself is a hopeless enigma, even more of a puzzle than Doc Thorn, who was, to put it bluntly, simply a liar. Thomas Miner came from nowhere and, as far as the record goes, ended nowhere. He is suspended in historical space. He appears first at Hamilton, Ne-

---

recollections of the old days glazed over. He was a border itinerant, trying his hand at this or that, and at various times was a printer, probate judge, prospector, legislator, writer of letters to newspapers, and self-anointed oracle on Arizona history. In nothing was he much of a success, but as he grew older he made more noise and his tales grew taller and he claimed to be and to have done many things. He came to believe, for instance, that he had been a key figure in Crook's early military successes in that country, but a painstaking search of the records fails to demonstrate that he had any part in them whatever. Despite his self-proclaimed proficiency as a guide, he is mentioned as such in none of Crook's papers that I have seen, and it is my personal opinion that he couldn't have guided a party down a creek. He makes interesting reading, but so does Tom Horn. Banta was born in Warwick County, Indiana, December 18, 1843, and died June 21, 1924 at the Arizona Pioneers' Home at Prescott.

15 This account was sent to the *Miner* on September 27, 1869, from Canyon Creek, but I have no record of the date on which it appeared.

As a captain, Adna R. Chaffee led the Big
Dry Wash fight, in which Sieber played
a key role.

Colonel Emilio Kosterlitzky and his rurales
waged their own war against the Apaches
in Old Mexico.

Dr. William H. Corbusier about
1875, when he accompanied
the Indians transferred
from Camp Verde to San
Carlos Reservation.

Sergeant Edmund Schreiber
worked with Sieber on Lieutenant
Schuyler's long scout in late 1873 and early 1874.

vada, as we have seen, and disappears from record in south central Arizona. It is anybody's guess where he originated, or where he departed this life, or what he looked like or what he had been or what he became, but this we know: Thomas Miner—if that was his real name—was sold on Doc Thorn's tale and to pursue that elusive wealth he inspired the greatest mining expedition in the history of the Southwest, where large, well-organized operations were traditional.

Miner had followed the White Pine rush and somehow made a living at Hamilton for the two years it took to gather followers and organize his invasion of Arizona. He had, one would suppose, three reasons for recruiting such a large party: (1) numbers meant safety in that desperately hostile corner of Apachería; (2) it is likely that he himself was no miner and needed the skills which veteran prospectors could provide; and (3) with many men fanning out over the countryside, the Thorn riches, if they existed, would more likely be found. And if they were found, you can be sure that Thomas Miner expected to profit most.

But what if Doc's gold and silver were not discovered? Well, everyone knew that rich placers existed in that area—they simply *had* to be there! The reason men knew placers had to exist there was because no one had been able to get in to find out, or at least not to leave with the knowledge if he did get in. No one but Doc Thorn. The country was sealed off by Apaches. Even if Doc Thorn was a damned liar, the chances were good that other placers would be found, and who could prove they weren't those Miner himself claimed to have seen? The idea was to get in there—do it with force—and make a strike. Profit would surely follow.

So, two years after he had first announced his intentions in Nevada, Miner arrived at Bradshaw to make final preparations for the grand excursion. He told of his plans and their background in a solemn prospectus he caused to be printed in the *Arizona Miner*, where, no doubt, it was seen and avidly read by Al Sieber and scores of others:

BRADSHAW, A. T., July 3, 1871.

To the Editors of the Arizona Miner:

In accordance with the provision of a resolution, which will be found at the close of this article, I pen you the following for publication in your paper:

It has long been the opinion of many, and the certain knowledge of a few, that rich placers exist in the eastern district of Central Arizona; and one Thomas Miner, recently from Nevada, belongs to the latter few. In the year 1861, Mr. Miner was one of a company of miners who went on a prospecting expedition—under the leadership of one Stephens—into that hitherto unexplored region; and they found placers which, in Mr. Miner's opinion, will yield from $20 to $150 a day, to the man, by sluicing, and extending over an area of country sufficient for 5,000 miners, or more, with timber and water in abundance. They were permitted to remain in the mining district only some two months, on account of the Indians. Since that time Mr. Miner has made several unsuccessful attempts to raise a company to get back, but has never had promise of success until now. Last April we left Hamilton, Nevada, with an organization called the Mogollon Mining Co., to go into this much coveted region, but realizing that our company was too small for the undertaking, we came by way of this place for recruits. We have had a meeting here and added 30 names to the roll; and we hope before starting to number from eighty to one hundred strong. We now number forty-eight.

It was decided at our last meeting to start from this place on the 1st of August next, and go by way of Adamsville and Fort [sic] Grant, and thence to the mines. All persons desiring to go with this company can do so by reporting themselves at Bradshaw on the day above named, with the proper outfit of arms and pack animals. Great saving in packing can be made by purchasing provisions at the Salt River settlements, especially flour.

It will be the dawn of a glorious day to the sons of Arizona when this company shall have planted its standard on the rock-ribbed hills of the Mogollon, where now exists no mark of civilization except the debris of walled cities, whose relics attest to the residence of the proud Aztec, long since laid waste by the ruthless hand of the savage Apache. Thousands of hardy frontiersmen will pour in from Nevada and California, and the days of the Apache will be numbered, and those lofty peaks which have for ages past echoed only the yells of the murderous savage, will henceforth send back the sounds of civilization; and those sunny villages and amaranthine plains which have so long been made hideous by the war dance, will soon become the seats of luxury and opulence.

The following is the principal business transacted in the last company meeting. Mr. Shively,[16] Mr. Maxwell and Mr. Price were appointed a committee to see that all members, on starting, were properly outfitted, or had the means to become so.

Mr. Miner was then called upon to give a short account of his former expedition, which he did, in substance, as set forth in the first part of this article. A resolution, instructing the secretary to write a communication for publication in the MINER, setting forth the general features, the time of starting, etc., was then adopted.

OLIVER STEWART,
Sec'y Mogollon Mining Co.[17]

Who could resist such an appeal? Not, assuredly, the adventurous-minded of Prescott. Not Ed Peck, nor Al Sieber, nor Willard Rice, Lew Ellit, Tom Stonehouse, F. G. Christie, Force Gregory, or Robert Groom.[18] Not similar spirits from elsewhere in Arizona. Not Governor A. P. K. Safford and scores of others.

The Miner expedition began to assume grand proportions, to draw recruits from all over the Territory. Leaving Prescott, the original party went by way of Fort McDowell, collecting participants on the way. From the fort it moved to Tucson, then the territorial capital, where the newspapers gave it a rousing welcome and final preparations were made. A pack train was sent to Adamsville, on the Gila River three or four miles west of modern Florence, for flour. Each man's equipment was checked to make sure he was armed and had plenty of ammunition, food, a good saddle horse, and a fit pack animal. Ultimately, seven companies were organized, captained by Ed Peck, a man named Rogers, Maxwell, T. B. Kerr, Francisco A. Gándara, José Durán, and Francisco Martínez. Sieber, Rice, and Groom, of course, were in Peck's company. Governor Safford was named commander, Mr. Miner graciously retiring into the background. Oli-

[16] Probably Jacob Snively.

[17] *Arizona Miner*, July 15, 1871. It is possible, but highly unlikely, that some such expedition as Miner reported could have taken place early in 1861, but not later than April or May. By this time, news of the impending civil war had reached Arizona and U.S. troops were already planning to withdraw; the Apaches were thus in ascendance and no one in his right mind would wander off prospecting in the heart of their country. Nor could such a find as Miner claimed have been kept quiet for a decade.

[18] Joseph F. Fish, *History of Arizona* (cited hereafter as Fish), 536; *Arizona Miner*, September 30, 1871.

ver Stewart was promoted to adjutant and Francisco Erwin named secretary, and the organization's name was changed to Mogollon Mining and Exploration Company. Enrollment had reached at least 267 men by now, some counting even more.[19]

A pep meeting was held at Tucson the evening before the cavalcade clattered out on its way to wealth and glory, and Governor Safford delivered the keynote speech, concluding:

> You have before you months of hardship and labor. You are going through a country that others have tried to penetrate and whose bones lie bleaching on far off mountains, while others have returned with broken ranks and wounds. You are going to endeavor to discover and report to the world, we hope, riches in a country almost wholly unexplored, that will be of value to hundreds and thousands of poor people.[20]

From Tucson the mighty expedition crossed the San Pedro and reached the Gila, by way of Mount Graham in the Pinalenos, about at the site of modern Safford. They prospected down the Gila to the mouth of the San Carlos River, worked up to its head, and crossed over to the Upper Salt River. By this time it was evident that Miner didn't know where he was, had no idea where he claimed he had been, knew nothing of prospecting or this part of the country, and was at best a fool, at worst a mountebank.

Some of the party turned back. Others, including Peck's company, with Sieber, went down the Salt to Cherry Creek and up it into Tonto Basin, which Al now saw for the first time, in company with Peck, who knew it better than any other white man. They worked up Cherry Creek, penetrated the Sierra Anchas without success, returned to Cherry Creek, and went down it to the Salt again. They followed the river to the well-known Wheatfields,[21] about ten miles northwest of

19 Williamson, "Sieber," 61. Mrs. Clara Woody, Globe County historian, believes the party eventually numbered "about 280." Notes lent to the author.

20 Mrs. Woody's notes.

21 So named by pioneer and Indian fighter King Woolsey. On his Indian hunt in 1864, he and his men found a field of wheat which they believed the Indians had raised—no doubt from seed originally brought to the Gadsden settlements by the Spaniards. At any rate, the whites threshed out enough grain for their own use, then pastured their horses on the remainder. An army expedition also destroyed a field of wheat here in 1870. Barnes, *Place Names*, 480–81.

Globe on Pinal Creek. At this point the Miner expedition finally broke up, Governor Safford taking his group back to Tucson and Peck, Rice and Sieber the other crowd back to Prescott by way of the eastern slope of the Mazatzals west of Tonto Creek.[22]

The party that returned to Tucson lost two men, one killed accidentally and the other slain by Indians, and had two horses killed by the Apaches. The Indians also heckled the Prescott men, emboldened by what they no doubt considered a retreat. A mule was killed, one man had his hat shot off, and another got a bullet through his whiskers.[23]

Newspapers failed to make much mention of the return of the unsuccessful searchers for "Mr. Miner's nugget fields." The *Arizona Miner*, however noted that "many energetic men, who at their own expense, have been prospecting the wilds of Arizona, have just returned, firm in the belief that, although they did not find the 'right place,' it does exist and will yet be found."[24] You just couldn't down optimism like that.

There is no record that Al Sieber ever retained a belief in either Doc Thorn's or Miner's fabulous discoveries, even if he held any stock in them at the outset, but he never quite rubbed out the prospecting fever, either, although it failed to clutch him as it did some men. For the rest of his life he was a part-time prospector, taking up many claims, making a few dollars on one or the other, and sometimes coming within a whisker of fabulous wealth. But he never made it, and I don't think he cared very much.

At the moment it was the Indian, not mineral wealth, that was stirring Arizona as a fresh, strong hand took the reins of her military establishment and a clear, analytical mind applied itself to the solution of her seemingly insoluble dilemma over the hostiles. The thing that brought about this hopeful change was what one authority calls

[22] Williamson, "Sieber," 61; Mrs. Woody's notes; *Arizona Miner*, September 23 and 30, 1871.

[23] Mrs. Woody's notes. The complete list of names of those taking part in the Miner expedition was not preserved, or, if it was, it has not been located, and the only party whose enrollment is known is that from the Gila settlements, whose names, as they appear on mining claims, have been collected by Mrs. Woody.

[24] *Arizona Miner*, September 30, 1871.

"the blackest page in the Anglo-Saxon records of Arizona,"[25] a page that is known to history as the Camp Grant Massacre.

The incident itself is beyond the province of this book, but it involved the slaughter, by Tucson whites and Gila River Indians, of more than one hundred Arivaipa Apaches, mostly women and children, all of whom were living under the protection of the Camp Grant military post south of the Gila. The incident so shocked the nation that a change in military command for Arizona was ordered. Lieutenant Colonel George Crook, brevet major general, was assigned to the post.

[25] Frank C. Lockwood, *The Apache Indians*, 178.

VI. Massacre!

GEORGE CROOK was already well on his way to becoming the finest Indian fighter America ever knew.[1] He arrived in Arizona in June, 1871, accompanied by his aide, Captain Azor H. Nickerson,[2] and Archie McIntosh, a halfblood Indian from the Northwest in whom he

[1] George Crook was born September 23, 1829, near Dayton, Ohio, and was graduated from West Point in 1852, being assigned to the Fourth Infantry. He served with this regiment on frontier duty in California, Oregon, and Washington State until the outbreak of the Civil War, taking part in numerous Indian actions, including the Rogue River Expedition of 1856 and the Pitt River Expedition of 1857, during the latter of which he was wounded by an arrow. By 1861 he was a captain. His Civil War record is a distinguished one: he was wounded at Lewisburg, was repeatedly brevetted for gallant and meritorious service, took part in the Battles of South Mountain and Antietam, did good work against guerrillas in Tennessee and West Virginia, and was captured by commando-type guerrillas at Cumberland, Maryland, but later exchanged. He commanded the cavalry of the Army of the Potomac late in the war and was in on Lee's surrender at Appomattox, by which time he was major general of Volunteers and a brevet brigadier general in the Regular Army. After a brief tour of duty in the East, he returned to the West late in 1866 as lieutenant colonel of the Twenty-third Infantry, commanding the District of Boise (Idaho). Again he was in the thick of Indian fighting, ⸝warring with the Snakes, Paiutes, and Pitt Indians and eventually assuming command of the Department of the Columbia. He was transferred to San Francisco late in 1870 and on June 2, 1871, was named commander of the Department of Arizona. By this time Crook was a seasoned soldier, accustomed to command, and probably the finest choice that could have been made for this most difficult military assignment. Cullum; Heitman; *Dictionary of American Biography*.

[2] A volunteer officer who remained in the army after the Civil War. Crook had met him aboard ship when returning to the West and had arranged his transfer to the Twenty-third Infantry, whence he was assigned to Crook's staff. He once wrote that Nickerson "was wounded 4 times & in the battles of Antietam and Gettysburg was left for dead & his recovery was regarded as almost a miracle. He has now a hole in his chest which you can nearly stick your fist in, & in consequence his health is delicate & at times he suffers terribly from this wound. Notwithstanding all this, his ambition & zeal to do

had unlimited faith—as a scout.[3] McIntosh and Sieber took an almost instant dislike for each other, but this feeling never interfered with

___

his duty has been so great, that he has been constantly on duty ever since the war . . . most of the time he has been performing the duties of Adjt. Gen. & a more competent one is not to be found in this service." Crook to Rutherford B. Hayes, 4 January 1871. This letter is in the Rutherford B. Hayes Memorial Library at Fremont, Ohio, which has a large collection of Crook's letters and reports, numbering hundreds of documents. Its director, Mr. Watt P. Marchman, has generously placed them at my disposal. References to them are cited hereafter as Hayes Collection.

[3] Crook, of course, used many scouts during his extensive Indian operations, but none so won his confidence as Archie, unless it was Sieber. McIntosh, whose name was sometimes spelled "MacIntosh" (although he signed it without the "a"), was born at Fort William, Ontario, on September 14, 1834, to a Scot father and a Chippewa mother. His father worked for the Hudson's Bay Company, moved west while Archie was a child, and, by the time the boy was ten, took Archie along on fur-gathering expeditions. Archie remembered that as he and his father paddled their canoe up the Fraser River and its tributaries, he learned spelling and arithmetic. While on one of these trips his father was shot through the head from ambush, dying instantly. Archie, his mother, and his three sisters and three younger brothers escaped the Indians, presumably, who had made the attack, ultimately reaching Vancouver, where Archie went to school until he was twelve, then sailed for Scotland by way of Cape Horn. After two years of study at Edinburgh, he returned to Vancouver and continued his schooling there until he was eighteen, when he became a Hudson's Bay Company clerk for a year. He apparently first entered U.S. Army service in 1855 as a guide with a small detachment sent by Captain Rufus Ingalls against the Columbia River Indians. The troops had a bad time, and McIntosh was credited with helping to salvage the command. Archie enlisted in a Captain Olney's independent regiment of Oregon Cavalry on July 12, 1864, but served only three months, being honorably discharged October 31 at Fort Dalles. On September 10 he was badly injured when a horse fell on him as he was galloping across broken ground "chasing an indian to get a better shot" at him. When he recovered, he resumed his work as scout and guide with increasing success. On June 19, 1867, he led a party of Indian scouts that killed a dozen hostiles, wounded one, and captured two others near Steins Mountain, Oregon. On August 22 of that year he led his Boise Indian scouts into action near Surprise Valley, California, killing two and wounding seven enemy Indians. On September 26–28, 1867, he was with Crook at the bloody fight at Infernal Caverns, where twenty hostiles were killed, twelve wounded, and two captured, but the whites lost Lieutenant John Madigan, an Irishman posthumously brevetted captain for gallantry, and six soldiers, plus a civilian killed and eleven soldiers wounded. Near Camp Harney, Oregon, on April 23, 1868, McIntosh's scouts killed another hostile. On one occasion, Archie, miraculously it seemed to the General, led Crook and his men for some thirty miles in two days across a plateau during a blinding blizzard when it was sometimes difficult to see a dozen yards to windward, bringing them to the precise point they were aiming for. Archie later confessed to a reporter that "I knew there was going to be a blizzard and watched the course of the wind. When [the blizzard] came upon us General Crook

the splendid work each performed, nor, for that matter, did it lessen the respect each had for the other's Indian-fighting ability.

Crook was traveling light. "The only thing with him which could in any sense be classed as superfluous was a shotgun," wrote John G. Bourke, "but without this or a rifle he never traveled anywhere."[4] He paid a courtesy call on Governor Safford at Tucson, and before nightfall, orders had gone out to every officer in southern Arizona to report directly to him. From each he gleaned what knowledge the individual possessed about the country and the Indians, and to each he said nothing. The officers were impressed, if perplexed, by the new commandant.

From the outset Crook was convinced that the Apaches were never going to be conquered by troops alone, nor by civilians, nor by any combination of the two. They would have to be beaten by their own people. This would entail not only the enlistment of Indians to serve as scouts—and in many cases to do the fighting—but also of extraordinary white men to lead them as chiefs of scouts—men like McIntosh, Sieber, Joe Felman. He may have tried halfheartedly to recruit some Navahos and he made an unsuccessful attempt to use Mexicans, but his great interest and determination was in the employment of the Apaches themselves.

Crook soon left Tucson on a survey trip of his new territory and from Fort Apache organized an expedition composed of three com-

asked if we had not better go into camp until it passed, but I said, 'Follow me and I will put you into Camp Warner . . . .' So the General said no more but kept close behind me and you bet I kept the wind on my right cheek . . . but had it changed its direction ten degrees my goose would have been cooked." At any rate, by the time Crook was assigned to Arizona, he was convinced that Archie would be invaluable to him, and, as McIntosh recalled it, he had General John McAllister Schofield, then commanding the Division of the West, keep "the wires hot and the mails busy" trying to locate Archie. He was found at Camp Owyhee, Idaho. George Crook, *General George Crook: His Autobiography*, ed. by Martin F. Schmitt (cited hereafter as *Autobiography*), 147n.; *Chronological List*, 6, 8, 11; Holbrook, Arizona, *Holbrook Argus*, April 9, 1896, a useful biographical article on McIntosh by a reporter who signed his name "Sim Plex"; National Archives, where McIntosh's application for a pension contains interesting details; and, finally, correspondence and personal interviews with Donald McIntosh, Archie's only son, who at this writing is an octogenarian and still living at San Carlos, Arizona.

[4] Bourke, *Border*, 108.

panies of the Third Cavalry, commanded by Captain Guy V. Henry,[5] plus the Mexican scouts and some newly enlisted Indians. The command was to scout the country toward Camp McDowell, fighting any hostiles they might meet and thoroughly testing the capabilities of the Apache scouts. The expedition was an unqualified success. Henry reported that the combination of Indian and soldier had exceeded "his most sanguine expectations; that the Indians were invaluable, and that they enabled him to kill 7 warriors and take 11 women prisoners, under the most unfavorable circumstances."[6] Crook had demonstrated his solution to the Apache problem.

The officer continued his reconnaissance, arriving at Camp Verde with his head athrob with plans and schemes to put his solution to work immediately. On arrival, however, he was informed that he must hold his program in abeyance, pending the outcome of a new effort toward peace with the Indians being conducted by Washington through the Board of Peace Commissioners under the guidance of its secretary, Vincent Colyer.

Colyer traveled through Arizona Territory, holding councils with many important Indians, arranging for reservations, and generally too busy making peace with the natives to explain to the white population just what he was doing. Thus he was misunderstood and cordially detested by nearly everybody in the Territory. Most of them were probably secretly pleased when, shortly after he left for Washington, there occurred a new tragedy that shocked the nation and seemed likely to undo a good share of Colyer's work. This was a massacre—of whites, not the other way around—and it led more or less directly to a hot imbroglio in which Crook nearly lost his life (he was saved only by the alertness of his aide and Dan O'Leary) and to a campaign in which Sieber won his first official commendation and a victory that marked the real start of Al's long and singularly successful career.

This celebrated incident became known as the Loring, or Wicken-

[5] Guy Vernor Henry was born in Indian Territory and was graduated from West Point in 1860. He had a distinguished Civil War record, earning a brevet brigadier generalcy for heroism. He transferred to the Third Cavalry in 1870, rose to command it by 1895, and died October 27, 1899. Heitman.

[6] Crook's *Annual Report* for 1871, Letterbook I, No. 3, pp. 6–9, Hayes Collection.

burg, Massacre and occurred almost within sight of that mining community: eight miles distant on the long slope by which stages reached the divide west of town. A stagecoach with eight people aboard was attacked on the morning of November 5, 1871, and six persons killed outright, another dying of wounds. Among the slain were three members of the important Lieutenant George M. Wheeler surveying party. One of these was Frederick W. Loring of Massachusetts, a young writer of some promise who was widely known in the East. Loring had had his hair cut short before leaving for Arizona and had remarked jocularly to historian Hubert Howe Bancroft "that the Apaches would find it difficult to take his scalp."[7]

Initially there was some confusion over who had perpetrated the attack. Many thought it was Indians, but some were not so sure. Colonel N. A. M. Dudley wrote Colyer from McDowell that "at first even the Prescott papers partially admitted that it was [the work] of Mexican bandits from Sonora. Indians, when they attack a stage, are not apt to leave the horses, blankets, and curtains of the stage behind; in this case they did. I do not believe there was an Apache near the scene of the murder. All honest men have the same opinion, if they dared to express it."[8] There were odd elements in the case which led some people to refuse ever to believe it the work of Indians. Charles Genung, for example, said: "I have no doubt that there were many murders committed by Mexicans and blamed on the Indian; the Loring massacre . . . came near being one of the cases. It was reported by government officers that Date Creek Indians did the work, but the citizens of Wickenburg and Phoenix knew better."[9] Will Barnes also recorded "some reason to believe" that outlaws instead of Indians had done the deed.[10]

Captain Charles Meinhold[11] was rushed from Camp Date Creek

[7] Bancroft, 560n.

[8] *U.S. Board of Indian Commissioners. Peace with the Apaches of New Mexico and Arizona. Report of Vincent Colyer, Member of Board—1871*, 27.

[9] Farish, IV, 72.

[10] Barnes, *Place Names*, 291.

[11] Prussian-born Charles Meinhold enlisted in the army in 1851 and was commissioned a first lieutenant in 1862 in the New Mexico Infantry. He resigned and was commissioned a second lieutenant in the Third Cavalry that year and ended the Civil War

to investigate the tragedy, and even he seemed puzzled by some aspects of it. He left camp the day after the outrage and filed his official report, dated November 9, with the post adjutant[12] the day he returned.

The Captain had reached Wickenburg on the sixth. There he interviewed a William Kruger, or Krueger, who had been wounded in the attack and who told Meinhold that the passengers included, besides the driver, John Lentz, and Loring, who rode atop the coach with him, a Miss Mollie Sheppard[13] of Prescott; P. M. Hamel and W. G. Salmon, both, along with Loring, of the Wheeler survey party; C. S. Adams, a businessman; and Frederick W. Shoholm of Prescott. At about 8:00 A.M. on the fifth the coach was jumped by ten or eleven Indians, who fired from ambush, killing one of the horses, the driver, and all of the passengers except Miss Sheppard, Salmon, and Kruger, who were, however, wounded. Salmon mortally. There was, it is said, seventeen bullet holes in the coach.[14] Kruger and Miss Sheppard escaped from the coach and fled. The assailants apparently were out of ammunition, although they followed the pair for a short distance. Five miles later the two met the eastbound mail buckboard, whose driver improvised a barricade, mounted one of his horses, and rode for help, which arrived about midnight.[15] Kruger was positive the assailants were Indians.

The Captain examined the site of the massacre, finding moccasin tracks "of the pattern used by the Apache Mohaves," two butter tins, apparently discarded at some military post and used by the assailants to carry water, and a pack of Spanish cards similar to those often used by Indians in their incessant gambling. He also found other signs indicating that the attack had been made by Indians.

Meinhold trailed the outlaws as far as he could. He followed the

---

as a regimental quartermaster. He was named captain in 1866 and died December 14, 1877. Heitman.

[12] Indian Bureau Files for 1871, Record Group 75, National Archives.

[13] She was called a "notorious courtesan" by Jackson, *The White Conquest of Arizona*, 26. Jackson says that the coach passengers carried "over $100,000" between them and infers that white men perpetrated the massacre.

[14] *Arizona Miner*, November 25, 1871.

[15] McClintock, I, 218–19.

tracks of seven individuals toward the Hassayampa River, where he lost them in a welter of other tracks of individuals coming and going.

The Captain added to his report some of the gossip he had picked up at Wickenburg. Some suspected Mexicans, but

> others assert that such a scheme had been planned for some time; that it was intended to rob the mail of the bullion generally shipped on, or shortly after, the first of every month. Others, and I found them rather in the minority, accuse the Indians living at this post [Camp Date Creek]. The woman Sheppard is under the impression that white men were amongst the robbers, but she had no other reason to advance than that she had heard that certain parties in Prescott, who disappeared suddenly about the time she left Prescott, had made inquiries about the time of her departure, and what amount of money she was likely to carry with her.
>
> I ascertained that no horses were stolen, nor any baggage, that even the persons of the passengers were not searched and robbed except Mr. Adams, whose pockets were found to be turned inside out. Mr. Adams . . . was likely to be thought carrying a large amount of money.
>
> I also noticed that while many letters were not interfered with, almost every one addressed to an A. Q. M. or A. C. G. was opened, and that all the letters I saw opened had been opened carefully at one end, and the contents restored in many cases.

Yet the work of Indians it proved to be, or at least Indians were deeply involved in it—a raiding party of Apache Mohaves, reported "to belong to the main group of nearly one thousand tribesmen who were being fed at Date Creek."

The question was, which Indians? Crook bided his time, although with bulldog tenacity he explored every avenue to ferret out those responsible. Meanwhile, he kept his "army" at a high level of efficiency and continued to build it up, waiting for the day when the Board of Peace Commissioners would fall from favor and he could move on with his own solution to the Arizona Indian problem. He kept Hank 'n' Yank's Pack Train, consisting of 145 mules, on the payroll at $1.25 a day per animal; Hank Hewitt and Yank (John) Bartlett had the finest pack train in the Territory, and Crook didn't dare let it go for fear it might not be available when he needed it. McIntosh was on the quartermaster's roll at $125.00 a month as "guide," and in March, Dan O'Leary was hired for that sort of duty at $135.00 a month, although he was kept on duty for only nine days, as we shall see. Tom Moore, Crook's veteran packer, was added in April as "master of transportation" at $150.00 a month, and James R. Cook, also a packer, was listed at $86.66.[16]

By midsummer, Lieutenant William J. Ross,[17] as Crook's quartermaster, had formed a nucleus of select men to serve as scouts, guides, and "interpreters." They are listed on the faded records of the War Department in the National Archives as Joseph Felman, Archy (sic) McIntosh, Francisco (Marijilda) Grijalba, William McCloud, and Al Seavers (which was a pretty good approximation of Al's name, considering some of the variants extant). Each received $125 a month, except Grijalba, who unaccountably got only $80 a month throughout his long service. By August, Al was listed as "Severs" and by December as "Al Seiber." His name was so commonly misspelled as "Seiber" during his life that the mistake almost became an accepted version; sometimes he was mentioned as "Sieber" and "Seiber" in the same story or report!

In the meantime, the Wickenburg Massacre case had come to a head. Late in January, 1872, a rancher named William Gilson told Crook that he had reason to believe that Date Creek Indians were mixed up in the affair.[18] The General at once sent spies, both white and Indian, to hunt up evidence.

The next real break came from an Apache Mohave boy who had been raised by Dan O'Leary. The scouts were always taking in and

16 U.S. Army Records, National Archives.

17 William J. Ross, born in Scotland, enlisted in the Eighteenth Connecticut Infantry on July 23, 1862, and was appointed captain of the Twenty-ninth Connecticut on February 3, 1864, and made major on May 12, 1865. After the Civil War he became a second lieutenant of the Twenty-third Infantry on May 5, 1868, and transferred to the Twenty-first Infantry on April 19, 1869. Heitman. Ross fought through Crook's great offensive, but after the General was transferred to the Department of the Platte, he resigned. He did some bookkeeping work in connection with such mining camps as the Dos Cabezas and once tried to secure appointment as Indian Commissioner but failed. He died at Tucson in mid-1907. Correspondence with Louis Menager of Tucson, Ross's stepson, to whom I am also indebted for a photograph of the soldier.

18 Unless otherwise specified, this account is based on the complete narration in the Arizona Miner of September 28, 1872.

rearing some hapless child, whose parents they may have been instrumental in sending to another world. Anyway, the renegades who had looted the stage sent for this youngster to ask him the denominations of the bills they had seized; he did so, then told Dan about it, and O'Leary told Crook.

Having found out how much money they had stolen and with an irresistible urge to spend it, the renegades descended upon the Colorado River Mohave Reservation, where they made nuisances of themselves with their boasting and drinking, to the disgust of Iretaba,[19] chief of the Mohaves and a persistent friend to the whites, despite the most irritating provocations. Iretaba, with one or two of his subchiefs and a party of warriors, came to Whipple to tell Crook of the renegades.

Satisfied that he now knew who the renegades were and that they were Date Creek Indians, Crook laid careful plans to round them up. Early in March, 1872, he hired Dan O'Leary for a few days and with Lieutenant Bourke and Lieutenant Ross rode out of Whipple, telling no one his destination. The party went to Beale's Springs, at the southern end of the Cerbats, and Crook, with O'Leary's help, per-

---

[19] Iretaba was one of the best-known Indians of Arizona at this time. The Colorado River Reservation set aside for his Mohaves in 1865, was the first Indian Reservation in the Territory and still exists. Iretaba was taken to Washington about that time and was so impressed that he remained a friend of the undeserving whites for the remainder of his life. He appears in many early accounts of Arizona. Daniel E. Conner, who mentions him frequently, describes him as a "tall and large man with a careworn cast of countenance, knitted brow, and of a quiet, observant and thoughtful demeanor," and reveals that he was of considerable value during the initial penetration of the country. Conner, 86–91. Iretaba was credited with having purchased the Oatman girls from the Apaches to bring to a happy end their tragic saga and having guided the Whipple party of 1854 and the Ives expedition in 1857. *Ibid.*, 78n. He persisted in his friendship for the whites, although sometimes it must have been difficult, as in June, 1867, when a La Paz saloonkeeper lured Iretaba's favorite wife into his establishment, got her drunk, and raped her. Iretaba sought out the white man, they had a fist fight, and the saloonkeeper won, whereupon Iretaba went to Indian Superintendent George W. Dent, "who had the white man arrested," but, there being no jail at La Paz, "he was soon discharged, and then attacked Iretaba again, hitting him over the head with a revolver. The matter ended with Iretaba leaving town with most of his followers." *Arizona Miner*, June 15, 1867. Had the chief reacted like a white man and killed the saloonkeeper, it would have been listed as another Indian outrage, no doubt. Iretaba died on May 3, 1874, on the Colorado River.

95

suaded some Walapais to go with him and urge the Apache Mohaves to come into Date Creek, "where they would be fed and taken care of by the Government. This was a ruse, as the General's main object was to get hold of the robbers and murderers belonging to that tribe."[20]

The weather was terrible. On foot, through snow and slush, Crook and his lieutenants trudged along toward a rendezvous where he was to meet the Walapai scouts under O'Leary and two companies of cavalry, but at the last moment a travel-stained messenger hurried up with orders to cease operations and let General Oliver Otis Howard's first peace mission be carried out uninterruptedly. Crook perforce called off the short campaign. Howard had succeeded Colyer as the man upon whom peace hopes lay; he roamed the Territory during the spring and summer, and it was not until September that Crook could indulge his determination to gather in the rascals he was after. He had not forgotten them.

Word reached him that the renegades were becoming suspicious that he knew who they were. They therefore laid careful plans to murder him and his officers. The idea was to call Crook to Date Creek under the pretext that they wanted a conference, to come to it armed, and at a given signal, which was to be the rolling and lighting of a cigarette, to open fire, first on Crook, then on his officers. The Indians would then take off for the nearly inaccessible canyons at the head of Santa Maria Fork of Bill Williams River.

The renegades' plans went awry through no fault of their own. Crook had become aware of the plot and was willing to use it for his own ends, but the untimely death of Captain Philip Dwyer,[21] at that time the only officer at Date Creek, brought the General and his aide, Lieutenant Ross, to the camp sooner than either he or the renegades

[20] *Arizona Miner*, September 28, 1872.

[21] Dwyer, born in Ireland about 1837, enlisted in the cavalry and was serving in Texas at the outbreak of the Civil War. He served throughout that war as a Union officer and afterward was commissioned in the Fifth Cavalry. Dwyer fought with this regiment against Plains Indians, mostly Cheyennes, and arrived at Camp Date Creek, Arizona, on February 11, 1872, where he served until his death, on August 29, from some unidentified disorder. George F. Price, *Across the Continent with the Fifth Cavalry* (cited hereafter as *Fifth Cavalry*), 412–13.

expected. Lieutenant Bourke had already arrived there from another mission.

In his official report, Crook stressed the painstaking care he used in order to keep his plans secret while "getting the individual Indians into position so as to capture them." He met Iretaba and an interpreter at Date Creek, but on arrival he found that "at least two thirds of the Indians, belonging on the reservation, were absent from it, and that one band had left in a defiant manner, stating that they were not coming back, while others had left with the permission of the agent to go to a certain place, with the promise to come in whenever he sent for them, both promises they had failed to keep."

Upon his arrival, Crook informed the Indians that he wanted a talk with them the following day at a place he designated. They hastened their plans to carry out the murders, and no doubt were relieved when the General arrived at the assigned place with only Lieutenant Ross, a few soldiers, and a dozen packers, but no formal escort. Obviously, they must have thought, Nan-tan suspects nothing! They failed to notice that each of the packers, among them giant Hank Hewitt and, I think, Al Sieber,[22] was armed to the very teeth, with "every revolver on the full cock, and every knife ready for instant use."[23]

The Indians seemed uneasy and suspicious, and in very bad temper, appearing with their weapons and in war paint. Some of those who had participated in the stage attack were there, but they, too, were restless.[24] They were led by Chief Ochocama.[25]

Crook now set in motion his counterplot. Some Mohaves under Iretaba had arrived, and they alone could identify all of the murderers. It was planned that they would circulate among the Ochocama

[22] There is no list of the civilians who took part in the ensuing free-for-all, but in view of Sieber's prominent role in subsequent events and the report that he had been a packer for Hewitt, plus his friendship for O'Leary, who was also there, and other considerations, I think it most likely he was a member of the party.

[23] Bourke, *Border*, 169. It is a little difficult to correlate the two major accounts— Bourke's and the *Miner*'s—at this point, since the latter indicates that the soldiers played a prominent role and the former that they had almost no part in it. Bourke was at Date Creek at the time, and I'm inclined toward his version.

[24] Crook to Assistant Adjutant General (AAG), Division of the Pacific, September 18, 1872, Hayes Collection.

[25] *Arizona Miner*, September 28, 1872.

party, handing out short twists of black tobacco, but they would hand it only to the murderers; as they did so, a white would ease himself into position so that at a signal each of the renegades could be seized.

The first piece of tobacco was offered to Ochocama himself, who, suspicious and aware that something was wrong, hung his head and refused to accept it. He was persuaded to take the tobacco, however, whereupon "his countenance changed rapidly from one blue color to another, and he finally dropped" it. The last suspect was given a twist and Crook gave the sign. When a soldier stepped up to arrest this Indian, the renegades decided it was their time and gave their own signal. A classic melee ensued.

The soldier who had attempted the first arrest was stabbed, almost fatally,[26] but drew his pistol and fired. The Indian next to Ochocama raised his carbine and fired at Crook, but Lieutenant Ross and Dan O'Leary smashed into the General, knocking him aside just in time, the bullet killing an Indian who had been standing behind him. Crook recovered his feet and rushed into the center of the fracas, seeking to stop the shooting, which now had become general, with bullets flying in all directions. The packers were in their glory. Three of them grabbed the ringleader, Ochocama, who fought like a man possessed and would have escaped had Dan O'Leary not twisted his fingers into the Indian's long hair, spun him to the ground, and tied him up, whence he was thrown into the near-by guardhouse. Ochocama's brother, already there for trying to smuggle arms, became so excited that he sought to burst out through the roof and was shot for his efforts. Most of the warriors fled to the rocks as the shooting commenced, but "those who had to remain fought like demons." Ochocama, still beside himself with rage and now untied, "fired old boots, iron wedges and other missiles out of his cell, at the guard, jumped through the canvas roof, was shot at twice, pierced with a bayonet once, and finally made his escape into the hills."[27]

Big Hank waded through the seething mass of wrestling, straining bodies to seize the huge Indian who had given the signal for assassina-

[26] So says the *Miner*. Despite the casualties, the *Chronological List* does not mention this battle.

[27] There, it was rumored, he had died of wounds, but he did not.

tion. He clutched the warrior in a viselike grip and dragged him toward the guardhouse, but thought better of it as the Indian struggled, bit, and kicked. Hewitt grabbed him by each ear and dashed his head against the rocks, breaking his skull, so that the hapless victim died during the night. Most of the Indians, however, escaped into the hills, where they gathered and made their way down into the canyons they had selected, refusing either to come in or to send in the murderers, despite Crook's message that if they didn't, the whole tribe would be punished.

Hewitt estimated that about seven Indians had been killed in the skirmish, with others wounded, and added that "many more could and probably would have been killed" but for Crook's desperate efforts to stop the fight and prevent a general outbreak. In this he was successful.

Typically, Crook made no official mention of how narrowly he escaped with his life, nor did he describe the spirited action. In his report to the Assistant Adjutant General, Division of the Pacific, he wrote: "When the Indians were assembled, I had some men detailed to make the arrests as soon as the Indians were identified. As they were designated, the soldiers stepped up to arrest them, when one of the Indian friends standing back of the soldiers, stabbed one of them in the back. A shot was fired, by whom I could scarcely say, but I think it was by the soldier stabbed, and in an instant firing commenced on both sides the Indians making for the hills. I made every effort, as did all the officers present, to stop the firing, but it was all over in an instant. I returned to Prescott on the 9th."[28] Even in his autobiography the reticent General writes merely that "on the eighth day of September, 1872, in attempting to make the arrest, some of the Indians were killed, and some of our party narrowly escaped being shot. Some of the parties were captured and killed, which stopped all further depredations in that section of the country."[29] One reason for his silence may well have been that he realized his unorthodox methods of selecting civilian personnel to do the work might be subject to censure, but whatever the cause, he said nothing, officially, about it.

[28] Crook to AAG, Division of the Pacific, September 18, 1872, Hayes Collection.
[29] *Autobiography*, 174.

99

Some fragments of the various bands did filter back to Date Creek, bearing in their hearts an implacable hatred for Iretaba and his Mohaves until Crook patiently explained that he had identified the murderers from other sources and that Iretaba's people were not to be held responsible for the denouement, nor was Iretaba to be killed. But of course he couldn't get through to the hostiles with this information. About the middle of September, a friendly Walapai arrived at Beale's Springs and told Tommy Byrne[30] that Ochocama and five other chiefs were so angry about Iretaba's part that they "talked of going to the Colorado River to fight the Mohave Indians."[31] Most important, however, was the fact that the Walapai brought in definite word regarding the whereabouts of the enemy.

After waiting long enough to blunt the hostiles' wariness, Crook sent out a column of the Fifth Cavalry under Captain Julius Wilmot Mason,[32] a vigorous officer with much experience. The command included Company B, led by Captain Robert H. Montgomery;[33] Com-

[30] Irish-born Byrne, a blarneying officer whom the Walapais loved because he was fair with them and always took their part in their frequent disputes with Indian agents, enlisted in the army in 1854, was commissioned in 1862, and was assigned to the Twelfth Infantry in 1871. He died January 11, 1881. Heitman.

[31] *Arizona Miner*, September 28, 1872.

[32] Mason was born in Pennsylvania, probably about 1835. He was graduated as a civil engineer and was a professional engineer when the Civil War broke out, at which time he enlisted in the Fifth—then the Second—Cavalry. His intrepidity was marked at First Bull Run and many subsequent actions. During Stoneman's drive on Richmond in 1863, he led "one of the most gallant dashes made by any part of the regiment during the war." He participated in many engagements and was brevetted up to lieutenant colonel. Mason served with his regiment on the Great Plains and arrived in Arizona in February, 1872. Subsequent to his first tour in Arizona, he served against the Sioux and went back to Arizona to take part in the Loco campaign in 1882. Plagued by illness periodically, Mason contracted typhoid fever during the Civil War, "inflammatory rheumatism" in Arizona in 1872, and died of apoplexy at Fort Huachuca on December 20, 1882.—*Fifth Cavalry*, 370–74.

[33] Montgomery, a Pennsylvanian, was a noncommissioned officer in the Fifth, stationed in Texas when the Civil War broke out, but received a commission in 1862. He was captured in 1863 while on picket duty "and his name was dropped from the rolls of the army; but when the circumstances attending his capture were fully understood, he was restored to the service" and rejoined the regiment. He had extensive field duty against hostile Indians throughout the West. He retired a major on April 8, 1892. *Fifth Cavalry*, 424–27; Heitman.

pany C, Captain Emil Adam;[34] and Company K, headed by Second Lieutenant Frank Michler.[35] Also with the command was Second Lieutenant Walter Scribner Schuyler[36] and eighty-six Walapai scouts under Al Sieber.

I find it significant that Sieber led the large force of scouts on this important expedition. It is the first time he is mentioned officially as guide for a military command, although he went on the payroll for that purpose in July, 1872. It would seem that by this time he was already a seasoned leader of Indian scouts. Sieber says that he had accompanied Dan O'Leary on civilian expeditions and had done some military scouting before Crook took command,[37] but I have found no documentary mention of him until this affair. It would be unlikely that leadership of so large a detachment of Indians would be given to a man insufficiently experienced, and both the success of the cam-

[34] German-born Adam enlisted in 1861 and was wounded at Shiloh. He led many daring raids behind enemy lines, and his adventures would fill a book. He joined the Fifth Cavalry in 1871, was promoted to major in 1886, and died January 16, 1903. *Fifth Cavalry*, 428–32; Heitman. Adam was court-martialed and convicted in 1874 for misbehavior in the face of the enemy, but this apparently had no effect on his army career. *Arizona Miner*, May 8, 1874.

[35] Michler, a New Yorker, was graduated from West Point in 1870, saw service in Arizona and on the Plains, and was an aide to General Schofield and adjutant at West Point. He died May 29, 1901. Heitman.

[36] Born at Ithaca, New York, on April 26, 1850, of a prominent family, Schuyler was a man of rare ability and intellect. He and Michler were classmates, both graduating from West Point in 1870; the former was promoted through grades to the rank of brigadier general, which he attained January 5, 1911. He arrived at McDowell in February, 1872, but served mostly in the field until 1875, becoming one of Crook's favorite young officers, and figured in the engagements at Muchos Cañones, the Red Rocks, Pinto Creek, Lost River, Black Mesa, Cave Creek, Superstition Mountains, Aravaipa Mountains, the Mazatzals, Four Peaks, and elsewhere, in most of which actions Al Sieber also took part. Schuyler was brevetted up to the rank of lieutenant colonel for his successive Apache fights. In 1875 he traveled to Europe, studying the Russian army and various military establishments, then returned to serve on the Plains as one of Crook's aides, where he made a daring march through hostile country to join the General and participated in the Big Horn and Yellowstone expeditions. He operated against the Utes, raising the siege on Milk Creek and relieving a small detachment of hardpressed troops. Schuyler also served in Puerto Rico, the Philippines, and Cuba during and after the war with Spain and was a member of the General Staff from 1904 to 1906. He retired in 1913 and died at Carmel, California, on February 17, 1932. *Fifth Cavalry*, 533–34; Heitman; *Who Was Who*.

[37] Sieber statement for McClintock, 1903, Phoenix Public Library.

paign and the high praise for the work of the Walapais attest to Sieber's efficiency and skill as guide and chief of scouts.

Fortunately, we have an eyewitness account of the operation in a graphic letter Schuyler wrote to his father a few days later:

Camp near Cp Hualpai A. T.
Septr. 29" 1872

Dear Father.

Last Sunday "B," "C," and "K" Companies of our regiment with about 80 Hualpai Indian scouts left this place to make an attack on a war party of Apache-Mohaves who had organized on Burro Creek intending to attack Camp Colorado. We marched 20 miles the first day to a spring in the mountains south of here. Next morning we marched 6 miles to a canyon where we lay hidden until 1 o'clock the next morning when we hid the command in a hollow and sent out Indian scouts. Just at dusk some of these returned and told us they had found the Apaches. So we left the pack-trains and all baggage in camp, and mounted, followed the Indian guides over a very tortuous and rough trail for about 10 miles, where we dismounted and left the horses with a strong guard. From this point we could just see the camp fires of the Indians about 8 miles off. The Indian scouts then went ahead on the trail and we followed in single file as silent as could be, and very slowly as the country was very rough and we had to climb either up or down steep rocks all the time. In the dim moonlight the column presented a very weird appearance, looking like an immense snake slowly dragging itself along. If you want to see the superlative in sneaking, you ought to see one Indian hunt another. They crawled ahead of us like cats, and every little while when they saw something suspicious, we had to lie down flat until they had reconnoitered the ground. Their signals were very pretty being perfect imitations of the calls of the whip-poor-will or a cricket. We crawled along in this way for 7 miles when the Indians told us we were very near the camps of which there were four. "K" Company with most of the Indians were sent across the Burro Creek canon to attack on that side and we ("B" & "C" Co's) moved about a mile further, crawling some times on all fours until we were within 150 yards of the first "Rancheria" (camp) where we lay down to await until the day should break. We lay there on the cold ground shivering with cold, but making no sound for over an hour, and just at daybreak deployed as skirmishers along the crest of a hill, making a large angle between the two companies. In this angle and opposite to the 1" Rancheria were placed a party of Indians. In front of my companies' right wing was the second Rancheria. We had just completed the deployment when the firing commenced on the other side of the canon. We jumped up and poured in a withering cross fire on the astonished hostiles, and then charged, firing rapidly. The few warriors who were not knocked over made for the canon, where Michler's men picked them off from the opposite side. We skirmished the canon thoroughly capturing 4 ponies, and returned to the rendezvous where the command separated, with the trumpets sounding the "Recall."

We killed in all about 40 Indians, captured a large number of children and 8 squaws. Most of the papooses we left to be picked up by their friends, but the squaws and *their* papooses (10) we took along. The Apaches were so completely surprised that they fired but few shots, most all too high. Only one man on our side was wounded, he being shot in the chin and neck by an Apache who had concealed himself behind a rock, but the latter was killed as soon as he had fired. After the fight everyone was so fatigued that we just dropped down on the rocks and waited for the horses to come up, which they did in about 2 hours. We then returned to camp and got something to eat. We burned the Rancherias with all their supplies, bows, arrows, blankets, etc.

We thus whipped one of the worst bands of Apaches in the country and performed the unparalleled feat of "jumping" four rancherias simultaneously. We arrived back here on Friday, and just as we came into camp one of the men killed an immense black bear, upon which we have been feasting ever since.

Love to all
Your affec son,
Walter . . . .[38]

This was the first major test of Crook's methods, those by which he planned to tackle the Apaches to the east and thereby end, once and for all, the threat they had held over the settlements for many years.

It was a triumph for Sieber personally. He had accomplished the little less than prodigious feat of getting the soldiers, as well as the scouts, into position in time for the fight. Experience would show that this was rarely brought about and, in much of the confused fighting that would follow, often virtually impossible. Nine times out of ten, or maybe ninety-nine times out of one hundred, only the scouts at-

[38] Schuyler Collection, Huntington Library, San Marino, California.

tained position in time to fight, and actually did the fighting, to the point that many times the scouts were sent out by themselves, or with only a token force of troops accompanying them.

In any event, the actual advance, or point of the column, would be led by a sprinkling of scouts. Perhaps the white guide would go out with the point, perhaps not. Most of the scouts, as in this case, where eighty-six went along, would be organized in regular fighting companies of thirty or forty men or so each and used for combat, but only the best trackers and keenest woodsmen among them would be the actual scouts. Their value lay in their ability to slither into position for the fight more efficiently and silently than white men, their ability to march farther, to endure wild-country hazards with better spirit, and their general out-country know-how, which was superior to that of any but exceptional white men and surely averaged higher than that of troops, no matter how experienced. They were hired and used in place of troops and were expected to be killers, for that is what they really enjoyed and what they sometimes seemed best at.

Captain Mason exultantly sent Crook a dispatch summarizing the results of the expedition. "Officers and men behaved splendidly and I cannot speak too highly of our Walapais scouts," he wrote. "Their scouting was excellent and when the fight came off they were not a bit behind the soldiers. I congratulate the Commanding General and the country in having secured so valuable an auxiliary. . . . Guide Seaber did excellent service."[39] In turn, Crook issued *General Order No. 32*, formally congratulating the command on its signal triumph and, incidentally, partially correcting Mason's spelling of Al's name, making it "Seiber" instead of "Seaber." But Al, at this point, was too sick to care.

As Al was bringing in his grinning, dusky scouts to Camp Hualpai for rations, his horse, frightened at the whooping and yelling, tucked its head between its forelegs and set to bucking. Nobody could predict, then or now, when a western horse would buck. They could all do it. On sufficient provocation, with some horses more, with others none at all, they would buck, some with more skill and violence than others. Any westerner could ride a bucker; it was one of the trades

39 *Arizona Miner*, September 28, 1872.

that had to be learned if one didn't care to walk, and in the Arizona of vast distances and few settlements, no one really desired to walk. But a man could be taken unawares, and such must have been Al's fate. At any rate, he suffered a rupture and was bedded, in considerable pain, until Dr. J. N. McCandless, who had an office on the north side of Prescott Plaza opposite Whiskey Row, could be sent for. The good doctor saddled up and rode the sixty miles or more to Camp Hualpai to treat Al, who must have been laid up for at least three weeks.[40] However, he recovered in plenty of time to take part in preparations for Crook's grand offensive, which was now finally and definitely shaping up.

[40] *Ibid.*, October 12, 1872; *Republican* obituary. I have been assured by specialists that this must have been a rupture of a disc or vertebra; if it had been a ruptured intestine, Sieber would have died without surgery.

VII. The Grand Offensive

CROOK HAD BEEN PATIENT. Twice, during the missions of Colyer and Howard, he had interrupted his plans for an offensive against the Indians until the completion of peace negotiations. Although the negotiators had placed hundreds of Indians upon reservations and had been instrumental in bringing peace to wide areas of the frontier, the hard core of Apache hostility remained. Within a single year from the time Vincent Colyer had entered the Territory, more than fifty raids and forty murders were attributed to the hostiles. Their depredations all but blanketed the Territory. Stock thefts, burnings, and killings were so commonplace as to warrant scarcely a line in the local newspapers. It was said, facetiously, that the whites lived on the reservations and the Indians ran the country.

Crook's plans for ending the Indian menace were complex, but in brief they entailed putting a number of small commands, officered by men up to the grade of captain, into the field to cross and crisscross the hostiles' territory systematically, fighting any Indians they could catch and keeping the others stirred up, ultimately wearing them down to the point where they would prefer to come in to the reservations rather than starve or be slaughtered in the wilderness. To do this, he would need many scouts and many chiefs of scouts. He therefore enlisted as many Walapais, Yavapais, and Mohaves as he could get. He even made a trip across the line into Utah seeking Paiute scouts and enlisted some who worked the early part of the offensive.[1]

---

[1] A. H. Nickerson, *Major General George Crook and the Indians.* Nickerson reports that Crook, endeavoring to secure scouts among Indians he calls the Utes, sat in on a council with a "Captain Jack." "Some days previous," Nickerson said, "Captain Jack

To the ranks of such white scouts as McIntosh, Sieber, Felman, Grijalba, and McCloud had been added other, equally competent frontiersmen: Dan O'Leary, Jack Townsend, Gus Spear,[2] Ed Clark, Lew Ellit, Mason McCoy (who, like Archie, had come from the Oregon country, where he had served Crook's cause before), and the great Willard Rice;[3] later, George G. Bromley was signed on. There may have been still others who were used briefly or for some particular expedition because of their special knowledge of certain country or Indian bands. Archie was post guide at Whipple, and Dan O'Leary was described as guide at Camp Hualpai. Al Sieber was "in the field," as were Townsend, Clark, McCoy, and Ellit. Rice operated in the field, but mostly out of Verde. Felman was probably with the southern columns from Grant or Apache, as was Marijilda Grijalba.

As a legal basis for his impending offensive, the methodical Crook used his famous *General Order No. 10*, which had been issued November 21, 1871, but the execution of which had been held in abeyance during the peace missions. It said that all roving bands of Indians

had captured a particularly plump" lizard to eat "and in lieu of a better place to carry it, had placed the reptile in the envelope containing his credentials . . . which the agent of his reservation had given him. [He] forgot all about it. . . . At the council he produced his credentials from an inside pocket of his filthy hunting shirt and opening the envelope with great pomp—almost under the General's nose—disclosed the malodorous body of the defunct reptile. [Trying to explain it away as an accident] he caught the reptile by the tail, tossed it contemptuously away . . . saying: 'Pooh! Damn Snake!' and handed the papers to the General who received them with due solemnity, unbroken by even a smile."

[2] After his service as a scout, Augustus A. Spear established a ranch four miles east of the Colorado and northeast of present-day Needles on a lake named for him. His brother, Benjamin S. Spear, had a sutler's store at Fort Mohave and was a prospector and the first postmaster of Beale's Springs. Barnes, *Place Names*, 2nd ed., 223.

[3] Willard Rice was born at Greensboro, Orleans County, Vermont, on October 22, 1832, but moved with his parents to Canaan, Wayne County, Ohio, in 1837. He traveled overland from there to California on March 18, 1852, and became a placer miner near Marysville. With a small party of prospectors, he came to Arizona from California in 1863 and was listed as a miner in the Arizona Territorial Census of 1864. Rice was employed by Lieutenant Charles A. Curtis at Fort Whipple as a "spy" and guide at five dollars a day on January 1, 1865, and later served with Lieutenant Antonio Abeytia and other officers, putting in ten years at this kind of work in all. At one time he owned the Cornucopia mine in the Cherry District. He died at Prescott on January 2, 1899, at age sixty-six.

would have to go to some reservation or "be regarded as hostile and punished accordingly." Further, "active operations will be kept up against the hostile Apaches of Arizona and pressed with all practicable vigor until they submit to the authority of the government, cease from hostilities and remain upon their reservations."

The General was no headquarters soldier. He himself would move incessantly from point to point around the narrowing perimeter, coordinating the movements of his junior officers. Winter would aid his operations, making it more difficult for the hostiles to replenish destroyed food supplies and subjecting them to the rigors of high-altitude cold and snow, so November 15 was established as D day. Crook's plan was ruthless but, at the same time, humane. Only a brutal, sledge-hammer blow would force the hostiles into submission, whereupon wise and kind guidance could show them the one way by which they could survive the white tide engulfing their ancestral homeland.

On November 16, three columns pushed out from Camp Hualpai, each composed of a company of cavalry and thirty to forty Indian scouts, with orders to scour Chino Valley, the headwaters of the Verde, and the vicinity of the San Francisco Mountains and thereafter to operate out of Camp Verde, which was on the Verde River just below the mouth of Beaver Creek. Crook also ordered the organization of two additional columns, with Date Creek Indians as scouts, then left for Apache to direct the southern columns.

Sieber's movements during this operation are obscure. No report I have seen mentions him, yet he was complimented, along with seven other guides, in a general order noting the conclusion of the campaign, for "good conduct during the different campaigns and engagements" and he was known to be active in the field. It is probable that he was with either one of the Camp Hualpai commands or one of the two columns, under Captain George F. Price,[4] which included the Date Creek Indians. In either event, he saw rugged service that winter in the northern theater of the great offensive.

---

4 George Frederick Price was a New Yorker who enlisted in the army in California in 1861 and made captain during the war. He joined the Fifth Cavalry as a second lieutenant in 1866 and made captain in 1872. Price died May 23, 1888.

The Camp Hualpai columns had varying luck west of the Verde. One of them, with Paiutes for scouts, ran into hostiles in the Red Rock country on the east side of Chino Valley, killing some and capturing a few women. The commands all suffered from lack of water, but at last the snows came and that problem, at least, was solved. Captain Price, moving eastward south of Verde, found more country than he could handle, lots of Indian sign, but no hostiles.

After thoroughly crisscrossing the area west of the Verde, some of the commands were sent east and northeast into Upper Tonto Basin, an area which in later years Sieber would scout again and again because almost as long as there were warpath Indians anywhere in Arizona, they were in the Tonto Basin. Meanwhile, a force headed by Captain George M. Randall[5] was scouting Lower Tonto Basin along the Salt, working from Fort Apache to Camp McDowell. Its scouts were led by C. E. Cooley, who, being married to an Apache or two, had mastered their rather difficult language. This command had a few sharp skirmishes but failed to make contact with any large body of the enemy.

While all of this was going on, Crook left Apache and went to Camp Grant, where he organized still another column, ordering it to rendezvous with one from McDowell in the Superstitions, scouting the Pinals enroute. It was this command which struck pay dirt.

Just after Christmas, 1872, the combined command, which had with it the quite literate Lieutenant John G. Bourke, who, years later, would write the story, was guided by an Apache over the stony mesa north of the Salt and down over an all but impassable bluff to a wide-mouthed and shallow cave. Here the soldiers and their Pima allies trapped nearly one hundred of the most inveterate raiders among the Apaches, and here, high above the rushing waters of the Salt, was fought an all-day battle which ended disastrously for the hostiles. They would not surrender, these red warriors, and they died in their cave—died when they exposed themselves, died when soldiers on the

5 George Morton Randall was born in Ohio on October 8, 1841, and enlisted in the Civil War, being commissioned almost at once. He rose to lieutenant colonel by 1865, dropped back to captain after the war, and rose through ranks to major general at his retirement. He died at Denver on June 14, 1918.

rim above dropped great boulders into the mouth of the cavern, died from ricocheting fragments of bullets fired at the sloping roof of their retreat. Seventy-six Indians were killed in the fight or died of their wounds, and eighteen women and children, most of them wounded, were taken to McDowell.[6]

Al Sieber almost certainly was not at this fight. One of his acquaintances said he thought Sieber had told him he was, but that was long, long ago and he couldn't be sure. An unclear passage from an article by Bourke suggests the possibility: "Captain James Burns and Lieutenant E. D. Thomas joined us. . . . We had three white guides . . . who, as well as Al Seiber, Mason McCoy, Al Speers, Lew Elliott [sic], Willard Rice, and others, attached to the other detachment, rendered gallant and invaluable service at all hours during the campaign."[7] The trouble is that there is no record of which white scouts were with Burns. Bourke's list of five of the best guides "and others" is obviously too many for that modest command. I think the key word in Bourke's comment is "detachment," which must be a misprint for "detachments." This would broaden the statement to include all units involved in the campaign and thereby change its meaning.

Results of the bloody scrap were far reaching. For one thing it totally annihilated the band of raiders who had been making life unendurable along the Gila and the Salt. But the shock went deeper. It proved that troops, properly guided, could penetrate to the heart of Apachería and destroy the enemy, no matter how well protected he was, and it demonstrated the unrelenting persistence with which Crook's offensive was to be carried on. Yet it failed to end resistance completely. This was partly due to the fragmented nature of Apache society: what happened to one band was of no immediate concern to another—until a storm of bullets brought the offensive home.

On through the winter the soldiers campaigned. Their small commands were everywhere, tracking, attacking, probing, testing, burn-

---

[6] The best account of this fight is by Bourke, a participant, although his description of the event, written many years later from memory and his field notes, is somewhat colored by the passing years. See Bourke, *Border*, 187–201.

[7] John G. Bourke, "General Crook in the Indian Country," *Century*, Vol. XLI, No. 5 (March, 1891), 656.

ing rancherias, destroying food stocks, driving the hostiles higher and higher into the frozen mountains, picking off a few here, some more another place, but always on the offensive. By mid-January, the Superstitions were cleared. The war moved across the Salt and concentrated in the wilderness areas east and west of the Verde. In spite of the pressure, however, Indian depredations against the settlers continued. On March 11 the Apaches slaughtered three whites, one by torture, not far from Wickenburg. The Tonto Apaches who did it were actually waiting to plunder the Arizona-California stage, but it was several hours late and to amuse themselves the raiders captured George Taylor, a 21-year-old Scot. They led him to a secluded place, stripped and bound him, and began shooting arrows into his naked body, taking care not to strike a vital spot. In his agony the young man rolled over and over, breaking off the arrows until more than 150 had been shot into him. When he could move no more, "they finished him in a manner so excruciating and beastly that I could not, if I would . . . hint of the method of his final taking off."[8] Even hardened frontiersmen winced at the details of Taylor's death, and Crook ordered punitive efforts everywhere stepped up in order to punish his slayers.

At least three commands seemed to be on the trail of the killers, and Captain William H. Brown's[9] column killed fifteen warriors and captured eight women, one of whom reported that the band's warriors had just returned from a raid in which they had killed three whites. It must have been another trio, for Captain Randall tracked down the assassins of Taylor and the other two.

Coming from McDowell, Randall had trailed some hostiles across Bloody Basin, then struck a far fresher trail and followed it, moving by night much of the time. His scouts captured a squaw and "per-

[8] Nickerson, *op. cit.*

[9] Brown, born in Maryland about 1837, enlisted in the cavalry and was commissioned at the outbreak of the Civil War, earning a brevet rank of major for gallant and meritorious service during the Battle of Five Forks. He saw quite a bit of Indian service on the Middle Plains and in Arizona, was made inspector general of the latter department, and later commanded Camp Grant and San Carlos. In the course of his Arizona duties he fought the Apache well, earning brevet ranks up to brigadier general. He died of an undisclosed ailment at New York City on June 4, 1875. Heitman.

suaded" her to guide the party, under cover of darkness, to the top of almost unclimbable Turret Mountain. On their hands and knees the grim troops inched through the blackness to the very summit, gaining it just before daylight and finding there an acre or two of fairly level ground seamed by cracks resulting when the lava which formed the peak had cooled. On it stood the brush-and-cloth huts of the Apache rancheria, its inhabitants sleeping happily in the wake of the butchery they had so recently performed and confident that the "white eyes" could never, never find them here. "Just at dawn of day our people fired a volley into their camp and charged with a yell," wrote Crook. "So secure did [the hostiles] feel in this almost impregnable position that they lost all presence of mind, even running past their holes in the rocks. Some of them jumped off the precipice and were mashed into a shapeless mass. All of the men were killed; most of the women and children were taken prisoner."[10]

If the rocky prominence now known as Turret Peak is the same as that identified as Turret Mountain in late March of 1873, and I assume it is, there is reason to doubt that many Apaches leaped wildly into space as the shattering charge overran them. Although part of Turret Peak is rimmed by an escarpment, at other points ready access to the summit may be had, even though the slopes are very steep.[11] It seems likely that most of the Indians who disappeared so hastily over the rim of the mesa slipped and scurried down into the brush rather than crashing, after a free fall, into jagged rocks below the cliffs. If so, they lived to fight another day.[12]

[10] *Autobiography*, 178. I have followed Crook in the description of the fight, for I have been unable to locate, either in the National Archives, early newspapers, or any of various other sources, any other account of this famous battle, although it is often mentioned as one of the two most important engagements of the entire campaign.

[11] Claude Wright, veteran mountain lion hunter and woodsman of the Bloody Basin–Turret Mountain country, told me that he had once ridden a mule to the summit of the mountain. The claim, which I accept, is more illustrative, however, of the truism that a good mule under capable guidance can climb anywhere short of heaven than that scaling Turret Peak, which I did one hot August day, is anything but rugged.

[12] As usual, there is wide discrepancy regarding how many Indians died and were captured on Turret Mountain. The *Chronological List* shows thirty-three killed and thirteen captured, but ten were killed and three captured in an earlier action "near" Turret Mountain. The first report to reach Whipple, picked up by the *Miner* on April 5,

Nevertheless, Randall's men, swinging down from that butte now reeking of death, could be secure in the knowledge that they had broken the back of Apache resistance everywhere in the Verde country. Until now the only prisoners had been taken by force of arms, but from this moment a strange thing began to happen. Bands of Indians, small groups at first and then larger ones, drifted in to the various military posts with offers to surrender. "In the first week of April," wrote Bourke, "a deputation from the hostile bands reached Camp Verde, and expressed a desire to make peace; they were told to return for the head chiefs, with whom General Crook would talk at that point."[13]

By this time the various commands, or at least most of them, had congregated at Verde, coming in one after another, riding down the white stone benches in long, swinging columns, working their way up the Verde or down it, down Beaver Creek, which joins the Verde right at the camp, down West Clear Creek or Oak Creek. From the points of the compass they came, "and a dirtier, greasier, more uncouth-looking set of officers and men it would be hard to encounter anywhere," Bourke recalled. "Dust, soot, rain, and grime had made their impress upon the canvas suits which each had donned, and with hair uncut for months and beards growing with straggling growth all over the face, there was not one of the party who would venture to pose as an Adonis; but all were happy, because . . . we were now to see the reward of our hard work."[14]

The full story of those winter months can never be told, of course, but Crook gave a hint of it in his *Annual Report* for 1873: "The examples of personal exertions & daring among the officers and men if all told would fill a volume." The hostiles, he said, complained that every rock had turned into a soldier "and that they were sprung from the ground, as was literally true in several instances when the troops

1873, said forty-seven had been killed. The next week, that newspaper said that Randall claimed to have killed twenty-three Indians, "but his soldiers—Indians and whites— claim to have counted 41 dead ones." Crook gives no total. Ralph Hedrick Ogle, *Federal Control of the Western Apaches: 1848–1886*, 116, says Randall captured "the entire group including some one hundred and thirty-six souls."

[13] Bourke, *Border*, 211.

[14] *Ibid.*, 212.

crawled down into caves to come up in the rear of the position between the Indians and the entrance to the caves in which they expected to take shelter in case of attack." The General continued: "In the campaign our Indian allies were invaluable; they possessed thorough knowledge of the country and of the habits and haunts of the Indians. To lead and manage them I had secured the services of some of my old guides and scouts who had been under my immediate command in other Indian wars and were thoroughly conversant with my mode of operating against Indians. I was materially assisted by Citizen guides of the Country, who only required to be generally informed of my wish to execute it with alacrity and ability." In the latter, of course, he was referring to Al Sieber, among others.

The first major triumph came when an Apache Mohave chief named Cha-lipun surrendered about 2,300 Indians to Crook. They gave up, the chief told the white officer, not because they loved him, but because they were afraid of him, because they had not only the white soldiers to fight, but their own people as well.

With the surrender of Cha-lipun and other chieftains, organized resistance crumbled, but it could not be wiped out until the worst of the Tonto Basin leaders, Delshay, was taken. Randall continued hunting him through the thicketed wilderness of the Mazatzals. Not until this Indian, as troublesome as his name, which means "red ant," was eliminated, could central Arizona breathe easily.

Delshay had plenty of reason to hate and distrust the white man. He was probably a Tonto, a fairly meaningless term, since it was applied indiscriminately to Apaches and Yumas who lived in the Four Peaks area of the Mazatzals. Old Camp Reno was established because of him in early 1867, and the next year, soldiers from there shot and killed his brother "while [he was] attempting to escape." In 1870, Delshay himself was wantonly shot and wounded by an army doctor. Vincent Colyer made every effort to contact him and almost succeeded once, but a false report frightened Delshay off "to protect his women and children from the Pimas," who were rumored to be hunting them. Delshay, too, was a mighty warrior. Every depredation which could in any way be linked with Tonto Basin Indians was credited to him, so that he seemed to be ubiquitous, the symbol of hostility. Little wonder, then, that Crook wanted him brought in.

Randall's scouts kept probing about the Mazatzals for this elusive Indian and his stubborn fighters. They crowded him out of his usual haunts and at last cornered him in the upper reaches of Canyon Creek, which flows southward from the Mogollon Rim toward the Salt. On April 25, Randall's command surrounded Delshay's camp and at dawn began firing into it. They had loosed scarcely twenty bullets, however, when Delshay raised a white flag and asked permission to surrender.

Too often had Delshay surrendered, growled Randall, only to break his word; the soldiers had lost confidence in him. The Indian began to cry, saying that he would follow any and all orders because he wanted to save his people from starvation. Every rock had turned into a soldier, he said. He would accept any terms. He confessed that "he had one hundred and twenty-five warriors last fall, and if anybody had told him he couldn't whip the world, he would have laughed at them, but now he had only twenty left. He said they used to have no difficulty in eluding the troops, but now the very rocks had gotten soft, they couldn't put their foot anywhere without leaving an impression by which we could follow, that they could get no sleep at nights, for should a coyote or a fox start a rock rolling during the night, they would get up and dig out, thinking it was we who were after them."[15] Randall hesitated, fingered his chin stubble, as though considering whether to accept the surrender or shoot the whole band, then took Delshay at his word. The hostiles meekly followed to the White Mountain Apache Reservation.[16]

Delshay found, however, as soon as his fears had vanished, his stomach was filled, and his people rested, that he didn't like the White Mountains any better than he liked McDowell, so once more his band fled, this time to turn up at Camp Verde. Delshay told Lieutenant Schuyler, then stationed at Verde, that "he was abused at [Fort]

---

[15] *Autobiography*, 180.

[16] *Arizona Miner*, May 10, 1873.

Apache by other Indians and could not stay there, and that he will behave himself at Verde."[17] He was permitted to remain.

Crook warned that after a short period of grace his troops would resume scouting after renegades and stragglers who refused to come in. On April 9, 1873, he issued his well-known *General Order No. 14*, commending his successful command upon virtual completion of their most arduous offensive:

> The operations of the troops in this Department, in the late campaigns against the Apaches, entitle them to a reputation second to none in the annals of Indian warfare.
>
> In the face of obstacles heretofore considered insurmountable, encountering rigorous cold in the mountains, followed in quick succession by the intense heat and arid waste of the desert, not infrequently at dire extremities for want of water to quench their prolonged thirst; and when their animals were stricken by pestilence or the country became too rough to be traversed by them, they left them and carried on their own backs such meagre supplies as they might, they persistently followed on, and plunging unexpectedly into chosen positions in lava beds, caves and canyons, they have outwitted and beaten the wiliest of foes with slight loss, comparatively, to themselves, and finally closed an Indian war that has been waged since the days of Cortez.

Crook concluded the document with several pages of names of officers and men, guides, Indian scouts, and civilians who had contributed importantly to the campaign's success. Among the names were those of Al Sieber, Dan O'Leary, Archie McIntosh, Gus Spear, Lew Ellit, Mason McCoy, Ed Clark, Joe Felman, and Antonio Besias.

---

[17] *Ibid.*, August 9, 1873. Dr. William H. Corbusier, post surgeon at Verde, who treated Delshay for tapeworm (as he later treated Geronimo for it), said that the Indian had heavy shoulders, usually "sort of lumbered along," in a half-trot, rarely walking, and wore an ornament in his left ear. He wore nothing in his right ear because, Delshay explained, it would interfere with the operation of a bow or gun. Information from William T. Corbusier, son of the Doctor.

VIII. The Long Scout

THE SURRENDER of the main bodies of the hostile Apaches did not mean the end of Indian troubles in Arizona, as the reports of scouts and military operations reveal. Crook's campaign was a success, no doubt about that, and only mopping up remained—but what a job that was to be!

Most of the white scouts were discharged at the end of April, 1873. Gus Spear, Lew Ellit, Ed Clark, Willard Rice, and others whose services no longer were needed either resigned or were let go. John Townsend had been dropped in March. Archie McIntosh was assigned to Camp Grant from May 1 and Al Sieber to Camp Verde on April 30. Walapai Charley Jaycox was also sent to Verde, but he apparently didn't like it there and within a month went back to his own country. From that time until late 1879, Sieber was the only regular guide and chief of scouts at Verde. He was almost continually in the field.

Crook's men had earned a rest, and scarcely had the surrenders been effected when the General sent a train of conveyances to bring his officers to Fort Whipple, at Prescott, for a round of parties and whoop-up. Lieutenant Ross bought a pair of fine horses that won fame as "the fastest team of trotters in the county,"[1] and the General, always mindful of the welfare of his Indians, took the money due the scouts and sent Dan O'Leary—and probably Sieber—to California to buy them horses.[2]

[1] *Arizona Miner*, May 10, 1873.

[2] *Autobiography*, 184: "I had a band of horses driven down from California, and took the scouts' pay due them, and bought horses for them, so as to get them owners of something, so as to anchor them to some fixed locality." The *Arizona Miner*, April 5,

Crook realized that for many months, perhaps years, management of the reservations would be a ticklish, exacting job, and he chose carefully the officers to be stationed on each. Walter S. Schuyler, perhaps the most able of the lot though still only a second lieutenant, had been sent to Verde on February 5 from Date Creek; he and Sieber worked closely together for a couple of years. Captain William H. Brown went to Fort Apache, while to the newly established San Carlos Reservation, to which the Indians formerly at Grant were moved, was sent First Lieutenant Jacob Almy, a courageous and highly regarded young officer.[3] He soon ran afoul of renegades captained by Chunz, Cochinay, and Chan-deisi, however, and was killed, the outlaw bands bolting the reservation to resume their old, free life in the mountains.

At Verde, because Indians of widely divergent origins were closely confined there, feuds, long smoldering, were likely to burst into flame at any time, but Schuyler and Sieber were taking things in hand, as Bourke put it.[4] Their position, the *Arizona Miner* noted, was "one of the most difficult and trying in the department, and requires the most unremitting labor and care" in policing the perhaps two thousand lately hostile Indians.[5]

Hundreds of hostiles were still out, although for the most part lying low, and on June 16, First Lieutenant John B. Babcock[6] struck

1873: "The Wallapais [having] accumulated considerable money, desire to invest in horses and livestock, [and] commissioned Dan. O'Leary, their interpreter and leader, to procure the animals. Dan and others of his choosing now are enroute to California to buy the stock."

3 Jacob Almy, a man of Quaker parentage and training, was born at New Bedford, Massachusetts, on November 20, 1842. In spite of the religious convictions of his parents—and of himself—he volunteered for combat service at the outbreak of the Civil War, but soon won an appointment to West Point and saw little actual service during the Rebellion. He was commissioned in 1867 and assigned to the Fifth Cavalry, with which he served with distinction against Plains Indians and in Arizona. During the Crook offensive, he participated in the Battle of the Cave, being recommended for a brevet rank of captain, and at Pinto Creek and elsewhere. At the time he was sent to San Carlos, he was thirty-one years old. *Fifth Cavalry*, 519–23.

4 Bourke, *Border*, 218.

5 *Arizona Miner*, July 12, 1873.

6 Babcock, born in Louisiana, entered the Civil War on the side of the North, and from that time until the end of the Indian wars, he was never very far out of earshot from combat, always acquitting himself with gallantry. He was brevetted up to colonel. At this time he was new to Arizona and was stationed at Fort Apache, assigned to

a large band of Tontos seven miles northeast of the forks of Tonto Creek in the Diamond Butte country. It must have been a hard fight, for Babcock and an Apache scout were wounded, the latter mortally, 14 Tontos were killed and 5 captured, while 160 more were frightened into surrendering at Verde and 40 at San Carlos.[7]

The summer of 1873 was a busy one at Verde. No sooner did Indians come in, or were brought in, than a few would bolt again and have to be chased. Schuyler, and, of course, Sieber, his chief of scouts, undertook "a pretty hard trip of 10 days through the Bradshaw Mtns." late in June but failed to strike the large band of hostiles rumored to be there. "Scouting at this season is even harder work than that of last winter on account of the scarcity of water and the intense heat," Schuyler wrote his father. "This is a comparatively cool place, yet the middle of the day the mercury usually rises to 106°–110° in the shade."

Schuyler also complained of the difficulty of working with the Indian Bureau agent at Verde:

> Things often run badly, and I have to devise means of straightening them out quickly in order to avoid trouble. . . . The consequence may be trouble similar to that at San Carlos where Almy was killed, but at the first sign of an outbreak I shall hang about six or seven Indians that I am watching and disarm the rest. . . . Most [of the agents of the Indian Bureau] are afraid of the Indians and are willing to do anything to conciliate them, thereby making them lose all respect and confidence in him and only sowing the seeds of insurrection. I am afraid of them myself, but have seen enough of them to know that the only way to insure my safety and their future civilization and prosperity, is to make them afraid of me. An Indian . . . only know[s] two emotions, fear and hate, and

almost continuous scouting operations in the Tonto Basin country. *Fifth Cavalry*, 456–58. Babcock was made brigadier general of Volunteers during the Spanish-American War (see Heitman) and brigadier general in the Regular Army on August 7, 1903. He died in 1909. *Who Was Who*.

[7] *Chronological List* gives the figures on this fight, in which Indian scouts, as well as Fifth Cavalrymen were involved. *Fifth Cavalry*, 458, says that Babcock was slightly wounded. The *Arizona Miner*, July 12, 1873, mentions the ingathering of the Tontos. In his official report to the post adjutant at Camp Apache, dated June 28, 1873, Babcock made no mention of his own wound, although he cites the wound received by the scout. Record Group 94, 3125 AGO 1873, National Archives.

unless they fear a person they despise him, and show in every way they can their contempt for his authority.[8]

In mid-July, Crook urged Schuyler to "make some scouts in the Red Rock country as well as any other districts where you may suspect there are any Indians who are off the reservations,"[9] and late in July or early in August the Lieutenant led a column north from Verde. They found some Indian women and Sieber's scouts "compelled them to divulge the hiding place of the bucks." This presented special problems, however, since it was a nest in the rocks that could be reached only through a cleft just wide enough to admit one man at a time. During the night, Sieber worked his way through the perilous passage, followed by the scouts. A misstep or a sound might have meant death for many of them, caught as they would have been more snugly than Leonidas at Thermopylae. But unlike Leonidas, they brought off their adventure and, according to Schuyler's terse report, "the Indians were captured and returned to the reservation."[10] Crook, somewhat disgruntled, wrote the young officer: "It is a great pity you could not have killed some of those Indians. . . . Nothing short of some severe examples will thoroughly settle your Indians."[11]

Delshay had again raised problems. Once more he was uneasy. About mid-August the alarming word reached Prescott that he had bolted the Verde reserve, and Crook hurried there, but was relieved to discover that Delshay had not broken loose after all; several hundred Tontos who had fled had already returned to the reservation, satisfied that the rumors of an attack upon them by Fort Apache Indians was false and having also heard that Sieber was on their trail and they had best come back on their own. As the *Miner* put it, "the Tontos would have been warmed up considerably if they had not returned. Al. Zeiber followed them, and the scouts were sent out in different directions to attend to their welfare, and if they were scared off the reservation . . . they doubtless were scared back."[12]

---

8 Schuyler to Schuyler, July 6, 1873, Schuyler Collection, Huntington Library.
9 Crook to Schuyler, July 16, 1873, Schuyler Collection, Huntington Library.
10 *Arizona Miner*, August 9, 1873. *Chronological List* does not mention this affair.
11 Crook to Schuyler, July 31, 1873, Schuyler Collection, Huntington Library.
12 *Arizona Miner*, August 23, 1873.

Crook used the occasion of his visit for a "big talk" with the disaffected Indians anyway, but he didn't stop the growing unrest of Delshay, who gradually gathered around him the more turbulent, more insolent Indians. By late summer, things had come to a head.

Schuyler knew something was wrong; he wasn't sure what. Nor could Sieber decide exactly what was brewing, although with his finely honed sensitiveness to Indian nature he was aware that something was amiss. The two became convinced that whatever the trouble, Delshay was at the bottom of it, and Schuyler wrote something of this to Crook, who hurried a reply:

> By all means arrest Delché & send him with a strong guard to Camp Verde [from his rancheria within a few miles of the post], so there will be no chance of his escaping. Get sufficient men from the post so as to prevent a collision & do your utmost to prevent one, but should one unavoidably occur, have your men so posted that they can kill all the ring leaders who support Delché in his opposition. As soon as you make the arrest tell Delché that if his people make any attempt to rescue him that he will be the first one you will kill & that he must prevent them from committing any overt act. . . . Don't attempt to make the arrest unless you are sure of success, as a failure will lead to bad consequences. . . . Make your disposition in such a manner that you will have the Indians completely in your power. . . . I shall feel very anxious about you until I hear from you again.[13]

Crook's fears were well founded, although his word of warning, if the Lieutenant and Sieber needed it, came too late.

The treachery was deep seated and carefully planned. If the whites had spies who reported on the brewing hostility among the surrendered Indians, Delshay also had spies who reported to him on the intentions of the whites. One of these was a treacherous Tonto interpreter named Antone, who thoughtfully unloaded Schuyler's rifle, so that when the time for action came, the Lieutenant was helpless (Schuyler offered a fifty-dollar reward for the interpreter, it is said, after this incident). The story, as recalled by a participant almost twenty-five years later, was told like this:

> Lieutenant Schuyler, having determined on the arrest of Delshay,

[13] Crook to Schuyler, September 15, 1873, Schuyler Collection, Huntington Library.

concluded that the best way to get the old rascal in his clutches was to summon the Indians to the parade ground to be counted. As this was a frequent occurrence, he thought the Indians would come unarmed. He confided his plans to his interpreter and gave orders to eight of the enlisted men of the command to assist him in arresting Delshay and seven of his principal warriors. Before going out to make the arrest, Schuyler cleaned and loaded his Winchester, after which he stood it in the corner of his tent.

The Indians were finally seated in a great semi-circle, waiting to be counted. Schuyler walked into his tent, got his sixteen shooter and walked directly up to Delshay, the eight soldiers following in the rear. Then the party halted and there was a moment of intense silence. Then the Lieutenant, through the interpreter, Antone, told the old war chief, in language more forcible than elegant, that he was a prisoner.

"Antone," says he, "you tell this old vagabond that I'm going to load him down with irons and hustle him into Camp Verde." The camp was eighteen miles distant.

At the same time, Schuyler's men took their positions in front of the men they were going to arrest. Old Del merely grunted when Antone interpreted to him what the Lieutenant was saying. He told Antone to say to Lieutenant Schuyler for him that he was not a prisoner and was not going to Camp Verde.

This made Schuyler fighting mad, and leveling his gun at the old rascal, he hissed, "You d—d thief, you'd better make your little prayer, and be quick about it, too!"

The old sinner only laughed at this, and Schuyler, driven to desperation, pulled the trigger of his gun when the muzzle was only about two inches from the Indian's nose. The gun missed fire. All at once Delshay's band jumped to their feet, and from every blanket out came a gun or a pistol.

Schuyler saw that there was going to be trouble and he began to pump the Winchester for all it was worth, only to discover it had been tampered with. Antone had stolen every shell.

Then we were in a predicament. Before you could count three, every soldier was surrounded by at least a dozen of the worst cut-throats that ever drew breath, and for a little time things looked mighty juberous for us Yankees. The soldiers were as brave as ever straddled horses, but when they were so suddenly surrounded by them wild Tontos, every last one of 'em felt his heart jumpin' up in his neck.

At this juncture, Mojave Charley, the big chief of the Mojaves, came to the rescue of the Lieutenant and his little squad of soldiers. He jumped to his feet and ordered his six hundred warriors to help the Lieutenant. But for him God knows what would have happened to us.

"Young men of the Mojave tribe," he said, "listen to one who has been the friend and also the enemy of the white man. Lieutenant Schuyler and his men are here for the purpose of preserving the peace and protecting us from the bad white men who would steal all we possess. He is here simply to help us in every way that lies in his power. You all know Delshay and the Tontos. They are thieves, they are murderers, and it would be better if they were all dead. Delshay runs away from the agency whenever he feels like it. He takes his young men and goes down into the valleys where the white men live, robs them of their cattle, robs them of their horses, robs them of their mules, burns their houses, and not satisfied with that, butchers their women and children. He comes back to the agency to draw the rations that the government gives him.

"When these are eaten up he goes out again. He has kept this thing up for years and he has got to thinking that the government is afraid of him. Lieutenant Schuyler was ordered by the big chief in Washington to arrest Delshay and bring him before a soldier council to be tried for his bad deeds. He arms his young men with rifles bought from bad white men and threatens to kill Lieutenant Schuyler and his little band of soldiers. If we allow Delshay to carry out his threat, the blame will rest on us, as well as on him. Shall we permit it? I say, No! Not while I and my young men are here! Chetlepan [Eschetlepan], and you, Hauvayuma of the Yumas, stand by me, and do not let this man add another to his bloody deeds!"

After this, there were other speeches upholding the Mojave chieftain, and it was finally decided that Delshay should go to his own camp as a prisoner and remain there until called for by Lieutenant Schuyler. The old rascal stayed just one week, and then stole off on another foraging expedition.[14]

[14] Carl P. Johnson, "A War Chief of the Tontos," *Overland Monthly*, Vol. XXVIII (Second Series), No. 167 (November, 1896), 528–32. The article, somewhat paraphrased here, is based on an interview with "Jim Duffy, the well known scout," writes Johnson. At the time of the incident, Duffy was a member of Company K, Fifth Cavalry; there is no record that he ever was a scout, but he was a member of Schuyler's detail to arrest Delshay. A "hostler," James Duffy was born at Birmingham, Connecticut, on October 31, 1849, and enlisted, for five years, in the Fifth Cavalry at New York City on September 13, 1872. However, he was discharged June 6, 1877, because of a reduction in the size of

The *Miner* said of the incident simply that "when an attempt was made to arrest Del-Che, the Apaches on the reserve were ready and eager to murder every white man—citizen and soldier—on said reserve, so Lieutenant Schuyler, having but a very small force, was compelled, much against his will, to desist from arresting the reprobate."[15] Delshay, it reported, bolted the reservation with eighteen warriors and twenty-four women, which moved John Marion to "pity," or so he wrote. "They will enter the limits of their final reserve before Spring," he predicted, and missed it by only a few weeks.

It was the start of a gloomy season for the settlers of Prescott and central Arizona. Reports from Camp Verde said that more than one thousand Indians had left the reservation, although most of them

the army. After that he lived largely in Indian Territory, working as a prison guard, police officer, newspaperman, and watchman; he died May 8, 1928, and was buried at El Reno, Oklahoma. Duffy served about three years in Arizona and was also in combat against the Cheyennes at War Bonnet Creek, Wyoming, on July 17, 1876, and against the Sioux in the Battle of Slim Buttes, Dakota Territory, on September 9 and 10, 1876. Captain Charles King spoke of him "as a faithful and deserving soldier." Old Army Records, National Archives. Duffy's facts generally check out on the Delshay incident, but the writer, Johnson, has added to and embroidered the story while leaving some interesting questions unanswered. Who, for example, interpreted what Mojave Charley said? With guns at the heads of the whites, whom Delshay seems to have intended to murder, why was there time for so much speech making? Where was Sieber? Is it likely that Schuyler would have attempted the arrest without the assistance of the veteran Chief of Scouts? These are some of the unresolved problems. I believe Sieber must have had an important—perhaps a decisive—role, in rallying the Mohaves and other Indians and nipping the attempted mutiny in the bud. I have been unable to locate an official account of this little-known adventure. It is referred to by J. P. Dunn, Jr., *Massacres of the Mountains*, 632; by McClintock, 227; by the *Arizona Miner*, September 27 and October 4, 1873; and by Crook, in a letter to the AGO written from Prescott on April 10, 1874, in which he says, "One large band of bucks with the head chief Delt-ché, surrounded with arms in their hands the whites on the reserve, and but for the coolness of the whites and the timely interference of some of our Indian scouts would have massacred the whole party" and in his *Annual Report* for 1874, Hayes Collection, in which he says, "A short time since while he [Delshay] and his people were residing on terms of peace on the Verde Reservation, he, with his warriors, surrounded all the whites on the reservation and would undoubtedly have put them to death, but for the timely siding with our people of a number of scouts and other friendly Indians who had learned long since that he could not be true to friend or foe."

15 *Arizona Miner*, October 4, 1873.

with no evil intent. But they were prowling everywhere. Once more there were silent murders of whites in the wilderness, among them that of John Townsend, who was slain while following his old Indian-hunting habits, and the *Miner* called for vengeance. It urged killing "the devilish foe until sufficient of them are offered as sacrifices to the spirit of the great departed."[16]

Autumn brought the usual blaze of color to the lowlands, along the Verde, with the cottonwoods turning yellow and the haze in the air reminding one of fall in Pennsylvania or Minnesota. In the high country the frost was already sharp of a moonlight night, and it wouldn't be long until the peaks would be splotched with the first snow of the season.

On September 18, Lieutenant Schuyler left Camp Verde with fifteen soldiers and twenty-three Indian scouts under Al Sieber. The command was rationed for twenty days, and planned to seek out hostiles said to be camped near Turret Mountain—who knew, perhaps they would find Delshay. Others might be camped on the East Fork of the Verde, so the command pointed east at first.

The country is as rugged today as it was then—and almost as un-settled—and one may reflect admiringly on the distances covered. The command moved swiftly some thirty miles to Mud Tanks, a wet-weather water hole probably named by Uncle Davy Horst of Camp Verde, who planned to establish a ranch there if the Indians ever left the place alone. Sieber's scouts turned toward the south, rounding the head of Fossil Creek above Fossil Springs, where you could almost always find hostiles, although not this trip. The column rapidly paced the ancient trail over the mesa to Hardscrabble Creek.

No fresh Indian sign had been seen as yet, which tended to confirm that the hostiles must be camped either to the south, along the East Fork of the Verde, or across the main stream, in the Turret Mountain area. Schuyler now sent out two parties, one of nine Tonto scouts under Sieber and the other with eleven Yuma and Mohave Indians under Corporal Snook;[17] each group had three days' rations. Sieber

16 *Ibid.*, September 27, 1873.

17 Snook was a minor Apache Yuma chieftain who was first enlisted as a scout on March 1, 1873, and continued in that capacity off and on into 1886. In 1873 he was said

was to scout the difficult upper reaches of East Fork and Snook the equally broken country between the East Fork and the main stream. Schuyler gave each party "explicit instructions to avoid any collision with hostile Indians except they should discover very small parties encamped at a distance from the main body."

On the twenty-third Snook blundered into a Tonto rancheria of four huts, and since he was discovered, he attacked forthwith, leading his screaming Indians in person. They fell upon their hereditary enemies with such fury that they killed everyone in the rancheria, numbering fourteen individuals. Snook's party was also favored with good luck on the return trip, for they located the main body of more than sixty hostiles on the southern reaches of Hardscrabble Mesa, or perhaps Polles Mesa. When the Corporal reported to Schuyler, the latter, since Sieber had not yet returned, left at once, with the Corporal leading the way, to stalk the enemy, knowing that Al would correctly size up the situation from the sign and track him down, perhaps before the anticipated fight.

Schuyler's men descended Webber Creek to the East Fork of the Verde, then turned downstream on that tributary's right bank to Pine Creek, from there sending scouts to "perfect their knowledge of the location of the hostiles." They had scarcely left when the Tontos arrived, minus four of their number, who had deserted after saying they were sick and going home, although their trail, later followed, revealed that they had joined the enemy camp and had no doubt warned them of the search party. More serious was the fact that Al was ailing, but he pushed on and refused to give up. The scout after the main hostile camp was futile, the renegades having fled two days before Schuyler's men were able to gain a favorable position from which to attack. "I then thoroughly scouted Turret Mt. and Range and having camped near the head of Sycamore Creek, on the west side of the range, I sent a small party of soldiers and scouts with Guide Sieber to scout the divide between New River and Lost River,"[18] wrote Schuyler.

---

to be thirty-three years of age and five feet, ten inches tall. AGO Records, National Archives.

18 This divide was probably in the New River Mountains, although "Lost" River

Schuyler himself took the remainder of the column and worked down Sycamore Creek and across the prairie to Townsend's ranch on the Lower Agua Fria, thence to Dripping Springs, where Jack had been killed, and from there to the mouth of Wolf Creek,[19] on to a tank on the northwest side of a mesa topped by the present Prescott-McDowell Road, and finally back to Camp Verde. The trip, by way of Squaw Peak and Copper Canyon, was not entirely fruitless, since it showed that for the moment this vast area north of the Bradshaws was free of hostiles, but then it was not a very productive scout, either. Sieber's expedition came to nought because Al was soon too ill to continue and the party had to turn back, leaving the possibility that some hostiles might be camped far downstream on New River, where game and mescal might be found.

The Lieutenant scarcely gave his men time to rest and Sieber to recover before he led another scout, this time with twenty men plus an informant who said a large band of renegades was camped near Stoneman's Lake, up on the Mogollon Plateau, where you could count on it being good and brisk in mid-October. The command left in late afternoon and marched all night, arriving at 8:00 A.M. at a tank about four miles northwest of the lake and staying there until sunset. The approach was perfect; if the stalk continued thus, a decisive result might be had.

As the late sun was filtering through the tall pines and the cool night breeze came up, the informant and Sieber led out of camp and at midnight reached a tank about ten miles northeast of the lake, where the hostiles were supposed to be, and found—not a sign of an Indian. The guide now admitted that his "information" had been "founded on conjecture," and Schuyler, disgusted, ordered the men to lay over most of the day at Stoneman's. About four o'clock the Lieutenant sent Al and ten men to scout the head of Wet Beaver Creek while he headed back to Verde with the remainder. Sieber's party found only one trail, and that led toward the reservation. The real news, the men

does not show on contemporary topographical maps or on the Smith map of 1879, nor is it mentioned by Barnes. The stream which bore that name in 1873 must be the one now called Squaw Creek.

[19] Probably the Turkey Creek of today.

found on their return, was that the day after they left on the second scout, about 150 Tontos under Chiefs Eskeltsetle, Cachee, and Naqui Naquis had jumped the reservation, so there were more out now than when they had begun operations. The scouts couldn't even pick up their trail.[20]

Crook, and Schuyler, too, remained convinced that somewhere between Verde and McDowell were Delshay and other hostiles—perhaps near Turret Mountain, maybe in the Mazatzals—and late in November the little Lieutenant prepared for a long scout, possibly to last two months or more.[21]

At 4:00 P.M. on December 1, under the lowering skies of an early-winter storm, the expedition crossed the Verde and Clear Creek above the struggling settlements and headed toward Sycamore Creek (a different Sycamore Creek from that near Turret Mountain where Schuyler had camped before; this one enters the Verde from the east below Cottonwood Basin). Schuyler's force included Sieber, José de León and his son, fourteen Tonto scouts, Sergeant Edmund Schreiber,[22] Corporal Leonard Winser,[23] nine men of Company K plus two other men named Shrewsbury and Houlihan, a prisoner as a guide, and twenty-five mules with packers.

20 The report of these two scouts was sent to Whipple by Schuyler on October 15, 1873. Indian Bureau Record File 75, National Archives. His fight on the East Fork, where fourteen hostiles were killed, is not included in *Chronological List*.

21 Fortunately, we have the entire log of this scout in Schuyler's own handwriting, preserved among his papers at the Huntington Library, as is a letter he wrote his father from McDowell with reference to it.

22 Schreiber was born about 1840 and enlisted in the Fourth Maryland Infantry on November 16, 1861. He was wounded at Second Bull Run and at war's end was a sergeant. He re-enlisted and remained on active duty until his retirement, as an ordnance sergeant, on September 14, 1891, at Fort Supply, Indian Territory. Schreiber was present at Buffalo Bill Cody's slaying of Yellow Hand on the Northern Plains and was severely wounded at Slim Buttes, Dakota Territory, on September 10, 1876. He and Sieber apparently became fast friends, for among Sieber's effects at the scout's death was an autographed picture of the Sergeant. *Fifth Cavalry*, 676, 678; Don Russell, *The Lives and Legends of Buffalo Bill*, 225.

23 Winser is described by Charles King, *The Colonel's Daughter*, 297, as "a tall, splendidly-built soldier with bronzed face, clear-cut features, and dark, thoughtful eyes." King, who served as a cavalry officer and was wounded in Arizona, included a number of his former acquaintances in his many novels.

At 11:00 A.M. the next day, Schuyler, Sieber, and some of the command hiked over to Fossil Creek, almost due east, to seek out a rancheria, but after they got there, they learned the guide had meant that the hostiles were on Hackberry Creek, back to the west, so they camped and waited for the pack train, which came in after dark. During the night, Jocko and another scout deserted and high-tailed it for the enemy camp, so Schuyler, with Sieber, Schreiber, and ten men, plus some of the scouts and José, hurriedly pulled out at 8:00 A.M. to try to head off the deserters, then dropped down to the East Fork, where there were supposed to be rancherias once more. You never could tell about an Apache camp. There would be nothing there one day, but the next there might be a lively rancheria with a dozen brush wickiups thrown together by the indefatigable squaws. The Indians might live in it for a few days or weeks, then move sixty or one hundred miles—no one knew in what direction—where they would establish a new camp. That was why scouts had to cross and crisscross the same area repeatedly and could never let down their guard.

Schuyler's abbreviated party took up the trail via Jaycox Crossing on Fossil Creek, probably near Fossil Springs, rode up over Hardscrabble Mesa, which they found very cold and windy, and down to East Fork, which they reached after dark, but Schuyler wouldn't stop there, although he agreed to a forty-five minute rest. Leaving the horses with two men, he and the others climbed a "very steep Mt. on the south of E. Fork. Very difficult ascent." From the top he sent José with some Indians to scout ahead, despite snow which in places was two feet deep on the level. They found nothing, so Schuyler moved cautiously ahead through the ghostly grayness of snow and moon shadow, where you weren't sure what you saw twenty feet away. After three miles he sent scouts out again. This time José reported he had seen a fire about half a mile beyond and had located two rancherias some distance apart. The Lieutenant agreed now to stop for the remainder of the night. It had begun to snow about 10:00 P.M., turning very cold, and his men were half-frozen. They had marched twenty-seven miles that day and night and it seemed they couldn't remember the last hot meal they had had, but they couldn't stop, even now, for if they did, they would freeze—and no fires could be struck. So the men marched in circles the rest of the night to keep their circulation up, clutching their rifles close to their bodies to warm them so that their hands wouldn't stick to the frigid metal.

Come daylight, Schuyler sent Schreiber, three soldiers, and some Indians to take the upper rancheria, which was supposed to contain only one old man and two women, while he, Sieber, and the rest of the command set out through a blinding snowstorm for the lower rancheria. Situated on a small stream in an oak grove, it was found to contain three wickiups and eighteen Indians; they belonged to Natotel's band. "We got within 20 yds of them and woke them up firing into the houses," the Lieutenant wrote, but the swirling snow made firing inaccurate and two men and a woman got away, one of the former being wounded. Fifteen Tontos were killed and no prisoners taken.[24] The avengers found no food and no arms of consequence, but burned the rancheria anyway and slogged through the snow to their camp on the East Fork, where they had a hell of a time trying to get a fire started with nothing but water-soaked wood to burn and the snow—and sometimes rain—wetting them to the skin all the time. Unfortunately, Schuyler noted, the rancheria Schreiber was after was three miles distant from the point of departure, much farther than he had supposed, and the Sergeant could not get into position before the sound of firing from Schuyler's attack alerted the Indians. They fled. In his log the Lieutenant noted that "Sieber & Lannihan[25] [sic] deserve credit" for their part in the fight and that the scouts "did well." The mother of one of the scouts was with the renegades and was killed, so it was necessary to lay over for two days in order that he might fulfill the required period of mourning for her.[26]

On December 5 the hunters returned to their camp on Fossil Creek. They found the mesa covered with snow a foot deep, "and all day long it snowed and rained alternately. It was bitter cold and we were all wet. I [Schuyler] walked about 18 miles of the way. Reached camp

[24] The log says eight killed, but *Chronological List* says fifteen, which agrees with Schuyler's estimate of the number of Indians at the rancheria.

[25] Just a year earlier, Private James Lenihan had been commended for "conspicuous gallantry" in an action on Clear Creek. *Fifth Cavalry,* 675.

[26] Lockwood, "Sieber," 23.

at dark." They remained in camp the next day to rest and dry out, although that was difficult, since the rain continued intermittently. With daylight on the seventh, Schuyler sent Sieber to find a trail down Fossil Creek Canyon to the Verde, and, of course, he found it. José made a fruitless scout to the northeast to seek a rancheria which was supposed to be up there somewhere.

The command gladly saddled up on the morning of the eighth, as swiftly as stiffened fingers permitted, eager to be out of the wet, freezing, miserable camp and convinced, like all soldiers, that the next one would be better. They followed Fossil Creek downstream for a mile and a half, then cut across the hills, great balls of mud collecting under their mounts' hoofs and the trail proving slippery and treacherous. They struck the Verde without incident, except, of course, those normally encountered in working with pack trains, about four miles above the mouth of Fossil Creek, probably near Verde Hot Springs. From here they worked downstream a mile and a half, crossed the river on the trail they had made in September, and followed it west to near the head of a creek Schuyler called Box Elder, possibly a tributary to Houston Creek. Al Sieber killed a couple of deer and the men roasted them for a more satisfactory meal than they had had in a week.

For three days the expedition stayed at this camp. Four scouts sent down toward Turret Mountain found nothing, rain kept everyone in camp another day, and heavy rain and snow did so the third day. The Indians killed two more deer, which were welcome.

At eight o'clock on the morning of December 12, Schuyler left the Box Elder camp, crossed Tule Mesa three miles south of his autumn trail, followed the canyon of Sycamore Creek west for about six miles down from its head, and camped in the snow, happy to note that at least there was less of it here than in the two-foot depths on the mountain above. The camp, the officer observed, was twenty miles due east of Townsend's ranch, notched between pointed peaks visible from that place, on the sky line north of Turret Mountain.

Ten scouts with a day's rations were sent ten or twelve miles due north by trail to scout Squaw Peak thoroughly, tackling any small party and bringing back what Indian women they could catch, although if they struck a large rancheria they were to send for the main command. "Hope to catch a squaw to use as guide," Schuyler jotted in his logbook, but the Indians returned the next afternoon, having found nothing. Sieber and two soldiers, restless at sitting around camp, scouted five miles down Sycamore Creek and circled back, but they didn't find anything either. On the fifteenth, Schuyler moved south a mile to a tributary of Sycamore Creek, followed it downstream a short distance, then crossed over to Badger Creek (probably Silver Creek on today's maps), and sent José with some Indians to scout Granite Mountain and Sieber five miles down Badger Creek, but neither found anything. That was the story of Arizona scouting in this period: scores of miles of the most backbreaking travel, and if any sign at all was uncovered, you were lucky, so elusive was the enemy. It was discouraging, but it certainly toughened the men, and when a trail *was* struck, the quarry rarely escaped.

On December 17, Schuyler selected Sergeant Schreiber, eleven men, some scouts, and Al Sieber to accompany him, had them stuff four days' rations in their saddlebags, and started off ahead of the main body. In a wash about two and one-half miles beyond where Sieber had scouted the day before, they found the tracks of two Tontos who had gone on toward the reservation. They backtracked them to the south and about dark reached Lost River (which must be the stream that is now called Squaw Creek), camping on its south fork at the foot of Cook Mesa. At dawn they scouted ahead some five miles to New River, touching it where it hooks to the north, and on foot marched swiftly downstream on the trail of some hostiles which led up New River Mesa, a brick-shaped butte lying northeast-southwest. "Very fresh sign," wrote Schuyler in his journal. "Took up onto the mesa, and followed sign until too dark to see. Camped on small rocky stream which runs into New River [this, no doubt, was Robbers Roost Canyon]. Nothing to eat except some of the Indians' tortillas, and very cold. Small fires."

Unknown to Schuyler, his scouts had betrayed him and now refused to guide him to the rancheria, the whereabouts of which they well knew. During the day the hostiles had seen the command, and lit out.

With daybreak, however, the Lieutenant sent Schreiber, José, and five men with some Indians to follow the trail. They found the rancheria in a cave under the rim of the mesa: eleven huts cleverly concealed. So perfect was the location that Schuyler believed the Indians would never abandon it permanently and therefore laid plans to outfox them—hostiles and betrayers alike.

The Lieutenant took his men back to the New River camp and on December 20 mounted them up and moved down that stream for a dozen miles to the vicinity of the road crossing. Then he moved across the Agua Fria as a feint, laid over a day while the Indians hunted, and marched back the following day to Cave Creek by road, sure that the hostiles were watching his every move. During the night of December 23, he mounted a scout with four days' rations and under cover of darkness worked north along Cave Creek toward the mesa again. At daylight the grim hunters hid out in the rocks, while to the south their pack train and the remainder of the column marched openly, and with plenty of dust, toward McDowell.

The ruse worked. Squaws were seen drawing water from Cave Creek, and thus the exact location of the rancheria was noted. During the night the attackers crept like wolves up through the rocks into firing position and at sunup greeted their adversaries with a crash of gunfire that slew nine hostiles and cleaned out the retreat. It was supplied with several tons of mescal, which was destroyed under the theory that hungry Indians were more apt to surrender at the reservation than fat ones.

The Indian loss had been more severe than numbers would indicate, for among the fallen was Nanotz, one of the bravest, most reckless, and therefore most admired and followed of the enemy. Thus on this basis alone the long scout was well worth all the effort put into it. "The business of reducing Apaches to subjection involves some of the most arduous, exhausting labor to be performed by troops," commented the *Miner*, "but such scouts as these are doubly beneficial; those Indians that are killed are peaceable forever, and the destruction of their stores in midwinter, will force those who escape to return to the reservation to get food, and when once again with plenty of food and safe quarters, they will not be likely to take to the mountains a second time."[27]

On the day after Christmas, Schuyler's fighters wearily entered McDowell, on the Lower Verde, bewhiskered, filthy, and nearly exhausted, but satisfied with the work done thus far. Schuyler wrote to his father, outlining the scout to this point and commenting:

> I have only 15 men but they are picked shots, and with two scouts we can make it lively for [Delshay] if I can catch him. His death will settle the business, as he is the king chief of them all.
>
> I hope that you will enjoy a merrier Christmas and happier New Year's than I, for I am doing hard work now, the hardest ever done here, on account of the weather. I have been marching and camping on snow from one to three feet deep, and sometimes suffering terribly from cold, sometimes sleeping on the ground without even a coat on my back. *But*, I have *succeeded*.[28]

Leaving McDowell on the last day of the year with the notion of scouting the valley of the Verde and its tributaries as he worked northward, Schuyler marched ten miles to the mouth of Blue Rock Canyon, where he made note that he had to fire Houlihan for theft and the next day that Private Terry, his blacksmith, deserted, "taking full cavalry equipment and 1 pair pinchers." The march on New Year's Day was fourteen miles up Blue Rock Creek to water. The following day he remained in camp until midafternoon but sent out the scouts and the inexhaustible Sieber to look over the country to the west. They didn't find anything live, although they did trail a horse thief who had stolen two animals near McDowell some time previously and driven them to the foot of New River Mesa, where they were butchered and the meat packed up the mountain. Schuyler speculated that the thief was Nanotz or one of his people, already accounted for. About 3:00 P.M. the Lieutenant saddled up and moved ten miles west to the Verde. Of course it rained again.

On January 4 the command moved up the river eight miles to Mesquite Bottom and let a packer named Sanford go back to the previous

27 *Arizona Miner*, January 4, 1874. This account has many details not available elsewhere, but they are wondrously confused, one fight with another.

28 Schuyler to Schuyler, December 29, 1873, Schuyler Collection, Huntington Library.

camp to hunt up his personal mount, which had wandered off. Sanford reported three Indians in the camp the command had left, but scouts later said that this was not true and that Sanford's horse had legged it back to Camp McDowell and a daily ration of grain and hay. Schuyler moved six miles farther upriver next day, sending scouts over to the head of Cave Creek to see what they could find. He laid over a day and then pushed on an additional ten miles over a terrible trail up the Verde, going into camp on an extensive bottom on the west side eight miles below the mouth of East Fork. He laid over on the eighth, and about 11:00 A.M. his scouts came in, reporting "they had found a probability." That was enough.

The expedition's scouts and a small detachment moved out at 2:00 P.M. on the ninth, crossed the river about three-quarters of a mile from camp, and about a mile and a half farther upstream came to the mouth of Graham Creek (possibly the area now called Goat Camp Canyon), laboring up it for two miles before halting for the night hard under a pointed mountain. Just at sundown the scouts spotted two hostiles, blazing like torches in the strong rays of the setting sun, atop the mountain, but they soon disappeared and no one could guess whether or not the command had been discovered. Schuyler waited until the moon rose, about midnight, then started up the mountain on foot, thinking he would strike a rancheria on top. The unit reached the summit at daylight, but all they found was tracks. These they followed, however, for the Indians who made them had moved rapidly along the rocky ridge toward the north. When the hunters reached the northern point of the ridge, they sat down in a secluded nook and surveyed the rolling canyons and breaks below them. After a while they discovered a party of hostiles moving toward the East Fork about two miles distant, waited until it had dropped from sight, and then rapidly slid and scrambled down the long slope in pursuit. They found the spot where the enemy had camped the previous night and judged from the three fires that the group was a small one. José and his Indians sped away in the advance, chased the hostiles six miles, and overtook them on the riverbank. They killed four, Natotel, who was second only to Delshay on the "most wanted" list of that day, two children, and a woman, and captured a woman and two infants.

Three men and two children escaped. José had personally slain Nato-tel and secured as well-earned booty the Indian's double-barreled rifle and other trophies. But not to enjoy for long.

The heavy rains and snows had caused the Verde and its branches to rise swiftly, and while awaiting an opportunity to cross, the command made a three-day scout to the east, finding nothing but children's tracks heading toward North Peak. Upon returning the party moved slowly up the Verde to its junction with East Fork, which was running twenty-five feet above normal. Schuyler used nine words for his log entry of January 22: "Jose and boy drowned at mouth of E. Fork." Lamented the *Arizona Miner*: "We sincerely regret the death, by drowning, of Jose de Leon and his son. True, they were not white men; but, what of that? The father was a gallant Mexican, thoroughly devoted to our country and cause. The son, a brave half-breed, who, like his father, had done noble service in the good cause." It added that José "was a native of Sonora, from which state he was carried away captive at an early age by the Apaches, among whom he lived for a great number of years, and with those on the Sierra Blanca [White Mountains] and Verde reservations had acquired great influence which he used to advantage on the campaign against those who refused to make peace. . . . His loss will be severely felt by our troops."[29]

John Marion probably obtained his information about José from Al, who, the newspaper said, had stopped in the evening before, a Thursday. "Mr. S.," Marion confided, "is one of the best and most effective of Gen. Crook's guides."

Al visited the Flanders Photographic Studio and had his picture taken, sitting stiffly upright, his hair seemingly combed with an egg beater and his young face sporting a ragged, square-cut beard that had the makings of a goatee. He wore a thick woolen jacket, a woolen shirt open at the throat, and red flannels underneath. The legs of his woolen trousers were lined with buckskin on the inside, which was as close to wearing *that* supposed scout's uniform as Sieber ever came.[30] He once posed for a couple of photographs in a full-scale

29 *Arizona Miner*, January 30, 1874.
30 I assume that Sieber had the picture which is in my possession taken at this time,

buckskin outfit, but it was new, perhaps made for him by some admiring Indian woman, and you can see that he was uncomfortable in it. He never wore it again.[31]

Sieber didn't spend much time at Prescott before he had to hurry back to Camp Verde, where Schuyler was organizing a much larger expedition for an extended campaign. Again Al was to be the Lieutenant's chief of scouts.

for the *Miner* of February 13, 1874, reports that Flanders' gallery, exhibiting the photographer's work, was open to the public, and he took Crook's portrait the following month. On the reverse of the original print of the Sieber picture is the legend "Flanders & Penelon, Photographic Artists."

[31] "As for my scouting costume," wrote Al in later life when asked for a photograph taken in it, "it was ever the same as that of any roving man; for, during my twenty-one years of fighting and hunting hostile Indians, I never wore long hair or buckskin clothes." Al Sieber in a letter printed as an appendix in Horn, 313–14.

IX. The Marrying Man

THE NEW CAMPAIGN was part of a full-fledged offensive organized by Crook to clean out, once and for all, the Tonto Basin and adjacent lands, now plagued not only by Delshay but also by Chunz, Cochinay, and Chan-deisi, among others. To accomplish this, columns would, as in the days of the grand offensive, start from various of the forts and camps and once more thoroughly search the breaks and uplands. Crook had determined upon these drastic measures after cruel depredations in the San Pedro Valley and south of the Gila by Chunz and some of his people.

For Sieber, this was the first real scout south of the Gila and probably his first visit there since the days of the Miner expedition. New country and new problems always fascinated him, and he eagerly looked forward to the extensive operation.

The Verde Indians, too, were interested. Although Schuyler needed only 100, half again that number volunteered, and in the end he selected 122, including 59 Apache Yumas, 41 Apache Mohaves, and 22 Tontos, Sieber's favorite Indians at this period. Also with Schuyler's column would be 30 men from Troop K of the Fifth Cavalry; a physician-surgeon, William H. Corbusier,[1] who was both amused and

[1] During his service at Verde, Corbusier became quite interested in his charges and thus something of an ethnologist. His accounts of various events in which he participated in Arizona, such as the scout in question and the later removal of the Indians from Verde to San Carlos, are lively, informative, and valuable. They have been utilized here for much of the information about this long scout. APHS Files. Corbusier was born at New York City on April 10, 1844, and was graduated from Bellevue Hospital Medical College on March 1, 1867. He served in the Civil War with General Benjamin H. Grierson and other noted officers. In the course of his work as army surgeon in the West, he

excited by the prospect of a scout; and, for Schuyler and Corbusier, a Negro cook, who proved to be a "trifler," driving the officers to mess with the packers, who, in the nature of their kind, always ate high on the hog. There was a pack train of 80 mules, led by a white bell mare (with whom each of the cargo animals became infatuated), to carry rations and ammunition, but Corbusier managed to get his medical supplies aboard. For the entire three months' journey, during which almost 200 men negotiated the most perilous terrain in the Southwest and fought its most savage foes, Corbusier's load of medicines and other supplies was "not over a foot square!" Not much like the field hospitals of today's military expeditions, but it was better than anything scouting parties in Arizona had ever had before.

Corbusier was interested in the pack train, and he and Schuyler were made welcome by the hardy packers at their mess. They "sat on the ground around the dirty manta on which tin cups, plates, etc., were thrown and boiled frijoles—Mexican brown beans—fried bacon, yeast powder biscuit and coffee were served from iron camp kettles, dutch ovens and other vessels that they were cooked in. Sometimes we had a little rasberry or other jam, called 'dope.' "

Each morning the knowledgeable mules would line up in proper order to have their *aparejos* fitted and cargo loaded, and each evening they trotted into the same formation to be unburdened. As soon as this was done, they would roll and dust themselves luxuriously, struggle to their feet, shake vigorously, and join the herd of loose mules for watering and a few hours' grazing or, if that were not feasible, wait to be led to the picket lines, where they would get a ration of grain, if available, or cut grass if it were not. Mules are the easiest of animals to herd; as long as the bell mare is with them, they will not stray. If a mule should graze out of earshot of the bell, however, or out of sight of the mare, it will be frantic until it gets back.

had become a student of Indian languages. He retired, but returned to duty during World War I, then retired again, this time with the rank of colonel, on August 15, 1919; he died February 7, 1930, at San Francisco. His son, William T. Corbusier of Long Beach, California, says that the Doctor had "absolute faith" in Al Sieber and that Mrs. Corbusier, the former Fanny Dunbar, thought the scout "as fine an individual as ever lived." Both knew him for several months while Dr. Corbusier was stationed at Camp Verde and also in later years.

Lieutenant Ross, with a good eye for livestock and imbued with Crook's personal interest in the matter, helped to organize the pack train, although he would not accompany it, and on February 22 he saw the expedition out of camp, across the Verde, and pointing south, a long, straggling line of men and mules, looking as unmilitary as could be but having about it, for all of that, an aura of confidence and seasoning which boded well for it and ill for the Indians.

Once free of the post, Sieber sent scouts to both sides of the Verde to search along the flanks and at the head of the column, but they found little of importance. The second or third day out, Corbusier noted, Schuyler met a command from Whipple on a similar mission, and it took about twenty of his scouts, leaving him with approximately one hundred, which seems to have been the standard number for such expeditions.

Sieber and the Lieutenant let the scouts hunt regularly until the party reached country that might fairly be considered enemy held. The doctor was an interested observer as the Indians happily pursued their second-greatest love—the first being depredating, now denied them. "At first the scouts were poor shots," he said, having noted that each was armed with a Spencer carbine, "and I saw twenty of them fire at a deer, not over a hundred yards away, and miss." This didn't mean that they went without fresh meat, he hastily added. When they didn't bag a deer or when, for some reason, hunting was prohibited, "they hauled wood rats from their holes under bushes and boiled them whole, after slitting up the abdomen." These little creatures were considered great delicacies by the Indians, although they would rarely touch ground squirrels or similar rodents. But then the Apaches often ate things which were odd to the taste of white gourmets; on the other hand, they would not touch some foods which whites delighted in. For example, an Apache would not eat bear meat, considering that animal an embodiment of some dead warrior, nor would he eat fish or, except in unusual circumstances, turkey, which abounded in Arizona at that time.

One of the Indians' favorite ways of hunting was noted by Corbusier: "We were hunting one day and the scouts formed a long line and gradually closed in on the ends so as to surround a small valley in which many deer were shot down." Sometimes an expert shot, such as Sieber, would be the central figure in such a hunt. He almost never missed, and as the Indians literally drove the deer past him, the kill would often tally up in scores of animals, all of which were greedily devoured around the campfire as a welcome relief from bacon and hard bread. Once the command entered the Tonto Basin, however, no hunting was allowed—"except for hostile Indians."

One day a shot was heard on the far side of a low ridge, and Sieber's Indians piled over the hill to investigate, returning with the carcass of a deer which the hostiles had killed. When they saw the scouts, they fled. "From here on we followed their tracks," wrote Corbusier, "and some of a horse were very plain for days and then were no longer seen, the horse probably having been killed and eaten." He also noted that "moccasin tracks were not so easily followed and would sometimes be lost for a time." But patience paid off:

> At length the scouts began to locate che-wa-kis or rancherias, and night marches were made to surprise the occupants about the break of day when the killings were made. Women couldn't be distinguished from the men at a long range, and especially when they had bows and arrows to take part in the fight, but usually they ran to shelter, yet some were found among the dead. The hostiles led us over high mountains and through the roughest country, but we followed.

They kept hard at it until they reached the Salt River flats, the column arriving at McDowell on Saturday, March 7. By that time they were quite a sight, Corbusier admitted, especially the Indians. "Black, stiff-brimmed hats had been issued and ordered worn," he recalled. "They no longer protected the heads of the wearers. The brims were completely or nearly gone, and the tops were full of holes, or absent, so that the men's hair stood out. Soft gray hats now replaced them, and were the forerunners of the present campaign hat." But the Apaches had learned to like the black, high-crowned, stiff-brimmed hat, and to this day it is a favorite item of clothing among the men, although without the holes through which their forebears' hair protruded in 1874.

In the middle of the week following their arrival at McDowell,

141

Schuyler's outfit left for the Superstitions and the Pinals.[2] Through the remainder of March and on into April, the command examined the rugged Superstitions with microscopic care. On March 25 or 26 somewhere in those mountains the Verde men struck hostiles, killing a dozen and capturing two. Other parties in the Superstitions also reported successes.

Sieber sometimes led his scouts on side expeditions, which might last a few hours, a day, a week, or several weeks, and on one of these an Apache was captured, even though the order had been to take no prisoners. Sieber wanted to get information out of this Indian, however, and kept him around for several days, despite the hole which his insatiable appetite made in the party's short rations. At length they turned back toward the main column. As Al told a friend, he realized that he couldn't bring in a prisoner after he had been ordered not to do so. Morning came, and the Indian scouts, the prisoner, a packer, and Sieber were sitting in a circle eating their sparse breakfast. Al figured there was no time like the present. "I motioned to some of my scouts," he said, "and they did not seem to understand— or didn't want to understand—so I took my rifle, laid it back of the packer's head and shot the Indian behind the ear just as he was biting into a piece of bread. He fell over backwards; his feet went up in the air. The packer turned to me and said: 'Al, if I had knowed you was going to do that to him, I would not have let him eat so much.' "[3]

En route to the Pinals the Schuyler-Sieber column combed the Sierra Anchas, where Al was to locate a gold claim that kept him sporadically occupied and constantly hoping for the rest of his life, then crossed the Salt River and entered the Pinals. This was a different sort of country from that in which Sieber had operated before. "Often the water at our camps was alkaline and we had to go unwashed or suffer with sore lips and chapped hands," complained Corbusier, not mentioning the debilitating effect of alkali, one for which

---

[2] *Arizona Miner*, March 13, 1874.

[3] Lockwood APHS; Lockwood, "Sieber," 23. There is nothing to indicate when this incident occurred, but it fits with this scout and there is no reason to suppose that it or something similar didn't happen on this particular expedition.

the soldiers had various names in English and the Tontos in Apache. The war party struck more Indians and gave the hostiles no rest.

They also made other finds of passing interest. "On our way up the west side of the mountains to the old abandoned Camp Pinal,"[4] noted the Doctor, "we came upon an old oven which had been built by troops when digging the trail. In it were entombed the bodies of two prospectors who had probably been jumped by Indians while they were asleep. The end of a box that had held tomatoes closed the opening and was inscribed with their names." This was an interesting but by no means singular discovery in the Apachería of that era.

Equally intriguing was a report one day from the scouts "that there were some dead Indians on a spur high above us." Corbusier describes the scene:

> I was given twenty of them to climb up and investigate. I wore government shoes and leggings and in places had to be assisted by the scouts who put on moccasins when climbing up steep mountains, and by the time we reached the summit I was dripping with perspiration. I found half a dozen co-wahs [huts] and the dead bodies of sixteen Indians with heads mashed in and bodies filled with arrows, most of them at the openings of their shelters, as if they had been killed as they attempted to come out. Many war clubs were lying around, some of them broken and covered with hair and blood. The che-wa-ki was in the open and their fires could have been seen miles away. The Pimas, their ancient enemies, had probably located them and jumped them early in the morning.

True it was that all Apache atrocities were not inflicted on the settled peoples, red and white, of the valleys. Whoever had started the bloody business, both sides now suffered.

Schuyler's command penetrated the Aravaipa Mountains east of Old Camp Grant, and on April 28 the scouts and K Company, with

---

[4] Camp Pinal was located as "Infantry Camp" on November 28, 1870, by orders of General Stoneman, who planned it as a major post, although it was abandoned in August, 1871, as a military establishment. It was originally situated on the north side of Hutton Peak near the head of Pinto Creek, about thirty miles northeast of modern Florence, but was moved to Queen Creek at Picket Post Butte when it became a civilian operation. Barnes, *Place Names*, 333–34; 2nd ed., 303.

hard-bitten Sergeant Rudy Stauffer[5] and other tough cavalrymen in the vanguard, struck a hostile camp and reported twenty-three killed and a dozen captured. Schuyler's instructions from General Crook had been to scout the Pinals but not to confine himself to them, "as I want you to hit them where ever you can & if you have good reasons to believe there are none in that range of mountains, go where you think they are."[6] In pursuance of these orders, he and Lieutenant John Babcock from Fort Apache, with whom he had joined forces, led their commands south and west of Mount Turnbull in the Santa Teresas and found "plenty of Indian tracks but the hostile Apaches [were] too scattered and on their guard to be caught."[7] The Verde command, Schuyler felt, could now turn homeward—with plenty of hard marching and fighting en route. At San Carlos they left "some disobedient scouts," who were mighty lucky they weren't killed as Sieber had often disciplined others, moved on to Hog Canyon and camped under a live oak "from which a Chiricahua Indian who had threatened to kill an officer had been hanged," camped on a succeeding night about a mile above what is now Roosevelt Dam on the Salt, lost a mule and load of flour over a cliff along the present Apache Trail, and finally made a camp at Fish Creek. The Salt was too high to be forded, and Schuyler worked on down the river to Marysville, not far above McDowell, where Charles Whitlow ran a ferry, and crossed the turgid stream in style. They reached the post about May 10 and left early on the fourteenth to sweep the Mazatzal Range once more for stubborn renegades reported still lurking in the soaring fastnesses of the Four Peaks.[8]

[5] Stauffer, who was born at Bern, Switzerland, on November 27, 1836, enlisted in Company K of the Second Cavalry (later the Fifth Cavalry) at Cincinnati on June 24, 1855, serving continually in the same outfit until December 11, 1878. He won a Medal of Honor for gallantry in action on May 20, 1872, near Camp Verde. Stauffer died at the Soldiers' Home in Washington, D.C., on June 8, 1918, at the age of eighty-one. Charles King, in a passage that apparently referred to Rudy, once called him "grim old Stauffer, the first sergeant." See *Tonio, Son of the Sierras*. A butte which Stauffer and a Fifth Cavalry contingent once cleared of hostiles was named Stauffer's Butte, but no one now knows where it was.

[6] Crook to Schuyler, dated "16th, 1874" (probably February 16), Schuyler Collection, Huntington Library.

[7] *Arizona Miner*, May 8, 1874.

[8] *Ibid.*, May 15 and May 22, 1874.

Although he never wore it otherwise, Sieber donned this buckskin outfit for the photographer at Camp Verde in 1877.

Al Sieber on crutches after the Apache Kid affair, which ended his active career as a scout and left him crippled for the rest of his life.

Captain Charles Porter led many scouting parties from Camp Verde, usually with Sieber as his chief of scouts.

Lieutenant Charles B. Gatewood, who talked Geronimo into surrendering, was one of the unsung heroes of the Apache war.

On the seventeenth Schuyler was camped on the west side of the Four Peaks about twenty miles east of the Verde while Sieber and his scouts were threading the foothills for sign. A courier brought in a telegram from San Carlos reporting (from a captured Indian woman) the presence of renegades near the Four Peaks, along with information about where they might be located. Schuyler called Sieber in, and they plunged off toward the indicated site. There they "found tracks of Apaches which led to a rancheria where the hostile Indians were attacked with a loss to them of eighteen killed and five captured. One of our soldiers was very badly wounded."[9] Nor was this the end of the fighting. The very next day, Sieber rooted out another rancheria, with a resulting ten killed and nine captured, making a two-day total of twenty-eight slain and fourteen captured—"a very good week's work," as the *Miner* put it.[10]

In three months of the hardest kind of campaigning, covering 1,500 miles, the command had accounted for 83 killed and 26 taken prisoner, and the credit was largely Sieber's. Other scouting parties from other bases had achieved single successes, but none whose reports I have seen burrowed so single-mindedly into so vast an extent of the frontier in so short a time, carried out one difficult approach after another, fought in half a dozen major affairs and no one remembers how many skirmishes, and produced such decisive results in each.

The column reached Camp Verde on May 25, bearded, grimy, tough as nails, and quite ready for the final ceremony, one which Dr. Corbusier noted with interest and some amusement:

> The scouts had captured many women and these were drawn up in a line and asked where they wished to go. About fifty of them crossed over to the scouts, who also were in line. The latter were asked if they wanted the women to live with them, and if they would take them as wives. The women were asked if they wanted the scouts as husbands. All replied, "Yes."

It seemed to Schuyler and Corbusier that this called for a little some-

9 *Ibid.*, May 22, 1874.

10 *Ibid.*, May 29, 1874. The *Chronological List* makes these totals thirty-eight killed and a dozen captured and says nothing about the wounded soldier. Perhaps Schuyler was counting only dead warriors, as was sometimes done, or it may be that wounded Indians later died.

thing of a ceremony, and they turned it over to their resourceful chief of scouts. He tugged a bit at his mustache.

Al Sieber explained that he was going to marry them in the white man's way and they must always remain faithful. He then told the couples to join hands and he pronounced them man and wife.

All left, apparently happy.

No, sir, you never knew what you were going to be called upon to do when scouting for hostiles in Apachería. But Al had demonstrated that he was game for anything, equal to any emergency.

One by one, Chunz, Cochinay, and Chan-deisi, were tracked down and slain, but Delshay seemed to lead a charmed life. Crook urged Schuyler to send out "your killers as soon as possible after the head of DelChé & Co. The more prompt these heads are brought in, the less liable other Indians . . . will be to jeopardize their heads."[11] Schuyler sent out three Tonto scouts, who claimed they killed Delshay near Turret Mountain on July 29 and brought in a scalp and part of the purported chieftain's distinctive ears as proof. Meanwhile, a column from San Carlos also claimed to have killed Delshay and had a head to offer as proof. Crook had offered a reward for Delshay's death. Now, he wrote, "being satisfied that both parties were in earnest in their beliefs, and the bringing in of an extra head was not amiss, I paid both parties."[12]

All during the eventful summer of 1874 and the following winter, while contentious John Philip Clum[13] became agent at San Carlos and

11 Crook to Schuyler, June 23, 1874, Schuyler Collection, Huntington Library.

12 *Autobiography*, 181–82.

13 Clum, born September 1, 1851, on a farm near Claverack, New York, completed one year at Rutgers and then secured a position with the U.S. Army Signal Corps' newly organized meteorological service as an observer at Santa Fe, arriving there late in 1871. A member of the Dutch Reformed church, which at that time was charged with supervision over the Apaches (and still maintains missionaries among them), Clum was offered, and accepted, the position of agent at San Carlos, to date from February 27, 1874. He arrived at his new post August 8, age twenty-three less one month, and was to remain there until July, 1877, when he left in a huff. He purchased the *Arizona Citizen* in November of that year, moved it to Florence, then back to Tucson, where it became the *Daily Citizen*. Clum sold out in 1880 and moved to Tombstone, where he founded the famous *Epitaph* on May 1, 1880, and became mayor and postmaster of the town. He sold the newspaper in 1882, held a position in Washington for a couple of years, and

inaugurated his tumultous three years in that post, soldiering continued as usual against dwindling but still stubbornly recalcitrant bands in the wild and remote Tonto Basin and elsewhere. The official list of engagements with the hostiles, a compilation that is by no means complete, shows little diminution of fighting during this period.

Sieber's Verde Indians were busy all summer long trying to ferret out the remaining renegades, most prominent among whom were Eschetlepan and Chapo, or Chappeau. In Crook's opinion, these weren't really incorrigible Indians. He urged Schuyler to press efforts to get them to surrender and then "I will confine them away from the Verde until all the Indian is worn out of them,"[14] but he had no interest in killing them. Nevertheless, Chapo was killed by a party of scouts from Fort Apache under C. E. Cooley in mid-August, which left Eschetlepan as the free Indian the whites wanted most to catch.

Among the newer officers assigned to Verde were Lieutenant Charles King,[15] who had already been in a scrap at Diamond Butte,

returned to Tombstone for a year in 1885. Clum was a postal inspector in Alaska during the 1898 gold rush, there renewing his acquaintance with and friendship for Wyatt Earp, whom he had known well and whose partisan he was during the violent Tombstone days. Clum eventually settled at Los Angeles, where he died at eighty-one of a heart attack on May 2, 1932. Woodworth Clum, *Apache Agent*; *Los Angeles Times*, May 3, 1932; Lutrell, *op. cit.*, 79; *Arizona Historical Review*, Vol. V, Nos. 1 and 3 (April and October, 1932).

[14] Crook to Schuyler, August 8, 1874, Schuyler Collection, Huntington Library.

[15] Charles King, born at Albany, New York, on October 12, 1844, won fame with his novels of frontier soldiering. Based on his own experiences and those of his Fifth Cavalry comrades, they enjoyed considerable popularity around the turn of the century; in fact, they are still being read. A few of the earlier ones mention Sieber, some as "Al Zeiber," and, in the literary style of the period, attribute to him a florid manner of speech that stemmed from James Fenimore Cooper, not from Al Sieber. King was graduated from West Point in 1866 and joined the First Artillery. He was promoted to first lieutenant and transferred to the Fifth Cavalry on January 1, 1871. He had been an instructor at West Point, and upon joining his new regiment, he was assigned as aide-de-camp to the general commanding the Gulf, who was headquartered at New Orleans, where King met and married a southern girl. In January, 1874, he took a party of recruits to Arizona, joining his company at Camp Verde on May 13. Subsequent to his Arizona service he saw action on the Northern Plains, on the basis of which he wrote his *Campaigning with Crook* and other pieces. In June, 1879, he retired because of disability caused by wounds received in Arizona, but served with the Wisconsin National Guard during the Spanish-American War and became a brigadier general of Volunteers. King died at Milwaukee on March 18, 1933. *Who Was Who.*

and Lieutenant George O. Eaton,[16] fresh out of West Point but so promising that Crook wrote Captain J. W. Mason, then commanding at Verde, urging that Eaton be permitted to go out with the veteran Schuyler on a scout, "as he has not had a show" and shouldn't miss the opportunity.[17] So Schuyler, Eaton, and Sieber left Verde on July 29 to work the Tonto Basin and Black Mesa once more. It was a short and not very rugged trip, except for the heat, and they returned August 5, having found a small number of renegades east of the Verde, of whom they killed one or two.[18]

Even beyond the fringe of civilization, Sunday is a day of rest, or, at least, for not pursuing one's normal labors. Prospectors and hunters, if they could remember which day Sunday was, used it for washing clothes, repairing tools, lolling around camp, hunting, or some other pursuit less backbreaking than working a rocker, although from sheer boredom they usually ended up with it by midafternoon. Thus it was that on Sunday, September 6, a party of prospectors on Humbug Creek, a tributary of the Agua Fria south of Camp Verde, were trying not to work. They soon became bored, however, and one of them, William Roberts, picked up a rifle, announced he was going to hunt deer, and strolled up the creek bed. A short time later his partners[19] heard a series of shots, not all of which could have come from Roberts' weapon, and snatched up their own guns and ran to his aid, but they were not in time. They found him stone dead, shot once

[16] Born in Maine on May 14, 1848, Eaton enlisted in February, 1865, but saw very little Civil War service and four years later was appointed to West Point. He arrived in Arizona in December, 1873, and soon distinguished himself in Apache warfare as a man of courage and judgment. Later, while on a Sioux campaign in the Black Hills, he was wounded by the accidental discharge of a pistol while trying to stem a horse stampede at night, and his subsequent service was periodically interrupted by sick leaves. *Fifth Cavalry*, 541–42. Eaton resigned on March 29, 1883, and was a mining figure of some importance at Cooke, Montana, thereafter, becoming Surveyor General of Montana in the early 1890's, but in 1896 he moved to New York. Eaton died at Fort Myers, Florida, on September 12, 1930.

[17] Crook to Schuyler, July 13, 1874, Schuyler Collection, Huntington Library.

[18] *Arizona Miner*, July 31, 1874; August 7, 1874.

[19] They were Martin Cummins, Daniel Quinlon, Edward Farley, and J. Ellis. *Arizona Miner*, September 25, 1874. Barnes says the Humbug was named in 1879 because reports that it bore gold proved false, but this record shows that it was so named at least five years earlier. Barnes, *Place Names*, 2nd ed., doesn't list the Humbug.

through the leg, twice through the body, and once through the head—and knifed twice. His gun, knife, boots, and hat were gone, and moccasin tracks indicated that at least three hostiles were to blame. After leaving the scene the renegades swept down on Charles Whitlow's ranch at Marysville Ferry on the Salt, killed or seriously wounded the herder, and drove off some cattle. A column out of McDowell picked up their trail, but lost it.

The gold hunters, meanwhile, had caused a message to be flashed from McDowell to Verde for Sieber and his Tontos; a detachment from Company K, headed by Sergeant A. Garner, and Sieber's scouts was hastily organized. They moved swiftly to the scene of the murder, arriving there exactly one week after the crime. By that time the site had been liberally trampled by the miners in their rough boots, but this meant less than nothing to the ferret-eyed Tontos, who promptly estimated the size of the hostile party, said they were Apache Mohaves, and, with Al and Sergeant Garner's troops, set out like bloodhounds on the cold trail. On the fourth day out the scouts rode about ten miles ahead of the soldiers to sift sign for that of the renegades on the headwaters of Cave Creek. A *Miner* headline of September 24 heralded what happened:

GOOD NEWS!

SHARP FIGHT AT THE HEAD OF CAVE CREEK!

FOURTEEN SAVAGES KILLED

OUR LOSS, ONE INDIAN SCOUT KILLED AND TWO WOUNDED![20]

As Al told it to the commanding officer at Verde later, he and his scouts were busily working out the trail when, rounding a bend in the wash they were following, they burst upon the hostile rancheria so suddenly that the only thing to do was to attack, without awaiting Garner and his men, so they fought. The enemy dove into the brush at the first fire and returned bullet for bullet, the battle raging furiously for a few moments. Two women were captured. "Sieber reports

---

[20] It is possible that Sieber was one of those wounded, although neither the official report nor any news dispatch I have seen says so. He took an arrow through the arm in a fight on Cave Creek on September 1, 1875, according to one notice. *Republican* obituary. That fight is not shown in the *Chronological List*, and there is a possibility that the writer was mistaken in the year.

that the Indians attacked were some twenty-five in number—that they had blankets precisely like those issued at the Verde Reservation and other stores which appeared to him to have come from there," said the official report. "He thinks that they must have been bartering with the Indians on the Reservation. They were Apache Mohaves—many of them were armed with guns—two or three had breechloaders and the Springfield ammunition."[21]

Sieber and Garner returned to Verde after this skirmish, but there were almost a dozen hostiles yet unaccounted for and on October 19, Rudy Stauffer and Sieber went back to the head of Cave Creek to see if they could stir them up. Four days after their departure they found a solitary Indian family trying to make its way from San Carlos to Verde, killed the man, and captured the woman. To bring such a disaster down upon a more or less inoffensive family pursuing a peaceful course was unfortunate, but in those violent days, all Indians off the reservation were presumed hostile; if they fled instead of standing to show authorization to be in no man's land, that cinched it. The killing undoubtedly was regretted, but many innocent men and women, red and white, lost their lives during those tragic years.

Sieber and his scouts went on alone to the head of Cave Creek and on the twenty-seventh struck a rancheria, killing seven warriors and capturing three women and some booty, including bows and arrows and two rifles, one unserviceable. "The seven killed," said the report, "were the last of Big Rum[p]'s band, and the same struck by Lieut. Schuyler last Christmas, and Sieber's scouts 17th of Sept'r last." The west side of the Verde between the post and McDowell was now entirely free of hostiles[22] and, for the most part, would remain that way. To accomplish this, the *Miner* noted proudly, "required patient toil and weary search that will be fully appreciated by the people of Arizona, familiar with the country traversed and the wariness of the Apaches hunted down."[23]

21 Captain G. M. Brayton, Headquarters, Camp Verde, to AAG, Department of Arizona, September 23, 1874, Indian Bureau Record File 75, National Archives.

22 Mason to AAG, Department of Arizona, November 1, 1874, Indian Bureau Record File 75, National Archives.

23 *Arizona Miner*, November 6, 1874.

While Sieber was active south of the Verde, a party of hostiles, thought to be Tontos, had slain a mail carrier named Kennison on the Little Colorado River northeast of the post. Lieutenant King was sent out to discover the culprits, if possible, and do something about them. Late in October he left Verde with Lieutenant Eaton, Sergeant Bernard Taylor, and a detachment of the Fifth Cavalry, along with six Indian scouts, but, unfortunately, with no Sieber to lead them. King arrived at Sunset Pass (about twenty miles southwest of present-day Winslow) early on November 1 and made camp. He and Sergeant Taylor set out to climb East Sunset Mountain, somewhat more than half a mile from camp, and ran into an ambush as a result of which the officer was brutally wounded by a rifle bullet through the arm and shoulder. He was recovered by Eaton, who tried hard to make his Indians scout for hostiles, but they wouldn't do it. "A more abject set of cowards it has never been my fortune to witness," he grumbled in his report. "They admitted it, and said, 'Tonto kill me.' "[24]

Nothing could illustrate more clearly that a very special hand was needed to make the Indian scouts do their best. Sieber's scouts sometimes—rarely—deserted, and sometimes they tried to murder him, but they never got away with mutiny, for he made it a point that they be more afraid of him than of their tribal enemies. In addition, they knew him for an intrepid, dogged fighter and they realized that if they didn't lead him, he would lead them. Such an incident as the failure of King's scouts would have been impossible had Al been along.

Years later, King, then a retired captain, wrote a novel he called *Sunset Pass*[25] in which he envisioned a small party being ambushed in the rocky confines of that defile, a description based, no doubt, on his memory of the site. A prominent figure in the novel is Al Sieber. King's description of Sieber is probably fairly accurate for the man at this period, and it is the only one we have for the decade of the seventies:

A stronger, firmer type of scout and frontiersman than Al Sieber never

[24] Eaton to Post Adjutant, Camp Verde, November 7, 1874, Indian Bureau Record File 75, National Archives.

[25] Charles King, *Sunset Pass; or, Running the Gauntlet Through Apache Land.*

sat in saddle in all Arizona in the seventies, and he was a noted character among the officers, soldiers, pioneers, and Apaches. The former respected and trusted him. The last named feared him as they did the Indian devil. He had been in fight after fight with them; had had his share of wounds, but—what the Apaches recoiled from in awe was the fact that he had never met them in the field without laying one at least of their number dead in his tracks. He was a slim-built, broad-shouldered, powerful fellow, with a keen, intelligent face, and eyes that were kindly to all his friends, but kindled at sight of a foe. A broad brimmed, battered slouch hat was pulled well down over his brows; his flannel shirt and canvas trousers showed hard usage; his pistol belt hung loose and low upon his hips and on each side a revolver swung. His rifle—Arizona fashion—was balanced athwart the pommel of his saddle, and an old Navajo blanket was rolled at the cantle. He wore Tonto leggins and moccasins, and a good-sized pair of Mexican spurs jingled at his heels.[26]

Failure of the King scout to corner and destroy the hostiles meant that still another party had to be sent out from Camp Verde to work in co-operation with scouts from Fort Apache and elsewhere, and Eaton was selected to command it. This time Sieber was sent as chief of scouts and there was no mutiny—quite the reverse. Rarely in the annals of these difficult years is found so sharp an example of the unflagging courage and endurance of Indian scouts when under competent leadership.

The column left on November 17 and almost immediately encountered terrible weather. The first day, they made it to Cedar Tanks, due east of Verde about ten or fifteen miles. During the night a violent storm blew up, bringing snow, sleet, and rain. It lasted without interruption until the morning of the twenty-first, and the command, poorly prepared for it, was miserable. Bedding and clothing were drenched and became stiff with cold. The weather began to clear on the twenty-second, but the whole area was flooded. On the twenty-third, camp was broken at daylight and the column slopped through mud for five miles along Apache Road, then bore left for nine miles and camped on the edge of the snow on the north side of Clear Creek. The day's

26 *Ibid.*, 6–7.

march through gummy mud and rock had been so rough that sixty-two horse and mule shoes were pulled off and two mules and three horses were strained and rendered useless through being mired and pulled out forcibly.

It took until noon on November 24 to reshoe the animals needing it, whereupon camp was broken and the command marched north of east sixteen miles into the mountains through snow from six inches to a foot in depth. At camp that night there was no grass and no water, save melted snow. The next day, camp was again broken at daylight and the weary, half-frozen column marched east three miles to a divide in the mountains, then north of east nineteen miles to below snow line and due east another ten miles to the bottom of a deep canyon. Here again there was no water and but little grass. Obviously, the animals could not continue like this and on the following day, the tenth out of Verde, Eaton had to hunt water instead of Indians—if he were to be able to hunt the latter at all. Nine miles due east he found a tank in a deep canyon which made a good hiding place, so he established a base camp there and the next day sent Sieber and the scouts out with two days' rations to see what they could raise.

About 1:00 P.M., Guide Eben Stanley[27] and twenty scouts from Fort Apache rode into camp, reporting that they were part of an expedition under Captain R. H. Montgomery, who was camped twenty miles to the east, which would make it unnecessary for Eaton to work farther in that direction, or so he thought. However, one of Sieber's Indians arrived at noon the next day to guide Eaton to where the Chief of Scouts was waiting on a fresh trail the Fort Apache party had missed but he had found. The main column joined him about two hours after sunset just as a party of two Tonto men, two women, and four children blundered into them. The men were killed and the others captured. There was no time to do more than cursorily question the captives in the flickering light from the small campfires. At this point, Sieber and his scouts had been on their feet for more than thirty-six

---

[27] Iowa-born Eben Stanley, while serving as a Fifth Cavalry enlisted man, had won a Medal of Honor near Turret Mountain the year before; now he was out of the army and becoming an outstanding guide and scout. He operated out of Fort Apache.

hours, but they seemed as fresh as if they had been curled around a fire and snoozing for twelve. The steel coils they used for muscles sent them bounding up the trail as soon as the troopers were ready.

Lieutenant Eaton describes the chase:

> Sieber reported that he was watched by Indians on distant points, but it was hoped that by making a rapid march that they might be surprised. Leaving a sufficient guard with the pack train, the command [dismounted] took the trail which was very fresh, and at 4 p.m. [*sic*] the next morning came to a deserted camp with eight fires still burning.

The Apaches and their tireless white chief had now rounded out forty-eight hours of the most exhausting toil, but that made no difference once they scented blood. They remained as eager as if they had left the post that morning.

> All hopes of a surprise were abandoned; each Indian scout dropped the blanket he wore, the soldiers did the same, and we followed up at the run. The trail for about four miles led almost due west, and it was hoped that they would take to the snow, but they soon swung around to the left, crossed our trail of three days previous in the canyon, and bore for the still larger canyon still further to the south.
>
> As soon as we came in sight of the rear of the pursued, they commenced to scatter and redoubled their efforts and came near getting away entirely but after running them about twelve miles, one buck was killed and three squaws captured, the chase was then abandoned.
>
> The Indian scouts had been on their feet two [*sic*] days and two nights and this run about used them up, while the soldiers were equally exhausted. In the scattered condition of the pursued, it was of no use to follow them further. We then returned, recrossed the canyon, and marched to a point previously designated to the pack train and camped.

This party of Indians, Eaton added, had occupied sixteen wickiups in a dense pine grove and could easily have been surrounded "had they not already been on the alert watching the movements of the other scouting party who scouted entirely around and on the outside without discovering them." Eaton said that in view of the weather, the Indians would soon have to go into winter camp, when it would be easier to corner them.[28] However, Montgomery struck either these same Apaches or another band of renegades in the basin of Canyon Creek six days after Eaton's chase, killing eight, wounding a couple more, and capturing fourteen.[29]

Conditions at Verde, meanwhile, were unsettled. This was partly due to chronic differences between army officers and the Indian agents of the Department of the Interior and now the situation had been stirred up by persistent rumors, which had even reached the Indians, that this reservation, which the government had promised them forever, would be nothing of the sort. Pressure for white ownership of the lands allotted to the Indians was increasing. It was a frontier truism that white pressure, once generated, would always be eased at the expense of the Indians. So it was to prove again.

[28] Eaton to Post Adjutant, Camp Verde, December 5, 1874, Indian Bureau Record File 75, National Archives.

[29] *Chronological List.*

X. The Rocks Melt

THE INDIANS herded onto Verde Reservation were assured, as the government always told its wards, that this was to be their home as long as the rivers ran, the grass grew, and the hills endured. However, as often happened with federal promises, the streams soon dried up, the grass withered, and the rocks of the enduring hills melted away. After a short time, during which they had become attached to their new home, the Indians were informed that they would be moved once more. To a less desirable place, naturally—one the white man could find fewer economic reasons to covet, yet within the clutches of such grasping contractors as had political friends at Washington.

All during the winter of 1874–75 and for almost a year preceding there had been whispers to that effect. Even the Indians had heard of it. The March before, for instance, it was reported that "rumors are current among the [Verde] Indians that they are to be taken to a reservation on the blistering Colorado" and they were worried. The San Francisco *Chronicle* reported that Verde Agency was to be abolished and the Indians taken two hundred miles east to San Carlos. "Should this prove true, trouble with these Indians may be looked for," warned the *Arizona Miner*.[1]

In late July, Delshay, the outlawed Tonto, had slipped back onto the reservation and "tried his utmost to induce an outbreak, saying to the Indians that . . . the Americans . . . were soon going to break up that reservation and move them off to a barren desert where the heat would speedily exterminate the tribe."[2] How Delshay, in some wilder-

---

[1] *Arizona Miner*, March 13, 1874.   [2] *Ibid.*, August 7, 1874.

ness lair which not even the scouts could find, heard this, by what means it was communicated to him, is an intriguing mystery. One thing is certain: he heard it from whites, not from Indians. He also heard it before the officials at Verde, or the military command in Arizona, for that matter, had positive knowledge of it. His reported phrase, that the Verde Indians were to be sent "to a barren desert where the heat would speedily exterminate the tribe," darkens the mystery, yet sheds some light at the same time. It leads one to suspect that during his last hegira, Delshay was in touch with renegade whites, presumably some with contacts among unscrupulous contractors who had high-level connections in Washington and whose interests would best be served by an Indian war rather than peace. The remark passed on by Delshay to his fellow tribesmen obviously reached him from some white scoundrel who was an agent of even more miserable wretches, and it was patently calculated to flush the Tontos out of Verde and onto the warpath. No other conclusion seems possible.

If greedy contractors were seeking to stir up strife at Verde in order to fatten army orders, others, equally selfish, though based at Tucson, were tugging at *their* Washington friends' coattails to get the Indians concentrated at San Carlos and hence within their grasp. As it happened, they had more influence than their unwashed competitors and so won out. "A 'ring' of Federal officials, contractors, and others was formed in Tucson, which exerted great influence in the national capital, and succeeded in securing the issue of peremptory orders that the Apaches should leave at once for the mouth of the sickly San Carlos, there to be herded with other tribes," wrote John G. Bourke. "It was an outrageous proceeding, one for which I should still blush, had I not long since gotten over blushing for anything the United States Government did in Indian matters."[3] J. P. Dunn, Jr., writing at almost the same time, sarcastically referred to "our humanitarian, sympathetic, religious, peace and civilization Indian Bureau," which he said was, according to repeated charges, "controlled by a corrupt ring, which manages to keep its hold on men of every profession and every party who are appointed to represent the government in this branch of its interests. It has been charged that they have had such a

[3] Bourke, *Border*, 216–17.

control over Congress that they can turn it whither they will, and break down any man who tries to stand up for honesty and justice. . . . It is but too evident that control of that department has been in the hands either of men who 'stole the livery of Heaven to serve the devil in,' or of errant fools who have been played upon like shepherds' pipes by the land-grabbers, who have secured the spoils."[4]

It is difficult to evaluate properly the removal policy and its consequences on the basis of contemporary accounts, but from the perspective of nearly a century, this problem is simplified. The removals themselves were effected at great risk, albeit with a minimum of bloodshed and deaths, but they led directly to and largely caused the long and dreary series of Indian wars that cost thousands of white and Indian lives over the next decade and necessitated the expenditure of untold sums before they were quelled. As a "peace policy," under which they were sold to various administrations and the public, the removals were abject failures; as steps toward economy in handling Indian affairs, they were a farce. John P. Clum, as the key man in Apachería, did not establish the policy, but enthusiastically welcomed it. He was the agent under whom the Tontos, Yavapais, various bands of Apaches, and even some of the Apache Yumas were to be concentrated. He favored it because it would make him the most important Indian man in the Southwest. He could see nothing but shining successes as each removal brought fresh bands of Indians to his extensive rancheria. Crook, who vainly hoped in the summer of 1874 "that the interests now at work to deprive these Indians of this reservation will be defeated,"[5] warned, correctly, of the dire consequences which would result, but he was not heeded. To Sieber, Schuyler, Randall, and others concerned with day-to-day control and management of the lately hostile, the decision meant added problems, but on an executive level. Their job went on and on, no matter which Indians they had to fight or under what policy.

There was a little scouting during the early winter, but nothing very important. On January 11, 1875, Rudy Stauffer and Sieber took K of the Fifth and some Indians into Tonto Basin, where they met a

4 Dunn, *op. cit.*, 633–34.
5 Crook, *Annual Report*, 1874, Hayes Collection.

scout from Fort Apache commanded by Captain Frederick D. Ogilby[6] of the Eighth Infantry. Rudy and Al continued with their own mission, thoroughly scouting North Peak and passing through the Mazatzals to the Salt before turning southeast to the Sierra Anchas, but found no hostile sign. On the way back, however, they killed two Tontos on the East Fork of the Verde and arrived safely at the post after a 230-mile trip.[7]

The first major test of the concentration policy, now approved, was to move almost 1,500 Tontos and other Indians from Verde some 180 rocky, difficult miles to San Carlos. L. Edwin Dudley, former Indian superintendent of New Mexico, was chosen to accomplish it. He left Washington on December 22 and after many delays had finally arrived at Prescott, where he immediately conferred with General Crook. That sagacious officer received him cordially but "thought it impossible to effect the removal," although he pledged the co-operation of himself and his officers in any way short of force. He would not use troops to force the Indians to make the unwise move, he said, and Dudley "answered him that I would abandon the effort as soon as it became apparent to me that military force would be needed."[8]

[6] Frederick Darley Ogilby, born in New Jersey, was commissioned from New York and fought throughout the Civil War. He died May 30, 1877.

[7] Brayton to AAG, Department of Arizona, February 5, 1875, Indian Bureau Record File 75, National Archives.

[8] Unless otherwise noted, this account of the transfer of the Indians to San Carlos is based on Dudley's report to Commissioner Edward P. Smith, dated from Tucson, April 3, 1875, Indian Bureau Record Group 75, National Archives; Corbusier's memoirs in the APHS Files and an article by him entitled "The Apache-Yumas and Apache-Mojaves," *The American Antiquarian*, Vol. VIII, No. 5 (September, 1886), 276–84; and an article by Eaton, "Stopping an Apache Battle," edited by Don Russell, in the *Journal of the United States Cavalry Association*, Vol. XLII, No. 178 (July-August, 1933), 12–18. Dudley's original report, now faded and hard to read, has many sections lightly scratched out, as though in preparation for publication. Some of these deletions contain interesting material, and I have used them along with his edited statement. Eaton's article poses an additional problem in that nowhere does he mention Sieber as having been along, unless under the somewhat nebulous term "interpreter." This is not merely a matter of editing, for Mr. Russell assured me, in correspondence dated April 21, 1962, that the original and lengthier manuscript, prepared by Eaton shortly before his death, doesn't mention Sieber either. This can only be due to the lapse of half a century between the occurrence of the events described and Eaton's writing of them. That he did not remember the circumstances too clearly is revealed by his statement that the transfer

Dudley received a mixed welcome on his arrival at Verde, early in February. He had already learned that many people in the Prescott area opposed the transfer and that everyone thought it could not be done, but he was still confident. At Verde he had to sell the idea to many hundreds of warlike and restless Indians. He ordered them assembled, and when they gathered, he emerged from his tent, swung a buffalo robe over a step leading into it, sat down, and with a lordly gesture somewhat reminiscent of a Roman potentate, rested on one arm as he harangued the multitude. He had come from General Grant at Washington, he said, with orders to move them from this "permanent" home to another.

Dr. Corbusier, something of a linguist and wise in the ways of Indians, lost no time in slipping among them, alert to hear what they said to each other. "I heard one buck say in a low tone, 'He is drunk,' and when he arose and went into the tent, another one said, 'He has gone to get a drink of whiskey,'" Corbusier recalled.

"Of course the Indians were opposed to going," Dudley conceded in his formal report, "but when told it was the order of the President, that the move was intended for the purpose of placing them in a more healthy and better country, and that . . . they were not to be driven by troops, their consent was obtained." Not easily, however, and not, although he didn't suspect it, entirely through Dudley's own efforts.

Snook, a chief and one of Sieber's most dependable noncoms, replied to Dudley as his people listened carefully, grunting their approval as the words rolled out of his powerful throat. He told Dudley he and his people would not go where they would be outnumbered by

---

took place in late spring or early summer, his description of difficulties caused by the heat when it was actually snow that bothered them, and his hazy recollections of the marching times between points, as when he believes it to have been "twelve or fourteen" days to the East Fork of the Verde, when, in fact, it was two days. There are many other discrepancies, and in general I have followed the rule of thumb that when faced with divergent accounts by participants of presumed equal integrity, depend upon the most nearly contemporary. Dudley's report was written within days, perhaps hours, of his arrival at Tucson and is thus the more reliable, at least in my judgment. It is worth noting that W. T. Corbusier, whose father was the physician accompanying the group and who received an account of it from the Doctor in person, said that Sieber "was the boss of the expedition. Both Dad and Eaton relied on Sieber." Interview with the author, May 5, 1963.

their enemies. This was their country and always had been. Their fathers and grandfathers, their children, their wives—all were born here where their ancestors had died. He reminded the Commissioner of the promises which had been made to them, the major one being that the country for forty miles along the river and ten miles on each side would be theirs forever. Then his face fell. As though hopelessness had overtaken him, he turned from defiance to pleading. Finally he chided Dudley: "Why did the commissioner call the Indians brothers, as he didn't ask him to take a drink?" Snook wondered (as Dr. Corbusier remembered it). "When the white man meets his brother he always asks him to take a drink." He urged Dudley not to drink any more whiskey "until after the conference of the next day, so that he might know what he was saying to them."[9]

After that first day's meeting, many Indians came to Corbusier and asked him to intercede with Dudley, who "was crazy or drunk, but when I told them that the order did come from General Grant, and they must obey it, they agreed to go quietly, providing I would accompany them to see that they were properly treated and not attacked by their enemies."[10]

Once he had secured the Indians' consent, Dudley "did not wait for a change of decision longer than was absolutely necessary to make arrangements for transportation." Dr. Corbusier "recommended that the tribes be taken by wagon road around the mountains, but he re-

[9] There is no other evidence that Dudley was a drinking man, but the Indians, having accepted the notion he was drunk, continued to believe it. Dudley appears to have been a conscientious and reasonably able man. W. T. Corbusier, however, says that Dudley "was anything but pleasant. He was recalcitrant, stubborn, and a drinking man." Interview with the author, May 5, 1963.

[10] Eaton states that Crook was aware of the decision to remove the Indians before Dudley's arrival and had already selected Eaton to accomplish it, adding that an "inspector" from the Indian Bureau would go along and report details of the transfer but "would have no authority and would be present simply as an observer. . . . The full responsibility would be on me." This seems at variance with Dudley's activities when he arrived at Verde and with Corbusier's account as well, although Crook may have told his young officer something which suggested that meaning to him. Dr. Corbusier's son told me that Eaton "was not in command and simply went as an escort. Anything the troops did had to await Dudley's approval. Dad was more or less a free lance." Interview with the author, May 5, 1963.

plied that they were Indians and used to the mountains, and he was going the shortest way; he had moved Indians before."

On February 27, 1875, the motley exodus got under way, and a sadder pilgrimage was never seen under Arizona skies. There were 1,476 Indians of all ages, sizes, and physical conditions composing the horde, with Oliver Chapman, special agent, in field command. Lieutenant Eaton led fifteen select cavalrymen as escort, and Al Sieber, whom Dudley referred to in his report as "Mr. Seaber," was along, with his Tontos acting as policemen.[11] Crook had supplied the Camp Verde pack train of 29 animals, and Dudley succeeded in hiring a civilian pack train of 26 more. These 55 mules were not enough to carry rations for the entire trip, so the Commissioner telegraphed John Clum to meet the caravan with rations from San Carlos, although, because the telegraph line stopped many miles short of the agency, Dudley feared that Clum hadn't received the message. He therefore contracted for 5,000 pounds of flour at McDowell, issued out to the already groaning Indians the rations which the civilian pack train would have carried, and sent it to McDowell to pick up the additional flour and meet the travelers somewhere about halfway. There would still be a shortage, but it couldn't be helped. Indians, Dudley reasoned, were accustomed to going hungry.

No one knew better than the Indians the hazards awaiting them on this long, painful journey. The mountains they had to cross were high. Rivers were numerous and at this season might rise many feet overnight, making a crossing impossible sometimes. They had to carry all of their belongings on their own backs; even the very old and the very young were under heavy loads. One ancient Indian placed his aged and decrepit wife in a basket, through the bottom of which he had cut holes so that her feet could stick out, then slung her on his bent back, supported the cargo by a tumpline across his forehead, and carried her the full 180 miles—and there were those who said an Indian was incapable of such fine emotions as love! The cavalrymen,

[11] It took three days to move the Indians from the reservation to Camp Verde, a distance of sixteen miles, where Eaton and Sieber apparently joined them. Sieber directed the Tontos to take the lead, which disappointed them because they didn't want their enemies behind them. W. T. Corbusier in an interview with the author, May 5, 1963.

for the most part, walked so that footsore children, cripples, and the weak could ride their horses. Sometimes an old man died along the trail; one day two babies were born, each wrapped in a blanket and carried to the next camp before any other covering could be provided. After a short rest, the mothers followed on foot. "No wonder," Corbusier marveled, "Indian women looked old so soon."[12]

Dudley made a flying trip to Prescott but returned in time to overtake the Indians on the second afternoon; he found them discouraged and sullen in the face of a bitter snowstorm which had kept them in camp all day.[13] The next day, Dudley, who had already earned the nickname "Come-along!" for his constant prodding and nagging, consented to a march of only five miles, to the East Fork of the Verde, and the horde went into camp early in the afternoon, tired, muddy, cold, and surly. As usual, the Tontos and Apache Yumas established themselves well apart from each other, for their hereditary hostility, having never been cured, rankled in their breasts.

Sieber smelled trouble. He had been through so much of it that it came to him as clearly as the dampness preceding a storm.

A deer ran along the side of a mountain above the camp and the Apache Yumas and Apache Mohaves by the creek, excited as children, blasted away—with no harm whatever to the deer. Sieber grunted at such awful shooting, and when the animal bounded down even with the tents of the whites, he dropped it with a single shot. The Indians below, who had been shooting at it, ran up, but the Tontos above dashed down and seized it and "the hungry ones were driven away very angry."

The next day, Lieutenant Eaton and Dr. Corbusier rode ahead of the column to hunt, leaving Sieber in command of the escort and the

[12] W. T. Corbusier informed me that "no less than 25 new babies were presented to the agent at San Carlos; the men paid no attention to this." Interview with the author, May 5, 1963.

[13] Dr. Corbusier's son says there was much difficulty in crossing Strawberry Creek, which flows south from the rim to enter Fossil Creek. "Sieber and Eaton were for delaying until the raging torrent subsided, but Dudley was insistent," he said. "The mounted soldiers ferried the Indians across the stream, with debris and rocks tumbling down it. Ropes were passed over to assist in the move. The crossing took all night. The doctor treated the injured." Interview with the author, May 5, 1963.

scouts. The surgeon killed a deer, cut off enough for the whites, and hung the rest of the carcass from a tree so that the Indians could get it as they came along, but again the Tontos took it all, leaving the Apache Yumas and Apache Mohaves none.

Camp that night, according to the Lieutenant, was made in a pleasant valley along the East Fork, with the supplies, horses, and pack trains farthest upstream, then, in order, the escort's camp, the Tontos, and, after an interval, the Mohaves and Yumas together. Eaton describes the scene:

> The half-grown boys began playing games on vacant ground between the two Indian camps. In course of time . . . they began to shout at and ridicule each other. Soon . . . the little rascals formed themselves in two opposing lines, facing each other. . . .
>
> They stretched themselves out on their stomachs, seeking cover, in true Indian style. . . . The vocal volley increasing . . . until a few unarmed buck Indians began to stray here and there from their respective camps and join their respective children. The numbers of these increased until there were more adult Indians in each line, all lying down and seeking cover, than there were boys. . . . Suddenly there came a sort of verbal explosion. . . .

Corbusier clearly heard the women scream out: "Kill the Tontos! *Kill* the Tontos!"

A flood of incensed warriors rolled past the tents of the white civilians. Dudley, limping from an old war wound, hobbled out to turn them back, but they overwhelmed him, passed him by, unheeding, and with sharp cries and whoops bounded up the slope toward their opponents. Chapman and the agency people dropped to their knees, praying and singing, while Sieber and the escort stormed up through the attacking Yumas and Mohaves, who had broken out on a small mesa where the Tontos were encamped. The assault force flopped on their stomachs and began shooting, wildly, fortunately.[14]

If Sieber paused to think of the risk he was taking, there was no indication of it. His face was red with emotion and his mustache

[14] Packers Sam Hill, Harry Hawes, and a couple of others flattened out as much as they could to avoid the bullets; fortunately, none of them was hit. W. T. Corbusier in an interview with the author, May 5, 1963; reminiscences of Fred W. Croxon, Sr., a former Forest Ranger, APHS Files.

bristled as he ran across the mesa, past the shooting Indians, and into the very center of no man's land amidst a hail of bullets, followed by Eaton's cavalrymen and some of the scouts. How they missed being killed it is impossible to say. Already the dead and wounded dotted the mesa. A general massacre seemed inevitable, and once it began, no human agency would be able to stop it. Warriors, women, children, and, inevitably, whites as well, would fall under the bloody scythe of internecine warfare. Casualties would be reckoned in scores or hundreds. One man, and one man alone, prevented this: Al Sieber. In all his checkered, adventurous, perilous career, Sieber knew no finer moment than when he stood between the impassioned, furiously shooting braves of these great Indian nations, his arms upraised, his blazing eyes literally cowing them into ceasing fire without he himself firing a shot.

Dudley, playing down the high drama of the moment (which he afterward referred to as "my 'circus' "), wrote it up quite prosaically for the Commissioner's eyes:

> A difficulty occurred . . . which resulted in a general fight between the two tribes. . . . The escort under direction of Mr. Al Seaber, Chief of General Crook's scouts, at once took position between the two contending parties and made every effort to send them to their respective camps, and success attended their efforts. When the loss came to be counted we knew of five dead, the Indians said seven, and ten wounded, not a great loss where so much lead was expended.

Anyway, they were only Indians.[15]

[15] Eaton has left a detailed account of this battle, in which, he wrote, "frenzy reigned" rampant. Crook, he said, had told him that if the Indians wanted to fight among themselves, let them, "but if it comes to a point where government property and the safety of your command are endangered, you will of course stop it if you can." The fracas soon reached that point. Eaton wrote that he led his escort, the "interpreter," the Inspector, and the Doctor into no man's land with his arm upraised, stopping the shooting. "Through the interpreter," he wrote, he called the three leading chiefs to the center and bawled them out, and, after some difficulty, called off the fight. He said his explanations "took time, as the interpreter had to make all parties understand," but he gives no other indication that anyone but himself was responsible for stopping the shooting. No doubt that is the way he remembered it. Dr. Corbusier reported that "I found 25 sprawled out in various positions and treated the 10 worst wounded. Estimates of the dead varied up to 30, but I found four." W. T. Corbusier in an interview with the author, May 5, 1963.

Corbusier had a professional interest in the outcome. He collected and treated the wounded, buried what dead he could find, "and on my way back to Camp Verde [after the Indians were delivered to San Carlos] I disinterred the heads and sent the skulls to the Army Medical Museum, as they showed the so-called explosive action of a bullet passing through the skull which it broke into many pieces."

On the morning following the battle the whites had difficulty stringing the Indians out on the trail. Once underway, they set a rapid pace in order "to tire them sufficiently to take the fight out of them for that night."

Cattle which had been driven along for beef now became footsore and many animals had to be left behind. The supply of beef and flour gave out. The Indians cooked and ate the stems of Canada thistles and such other greens as they could find in late winter, and the women and children began to cry with hunger. On Saturday, the thirteenth day of March, the swaying, exhausted column staggered down to the banks of the Salt. Dudley feared it would be too high at this season to be crossed without a raft or boat; material for neither was abundant, since the only timber along its course was cottonwood, which was difficult to work, and often the stream was wide and its current swift. Fortunately, however, the spring floods had not yet set in. "We found that the stream could be forded, but running as swiftly as it does in the month of March it was a sad duty to compel men, women and children to wade through the cold water, even though they *were* Indians," Dudley wrote compassionately. "The water was about waist deep to a tall man and the crossing was a pitiable sight, one which I could not witness without a feeling of pity, which brought tears to my eyes. The crossing of the river reminded me of another exodus, and I wished that the waves might again be rolled back."

In the morning, after the emigrants had passed a soggy and frigid night, Corbusier noticed that the Mohaves and some of the Yumas had their faces painted, "their noses red and the rest of the face black with galena as when they prepared for war." He went to a chieftain friend to inquire about the reason and was gruffly told, "Kwa-wa-o-pie"—no talk! Obviously the chief was disgruntled to the point of violence because of hunger, exhaustion, and exasperation with the move, and Corbusier hurried to Dudley to report the alarming turn of events. He didn't have time to complete his recital, however, before a bullet whizzed their way, "as a warning for him [Dudley] to get busy, or the next one might be for him." Corbusier yelled to the interpreter to call out that Dudley would go ahead and send back some food which would soon arrive, and the irate chief grumblingly let him off with that promise.

Dudley, said Corbusier, "could not see the looks of hate beneath the paint that the man cast at him, nor had he understood what the men and women said on the trail and, when he asked me, I wouldn't tell him, as most of it was not fit to be translated. Once a buck shook his fist in the face of a companion as they passed us, and called him a vile name in English, and then looked up into the Commissioner's face and grinned. He then gave me a knowing look, as if I knew to whom the name really applied."

The Commissioner lost no time in mounting his horse and trotting away, and he was pleasantly surprised to encounter, just beyond the camp, a drove of twenty-five cattle and mules with more than half a ton of flour sent out by Agent Clum, who had received Dudley's message after all. The Indians were moved a mile to better water and sent into camp with plenty to eat, "and all were in good humor again." The rest of the way was by an easy trail, most of it downhill.

Clum met the caravan in Pinal Canyon, thirty-five miles from San Carlos, among the mountains and gorges which later became the site of Arizona's most promising mining camps but then contained not a single human being save those hapless ones being driven from their homes to the newly promised land. "It was a dark, blustering March night, with flurries of snow," Clum recalled. "Campfires flickered up and down the canyon; occasional echoes sounded very much like Apache war talk. But the night passed uneventfully, and the following day we hiked to San Carlos."[16] It was on this trip that Clum first met Sieber. He was so impressed by the scout, and by Dudley's recounting of Al's part in quelling the near-disastrous battle, that he later offered Al a key position on the growing San Carlos Reservation.

By now Sieber was a mature scout, not as famous as he would be

16 Clum, *op. cit.*, 150.

a decade later—outside Arizona, that is—but as well known within the Territory as any man not engaged in politics and better known than even some politicians. His fame had not spread widely because of the nature of the operations in which he was engaged. These had not yet assumed the spectacular proportions which would lead to national headlines; that had to await the arrival on the scene of Victorio and Geronimo. But in all the war there was, Sieber was superb.

Army men liked Al not only for his mastery of all the intricate knowledge that a scout must possess but also because he took orders and never pushed himself to the fore. He was popular with the Indians, and he was determined to understand what the army wanted done with them, and to do it, letting the officers, many of them green and inept in the ways of the frontier, take the credit. Perhaps this accounts for his astonishing popularity with officers of every stripe over more than two decades—his ability and his unwillingness to push himself forward at the expense of those who would get the credit. He had no women, or none that he allowed to enter into his life; he had no love but scouting, no interest except carrying out orders or seeing to it that army men did, and no taste for glory or fame or anything outside of the military—save a little liquor and funning now and then.

The immense task of transferring the Verde Indians was now complete. "The move was a difficult one," understated Dudley in his formal report of the exodus, "and was successfully made. No one at Prescott thought it could be made without many of them going to the mountains. I do not ask for any consideration for success. I know I should have been the recipient of much abuse for failure." And there is no doubt that the transfer of these fifteen hundred Indians was a remarkable achievement, though poor Dudley got less than his due from it. He found, in fact, as have so many others who have sacrificed much for their government, that he was to be gypped out of even his expense money. "You have refused . . . to send me funds necessary to pay for the move," he complained to Commissioner Edward P. Smith, whose reaction to Dudley's feat is incomprehensible. "I have made the move for as little money or maybe less than any similar move was made for." Nor was that all:

Myself, the Indians, employees who were with me, the military escort, the pack train all took their lives in their hands and all knew that at any time during the journey they might be in danger of losing their lives. You can sit in a nicely carpeted office and forget more in one day about this miserable place than those of us who came over it ever knew. . . . I feel aggrieved that you should fail to give me the small amount of money that was necessary. . . .

The count of the Verde Indians actually arriving on foot at San Carlos was 1,361, or 115 fewer than those who started. Of these, 25 had been sent by wagon on the roads encircling the Tonto Basin, a few oldsters had died on the march, some had taken off for the Colorado Reservation rather than risk the unknowable perils of San Carlos, and the remainder had fled into Rattlesnake and Hell canyons to pick up the threads of the old, free life. These would be Sieber's problem in the months ahead.

Verde Reservation was closed out as a subagency, although Camp Verde would continue to be an important military post until 1890 and for years Sieber and from forty to one hundred Tonto scouts would be based there. "The Verde removal . . . ended the Apache question in west-central Arizona from the geographical standpoint; but in concentrating the Verde bands upon the San Carlos Reservation, the real problem of their control was perhaps more difficult than ever before."[17] And this was John Philip Clum's concern.

[17] Ogle, *op. cit.*, 126.

XI. The Scouts Come to Town

PRESCOTT HAD SEEN NOTHING like it before—nor has it since. Al Sieber was in town with about forty of his Tonto scouts, brought to Whipple because the Walapais were grumbling and it was thought they might make trouble. The scouts were enlisted at San Carlos, where all the Indians now lived, but were stationed at Verde.

About half a dozen of them visited the *Miner* office, prowling around like children, wide eyed with curiosity, examining the type, watching the meticulous composition of a story in the form sticks of type in those pre-Linotype days, fascinated by the flat-bed press as it ran off thousands of sheets of printed paper, and winding up their visit with the unabashed demand of every white in the shop, from proprietor to devil, to give them clothes, "which, though the weather is warm and pleasant, we felt obliged to decline," noted Thomas J. Butler,[1] who had succeeded John Marion in the editorship. "Our best pants were so recently presented to us that we couldn't think of parting with them, though one brawny savage had his hands on them and insisted, as well as we could understand him, that we could spare them, else why were they hanging idle against the wall instead of being worn?"

[1] Butler was born in Indiana in 1826 and in 1849 went to California, where he endured more than his share of hardships in the mining camps. He was connected with newspapers which he owned or edited at Red Bluff, California, and in Idaho, Montana, New Mexico, and Nevada, and he arrived at Prescott in December, 1874, just when John Marion was thinking of retiring to a ranch. Marion, however, could remain out of a print shop only a couple of years, and bought back into the *Miner* in 1877 when Butler turned to other pursuits. Butler was territorial treasurer for several terms and became vice-president of the First National Bank of Prescott before his death in 1902. Lutrell, *op. cit.*, 78.

To humor them, Butler had proofs run of a lot of stock woodcuts of bears, deer, Indians, guns, and so on, and this delighted the Tontos, who seized them, grinningly compared one with another, and stalked off clutching one apiece to show to those of their red brethren who had been inspecting some other nook of the white man's town.[2]

Sieber really didn't think there would be much to fear from the Walapais. For one thing, Dan O'Leary had gone out to see them, confident that he could "talk them in."[3] However, with so many nominally friendly Indians in town, it was inevitable that someone would suggest a show, and Al was certainly willing. He was never an exhibitionist, did no bragging, wore no long hair nor buckskin clothes, had no pet rifle with silver mountings nor fancy moccasins nor beading on his hatband. He was just a man who liked his work. But he enjoyed funning even more, and this sounded like a great idea. He would be the white "victim," and his scouts would be the "hostiles."

It had to be realistic because the "performance" would be presented before the critical eyes of the most Indian-battered audience on earth; there was scarcely a man in the crowd who had not had some narrow escape or knew of someone who had—or someone who hadn't escaped at all. That the show was a success was revealed by a mildly disapproving article which appeared in the *Miner*. Butler, who wrote it, thought the show was too realistic and that Al ran too great a risk.

One hardly need be gifted with a very vivid imagination to fancy himself surrounded by hostile Apaches bent on securing a trophy in the shape of a lock of his hair while attending one of their unearthly orgies, such as the denizens of Prescott were treated to. . . . Al. Seiber with his forty Scouts in war paint, armed with needle guns, etc., gave quite an exhibition on the Plaza, Al. personating a victim in one of the dances and they pursuing him with savage yells, almost made the hair stand on end with those who had met the red devils on former occasions enacting similar tragedies under less pleasing circumstances. It was the first Apache frolic we ever attended. . . .

These are in the service of the United States, under perfect discipline

[2] *Arizona Miner*, May 14, 1875.
[3] *Ibid.*, April 30, 1875.

and invaluable allies . . . but it seems so unnatural for them to have any sympathy with the whites, as against their own kind . . . that we should really, while we feared them, have more respect for them if they remained enemies. . . .

The conviction forces itself upon us while witnessing their mimic scalp-dance around an imaginary victim, that it would add zest to their enjoyment if it was real hair from the head of some miner, ranchman, teamster or soldier, rather than the old coat or hat that is pressed into service to represent a genuine scalp.

Seiber has them under apparent perfect control. They evidently fear him, and no doubt respect him as much as it is in their nature to reverence anything; but it really looks as if he was taking desperate chances. Their estimate of the value of the life of a white man is measured by the fear of punishment for destroying it, and were we in Seiber's place we should always try to make it a point to show them that it would be to their advantage to let us live.[4]

During the course of his work with the scouts, Sieber had come "to have remarkable insight into Indian character and psychology," wrote one who studied him thoroughly. "The very bravest of the Indians he fought and conquered today he would enlist as scouts tomorrow. His position was the most eminently hazardous post held by any white man in the Southwest; yet rarely did one of these Army scouts whom he commanded prove false in time of need. He held their complete respect. Although his domination over them was inflexible, he was honest with them and always treated them fairly. Moreover his powers were so absolute, his courage so unflinching and invincible, that they felt confident under his leadership."[5]

Now thirty-one, Sieber was at the very peak of his physical development. He was about five feet, ten inches tall, but appeared taller; he weighed about 175 pounds, and there was not an ounce of fat or excess flesh on him. His shoulders, broadened by farm work and timber cutting in his youth, were heavy and strong, but not unsightly with the freakish muscles of professional strong men, and his lungs were developed for endless endurance rather than exhibition purposes. He had a "hand like an elephant." He used a little tobacco

4 *Ibid.*, May 21, 1875.
5 Frank C. Lockwood, *More Arizona Characters*, 20.

now and then, to chew or to stuff into a sour-smelling pipe, and he loved good whiskey, or any whiskey, a poker game, a dance (and he didn't care whether it was an Indian or a white dance), or a night of carousing.

Al was a practical joker at a time when that was looked upon by most men as the highest form of humor. When he and his pals set out to tree a town, the *Miner* could dryly report that "by all accounts, Al and his friends had a fine time." Once he played billiards and drank through the night during such an evening on the town at Prescott. Toward morning, he and his companions left the saloon and went hunting for something to eat. They passed a butcher shop with a porch over which were scantlings for meat to hang on. There was a drunk passed out on the porch, and Al allowed he might get frozen stiff in that position, so he picked him up and hung him, by his coat collar, on a meathook. There the unfortunate man was, helpless to free himself, when the proprietor came around later to open the place.[6]

Al's sprees were merely interludes in a life of almost constant danger, a life full of the perils he loved, which gave him his real zest for living. His profession demanded that he sometimes be utterly ruthless in disciplining his wild and often turbulent charges. More than once he is known to have shot down some disloyal scout in the presence of the Indian's companions, although he did so only with the gravest provocation and he never became a killer in the sense of becoming addicted to that failing. No man but Sieber could have got away with such summary executions. It is a testimony to his control over his scouts and their faith in him that they never reacted in such a way that they put him in an untenable position, nor did his disciplinary actions lessen their liking for him.

Sieber's control over his Indians sometimes seemed almost uncanny. One of his acquaintances reported having "seen him go into a camp of 'tizwin' crazed Apaches at Fort Apache and kick and slap them about as if they were a lot of children. Not one of them resisted or showed any resentment or anger."[7] Sieber himself attributed his weird hold on the Apaches to his habit of never lying to them under

6 Lockwood APHS.
7 Barnes, *Place Names*, 403.

any provocation, thus winning their complete confidence. "I do not deceive them but always tell them the truth," he told an interviewer. "When I tell them I am going to kill them, I do it, and when I tell them I am their friend, they know it."[8] But it was even more than that. He was a better woodsman than most of the Apaches. He was stronger. He could hike farther and ride longer and run a greater distance than any of them. He was braver than all but the boldest warriors, and no one ever knew him to show fear in any situation. He could be kind and murderous and gentle and firm in rapid succession. And he left their women alone. Sieber was a bulldog on a trail and a mastiff in a fight and as alert as a terrier all the time. He rarely held a grudge; he could get along with almost anyone. There were men in the Territory who were jealous of him and he had a rare enemy, such as Archie McIntosh, but few men anywhere were so positive in their accomplishments and at the same time so nearly universally esteemed by men and women alike as Al Sieber.

His adventures during these years were uncountable; most of them, after becoming campfire yarns, gradually were lost, so that only a sampling remains. On one occasion he was hunting renegades with his scouts, under orders to bring in no prisoners. His party jumped a band, killing sixteen, and returned to camp minus one scout, who was thought to have been killed. Al decided to lay over a day to recover the body and give it a proper burial, since such things were a great aid to his Tontos' morale. He led his men back to the scene of the fight the next morning; seeing heads pop up from behind the shrubbery, he realized that he had missed some of the renegades, who had now laid an ambush for him. What did Sieber do?

> Giving the order to charge, he led his scouts a little distance toward an arroyo. As he approached he suddenly came to a steep jump-off, and looking down from the bank he saw right below him a big naked Indian lying on his side with his bow drawn taut to shoot. On the brave's back was a little baby with its arms about his neck. The arrow was discharged and carried Sieber's hat from his head. Without taking time to throw his rifle to his shoulder, he fired. He said he was sure he had wounded the Indian, but had not killed him. So he jumped down into the bed of the creek ran

8 *Republican* obituary.

around to one side, and finished the work. He did not like to tell what became of the baby. When pressed, he explained that one of the scouts seized it by the heels and dashed its head against a rock.

The body of the missing man was not found. The reason, Al discovered when he returned to his base, was that the Indian had captured two women and didn't want to kill them, as orders had insisted he do. Instead, he had slipped off with them through the brush, taking them into the post alive.[9]

In a battle on the Verde, Sieber salvaged a youngster three or four years old and boosted him up behind him on his white mule. For a little while the child sat quietly, clutching the tail of Sieber's shirt so that he wouldn't fall. Suddenly Al felt a sharp sting in his side, grabbed at it, and caught the hand of the boy, who had silently drawn Sieber's bowie knife and was digging it into his side. A scout rode up and grimly snatched the boy off to no one ever told what fate.[10]

On another occasion Sieber and some of his scouts were sent out after a band of hostiles, whom they discovered camped on a bench above a gorge choked with boulders and stunted trees. During the night the scouts slipped cautiously down this gorge, waiting out the remainder of the darkness close under the bench where the enemy was sleeping peacefully. It was a moonlight night. Sieber, like his scouts, was hidden, but ceaselessly watched the edge of the bluff for any sign of movement there. At last an old chief got up and walked toward the lip of the bluff, his blanket clutched tightly around him in the early-morning chill. He stood on the edge of the little cliff and stared down the canyon, where the morning mist was just rising from the jumble of freshet wreckage, softening and smoothing over the scene. He cocked his head as if he had heard some sound of danger, but it was just a distant coyote yelp from the valley below. All else was fresh and damp and silent. The Indian squatted on the ground near the fire for a moment. Then, for some reason, his suspicions were alerted once more and he crept over to the lip of the gorge and peered down into it. Sieber figured it was now or never and, although the light was not of the best, drew a bead and shot him.[11] With this the battle

9 Lockwood, *More Arizona Characters*, 21–22.
10 *Ibid.*, 22.   11 Lockwood APHS.

burst like a storm over the impromptu rancheria and several hostiles were killed before the rest scattered.

Al was well known as a marksman. He had that natural shooting gift which the most expert hunters possess, rarely taking long aim, usually shooting almost instinctively, most often unerringly. Once, riding a stage, the team horses flushed a jack rabbit and Sieber killed it with a single bullet as it bounded across the desert in long, zigzag leaps and while the stage was rocking and swaying in the manner notorious for those vehicles. He once told an acquaintance that the best shot he ever recalled was at an Indian running up a hill at a measured distance of five hundred yards. The bullet hit him in the head. Of course there was a great deal of luck in any such feat, but Sieber made enough remarkable shots on other occasions to prove that even this one was not all luck.[12]

During the years that followed the major military operations, Sieber became so closely identified with the Apache scouts in central Arizona that they often were called "Sieber's Scouts" or "Sieber's Apaches," and many were the tales told by pioneers about this singular aggregation which was largely responsible for keeping the peace and running down the renegades who were forever slipping away from the reservations and depredating until they were caught. Some of the stories were true, no doubt. Others were true in the sense that they honestly reflected the man, his scouts, and their job.

One daughter of pioneers recalled, in a newspaper interview, how, when she was twelve years old and "deathly afraid of Indians," she had arrived by wagon at the Verde, where her father had decided to homestead. "One day when mother was reading, I looked up and saw 12 Indians on horseback. They were painted and had feathers in their hair. I said, 'Mother, yonder comes a band of Indians; I think they are going to kill us.' My mother was a brave woman. She reached up and got a rifle, but they rode up, jumped off their horses and reached out to shake hands. They showed us a paper telling us that they were [Sieber's] Indian scouts."[13]

In his *Apache Land*, Ross Santee tells a story he picked up from a

[12] *Ibid.*
[13] *Arizona Republican*, April 16, 1930, article by Mrs. Charles Dickinson.

Lieutenant Charles Morton (here shown as a captain about 1880) joined Townsend on a successful raid against Tonto Basin hostiles in 1871.

The epithet "Indian killer" aptly describes John B. Townsend, whose obsession with slaying Apaches—or any other Indians for that matter—made him well known throughout Arizona Territory.

Lieutenant George O. Eaton of the Fifth Cavalry commanded the military escort when the Indians at Camp Verde were moved to San Carlos.

Walter S. Schuyler led many scouting expeditions on which Sieber acted as guide and chief of scouts. The combination of Schuyler's military skills and Sieber's superior knowledge of the Apaches yielded a long string of victories.

cowboy about how, when the rider was a child, he and his parents were surprised at their Arizona ranch by Indians—Apaches—all men, with long moccasins and rags tied around their heads. They moved up to the cabin single file as the frightened family barricaded itself. His father cocked his rifle, then relaxed. "It's all right, Mary," he called to his wife, "it's all right—it's Al Sieber an' his scouts." The story, told in Santee's fluent, vivid style, probably gives a better picture of Sieber and the Arizona of that day than a thousand pages of history.[14]

Columnist J. F. Weadock of Tucson's *Arizona Star* heard a similar story from an old-time stage driver named Jeb Sands. He was rolling eastward with an empty stage from Dragoon Springs in Apache days. At Ewell's Springs he found that the Apaches had burned the station and killed the attendants, so he was understandably worried as he ground on toward Fort Bowie in Apache Pass. "Suddenly he thought his luck had run out," wrote Weadock. "Over a crest came a group of riders, their seat on their ponies leaving no doubt of their identity. They were Apaches. Sands plied the whip and made his run for it. The Apaches, while they followed him down the trail, did not seem to be attempting to gain. But they followed right to the gate. They were a detachment of Al Sieber's Apache scouts, looking for the Indians that had burned Ewell's Springs station."[15]

Some years ago, in a letter to the editor of the Tombstone *Epitaph*, a retired army officer took issue with this general impression of Sieber's role with the Indian scouts and in Arizona fighting generally. Colonel Cornelius C. Smith[16] wrote in this vein:

> Sieber was a civilian scout, so had no . . . "command." . . . A civilian scout is simply a laborer of the Quartermaster Department of the army;

[14] Ross Santee, *Apache Land*, 103–11.

[15] Tucson, Arizona, *Arizona Daily Star*, September 22, 1958.

[16] August 21, 1934. Smith, born April 7, 1869, at Tucson, was a grandson of William S. Oury, prominent southern Arizona pioneer and one of the instigators of the Camp Grant Massacre in 1871. Smith enlisted in the Montana National Guard about 1890, was commissioned in 1892, and served in various cavalry regiments, among them the Sixth, Second, Fourth, Fourteenth, and Tenth. He was retired a full Colonel and died at Riverside, California, on January 10, 1936. Information from Smith's son, Cornelius C. Smith of Riverside, California.

and a chief of scouts was one of those men in a position of nominal authority only, over other civilian scouts, for the purpose of aiding the Quartermaster . . . to carry on such work as scouts were supposed to do, principally to carry out the orders of the officer in command. The scout gave no instructions, no orders, no advice, or in any way assumed any authority. He was taken along with the troops rather for his knowledge of the country than for anything else. But as to exercising command of any kind, never—that was an officer's job. . . . I would like to see any officer commanding Indian scouts . . . put up with a civilian scout administering discipline or punishment to one of his men—"it simply is not done," or was not done.

All of which is reminiscent of an observation attributed to Woodrow Wilson: "You may know all about the Constitution and the decisions of the high courts, but unless you know how a county Sheriff operates you don't know much about jurisprudence."

Colonel Smith saw a little service at the very end of the Indian wars and won a Medal of Honor at White River, South Dakota, on January 1, 1891, while an enlisted man. He subsequently served a full career in cavalry regiments and obviously knew the regulations and how they were applied after the skirmishing, patrolling, and fighting of Indians was all over. But unless he had spent several years hunting wild Indians far beyond the limits of the few and feeble military posts of the nineteenth-century frontier, he didn't know much about how such campaigning was done—and it was not often done according to the book.

There is abundant official support for the thesis that chiefs of scouts, or guides, as they sometimes were called, did in fact command Indian scouts, led them into battle, took prisoners, disciplined their men, punished and even executed them when necessary, and often were sent by ranking commanders to lead green officers around by the nose until they were blooded, until the youngsters learned their trade. The United States government's *Chronological List of Actions, &c., with Indians, from January 1, 1866, to January, 1891* notes many actions in which the commander was a civilian guide or chief of scouts. On page 40 is this entry: "1876, Sept. 18; 'Caves' (east of Verde), Ariz.; Indian Scouts, det., B; Commanding officer: Guide Al

Seiber; Indians killed: 5; Captured: 13." Officers' reports indicate that such chiefs of scouts as Sieber, McIntosh, Stanley, and O'Leary were far from the simple "laborers" Colonel Smith believes them to have been. To suggest that these men gave "no advice" is sheerest nonsense. Often the success of entire expeditions depended solely on the advice and suggestions of some veteran scout, and the wise commander invariably sought it out and encouraged it and listened to it. Those who didn't were apt to end up like Lieutenant King, Lieutenant Cushing—or Custer. As far as regulations were concerned, Colonel Smith was correct, but with respect to what actually went on in border campaigns, he was not.

If Apache scouts were necessary for the successful termination of Indian hostilities in Apachería, and Crook proved that they were, then the key figures in that triumph were the men who managed, led, and inspired those scouts. They were not usually the officers nominally in command, but the chiefs of scouts, who actually were in command.

In the spring of 1875, Colonel August V. Kautz[17] succeeded General Crook in command of the Department of Arizona. Although an able, even brilliant, officer, he soon became mired in the territorial political swamps as well as embroiled in an acrimonious and futile exchange of charges and countercharges, much of it aired in the public press, with contentious John P. Clum. Partly as a result of this, both

[17] Kautz, who was born January 5, 1828, at Ispringen, Baden Duchy, Germany, and came to the United States in July of that same year, was more of a student than most army officers: methodical, industrious, energetic—and a great writer of letters to newspaper editors. He had settled in Brown County, Ohio, had served in the Mexican War, and was later graduated from West Point, whereupon he was assigned to Vancouver Barracks, Washington. During his service in the Northwest he made the first recorded ascent of Mount Rainier, where a glacier is named for him, and was wounded twice in Indian skirmishing. His Civil War record was brilliant. While in command of a cavalry brigade he was instrumental in the capture of Confederate raider John Hunt Morgan. Kautz eventually commanded a cavalry division with the Army of the James and for gallantry was successively brevetted up to major general, both of Volunteers and in the Regular Army. He was a member of the military commission that tried Lincoln's assassination conspirators. After the war he was sent back to the frontier, where he had some Apache experience in New Mexico before being assigned as commander of the Department of Arizona on March 22, 1875. He was relieved March 5, 1878, and died at Seattle on September 4, 1895. Cullum; *Dictionary of American Biography.*

were to give up their jobs. But that was on a level far removed from the Indian fighters and therefore of little concern to Sieber. He got on well with Kautz, as he had with Crook; his war was within his own sight and smell and hearing, not in newspaper columns or federal mail pouches.

In the summer of 1875, Captain G. M. Brayton and Sieber scouted up East Fork and on July 1 interrupted a rancheria feast whose main dish consisted of the flesh of mules stolen from the settlements. The diners didn't get to digest their meal: twenty-five of them were killed and nine captured. The command celebrated the Fourth of July by striking another rancheria, this one at the head of Red Rock Canyon, where five more were killed and six captured from a party which had fired on some prospectors not long before. Brayton and Sieber stopped in at the *Miner* office after the scout, "looking none the worse for the campaign."[18]

So much killing seems brutal—and it was. But there were reasons for it, and not entirely fatuous ones, either. The Tonto Basin was vast, several thousand square miles, and almost completely unsettled by whites, yet the Indians who dwelt within its borders could not, or would not, remain there. They depredated regularly and persistently in all directions. As long as they lived remote from the whites and lived in the old ways, which were not bad ways, all went well, but this they would not do. Collisions were frequent and painful. Many alternatives were tried, but the only one that seemed to offer a lasting solution was the reservation system.

The task of the military was to drive the Indians onto reservations or talk them in. Those who acceded were not further molested. They were rationed, after a fashion, and assisted, at least in some cases, in raising their own food to supplement their rations. For those who found it too distasteful to give up the old ways, there was provision for passes and the issuance of arms and ammunition so that they could go hunting far from the reservation—for limited periods of time, of course.

From the beginning of the system until even the 1880s, or possibly

18 *Arizona Miner*, July 9 and 16, 1875.

after that, there were small bands which had never come in. They continued to live in one or another of the hidden canyons of the wilderness. As long as they lived far removed from the whites and followed their traditional ways, all went well. But when, as was inevitable, they could no longer resist the lure of economic betterment and therefore committed depredations, they had to be sought out and destroyed.

Such groups traded buckskin and jerked venison to the Moquis for arms, and once they had them, the young men could not withstand the sporting urge to tackle some lone white man or perhaps a small party. Invariably, punishment fell on the whole band. And if these reasons were not sufficient, there were always some itinerant whites wandering about Tonto Basin. They were filled with tales of real or imaginary atrocities. They were imbued with the frontier adage that the best Indian was a dead one, and they were scared half to death of any Indian. It was a fortunate warrior who had an opportunity to show his pass, if he had one, to such a white before the latter started shooting. If, as sometimes happened, the whites killed an Indian and the Indians, either in retaliation or in self-defense, killed a white, the same inexorable punishment was meted out to them as if they had begun the imbroglio themselves.

Always, or almost always, the kills were large and complete and done with no loss to the attackers. This should not be construed as meaning that the hunters were in no danger; they were in almost incredible peril day and night, but their formula of a night approach and dawn attack was all but invincible. Never did the Tonto Basin hostiles learn to put out a guard, and this failing cost them hundreds of lives. The reason was due less to lack of foresight or intelligence than to the organization of their society, which left no room for authority of any real meaning. No one could organize and enforce a guard system. Discipline was the one fighting quality they lacked, and because they lacked it, they died—and they lost their war.

For the rest of the summer and early autumn there wasn't much doing, but in November, Brayton, now commander at Camp Verde, went with Sieber to San Carlos, where they mustered out the current scouts, whose enlistment had expired, and signed on a new company.

On the return trip they detoured by way of Stoneman's Lake, seeking some renegades who had fired on mail rider Ben Baker the week before, wounded him, and killed his horse. They found no one.[19]

Christmas and New Year's passed with the usual garrison frolics, but Al missed out on them. Indians had stolen valuable oxen from George Hance, brother of John Hance, the picturesque guide and teller of tall tales who figured prominently in the early development of Grand Canyon National Park.[20] Hance's oxen had been driven east, and their trail was easy for the Tontos to follow: across the Verde, across Tonto Creek, and still farther east—to within twenty miles of Fort Apache. On his return, Sieber reported that the raiders were undoubtedly White Mountain Apaches who didn't want to move to San Carlos but were having tough going on skimpy rations. The scouts found the spot where the thieves had killed all of the cattle, taking only the hides and enough meat from one animal to last them home.

The only real adventure of the trip came on the way back when Al's scouts descended like fury on a rancheria, scaring the lights out of three innocent prospectors whom they took to be hostiles. No one was hurt.[21] It was therefore a rough, monotonous, wearying trip, and Sieber no doubt would much rather have gone hunting with Dan O'Leary, Charley Spencer, Tom Barbum, and Hank Herbert in the Bill Williams Mountain country. They were out three weeks or so and returned with one bear, five deer, and two or three dozen turkeys, and if Al had been along, the bag might easily have been doubled. On his return, however, Al dropped in at the Johnson and Maxwell ranch, three and one-half miles east of Verde, where "the light fantastic toe was indulged in" as "the youth and gaiety of the neighborhood gyrated to the sweet music made by the Camp Verde string band." The excuse for the party was dedication of the ranchers' new home and, the *Miner* reported, "Camp Verde was represented by . . . Al Seiber."[22]

It was the season for dancing, all right. The best one of the winter

19 *Ibid.*, November 5, 1875.

20 John Hance was a friend of Sieber during his Prescott days. For an entertaining biographical article on Hance, see Lockwood, *More Arizona Characters*, 41–52.

21 *Arizona Miner*, January 7, 1876.

22 *Ibid.*

was held a month later when even Tom Butler, as tall as an aspen and about as fat, came down from Prescott to attend. He wrote of it:

> The grand ball of the season took place . . . at the residence of Joseph Melvin, three miles south of the post. As a matter of course it was well attended by the youth and beauty of the valley, and excellent music was furnished by two of Verde's most accomplished musicians. At 11:30 dancing was temporarily suspended and the company repaired to a dining room where a splendid collation was spread. It is but justice to Mrs. Melvin and her assistant, Miss Roberts, to say that the repast was all the most fastidious epicurian could wish.
>
> Soon after, dancing was resumed and Mr. Seiber, the efficient floormanager, announced a Virginia Reel; the music commenced, and for a short time all went merry until the partner of the best looking young lady in the room, not being accustomed to *reel*, came to the conclusion that dancing a Virginia Reel was not his forte, being a little too complicated for his shallow brain, therefore gave it up. The company dispersed at an early hour, all apparently well pleased.[23]

Things remained quiet in Apachería during most of 1876, but in August a prospector, Thomas Hammond, was killed somewhere on Tonto Creek by renegades who had presumably slipped away from San Carlos. Captain Charles Porter[24] of the Eighth Infantry, no doubt with Sieber in charge of his scouts, attacked them inconclusively on the fifteenth, having an enlisted man wounded but killing seven

[23] *Ibid.*, February 11, 1876.

[24] Dublin-born Porter and Sieber made many scouts together and shared many an adventure, but, unfortunately, the logs of some of the most interesting of these have disappeared from National Archives files. Apparently the two men were good friends, for among Al's effects at his death was an autographed picture of Porter which he had saved for thirty years. Porter, a literate man of an inquiring turn of mind, enlisted in the Fifth Infantry in 1858 and became quartermaster sergeant for the regiment. In late 1863 he was commissioned, transferred to the Eighth Infantry in 1870, and became a captain by the time it reached Arizona, where he earned a brevet rank of major for gallantry in several engagements. He was sent to Idaho for the Bannock War. He attained the rank of lieutenant colonel by 1898, but retired late that year and died October 15, 1902. Heitman. Porter was handsome and, according to Martha Summerhayes, "charmingly witty." Apparently, he was also quite persistent, since it took him seven years of devoted effort to win the hand of "the beautiful and graceful Caroline Wilkins, the belle of the regiment," but, happily, he succeeded. Martha Summerhayes, *Vanished Arizona*, 15, 28–29, 262.

hostiles and capturing as many more. Al was sent back with his Tontos to find and re-engage those who had escaped. He left Verde on September 15 with Company B, Indian Scouts, and of course, found his quarry. Three days out he struck them at The Caves somewhere east of Verde, killed five, and captured thirteen, bringing the prisoners back to the post on September 22. Sieber and Joe Marr, by way of celebration, rode into Prescott and "from all accounts made things lively,"[25] but were back at Verde in time to leave with Porter on a two-week scout the last day of the month. Again they were successful, finally running down the last of the band responsible for killing Hammond, shooting eight warriors at the head of Tonto Creek, and capturing a couple of women.

It was midautumn now, and it was necessary once more to take the scouts whose enlistment was up to San Carlos and enroll a fresh batch. Sieber brought back his new crowd by way of Fort Apache, there picking up a horse thief named Janes who had escaped from the Prescott jail and returning him to his "old quarters." There was no risk—no horse thief in his right mind would attempt to escape the company of half a hundred dusky Apache scouts and Al Sieber.[26] The *Miner*, commenting on Sieber on the occasion of his return to Prescott, said the visit "reminds us that Lieut. [William C.] Roundy gives [Al] credit for being the best shot at a deer, of any man in the mountains." As if to demonstrate this, Sieber and Captain Brayton went on a pre-Christmas hunt, returning "with 33 deer, a large number of turkeys and other small game."[27]

Late in December, Martin Sweeney, acting agent at San Carlos during the temporary absence of John Clum, had formally requested the department commander to provide military assistance in running down "three Tonto bucks, accompanied by three women," who had escaped the reservation and were heading for Four Peaks. Sweeney wanted them "pursued and punished," and on the tenth of January, Brayton (who was now a major), Sieber, a medic, nine enlisted

---

[25] *Arizona Miner*, September 29, 1876.
[26] *Ibid.*, December 1, 1876.
[27] *Ibid.*, December 1 and 22, 1876.

men, twenty-one scouts, and Mickey Free as interpreter[28] left Verde, crossed the river, and struck out east by south.

The command spent the first night on Fossil Creek, and next morning, Brayton sent a side party of nine Indians "to scout the country between regular trail and Verde River, with instructions to meet me on Pine Creek at night." Darkness fell, and no scouts. The moon rose, was clouded over, and still no scouts. It was very cold. The upper hills were white with snow that gleamed in the chill night—and then a single scout trotted into camp. He said the Indians had jumped a rancheria but the hostiles had slipped into a cave, where the scouts were holding them by their fire, despite the rain and snow that had begun to fall. Brayton ordered out the remaining scouts that night and at dawn followed with Sieber and two white soldiers, slopping through mud and slush to the hideout.

"I found the cave in a canyon which opens into the east fork about six miles from its mouth and about eighteen miles from my camp," Brayton later reported. "The top of the canyon was a palisade of rock for about six or seven hundred feet down before the ground commenced sloping. About fifteen feet above the top of the slope, in the rock was the cave, with a narrow winding ledge running to its en-

[28] Captured as a boy by Apaches in southern Arizona, Free apparently lived with them for some years. After his liberation, he had put in several hitches with the Indian scouts. He was signed on as an interpreter at San Carlos on December 4, 1874, at a salary of $125 monthly, transferred to Verde on July 1, 1875, discharged November 1, and re-hired, at $100 per month, in May, 1876. From then until 1880 he was apparently on and off the payroll at Verde, San Carlos, or Fort Apache, but on October 27 of that year he was officially hired at San Carlos for a dollar a day as a "spy," which he had been most of the time anyway. The earliest newspaper mention I have found of Mickey Free, by that name, is in the *Arizona Miner* of August 29, 1874: "Private Mickey Free to be sergeant, in Maj. G. M. Randall's Indian scouts." It was taken, no doubt, from orders issued at Whipple. By January, 1877, Mickey had grown to manhood, his beardless face permanently disfigured in combat with a bear in which he had lost an eye, his red hair long and tangled as an Apache's, and probably as thoroughly inhabited, too. No one knew for sure how he had acquired his new name, but the fact that there was an Irish cast to his countenance possibly accounts for his first name, and the fact that he was liberated by the troops may well be the origin of the second. He had probably been freed during an attack by Randall on some hostile camp. Mickey was promptly signed on as a scout and then, because he knew Spanish and may have remembered a little English, became an interpreter. At any rate, from this time forward he was as much a fixture in Apachería as Sieber or Archie.

trance, which was about large enough for two persons to enter at once. ... I found my scouts in front of and about 150 yards from the mouth of the cave." The officer also noted that "about 50 yards in front was a broken ledge of rocks, good cover for the scouts." The ledge was crescent shaped, with the ends about thirty yards from the north and south ends of the cave. Under heavy fire from the cave, the scouts were advanced to the cover of the ledge. Brayton, leaving Sieber in charge, then returned to camp and sent rations back the same night. Now that he had the Indians trapped, they would never get out—if he could prevent it.

Sieber found, to his delight, that the cave Indians were led by old Eskeltsetle himself, the Tonto chief who had perhaps lured more braves from the reservations and onto the warpath than anyone since Delshay. The whites, during a brief cease-fire, offered to save him and all his people, sending them to San Carlos, if they would surrender. The chief thought it over and decided he'd keep on fighting.

This cave was better able to withstand a siege than the Salt River cavern. Its floor sloped downward from the mouth. The hostiles had built a stone rampart along it, leaving loopholes through which to fire. There was a side chamber into which they squeezed their women and children. They had one pistol and four rifles, one of them a Springfield lost by a scout who was wounded with Porter in the Red Rock fight in August, and plenty of ammunition.

All through the second night the scouts held their erring brethren tight in their sanctuary, doing they could not tell what damage. It rained for a while, then snowed for a while, and snowed some more. The snow whitened their hair and lay heavy on their backs and frosted their fingers, but they kept to their posts. By the second morning the snow was nine inches deep on the level, "but the Indian scouts with nothing on but their shirts and drawers never once left the point they had been stationed at." A box of ammunition proving worthless, Brayton sent a packer to the post for more.

Finally, at 3:00 P.M. on January 14, the besieged Indians had had enough. What really decided them was the abrupt death of Eskeltsetle, who, with three of his warriors, was slain by scouts firing more or less blindly at the rampart and into the cave. Eight other Tontos surrendered. "The Indians had a scalp dance that night," a soldier with the party recalled many years later, "and Seiber danced with them."[29] It might have been a dance, but it could scarcely have been a "scalp dance," since the Tontos, like other Apaches, took no scalps. Noting the success of this difficult fight, the *Miner* said hopefully:

> The day for Indians to leave their reservation, commit depredations, reign supreme throughout the land has passed and gone and whenever another party breaks away from their reservation, if they do, we hope Maj. Brayton, Al Seiber and their scouts will get on their trail.[30]

But the campaign was not nearly over yet. With the fresh ammunition had come orders from Kautz to pursue hostiles who had just stolen stock from the Hill ranch in Spring Valley, south of the cave where the last fight was concluded.

On the fifteenth the command marched to the crossing on East Fork, sending a side scout to the right, again to return by nightfall. This patrol found a recently deserted rancheria, overtook its fleeing residents, "who evidently had been waiting to see the result of the cave fight," and in a running fight killed one, but then returned to camp. Next day, Brayton laid over to permit his hungry animals to graze for the first time in two days, and the following dawn found him saddled up and riding over to the Hill ranch. Here he learned that the stolen livestock had been killed and that the renegades' trail was covered with snow, so that it was almost impossible to tell which way they had gone. Brayton and Sieber conferred on the probable direction of flight, and the Major moved, with his pack train, on that course, sending side scouts to the right and left to see what they could find. "Finally Guide Seiber discovered the trail just as we were going into camp," Brayton reported. "I pursued the trail and jumped them on the morning of the 21st on Tonto Creek about 12 miles south of crossing of Apache trail, killing seven and capturing three" and recovering four horses and mules stolen from another ranch the night before and not yet eaten. Three of the animals had been shot with arrows, and one was expected to die.

[29] Notes from the dictated biography of Charles F. Bennett, APHS Files.
[30] *Arizona Miner*, February 5, 1877.

Brayton's command then went into McDowell for rations and grain, remaining three days and leaving on the twenty-eighth. Two days later, some six miles south of North Peak on the western slope of the Mazatzals, he struck the band of Indians his scouts had quit trailing after killing one, and this time they killed half a dozen and captured nine. Scouting both sides of the Verde, Brayton reached the post on February 4 and reported on the eighteen Indians killed and twenty captured and his 360-mile scout. The *Miner* gratefully commented: "To Maj. Brayton, Al. Seiber, his guide, the soldiers of his command and the indian allies that accompanied him, is due the greatest credit, and we believe will be appreciated by all good citizens through the territory."[31]

When he sent a copy of Brayton's report along to higher headquarters (Military Division of the Pacific), Colonel Kautz had some interesting comments to add:

> The scouts from Camp Verde and Camp Apache have almost invariably been successful in overtaking and punishing the renegades.
>
> An investigation of the number of Scouts that have been made in the Territory since I have been in command . . . reveals the fact that one hundred and seven Indians have been killed, and seventy-nine captured. The fact that they are almost invariably killed or captured excites the inquiry why do they leave the Reservation in the face of such dangers, where they are supposed to be provided with plenty to eat, security to life and property, and the opportunity for civilization and improvement?
>
> The popular explanation is that they are badly treated on the reservation, do not get enough to eat, and fly to escape the pangs of hunger. Another explanation is found in their innate savage nature and aversion to restraint.
>
> This last finds strong plausibility in the fact that the scouts employed to hunt them up are their own people, frequently their own tribe and kin, enlisted in the service, who pursue them with the unerring instincts of the bloodhound, and kill them as remorselessly as they ever did the whites, and it is only through the presence of officers and soldiers that women and children are spared.
>
> Is there not ample room for doubt whether such savageness has yet reached that degree of development which will admit in another genera-

[31] *Ibid.*, February 9, 1877.

tion of a material approach to civilization of the white race, and is there any hope that the present generation can be controlled by any other influence than overpowering force, such as the military service alone can furnish?

Other experience indicated that Kautz was overpessimistic, and evidence from many parts of the Indian country where the Indians were first corralled, then assigned to reservations and treated fairly, progressively demonstrated that civilization is largely a matter of training and habit and that a single generation can establish it.[32] But Kautz voiced the opinion of much of the nineteenth-century frontier.

[32] This comment by Kautz, Sweeney's request for a military pursuit, and Brayton's scout report are in Indian Bureau Record File 75, National Archives.

XII.   To See the Wizard

AFTER THE LONG SCOUT with Major Brayton, Al Sieber, as was his custom, picked up some pay and came to Prescott for a few days of such winter sports as the place afforded—mostly in the immediate vicinity of his favorite saloon. While there he learned that Janes, the prisoner he and his Tontos had brought back from Fort Apache after the fugitive's escape from the Prescott jail, had fled its hospitality once more, this time in company with somebody named Hunt. Whether because he resented Janes's flight after he, personally, had turned him in or perhaps simply because it was something to do, Al readily agreed to ride with an Indian tracker and U.S. Marshal W. W. Standefer on the cold trail of the outlaw pair, which led almost due south toward Sonora. It was no use. By late February the trio had returned from the vicinity of Gila Bend, which was as far as they could make out the sign, and Standefer told the *Miner* that the "trail was too 'cold' to afford any hope of his party catching up with the rascals."[1]

A quiet as thick as a heavy snow settled over most of central Arizona. Al spent a relaxing season that lasted well into the following summer. He and Captain Porter came to Prescott in June for a few days, and Al went back to Verde with John Hance.

Life for army personnel at Whipple, never since the early days very strenuous, had by this time settled into a pleasant routine. There was very little to do except indulge in such entertainment as the talents of the men and their wives suggested. In his diary, Colonel Kautz records a procession of days, all pretty much alike, marked by such

[1] *Arizona Miner*, February 23, 1877.

incidents as the arrival of mail; an occasional tour of mining properties, in which most army officers interested themselves, or the assaying of ore samples, which Kautz did as a hobby; garrison duties; dances; the death of an infant or the illness of some adult; letter writing, and so on.[2]

Early in July, Mrs. Kautz began making preparations for an eagerly anticipated trip east—the highest point of the existence of any frontier army wife was the point of departure for a vacation in the East—while the Colonel was making such diary entries as "Mrs. Maj. Smith took carbolic acid today for Squibbs, a mistake that will teach her caution hereafter as she is suffering much pain."[3]

In mid-August, Kautz finally completed his annual report, saw it printed, and on Saturday, August 18, his party left Whipple at 10:00 A.M. by ambulance, the most comfortable conveyance of the times, reaching Verde at 5:30, heavily powdered from the dusty Verde end of the road but "well received" by the officers at the post. It was hot, but Fannie Kautz was too excited about her journey to care for such trifles, and the Colonel took heat as a simple tribulation of soldiering in Arizona.

The wagon with the baggage was sent out early the following morning. The Kautzes, an escort under Lieutenant William Baird,[4] Al Sieber as guide with half a dozen Tonto scouts, Mickey Free as interpreter, and a pack train carrying forage (for the weather had been so dry that grass was poor) got away at 10:00 A.M. The escort included, as a soldier, young Charley Bennett, who, in his brief account of the trip,[5] described the Sieber of that time as "probably the greatest scout in Arizona—he was a fine-looking fellow—the kind of type

---

[2] Kautz's day-by-day diary of these years is in the Library of Congress.

[3] Diary, Sunday, August 5, 1877.

[4] Baird, graduated from West Point in 1875 and assigned to Apache, had been moved to Verde in 1877—just in time for this trip.

[5] This version is based on Judge Bennett's reminiscences in the APHS Files, Kautz's diary, and the *Miner*. This is the first indication I've seen that Sieber had been as far east as Fort Wingate; he would scarcely have been taken along as guide, however, if he had not. Judge Bennett suggests that other women besides Mrs. Kautz and her children went: "General Kautz . . . decided to let all the ladies who wanted to, go east. The only way to get them out of this territory was to send an escort—and we were ordered to go with them."

Fremont was. Al was a big fellow—one of those good-natured men."

At any rate the party camped that night at Beaverhead, on Dry Beaver Creek at the foot of the Mogollon Rim, the troop escort efficiently raising white wall tents for the ladies and, since it was clear and hot, rolling up in their own blankets at a suitable distance from the cheery fires. Sieber and his scouts slipped off into the dark to bivouac by themselves.

On August 20 the group had to negotiate the steep and rocky road to the plateau, and Kautz, not trusting his soldier driver where his wife's safety was at stake, took the reins himself. The ascent was made without incident and the group reached Stoneman's Lake at three o'clock, although the baggage wagon didn't get in until after six. Kautz interestedly noted that the lake was an extinct crater and was two hundred feet deep. "We had a romantic camping ground; the scenery is very beautiful."

Many emigrants with their wagons shared the water and campground at Jaycox Tanks. The next night, the party threaded Chavez Pass,[6] where Kautz observed interesting Indian ruins, and reached Rock Station, just east of Sunset Pass, for a cold and windy camp. The cavalcade started at 7:00 A.M. the following day and in a couple of hours made the dozen miles to the Little Colorado, forded it, and continued up its right bank for thirty miles to Barado's Store, where the Colonel and Sieber were glad to run into C. E. Cooley and hear the latest news from Fort Apache.

Again leaving at seven o'clock, the Kautz party made an easy march of some eighteen miles to Carrizo Creek on the twenty-fourth and could have gone on, no doubt, but Kautz wanted to spend the afternoon hunting more of the interesting fossils and pieces of petrified wood he found scattered about. He noted casually that a deranged German, Karl Stagle, had been murdered there a couple of weeks earlier and was buried by the mail courier. Water was secured by sinking holes in the dry creek bed, but even so, it was "very muddy water."

[6] Sometimes called Jarvis Pass. It was named for Colonel J. Francisco Chávez, who, in 1863, commanded the military escort for the first gubernatorial party to reach Arizona. Barnes, *Place Names*, 88.

Following up the Puerco, Kautz camped the next night at Houcks Tank[7] and the following night two miles into New Mexico and thirty from Fort Wingate. During the day the travelers had passed a number of Navaho villages and cornfields and had camped at a trading post, where the goods of civilization were swapped for Navaho wool, even then a major product of that Apache-type people, who had taken to pastoral pursuits like ducks to water.

On the final day the party reached Wingate at noon, but before arriving met a small command en route to Fort Defiance[8] to inspect Navaho goods and from them learned that Kautz's letter to the commander at Wingate, announcing his arrival, had not yet reached the fort. Nevertheless, the Kautzes and their party were warmly welcomed and given the utmost hospitality of the place. A dance, or "hop," as the Colonel invariably refers to them, was given and he met most of the people at the post, including a trader's clerk "who is from Prescott. He was Parker there, here he is Mr. Dudley."

Kautz sent his wife on to Santa Fe and the East on August 29[9] and, with his escort and pack train, Sieber and scouts, headed toward Fort Defiance, where he learned much about the Moquis, Zuñis, and Canyon de Chelly—enough to intrigue the Colonel, whose curiosity was ever easy to arouse—and he determined to return to Prescott by that little-known route.

The party was delayed on the first morning, seeking a guide at least as far as Canyon de Chelly, approximately in the center of the then small Navaho Reservation.[10] At last a start was made without a guide. "As we started up there," Charley Bennett remembered, "we came to a creek, and there was an Indian watering his sheep. So Sieber hired him for a guide. He was a Navaho." The Apaches, who had little but

---

[7] The Smith map of 1879 shows it as "Hauks." It was named for a sheepman, James D. Houck, who committed suicide in 1921. Barnes, *Place Names*, 213.

[8] Fort Defiance, established in 1851, was abandoned by the military ten years later, but had earned the distinction of being the first military establishment in Arizona, as it later became the first post office. Ray Brandes, *Frontier Military Posts of Arizona*, 29–32.

[9] "Mrs. Kautz and the little Kautzes all returned to Headquarters yesterday evening, after an absence of some months, at the East." *Arizona Miner*, January 11, 1878.

[10] It then occupied a rectangular patch, thirty miles east and west and fifty-five miles north and south, in the extreme northeastern corner of Arizona.

contempt for their sheep-herding cousins, couldn't resist exploiting this fellow, who no doubt felt uneasy among the rough and tumble scouts. First they forced him into a foot race (for stakes, of course) and soundly beat him. Then, when he protested, they offered him a monte game, "to get even," and all but stripped him. Having nothing left but his knowledge of the country, he led the way toward Canyon de Chelly.

The group traveled "in a north of west direction and camped in a pretty little valley, where there was plenty of wood, water & grass," Kautz wrote in his diary. "For an hour or two the road was over a broken country covered with pinion and cedar. We then entered upon a high mesa covered with pine. From this mesa we had a fine view to the northeast. I spent the hour after dinner examining the vicinity of camp. It is all a red sandstone formation."

Setting out very early on September 1, the party continued northward, the trail cutting across valleys and canyons, and about 11:00 A.M. came out on a mesa yielding an extended view of a broad valley leading to the north as far as they could see. They rode on to it and continued until about 3:00 P.M., when camp was made by a "pond of dirty-looking water," where, fortunately, they watered themselves and their stock before the Indians arrived. Suddenly it seemed that Navahos were everywhere. Kautz later told the *Miner* that at this camp he saw "two or three thousand sheep and goats and several hundred head of horses driven to [the] waterhole,"[11] churning mud and water into an unpalatable soup of gritty brown. The group had hoped to reach Canyon de Chelly that evening, but did not, and "began to lose faith in our guide."

Within two miles the next morning, "we entered the mouth of a canyon whose walls of red sandstone rose rapidly to five or six hundred feet three or four miles up where we put the train in camp and Sieber & Baird accompanied me for about two hours up the canyon where it became quite narrow and the walls more than a thousand feet." They were in the Canyon de Chelly. "We returned to camp and after dinner I walked up a canyon coming in from the north opposite our camp several miles," wrote Kautz. "It was near sundown when

11 *Arizona Miner*, September 14, 1877. This issue contains a summary of his trip.

I returned quite tired." He found Canyon de Chelly well populated with Indians having large cornfields, peach orchards, flocks of sheep and goats, and herds of horses. Everywhere the Indians seemed to be "thrifty and industrious."

Although it was late summer, it grew very chill in the evenings and when the sky clouded over. The Navahos warned Kautz that this was the wrong time of year to try to get to Grand Canyon, which he wanted to visit on his return to Prescott, so, hiring a fresh guide, he left the mouth of the canyon on the following day and headed due west, or a little south of west, aiming for the Moqui villages and the San Francisco Mountains.

It had turned very cold, as Bennett, who was with the pack-train escort, remembered it. Kautz, Sieber, and the scouts had gone on ahead and by ten o'clock were well up on the side of a pine-covered mesa. A tent was pitched for the Colonel and a huge fire built—just in time. Bennett tells what happened:

> It turned cold; it sleeted; we got to a rock bank and oh, but it was cold; it rained and then it sleeted; the sleet was an inch or two thick.
>
> When we got to the camping place Seiber and another fellow had a big fire going; we were pretty near froze to death; we had a mule with us which carried about "ten gallons." Seiber saw us coming and bellowed out, "Catch the whisky mule!"

Stiff fingers uncorked the jugs and everyone downed a warming jolt of raw whiskey. The sleet stopped, the sun came out, and things took on a brighter hue. Kautz took the most optimistic view, noting that the storm "supplied us with water," which was one way to look at it. After lunch, he and Baird climbed a small but very high mesa and were rewarded by a magnificent panorama of desert whose natural colors had been washed clean and retouched by the violent tempest, traces of which remained in a turbulent sky of broken white-to-black clouds and growing patches of deepest blue.

Now on a southwesterly course, the party crossed mesas and valleys before camping near Moqui Agency, where, of course, thanks to burros and sheep, grass was almost nonexistent, although there was plenty of wood and a fine spring. By half-past-ten the following morning they had ascended the mesa on which stood the first three of the scattered villages. Kautz naturally examined them but, to his orderly taste, found them "filthy and unprepossessing in the extreme," which left him "no desire" to see others. He did enter the home of a chief in the middle village, however, accepting some boiled corn and baked corn meal, and many Indians visited the whites; some of them, having called at Prescott for rations, were acquainted with the Colonel.

He found the Moquis well to do, with fine looking crops of corn and herds of sheep. They labor under great disadvantages for wood and water. He thinks the Moquis offer a fine field for the humanitarians and missionaries who are so anxious to civilize the Indian. Removed to a more favorable country with their present industry and economy, they would soon become rich. Under present circumstances they have a hard struggle for existence.[12]

September 6 was the toughest day of all. The party started at 6:00 A.M., watered their horses and mules at a walled tank of dirty water at 10:30, and continued on until 9:00 P.M., when, after covering about fifty miles, they reached the Little Colorado after tramping the last twelve or fifteen miles down the sandy bed of Moenkopi Creek. The river was dry, although there was water in holes; Kautz believed that anywhere along its course sufficient water could be brought up to irrigate small farms. It rained during the night, and since the men were too tired to pitch tents, Kautz got his best clothes wet.

Threatening skies kept them in camp until after eight o'clock the next morning. A start was then made, and after wandering about a bit, they struck a wagon road which would lead them south of the San Francisco Mountains, missed a hailstorm which passed to the north, and made camp about six in the evening southeast of O'Leary Peak, a 9,000-foot mountain named for Dan,[13] where they feasted on the meat of an antelope an Indian had killed.

[12] *Ibid.*

[13] The peak was so named at least by 1868, for it appears on a map printed that year to accompany the report of William Jackson Palmer's survey for a railroad along the thirty-fifth parallel. The map is entitled *Map of the Route of the Southern Continental R.R. with Connections from Kansas City, Mo., Ft. Smith, Ark. [and] Shreveport, La., giving a general view of the Recent Survey of the Kansas Pacific Railway Across the Continent, made in 1867–1868 under direction of Gen. Wm. J. Palmer.*

The Colonel didn't want to take time to hunt, but, fortunately, the game came to them. Early the following morning they "saw quite a herd of antelope that got away from us, although Sieber wounded one or two of them. A little while after he killed two." They passed a deserted ranch at Antelope Springs, just east of present-day Flagstaff, and "during the afternoon Sieber shot a turkey out of a flock that covered the road before us." By 4:00 P.M. they had come to springs of good water, which Kautz took to be Snider's Holes, but actually the party was ten miles east of Snider's Holes at a place called Volunteer Valley, or Volunteer Spring. Here the road ran through a broad valley, with timber on either side, quite the prettiest country the men had seen since leaving Prescott.

They camped that night, probably at Bear Spring, and the following day crossed Hell Canyon and reached Banghart's Ranch in Chino Valley by 2:00 P.M. After an excellent lunch, Kautz saddled his horse, and "arrived at my lonely quarters about half past nine," after a round trip of almost one thousand miles in twenty-four days. Lieutenant Baird and Sieber brought in the rest of the party the following morning.

Al didn't have long to enjoy the relaxing pleasures of Prescott. The night before, Kautz had received a telegram from Captain Porter at Camp Verde stating that reports were that the Indians were troublesome in Green Valley, on the head of Tonto Creek. Several horses reportedly were found shot with arrows, three others driven off. Kautz immediately sent Sieber to Verde "with orders to Capt. Porter to have the matter attended to at once, and to recover the horses and punish the thieves if possible."[14] A two-week scout was organized.

The command left Verde on September 16 and camped that night on Fossil Creek at the crossing of the trail to San Carlos and Fort Apache. Porter sent out scouting parties, and these scoured the numerous tributaries of the East Fork, Tonto Creek, Green Valley, and all the way to the Mogollon Rim without finding any recent sign. By the twenty-second, the scouting parties united at Church's Ranch in Pleasant Valley. The only discovery of importance was by Porter's own party: seven of eleven head of cattle which settlers had reported

[14] *Arizona Miner*, September 14, 1877.

stolen by "Indians" but which had merely strayed. The others were recovered later, having been permitted, "through the carelessness or laziness of their owners," to wander off.

In Green Valley, Porter found that the trails, if any, of Indians charged with depredations had been washed out by heavy rains and that "no information of any value could be obtained from the settlers" regarding the direction the alleged Indians had gone. "Excess of caution and deficiency of enterprise," as Porter put it, "had prevented those parties from following the trail for any distance."

Because White Mountain scouts had worked the country to the east, Porter decided to move south toward the Four Peaks and cross the Sierra Anchas between Pleasant Valley and Tonto Creek. The party crossed Spring Creek late on the twenty-third, when "our scouts discovered the trail of a party of Indians, and were forthwith dispatched in pursuit. Just as the command was making camp on the 24th of September in Greenback Valley on Willow Creek, on the western slope of the Sierra Ancha, my Indian scouts came in bringing with them seven Indians—all bucks—whom they had overtaken that morning." The Captain noted that "these Indians had offered no resistance when captured, and had somehow been able to exhibit in time to save their lives what they represented as passes from the Indian Agent at San Carlos. . . . Their passes were examined and found to be all right as regarded time," but the Indians were well beyond the limits prescribed for their proposed hunting trip. "I dismissed these Indians and ordered them back to the reservation, with a gentle admonition that it would not be healthy for them to again go beyond the limits assigned in their passes." Porter added: "It is little short of miraculous how this party escaped extermination at the hands of the scouts, as the latter seldom allow their prey a chance to surrender or time to offer explanations. . . . I would have been justified in treating this party as renegades, but . . . common humanity prevented me from turning them over to the tender mercies of the Indian scouts. They were manifestly badly frightened."

Porter learned from the San Carlos Indians that other hunting parties were in the Four Peaks area. "Dreading to trust to good luck to favor the escape of another hunting party if encountered by my Indian scouts," he sought to avoid that portion of the Mazatzals and turned north, scouting their eastern slopes. He sent out various parties, but none found any recent sign and the command rode up the Verde to the post, having covered about 235 miles, not including side scouts.

Porter hadn't expected the command to accomplish much, partly because of the rains, which had obliterated most of the tracks, and also because he didn't think the reported depredations had much basis in fact. "I knew from experience that great exaggeration almost invariably pervades all reports of Indian operations and conduct when circulated by settlers interested in having a military camp established in their vicinity," he wrote cynically. "The scout was undertaken principally to satisfy public opinion." He couldn't find anyone in Green or Pleasant valleys who had seen or spoken to an Indian, while a settler he ran across in Greenback Valley, twenty-five miles from the nearest neighbor, said he had often seen and conversed with Indian hunting parties and had found them "as well-behaved and inoffensive in every respect as white hunters would be." Observed Porter: "In the light of this testimony the frequent reports from the Tonto Basin that the Indians are 'insolent and disposed to be belligerent' seem mere fabrications." Those depredations actually occurring, he thought, were due mostly to the settlers' permitting their livestock to roam at large over a vast extent of remote country, where they presented an almost irresistible temptation to parties of hungry Apaches out of the reservation on hunting passes. "Until a new order of affairs is somehow instituted, or until the Apache character is regenerated, I see no prospect of a millennium," he concluded.[15]

The command returned to Verde about the first of October, and almost immediately Al went to Prescott and on to California for horses, which he drove back to Prescott, reaching that place again probably early in November. He arrived just in time to meet Dan O'Leary's Walapai scouts, their pockets full of money and their feet

[15] Porter to AAG, Department of Arizona, October 2, 1877, Indian Bureau Record File 75, National Archives; *Arizona Miner*, September 21 and October 5, 1877.

sore from a 5,000-mile scout through southern Arizona. So he sold them "a number of the steeds," and there is no reason to suppose he didn't turn a handsome profit in doing so.[16]

He also met Alex Graydon at Prescott again, Graydon having been blacksmith at Verde and Sieber's drinking companion on many a bout. Over a glass at the saloon they must have laughed about the time they found a drunk and a spare coffin adjacent to each other, loaded the drunk into the coffin and fastened down the lid, then stood it on end against the porch railing of the commanding officer's cottage. Only just in time was it learned that they had made one little mistake: they had stood the unfortunate inebriate on his head, and by the time he was released, he was purple faced and almost dead.[17] Now Graydon was moving to Fort Apache, where he would become the post blacksmith, and that called for another drink. Or two.

A few days in town were plenty, and Sieber soon returned to Verde, where he found things quiet, too.

It was midautumn and the hunting season. As Thanksgiving approached the *Miner* reported that Sieber, "who has no superior and few equals as guide and scout," had gone after turkeys and anything else he could scare up in the breaks under the Mogollon Rim. He returned with a "large number" of the birds and having "succeeded in taming several very wild deer." That the game was having hard sledding with the growing number of hunters was suggested by such newspaper items as: "A wagon load of wild geese and ducks came up from the Verde yesterday, and were purchased by Cheap John, who found no difficulty in retailing them at a good profit."[18]

So passed much of the winter. In February, Sieber made a quick trip to Prescott and then for a month more had little to do. His efficiency as a scout was about to run him out of business, and perhaps that is why he turned his thoughts to politics, for him an unfamiliar field. He scarcely noticed when Kautz was relieved, on March 7, 1878,

16 *Arizona Miner*, November 2, 1877.

17 Mrs. Woody in correspondence with the author. Graydon and Sieber remained close friends for the balance of Alex's life; one of his rare letters is written on the letterhead of Graydon's carriage shop at Globe twenty years after this incident.

18 *Arizona Miner*, January 18, 1878.

by brevet Major General Orlando Bolivar Willcox,[19] who was but little more fortunate than his predecessor in Indian dealings but who, by remaining out of public print, did not arouse the antagonism of territorial powers as had Kautz.

At some time during the following two months, Al decided to run for sheriff, perhaps because of such needling notes in the *Miner* as this, from its Verde correspondent: "Mr. Seiber seems to be the favorite [among several suggested candidates for sheriff of Yavapai County], and if he can be induced to run, will get the hearty support of the Valley." While he was mulling over the notion, Sieber was ordered out with Porter on what appeared to be more or less a routine scout but which turned out to be one of the most demanding ever made in Arizona, not so much because of hostiles as because of the ferocious weather encountered.

The command left Verde on April 2, traveling north up the river for two days and going into camp on a small tributary entering the river from the east. Their initial mission was to locate and destroy a rancheria of Mohaves and Yumas, supposedly under leadership of Mi-ra-ha, whom Porter called a "noted renegade." To locate this camp the command had brought along a captive Mohave, who described the exact location of the rancheria. All possible preparations were made on the evening of the fourth and at dawn the rancheria was attacked by Sieber and the scouts and "captured after a brief engagement in which seven Indians were killed." One of these, badly pitted by smallpox, was believed to be Mi-ra-ha's brother. One of the bodies bore a pass, signed by the San Carlos agent, for a hunt in the

19 Willcox, born April 16, 1823, at Detroit, was a descendant of the earliest Connecticut pioneers. He was graduated from West Point in 1847, joining his artillery regiment in Mexico. He later fought the Seminoles and western Indians but resigned his commission to practice law in Detroit before the Civil War. In that conflict he commanded a brigade at Bull Run, where he was wounded, captured, and held prisoner for a year, but was exchanged in 1862 and made a brigadier general of Volunteers. He served with distinction at Antietam and eventually commanded a division, sometimes a corps. After the war he resumed his law practice at Detroit, but rejoined the army in 1866 with the rank of colonel. He commanded the Department of Arizona from 1878 until September 4, 1882. In 1886 he was made a brigadier general and for a time commanded the important Department of the Missouri. He died at Coburn, Ontario, on May 10, 1907. Cullum; *Dictionary of American Biography.*

Pinals. Willcox, in forwarding Porter's account to the Division of the Pacific, noted how far to the south those mountains were.

Anyway, one grown boy, three women, and three infants were captured; five warriors, who had been out hunting at the time of the raid, escaped, to the country of the Walapais, it was said.[20] The fight took place about a dozen miles west of Bill Williams Mountain near Hell Canyon. The camp, in a dense thicket of cedar and piñon, was almost totally concealed from view, although the Indians had an excellent observation point. Much loot was taken, including Navaho blankets, buckskin, many guns, and much ammunition. After the scouts had helped themselves, the remainder was burned. Burro trails showed where the renegades had been trading buckskin and venison to the Moquis for blankets and ammunition, according to the captured women.

On the morning of the seventh, Porter sent the captives back to Verde and led the rest of his command east across the Mogollon Plateau by the old wagon road, camping near Volunteer Flats the second day. From here he struck out toward the southeast, after having discussed the route with Sieber and hearing the scout's prediction of where the column would strike the Verde–Little Colorado Road. Neither Sieber nor Porter had been over this precise route before, and they found the going very difficult. Often they had to swing out to head steep and impassable canyons sliding in from the Rim, especially Oak Creek Canyon and its tributaries, and just as often they were forced to detour in order to avoid low places which recent rains and melting snows had converted into lakes or untraversable swamps. On the morning of the twelfth, however, the command struck the road between Stoneman's Lake and Pine Springs Mail Station, a dozen miles northeast of the lake, and "within a very short distance of the point where Guide Seiber said he would strike" it.

Porter had brought along two Indians the San Carlos agent had sent him, assuming they would guide him to rancherias purportedly occupied by renegades from the reservation, but he now discovered that they knew of no such outlaws. It was all a mistake, they said.

[20] Porter here probably meant Havasupais, for he says it was to "Hualpais inhabiting the big canyon of the Grand Colorado."

They thought they had been sent out because they were supposed to know the country, but, Porter grumbled, they showed they didn't know it as well as Sieber and "were of no assistance to my command." "In default of accurate information I was thus obliged to scout the country as I proceeded," Porter continued. He left Pine Springs on the thirteenth just as the first flurries of what was to become an incessant snowfall filtered down through the dark-green conifers. The command traveled eastward along the base of the mountains until it reached the vicinity of the main branch of Chevelon Fork three days later.

For all that time the snow had been falling, slightly, though without letup. It melted as fast as it fell, except at night. The country was a quagmire. Many of the mules and horses had lost shoes to the sticky gumbo; all were exhausted by their extreme labor and short rations. Now the snow came faster. On the morning of the sixteenth it began to fall heavily and "before 1 P.M. every vestige of vegetation was covered and by nightfall was buried under eighteen inches of snow. For forty-eight hours the animals were absolutely without any pasturage or food of any character whatsoever, for there were no cottonwoods to furnish them even a temporary sustenance." By now the Captain was convinced that he could proceed no farther with his pack train. Even the scouts' physical endurance, which seemed fathomless, "was unequal to the task of foot scouting in such weather over a country of that description."

On the morning of April 18 the storm broke, the sun came out, and the snow began to disappear swiftly, and, thinking the improvement permanent, Porter stubbornly decided to continue his scout. He hunted up a spot where there was some grazing for the animals and sent out the usual foot patrols to examine the country between Chevelon Fork and Chiloé Creek, his assigned goal. But the weather had lured him into a false complacency. On the morning of the twentieth a storm of unrivaled fierceness swept down out of the north. Neither Sieber nor the Indians could remember such a tempest in Arizona. "Its severity and magnitude were . . . unsurpassed [even] in the memory of several citizen employees who had passed winters among the snows of the Sierra Nevada" in California. The animals were again left without food. By now they were plainly starving. "Something had to be done, and that speedily," Porter wrote.

To have advanced farther would have been insane under the circumstances, for still deeper snows lay ahead. To attempt to cross over to the Little Colorado would have been futile, for muleshoes and rations would still have to be drawn from Verde. There seemed nothing for it to do but retreat, and during a brief lull in the storm the command made its miserable way back to Pine Springs, where Porter luckily secured two hundred pounds of corn, "actually the only food the animals received from the morning of the 20th until the afternoon of the 22nd."

By the twenty-fourth the hunters had descended to the Verde, across from the post, but the river was running so high with flood waters from the melting snow that they had to wait there for twenty-four hours before crossing. One side scout, sent out when Porter thought the storm was over, now returned, having seen Indian sign, but because of the renewed severity of the storm and many flooded streams, it couldn't track down the hostiles.

Porter regretted not reaching his objective, Chiloé Creek, but he had done the best he could, and in passing Porter's report on to department headquarters, the commander at Verde noted that "Capt. Porter has been out during one of the most severe storms ever known in Arizona. For his prompt and energetic execution of orders, indomitable pluck and perseverance, and good judgment displayed, he is deserving of great credit." And, of course, in so complimenting the commander, he was praising the command.[21]

By early May, Sieber had thawed out and made up his mind: he would run for sheriff. He went to Prescott on May 9 and dropped in at the office of the *Arizona Miner*, whose editor now was Charles W. Beach.[22] The new man noted that "Al. Seiber, the scout, guide and best Indian fighter in the Territory," had come to place a political

[21] Porter to Post Adjutant, Camp Verde, April 25, 1878, Indian Bureau Record File 75, National Archives; *Arizona Miner*, April 12 and June 7, 1878.

[22] Beach was born in Connecticut about 1849 and learned the printing trade at Watertown, New York. He went to Santa Fe as a youth and in 1864 came to Arizona, where he first worked as a teamster, then took up printing, publishing, and stock raising. He was slain in 1889 by a personal enemy. Lutrell, *op. cit.*, 76.

advertisement as Independent candidate for sheriff. Also running, either at the time or announced later, were W. C. Dawes of Prescott; Joseph Drew; J. W. Kelsey of Kirkland Valley; Joseph R. Walker, Jr.,[23] of Gillett; and Ed F. Bowers of the Agua Fria country. Sieber's statement read: "I respectfully announce to the voters of Yavapai County, that I am in the field as an Independent Candidate for the office of Sheriff of Yavapai County, at the coming election Nov. 5th, 1878, and if elected, shall perform the duties of the office to the best of my ability. Gentlemen, your support is solicited."[24] Obviously a routine announcement. But Al did no campaigning, or none, at least, that was recorded in the press, depending on his stock ad in the *Miner* to carry the freight—along with his continued effective service as chief of scouts. Late in May he brought to Prescott a dozen or so Tonto scouts, who, the newspaper reported, immediately set about "laying in a supply of cast-off clothing, etc. One martial looking son of the forest presents quite a dandy appearance with his legs encased in a pair of Will Vandevoort's tight lavendar pants." Others visited the *Miner* office, being more interested in a woodcut of an Indian than in the complicated, clanking presses.[25]

Early in July, Sieber again came to Prescott, allowing "his chances are A 1," and on July 12 the *Miner's* Verde correspondent wrote that "the political fever is about 86 in the shade. . . . Al Seiber is the favorite for Sheriff." Then in August the newspaper printed this terse dispatch from Sieber:

> EDITOR MINER:—Withdraw my name from your paper as candidate for Sheriff. I make no compromise with any person, and therefore my withdrawal is in favor of no particular one.
>
> AL. SEIBER.

A friend, not content with that wire, telegraphed Al to reconsider and received this reply:

[23] Joseph Rutherford Walker was a nephew of Joseph Reddeford Walker and a member of the party, led by his uncle, which established the first gold camp along Granite Creek. He was born in Missouri, had been an Indian fighter and miner ever since, and, after a two-year term as sheriff, engaged in stock raising and ran a Prescott butcher business. Bancroft, 612–13n.

[24] *Arizona Miner*, May 10, 1878.

[25] *Ibid.*, May 31, 1878.

It is impossible for me to run any longer. I know right where I stand. I have made no compromise with Dawes, and want nothing to do with the Sheriff's office whatsoever. This is final.

AL. SEIBER.

Dawes, incidentally, also withdrew, and Walker ultimately won.

Why did Sieber act as he did? Whether it was because of the development of some local political situation or for some deeper reason, Al never publicly stated. It is possible, although unlikely, that the question of his citizenship arose at that time,[26] but whatever the cause, Sieber bore no grudge against the winner and served him when called upon, and well, as a reliable deputy.

Sieber's abortive political adventure made no real difference in his life, except perhaps to increase his restlessness. There was simply not enough work for a scout to do these days—at least not in central Arizona.

In the spring of 1879 a few more depredations were reported from the Tonto Basin. George Hance wrote the *Miner* in May from the Ciénaga, about eleven miles west of Verde, that Indians had sacked Henry Sidler's place on the East Fork, driving off his stock, burning everything they could, and shooting at his employees. Then they galloped through a herd of fine horses belonging to the Houston brothers, killing seven of the best mares and a stallion that cost five hundred dollars in Tulare County, California. Al Sieber, on his way to Verde from the east, passed the Indians and eyed them curiously, but he didn't yet know of the trouble so did nothing about them. Isolated ranchers started rounding up their stock, petitioned General Willcox for troops, and also asked for Sieber and his scouts as "the best Indian peace commissioners the Government has ever had in that part of the footstool."[27] Heeding the outcry, Willcox wired Verde and urged the commanding officer to investigate, to pursue the Indians if they, indeed, had committed outrages, and to co-operate with San Carlos scouts, as well as to probe the advisability of establishing a temporary station somewhere in that area. "If necessary you are authorized to employ Sieber as guide," said the telegram, "who may be able to

26 For a discussion of Sieber's naturalization and citizenship problems, see chap. XXI.
27 *Arizona Miner*, May 23, 1879.

utilize any friendly Indians on the reservation." This was because Al was now following other pursuits. A scout, however, found little to indicate which Indians committed the deviltry, although it was assumed that they were from San Carlos.

Only a few days later two riders were ambushed about three miles from Baker Springs, at the foot of Baker Butte on the Fort Apache Road east of Verde, and one of them was killed. A scout from Verde struck the hostile rancheria within two weeks, killed six warriors, and captured a woman. But this was of no direct concern to Al, since he had quit (he thought for good) on April 17, 1879. He was succeeded by P. M. Keogh, a man competent enough, but no Sieber.

Al now was one of the elder statesmen among the scouts, whose principal occupation, it seemed, was to add color to the local scene. They often dropped into Prescott or the other towns—Dan O'Leary, Charley Spencer, Archie McIntosh, Sieber.[28] Some had passed on. Tom Roddick died at the age of forty-two at Tucson,[29] and King Woolsey died at forty-seven on June 29, 1879, leaving an estate of $37,403.80 and debts of about two-thirds of that amount.[30] Dan Lount died of disease and old age in August.[31]

Even the editor of the *Miner* became reminiscent, noting the vast change from the time a scant decade earlier when "no one ever thought of venturing 500 yards outside of any town without carrying a regular arsenal . . . and generally parties of not less than three to ten men ventured on any expedition, even if it were ever so trifling. Now we have no Indian wars, our people travel with as much safety as if they were on the streets of New York, Chicago or any other large city, and fire arms have been replaced by the shovel and pick with which many are now producing the precious metal."[32] Not quite *all* of the frontier flavor had left, however, as the editor observed in a learned discourse on a common oath which had recently led to a San Francisco shooting but which, in Arizona, was regarded as a "term

[28] For samples of respective newspaper items about them, see the *Arizona Miner* for July 4 and 18 and August 1 and 22, 1879.

[29] *Arizona Miner*, June 13, 1879.

[30] *Ibid.*, September 19, 1879.

[31] *Ibid.*, August 22, 1879.

[32] *Ibid.*, June 27, 1879.

of endearment," or, if uttered with serious intent, might lead to nothing more violent than a street fight.[33]

Among those who had swapped the rifle for the pick was Al Sieber. "Capt. Al. Seiber, the valiant scout, who has led the enlisted Apache warriors in a hundred campaigns against the bad Indians of their tribe [has] cast aside his armor, thrown down the sword and retired to the peaceful pursuit of mining in the Tonto Basin," noted the *Miner*.[34]

During his countless expeditions, Al had always kept a weather eye out for likely ore-bearing ledges, and once or twice he came within an eyelash of discovering deposits worth millions. "Once, when the Tontos came as usual to the 'Place of the Bitter Water,' a white man came with them—Al Sieber," writes a historian of central Arizona about the discovery of the fabulously rich United Verde copper deposits at the present-day site of Jerome.

> Far below the present mine, the little stream passed over a ledge of lime rock, and had built up through uncounted years a rich deposit of copper. To this Sieber came again with George B. Kell and made a location, calling it the Copper Queen; and here, long after, a quantity of the rich ore was taken out.
>
> Sieber and Kell and George W. Hull were probably the first prospectors to follow the little thread of colored water up to the cliff-rimmed peak, though as early as 1858, renegade Mexicans . . . brought word to Charles D. Poston . . . of rich gold and silver and copper in the hills along the headwaters of the Verde River.[35]

It was probably in 1874 that Sieber made his Copper Queen find, but he evidently did little about it. He had been a member of the Miner expedition, which, while it discovered no riches, passed right

---

[33] *Ibid.*, September 12, 1879.

[34] August 22, 1879.

[35] Sharlot Hall, "The Making of a Great Mine," *Out West*, Vol. XXV, No. 1 (July, 1906), 3–26. According to Edward Hadduck Peplow, *History of Arizona*, II, 224, the first claims on the actual United Verde ore body were located February 17, 1876, by John O'Daugherty, John P. Kelly, and Josiah Riley. The site had probably been worked lightly even in Spanish days, perhaps by Antonio de Espejo in 1583 and other adventurers later. See Jack D. Forbes, *Apache, Navaho, and Spaniard*, 60–61, 86–87, 93, and 104.

over or close to future finds of importance. During his early army scouting days he had no doubt visited the spot where later arose the camp, then town, called Globe,[36] which he was to make his headquarters for the last twenty years of his life. The first claims at the site were made in 1873, but little work was done for three years, and Globe as a permanent settlement dates from 1876. The first house, of adobe, also became the first store, where the merchant sold potatoes at a dollar each and gave a bottle of whiskey with each purchase of two of them. Located originally as a silver camp, Globe's great wealth came from copper. By 1929 its mines had produced upwards of $10,000,000 in gold and silver, but more than $360,000,000 in copper.[37]

About the most important establishment in Globe, from Sieber's viewpoint, was the Champion Billiard Hall and Saloon, run by Bill McNelly[38] and Felix B. Knox. The latter was to meet his fate at the hands of Apaches within a few years, but McNelly and Sieber became the closest of friends and remained such as long as Al lived. Both McNelly and Knox had served in the Eighth Cavalry, the latter, because he was small, becoming drummer boy in the regimental corps.

Bill McNelly was physically the opposite of Knox. He was tall, straight as a ramrod, slender, with dark-red, almost black, hair, a red mustache, and a quiet voice that belied his service as a cavalry sergeant. He was handsome and one of the most popular men in Globe.

McNelly and Knox ran a clean place. It was on the corner of Broadway and Push streets. It had no batwing doors, no dancing girls, but it did have poker tables in front and in the wine room in back. It

---

[36] To this day no one knows where the name "Globe" came from, although the city was evidently called that after the Globe and the Globe Ledge mining claims; no one knows how those names originated, either. My information on Globe comes from Mrs. Woody, pre-eminent historian of the Globe-Miami area, and from the May 8, 1958, *Arizona Silver Belt*, an eightieth-anniversary edition of this important newspaper, rich in historical lore, some of whose articles Mrs. Woody wrote.

[37] Barnes, *Place Names*, 180–81.

[38] William T. McNelly was born at Avalon, Maryland, on April 3, 1849, enlisted in the Eighth Cavalry at Chicago, probably in 1870, and was mustered out as a sergeant at Fort Bayard, New Mexico, in July, 1875. He arrved at Globe in 1876, thereby becoming one of its first settlers, and opened the Champion soon afterward. He was "much too generous," always willing to help those in need. He died February 2, 1938, and is buried at Globe. Information from Mrs. Ben McNelly, Bill's daughter-in-law.

advertised "the finest wines, liquors, cigars, to be found in the Territory" plus a billiard table (first class) and the latest periodicals "for the accommodation of customers and the public generally." Occasionally a dance would be held, and with it a problem often arose over what women to invite. "We had a town drunk, an educated Frenchman everyone called Muldoon, who used to hang around McNelly's," Bob Riell recalls. "Once we decided to throw a respectable dance and the problem came up. For weeks the argument went on, whether to invite this one or that, and whether such a one would be insulted if we invited so and so. Finally the deadline approached and someone warned that we had better complete the list or we wouldn't have any dance at all. Muldoon, asleep in a corner, stirred and said, 'Gentlemen, I believe I have a solution to your problem.' 'What is it, Muldoon?' asked Al Sieber. 'Settle the issue along financial lines,' said Muldoon. 'Confine your list to those ladies who charge $5 or over.' "[39]

Sieber's alleged part in the naming of Tombstone is an oft-told though dubious story.[40] He had scouted with Ed Peck, whose Peck mine, one of the greatest in early Arizona chronicles, was discovered while Ed was hunting Indians. It soon earned more than one million dollars, but Peck lost it all through litigation and died broke. The glimmer of that possible wealth must have quickened Sieber's breathing, although money never interested him much except to use for his Spartan necessities: a good horse, a little whiskey, a poker stake, and decent food, with no frills. If he had found the richest mine in the world, he probably would have continued to live just as simply—and well—as he did now.

At this point, however, mining seemed the thing to do. Anyway, it beat farming. Over in the Tonto Basin he had seen a little rock that looked good, so he staked a couple of claims[41] and set about the labori-

---

39 Information from Bob Riell of Globe.

40 See, for instance, Walter Noble Burns, *Tombstone: An Iliad of the Southwest*, 1–3. According to this widely accepted version, the impetus to naming the place was given in 1877, and Burns says it came from the chief of the Walapai scouts recruited and sent to the Huachucas. If he is right about that, the scout in question would have been Dan O'Leary, not Sieber. Frank Waters, *The Earp Brothers of Tombstone*, 82, says, in fact, that it *was* O'Leary, but does not give his source.

41 He had half a dozen when he died, only a few of which were worth anything.

ous task of sinking shafts and running laterals. He named his best prospect "Last Chance," although it was anything but that, and from it, late in November, brought into Prescott ore worth three hundred dollars a ton.[42] A later report said that Sieber's works would pay five dollars per day per man, and by that time he had sunk his shaft 84 feet and run a crosscut, reporting 8 feet of solid vein matter. He had also stripped the surface from his claim for the whole 1,500 feet, with "splendid" shows of ore.[43] His work was slowed on occasion when some of his old scouts from San Carlos came up on pass to see him, but he put them to work hunting, and venison and antelope were always plentiful at his camp.

There is evidence that Sieber was hired, at least temporarily, as a guide by the army late that year, but generally he stubbornly continued trying to convince himself that he had become a miner.[44] Even Al would have to admit that there was not much adventure to it, but such could be had in other ways, by men looking for it, and he wasn't averse to a little excitement now and then.

Sometime in the fall he was deputized briefly by Sheriff Walker following a stage holdup near Prescott. Two of the robbers, named Williams and Frank, were believed holed up on a ranch that was "admirably located for making good their escape." Walker, Sieber, City Marshal James M. Dodson, and a man named Thomas Simmons "induced" the pair to come to a neighboring ranch, where the lawmen lay in ambush. As the outlaws neared the house, they were jumped and ordered to throw up their hands. Williams did so, but Frank went for his gun and was shot dead by Dodson. Williams later confessed that the pair intended to rob a bank at Prescott and another at Phoenix.[45]

Not long after this a stage was robbed near Gillett by three Mexicans. Billy Thomas, erstwhile foreman at the Tip-Top mine, was shot and killed. Among several who took up the chase was Sieber, who left Prescott with the famous Bob Paul, a Wells Fargo & Company

[42] *Arizona Miner*, November 21, 1879.

[43] *Ibid.*, April 13 and 22, 1880.

[44] Cruse to Lockwood, January 6, 1934, Lockwood APHS, says Sieber went to San Carlos from McDowell as a scout in late 1879, as will be shown.

[45] *Arizona Silver Belt*, December 6, 1879.

special detective and one of the Southwest's most successful man hunters. Johnny Behan and a party came from Gillett and still another group from Phoenix. "If these *caballeros* from Sonora get away without being killed or captured it will be a miracle and really too bad," said the *Miner*.[46]

Sieber took the trail and reported that the tracks led southeast, crossed the Verde six miles above McDowell, continued on course, and struck the Salt ten or twelve miles above the Verde. Here the bandits had entered an Indian camp and all tracks were lost, save those of four horses heading for Sonora. Soon they had been washed out by a storm. And that might have been the end of it, with ordinary man hunters, but Bob Paul never gave up.

One Sunday morning in February, 1880, Paul brought to Prescott one Demetrio Domínguez, who admitted being one of the bandits. Paul had heard that Domínguez was at Maricopa, then had gone to Tucson, whence he had left with David F. Harshaw, an Indian fighter and mining figure who was en route to Patagonia, a mining district in the southern part of the Territory. Paul hurriedly hitched up his buggy and overtook the pair twenty miles out of Tucson before Domínguez had an opportunity to add the unsuspecting Harshaw to his toll. The Mexican had a watch taken from the slain Thomas.[47] One year to the day after the killing of Thomas, Domínguez was hanged at Phoenix. Although he named his two accomplices in the crime, he died game.[48]

Sieber's mine continued to show promise, but Al was getting restless. He placed some "very fine" ore specimens on exhibit at the popular Black Canyon Stage office at Prescott, where they would be sure to catch the eye of any traveler interested in picking up likely property. The *Miner* reported that Al was putting his mine in shape "for working or sale,"[49] and there wasn't much doubt about which of the two propositions he wanted.

46 *Arizona Miner*, December 5, 1879.

47 From the Tucson *Arizona Star*, reprinted in the *Miner* on February 9, 1880.

48 The Phoenix *Arizona Gazette* printed his confession the day he was hanged, November 27, 1880, and the *Miner* reprinted it on November 29.

49 *Arizona Miner*, December 7, 1880.

On September 1, Cal Jackson, who had come to Arizona back in 1857 with the Butterfield Stagecoach Company, died, an event calling for one of the finest funerals in Prescott's history. Some thirty carriages were in the procession, followed by a straggling line of pioneer prospectors, Indian scouts, and early settlers. Among them, leading his horse, was Al Sieber.[50] With the passing of so many of his friends, Al must have felt less rooted to Prescott, which was getting to be too civilized, anyway. Over across the line in New Mexico, and Old Mexico, too, there had been much doing recently; probably there would be more.

At some point Sieber's wild streak got the better of him; he saddled up and headed out of town. Toward the southeast. Toward San Carlos, where the Apaches were restless enough to give a man thought— and action. He was riding into a new kind of war, quite unlike anything he had fought until now, with a new kind of Apache as opponent. And he rode toward it with a lift in his heart. He was through with mining; he was through with drudgery. He was off to see the wizard.

[50] *Ibid.*, September 1 and 2, 1880. Calvin Jackson was born in 1824 or 1825 in Schuyler County, Illinois, and arrived at Lynx Creek in 1863; he may have come to Arizona with King S. Woolsey.

XIII. Victorio

THE WESTERN APACHE CAMPAIGNS fall into two categories. The one, as brought to a climax by Crook in his operations of 1872–74, consisted of innumerable expeditions against almost as many fragmented bands. Sharp, murderous attacks resulted in the destruction, one by one, of family and community groups. It was a laborious, merciless sort of war filled with danger and heroism and pursued until the enemy, in the phrase of the times, had "a belly full" and was willing to come in and starve on the reservations rather than endure further punishment in the mountains. The other sort of Indian campaign grabbed the headlines. It was far more spectacular—and exasperating—and it was led by Apaches who became famous: Geronimo, Victorio, Cochise, and Mangas Coloradas, for theirs were the deeds of which sagas are made.

Greatest of these Apache leaders was Mangas Coloradas, who was killed by soldiers after his capture in 1863. Cochise, an outstanding leader of the Chiricahuas, died at peace in 1874, and it became Victorio's turn to lead the Warm Springs and some Chiricahua Apaches, and he led them to war. By late 1879 he had been led, or driven, or frightened, onto the warpath, and his braves were ravaging southern New Mexico, and sometimes Arizona and Texas, almost at will.

The various references to Sieber during this time are, to a degree, confusing. He said in his statement for James H. McClintock that he had been in government employ continuously from 1871 until 1891 "with the exception of six months." If that six months extended forward from April of 1879, as I assume it does, he would have rejoined the government service in late October or early November.

Lieutenant Tommy Cruse,[1] who was to cut quite a swathe for himself in Apachería, said that he first met Sieber in November of 1879 when he, Cruse, arrived with Captain Adna Romanza Chaffee[2] at San Carlos, where Chaffee was to take over from H. L. Hart as temporary agent, although the army officer had actually replaced the civilian agent the preceding July.[3] As Cruse recalled it, Chaffee found little in order on the corruption-plagued reservation. He and Sieber discovered that the scales used to weigh beef cattle had been doctored so that underweight steers could pass muster. "I accused the contractor's agent with having committed the act," Chaffee wrote. "He of course denied it, when I lost my temper and from all accounts did not comply strictly with the commandment which forbids swearing on all occasions."[4] Cruse, who had arrived at San Carlos that day and met Chaffee for the first time, said that, "finishing his supper, Sieber rushed out and returned in a short time. Chaffee glanced up and in a voice like a rasping file, queried: 'Is the son of a bitch gone yet?' Sieber replied in the negative," although the contractor's agent was leaving the reservation by sundown as ordered.[5] It may well be that Cruse is mistaken in his dates and that Sieber was hired temporarily

[1] Cruse was born at Owensboro, Kentucky, on December 29, 1857, and was graduated from West Point in 1879. He became a brigadier general in 1917, retired the following year, and died June 8, 1943. He was in many Apache fights, always acquitted himself well, and was awarded a Medal of Honor for his exploits in one of them.

[2] Chaffee was one of the outstanding soldiers between the Civil War and World War I. Born at Orwell, Ohio, on April 14, 1842, he enlisted in 1861 in the Sixth Cavalry, where his record was such that he was commissioned in 1863 by direction of the Secretary of War. Chaffee was wounded twice and emerged from the Civil War a first lieutenant. He made captain in 1867, served with distinction with his regiment in the Southern Plains region and went with it to Arizona, and was promoted to major in 1888. He was appointed brigadier general at the outbreak of the war with Spain and promoted to major general of Volunteers, becoming a colonel in the Regular Army. In January, 1904, he was named lieutenant general and Army Chief of Staff, but retired in 1906, dying at Los Angeles on November 1, 1914. "He possessed military abilities beyond anything demanded by the operations in which he commanded." *Dictionary of American Biography*; *Who Was Who*; William Harding Carter, *The Life of Lieutenant General Chaffee* (cited hereafter as Carter, *Chaffee*).

[3] *Arizona Star*, July 6, 1879.

[4] Carter, *Chaffee*, 88.

[5] Lockwood APHS.

to take Chaffee to San Carlos from McDowell in July; the incident could scarcely have occurred as late as November.

Sieber's activities during the latter days of Victorio were mainly peripheral. He was chief of scouts under Lieutenant Augustus P. Blocksom,[6] who commanded Company C of the Apaches, and their operations were along the Arizona–New Mexico border, where they sought to prevent the infiltration of Arizona Territory and to fight what hostiles turned up.

In the spring of 1880, Victorio sent one of his ablest lieutenants, Chief Washington,[7] and fourteen[8] well-armed warriors on a flying raid toward San Carlos Reservation to kill and destroy. Washington encountered some hunters before reaching the agency, and his hand was called. Captain Adam Kramer heard from a sweating runner that "hostiles of Victorio's band" were fighting with "peaceful" Indians about eleven miles from the soldiers' camp on Ash Creek, whereupon he swept up a score of enlisted men and as many scouts and raced to the rescue. The cavalry soon outdistanced the scouts, who were afoot, but, bursting into the fight, "we received a volley from the hostiles compelling us to withdraw to a reasonable distance, where I skirmished with them until the arrival of my scouts, whereupon the enemy broke and ran, gained their animals, and made off at a run."[9] In this action the hostiles killed Sergeant Dan Griffin, "a magnificent specimen of the old-time cavalryman," severely wounded an Indian scout, stole some ponies, but got no ammunition before fleeing south.

Kramer pursued the raiders for nine miles with scouts and his soldier force, reduced now to fourteen men, coming upon the enemy well forted up. "I sent Lieutenant Blocksom with his scouts to make a detour to the enemy's rear," reported the Captain, "when, under the heavy fire of the scouts [presumably led by Sieber], they again

---

6 Ohio-born Blocksom was graduated from West Point and appointed to the Sixth Cavalry, then the Second, and finally the Third, of which he was colonel. He made brigadier general before his retirement on November 1, 1918. Blocksom won a brevet for his action at Ash Creek. *Who Was Who.*

7 Reportedly a son of Victorio.

8 Captain Kramer, who fought this band, estimated it at between "forty and fifty bucks, no women or children, with thirty-five animals." *Arizona Star,* May 9, 1880.

9 Kramer's report was printed in the May 9 issue of the *Star.*

broke and ran off at a very rapid pace. I followed them until nearly dark, they taking an easterly direction for the mountains." He could not follow them in the darkness, and the raiding party got clean away, pillaging, raping, and burning their way back to Victorio's camp, which they reached without losing a man, as far as was known.

Kramer's command, with Blocksom's scouts and the outfit headed by Captain Tullius C. Tupper,[10] put in at Camp Thomas for a rest and to refit, although Sieber's Indians were soon sent out patrolling once more. Al found time to be a witness (August 8, 1880), however, to the wedding of his old friend Bushrod Crawford[11] out on the Tonto, the rite being performed by a justice of the peace named Bland. The ceremony was conducted under a big walnut tree, and Sieber stayed for the party that surely followed—he wouldn't miss *that*—but he couldn't remain long: an offensive operation was being prepared and he was needed in the staging area.

Lieutenant Cruse also was en route to Thomas, focal point of the staging and "the most God-forsaken camp on earth," according to the Lieutenant. He was disgruntled anyway, having been named to succeed Lieutenant Charles B. "Beak" Gatewood[12] as commander of Company A, Indian Scouts, "much to my surprise."[13]

It was not easy to get promising officers to take this sort of post, or to do a good job when they did accept, for not many of them were as fascinated with working with Indians as was, say, Al Sieber. The job

10 Tullius Cicero Tupper was born in Ohio and enlisted in the army during the Civil War, being commissioned in 1862 and reaching the rank of captain in 1867. He retired in 1893 and died September 1, 1898. Heitman.

11 Bush Crawford, a short, stocky man who remained Sieber's friend from 1873 or 1874 until death, was born in Shelbyville, Missouri; his wife, Cordelia Adams, was born at Lampasas, Texas. They lived in the Upper Tonto Basin, just south of Payson, on a horse and mule ranch from 1880 to 1893, when they moved to Globe. Nona was born at Globe in 1881, Oran Sieber Crawford in the Basin, and Emily at Phoenix in 1896. The Crawfords operated several rooming houses and hotels in Globe, and Sieber often stayed at one or another of them.

12 Gatewood, given twenty-four words by Heitman, was a West Pointer from Woodstock, Virginia. Born in 1853, he became a second lieutenant of the Sixth Cavalry on June 15, 1877, and a first lieutenant January 3, 1885. His services to his country during his short lifetime were without parallel, and the nation's neglect of him is also somewhat unique. He died in May, 1896.

13 Cruse to Lockwood, January 6, 1934, Lockwood APHS.

required qualifications not commonly possessed. Cruse was correct in his opinion that it would do little for his career, as his predecessor, Gatewood, could attest. Yet for the right man, the rare man, it could offer big returns in high adventure, a satisfying dip into the wild, wild life now passing so rapidly from the American scene. One finds it difficult to believe that Cruse was too unhappy about his assignment.

At any rate, when Cruse arrived at Thomas, he found the place "celebrating to fare-you-well with champagne and ice from Tucson by special wagon," and at the heart of the celebration was Sieber. The scout was "having the time of his life relaxing and more joyous every minute. Captain [Thomas J.] Jeffords[14] . . . had just sold a mine in Tombstone for something over sixty thousand dollars cash [he had the money with him], and had called in all his old friends to share his joy." When Cruse, a teetotaler, entered the post trader's shack, "I was greeted with cheers as a welcome addition; but came near offending the host and some strangers by turning down all liquids, whereupon the trader, Will Wood, brought me a pound of candy and I nominated Al to drink my share. I was never more puffed up in my life when he told me that Gatewood and the packers had praised my actions in the Victorio fights—and that I *would do*."[15]

Day after day was spent in readying the expedition for the field.

[14] Thomas Jonathan Jeffords was one of the most remarkable men of the Arizona frontier. Born in Chautauqua County, New York, in 1832, he is said by McClintock to have been a Mississippi River pilot, but went west before the Civil War, laying out the road from Leavenworth to Denver in 1858. In the fall of 1859 he arrived at Taos and prospected in the San Juan Mountains the following spring. In 1862, with the Civil War under way, Jeffords carried dispatches from General Edward R. S. Canby at Fort Thorn, situated at the upper end of Mesilla Valley, to General James H. Carleton, whose California Column had reached Tucson. He then guided the Californians back to Thorn. Jeffords is said to have taken part in the Battle of Valverde. After the war he drove a stage for a time over the Butterfield Route, was ambushed by Apaches, and carried to his grave the scars of their arrows. He became superintendent of mails between Fort Bowie and Tucson and in sixteen months suffered the loss of fourteen men killed by Indians, which led him to negotiate his singular one-man peace treaty with Cochise, a pact that was never broken while Cochise lived. Following his Indian service, Jeffords settled at Owls Head Camp, in Pinal County, forty-five miles south of Florence. He died February 19, 1914, and was buried at Tucson. Farish, II, 228–40; McClintock, I, 217; Lockwood, *The Apache Indians*, 110–29.

[15] Cruse to Lockwood, January 6, 1934, Lockwood APHS.

Colonel George Pearson Buell, commanding several companies of the Fifteenth Infantry, part of the Ninth Cavalry, and Indian scouts, was to form a thirty-mile skirmish line and push south from Fort Cummings, New Mexico, advancing until he ran into hostiles or passed Lake Guzmán, about thirty-five miles south of the line. Colonel Eugene Asa Carr[16] had six troops of cavalry, three companies of Indian scouts, and three pack trains and was to move southeastward from Thomas until he contacted Buell. The scouts were ten miles in front of the troops, with Lieutenant Albert L. Mills[17] on the right, Cruse, with Gatewood's old company, in the center, and Blocksom, with Sieber and Company C from McDowell, on the left.

This giant expedition, like others before it, found nothing except deserted campsites. Victorio had skimmed eastward. After four days out, knowing that Victorio was at least a hundred miles beyond them, the soldiers turned back. Their enemy ravaged and plundered almost at will in northern Mexico, and even in New Mexico, until mid-October, when he was trapped and massacred with most of his force by a large body of Mexicans far to the southeast of Thomas in the Tres Castillos Mountains—well beyond the reach of Sieber and the Arizona scouts and soldiers.

The death of Victorio did not mean the end of scouting, or anything approximating it, and Sieber and his Indians were kept busy patrolling not only the reservation but also its environs as far east as western New Mexico.

Nor were Indians the only people to be ambushed. The following summer the veteran Nana, an incredibly tough old warrior whom

16 Carr, born at Concord, New York, on March 20, 1830, was graduated from West Point in 1850 and saw much frontier service before the Civil War. In that conflict he took part in a considerable number of battles and was promoted to major general of Volunteers by war's end. He then returned to the frontier and became what one writer called "perhaps the most famous and experienced Indian fighter of the quarter of a century following the Civil War," fighting against the Cheyennes, the Sioux, and the Apaches. He retired in 1893 a brigadier general and died at Washington on December 2, 1910. *Dictionary of American Biography.*

17 Mills was a West Pointer, graduating in 1879 and later (1898) becoming superintendent of the Military Academy, a post he held six years. He earned a Medal of Honor at Santiago during the war with Spain, made brigadier general in 1904, served on the General Staff, and died September 8, 1916. He was born at New York in 1854.

most people believed to be in his seventies and some in his nineties, led a handful of warriors over more than one thousand miles of enemy— that is, white—territory, sometimes pounding seventy miles or more in a single day. The remnants of Victorio's band, Nana's Apaches swept northward out of the Sierra Madre, crossed the border into eastern New Mexico, and gradually ravaged their way west as virtually all the troops of the New Mexico command looked for them and occasionally, to their sorrow, caught up with them. During the campaign the Apaches foraged on the countryside, fought a dozen skirmishes with the troops, and won most of them. They killed from thirty to fifty Americans and wounded many more, captured two women and not less than two hundred horses and mules, eluded pursuit, and did it with a group that numbered fifteen at the outset and probably never counted more than forty.

It was a grand raid, from the Indian viewpoint, but it was almost all in New Mexico and it didn't involve Sieber and his scouts, at least directly. Nor did the white ambush on Cibecue Creek late in August, a disaster in the making even before the dust settled from Nana's raid.

Cibecue Creek lies northwest of Fort Apache more than a day's travel by pack column. On the creek lived a medicine man named Noch-ay-del-klinne who during the summer of 1881 began to acquire considerable influence over a widening circle of Indians, and because of it, the whites came to the conclusion that he was preaching dissension. A column of seventy-nine soldiers, twenty-three Apache scouts, and several officers, commanded by Colonel Carr, went to Noch-ay-del-klinne's camp and arrested him on August 30. The command was attacked within a few miles of the Indian's camp, and eight men, including a captain, were killed and others wounded. The Apaches followed up the Cibecue attack with a long-range fusillade on Fort Apache, wounding an officer, and ravaged the countryside, killing a number of people. A hard core of recalcitrants then moved up into the Tonto Valley, where they lay low for some time.

The whole Cibecue affair was a mess. The operation was unnecessary to begin with, and badly handled; it was a bloody bit of business that did no credit to the officers and officials involved. It is probable that Al Sieber was not present, although he is placed at the battle by

Tom Horn, who wasn't there either but claimed to have been.[18] Sieber and his scouts were soon on the scene, however, though what effect their operations had is now unknown.

The course of events at Cibecue unnerved a good part of the southwestern frontier and upset those who had believed that with Victorio's death the Apache wars were won. So great was the impact of this relatively minor engagement that troops were sent to San Carlos and other troubled spots from many areas, and they may be directly charged with making matters a great deal worse. John P. Clum asserted that the twenty-two companies of troops rushed to southern Arizona made all of the Apaches edgy and brought terror to the ever suspicious Chiricahuas and Warm Springs Indians gathered at San Carlos.[19] It took very little to cause them to bolt the reservation, and that little occurred late in September.

For the first time in five years troops were actually on the San Carlos Reservation, and they were everywhere. Repeatedly the wary Chiricahuas demanded assurances of Indian Agent J. C. Tiffany that troop movements were not directed at them in retribution for their glorious raids from Mexico in times past. Each time he told them that they were not the subject of the maneuvers. Two White Mountain bands, under Chiefs George and Bonito, were encamped close to the subagency, near Camp Thomas, with the wild Chiricahuas near by. They had surrendered, when ordered to do so, following the Cibecue affair and then had been released on parole. Five days later, General Willcox, for reasons not made clear, decided to terminate their parole

---

[18] Horn, 94–102. Will Barnes, with an excellent opportunity to learn the details of this fight, asserted that Horn's "long yarn in his book telling of his presence at the Battle of Cibecue is an outrageous, barefaced lie from start to finish. I knew every soldier, officer, packer and scout who took part in that fight. I saw the command leave Fort Apache and met it four or five miles west of the post the afternoon they returned from that unfortunate affair. Tom Horn was not with the command at any time." Will Croft Barnes, "The Apaches' Last Stand in Arizona," *Arizona Historical Review*, Vol. III, No. 4 (January, 1931), 58–59. It might be questioned whether anyone could, after fifty years, remember clearly the names of 125 men comprising a chance military expedition of which he was not even a member, but Barnes was a man of integrity and he would not have made this statement were he not positive of its truth.

[19] John P. Clum, "Apache Misrule," *New Mexico Historical Review*, Vol. V, No. 2 (April, 1930), 141.

and "unnecessarily, stupidly and fatally," as Clum put it, sent cavalry, in battle dress, to arrest the chiefs and bring in their people. Seeing the military descending upon them, the most nervous of the White Mountain people fled to the Chiricahua camp, blurted out their version of the situation, and "so alarmed them that during the night seventy-four Chiricahuas and Coyoteros, including women and children, fled from the reserve."[20] All were under leadership of fat old Juh and Nachez, son of Cochise.[21] Sieber, for one, was convinced that the only reason the rest of the Warm Springs and Chiricahua Apaches did not make a break, too, was "that troops were stationed so near their camp,"[22] but they were under Loco, a wise and deliberate chieftain, and other evidence points to a genuine reluctance on his part to flee south.

The hostiles, after one hard fight between their rear guard and troops near Cedar Springs (about sixteen miles from Camp Grant), fled across the border. Once more the Southwest could brace itself for raids. For one thing, there was irresistible loot to be had north of the line, and for another, the hostiles still had friends at San Carlos and would make every effort to lure them onto the warpath. Prime target was Loco and what was left of the Ojo Caliente, or Warm Springs, warriors who once had followed Victorio. The troops, and especially the Indian scouts, must make every effort to prevent the wild Apaches from contacting their reservation cousins. To do this required incessant patrolling of the gloomy and little-known mountain corridors by which the hostiles might move: the Dragoons, the Mule Mountains, the Whetstones, the Chiricahuas.

Despite all precautions, about the middle of January, 1882, messengers from the south filtered unnoticed into Loco's camp, about a mile from the subagency, which was eighteen miles from San Carlos toward Camp Thomas. They said they had come from Juh and Nachez, which Loco already knew, and warned that in forty days the

[20] Lockwood, *The Apache Indians*, 244.

[21] Although the record is confused, I believe Geronimo was with this fleeing party, although he is not mentioned by name in any contemporary account I've seen.

[22] Sieber to Willcox, June 8, 1882, AGO, Letters Received, 2924, Department of Arizona, 1882, National Archives.

hostiles were coming on a raid and would force Loco and his people to return with them to the Sierra Madre. Loco grunted and kept his counsel. But others talked. By the middle of February, Al Sieber had heard of it. He, Lieutenant John Y. F. "Bo" Blake,[23] and ten scouts were ordered to search the Dragoons for hostiles, but found none, nor any signs of them; obviously, they had not come up from Mexico via those mountains.[24]

Everyone was uneasy, awaiting the explosion. Willcox sent two troops of cavalry to the border, not with the hope of heading off any hostile mission, but to be nearer the critical point of action when it came. In New Mexico, Colonel George Alexander Forsyth[25] was in the field with six troops of the Fourth Cavalry patrolling the Southern Pacific Railroad from Separ to Lordsburg[26] and beyond. Toward the end of March, Al Sieber was sent with some scouts to examine the Stein's Peak range of mountains, which runs north and south along the New Mexico–Arizona border, and here he struck pay dirt. "I, on the north end of the Las Animas Mtns., discovered fresh Indian signs

[23] Missouri-born Bo Blake was a West Pointer assigned to the Sixth Cavalry and Arizona upon graduation in 1880. He saw several years of active service before resigning on August 19, 1889. Attracted to—and attractive to—women, he fell in love with one who jilted him in the mid-eighties. Later he married another, and she persuaded him to resign, then divorced him. Blake was in South Africa for the Boer War and was wounded in one of its battles; he died and was buried at West Point. Cullum; Cruse to Davis, November 15, 1929.

[24] *Arizona Star*, February 22, 1882.

[25] Forsyth was a distinguished soldier and Indian fighter who won national fame by his heroic defense of Beecher Island during a long and bloody engagement with Roman Nose's Cheyennes in 1868, in the course of which he was wounded three times and for which he was brevetted brigadier general. A Civil War volunteer, he rose from enlisted man to brevet brigadier general of Volunteers, earning several citations for gallantry in action and taking part in sixteen pitched battles, two sieges, and sixty minor engagements. After the war he was commissioned a major of the Ninth Cavalry and on June 26, 1881, a lieutenant colonel of the Fourth. A bullet wound in the head caused him to exhibit mental unsoundness in financial and other transactions and led to his eventual retirement on March 25, 1890. He died at Washington on September 12, 1915. Although a brave and, at this time, competent officer, he failed to close with the Apaches and let them get away, exhibiting ineffectiveness and hesitance to the point of timidity. *Who Was Who*; Crook to AGO, December 3, 1889, Hayes Collection.

[26] Today, Separ is little more than a railroad siding and cattle-loading point about twenty miles east of Lordsburg, but for a brief time during the Apache wars it was a busy army camp. Lordsburg was already an important town.

of the Chiricahuas making their way toward the San Carlos Agency," he wrote Willcox. "This I found out afterwards was the same band of Chiricahuas Indians that came from Mexico to aid the Warm Spring Indians to leave the Reservation and join them in Mexico."[27] But by the time he found the sign and evaluated it, it was too late. Before Sieber could warn Willcox, the big break came.

Raiders under Chato, Chihuahua, Nachez, and possibly Geronimo cut the telegraph wire a short distance west of the subagency and during the night moved on toward San Carlos, no doubt planning a dawn massacre of the whites and what tame Indians they could catch. But they ran into Chief of San Carlos Police Albert D. Sterling and one of his Indian officers, who had been alerted to the raid, and killed them. Then, the element of surprise gone, they boiled back to Loco's camp and forced him—some said at rifle point—to take his seven hundred people out on the trail to Mexico.

It was too late for reflection, too late for indecision, and Loco acceded, leading the grand exodus eastward toward the Upper Gila, then curving south along the Stein's Peak Range, where they ambushed an element of Forsyth's command, killing four scouts, had a major fight with the whole of his troops in Horseshoe Canyon, and forced him to withdraw. Forsyth maintained, none too confidently, that the whites had won this engagement, but the southwestern frontiersmen, Al Sieber among them, rose in wrath to deny him, to argue faintheartedness on his part, and to accuse him of having no stomach for a battle with the Apaches once he had them cornered. He had lost two men killed, four men, including an officer, wounded, and thought he had killed at least two of the enemy. On the other side of the ledger, Loco was free to pull out, cross the broad San Simon Valley to the mighty uplift of the Chiricahuas, and be on his way to the relative safety of the rugged Sierra Madre.

[27] Sieber to Willcox, June 8, 1882, AGO, Letters Received, 2924, Department of Arizona, 1882, National Archives.

XIV. The Loco Fight

MAJOR DAVID PERRY,[1] commanding field operations in southern Arizona, had several troop elements posted in strategic places, far to the south, waiting to fall upon the hostiles when opportunity should present itself. He "so distributed his troops in small commands that it was actually impossible for the Indians to escape without striking one of them," wrote Sieber.[2] Captain William Augustus Rafferty[3] was at

[1] David Perry, born at Richfield, Connecticut, on June 11, 1841, was commissioned during the Civil War and arrived in Arizona in the late summer of 1879 after years of hard Indian fighting elsewhere. He was placed in command of the Sixth Cavalry, with headquarters at Fort Bowie. On April 5, 1868, he had led a strong detachment that killed thirty-two Indians, with no loss to itself, on the Malheur River in Oregon. He was wounded in a battle with the Modocs on January 17, 1873, but by June 1 had recovered sufficiently to lead F Company, First Cavalry, in the capture of the notorious Captain Jack. He lost a lieutenant and thirty-three men killed at White Bird Canyon, Idaho, on June 17, 1877, to start off the Nez Percé campaign, in which he figured prominently. He ultimately became colonel of the Ninth Cavalry and was retired for disability July 5, 1898. Perry died in 1908. Heitman; *Who Was Who*.

[2] Al Sieber wrote, or at least was by-lined on, a detailed description and analysis of the entire campaign, from the Battle of Doubtful (or Horseshoe) Canyon to the ambush of Loco in Old Mexico. It appeared under the heading "MILITARY AND INDIANS: Al Sieber Tells What He Knows About the Late War" in the *Prescott Weekly Courier* of Saturday, May 27, 1882. This newspaper, run by Al's friend John Marion, had been started in February of that year, and it is likely that Marion heavily edited or at least greatly assisted Sieber in presentation of his critique. It has been used extensively here.

[3] Born in New Jersey, Rafferty was a West Pointer, joining the Sixth Cavalry as a second lieutenant in June of 1865 and being named captain three years later; he eventually became colonel of the Fifth Cavalry. Rafferty earned the brevet rank of major, partly for his action against Loco, but also for an Indian fight on the Little Wichita River in Texas. He died September 13, 1902. Heitman.

Fort Bowie and Captain Tupper at San Simon Station. Each had a screen of scouts out working sign.

While Forsyth wandered aimlessly between the east face of the Stein's Peak Range and the Gila, hunting first water, then his scouts, and finally the hostile trail, Loco had crossed the San Simon Valley with all of his people and was headed toward Galeyville,[4] on the east side of the Chiricahua Mountains. The greatest confusion reigned as the whites grew frantic at the reported approach of the enemy. It was published in the nation's press that the Indians had attacked Galeyville and had killed thirty-five whites, a rumor that was entirely false. Lordsburg was guarded all night by armed men. Elsewhere, confusion was rampant. The Indians did come within plain sight of Galeyville, killed a deputy sheriff, and ripped down some tents bordering the community, but they then disappeared into the southern reaches of the San Simon Valley once more.

Tupper and Rafferty promptly learned that the hostiles were near Galeyville. Both commanders started there at once, and both arrived at about 5:00 P.M. on a Tuesday. The story they picked up was that the Indians were making generally for Cloverdale, or in that direction, Cloverdale lying beyond the Peloncillo Mountains, which bounded San Simon Valley on the east.

Tupper was too wise an Indian fighter to drop down into the valley and make dust following the hostile trail, for he knew such a cloud could be seen by lynx-eyed Apaches for thirty-five miles or more. Then there would be no catching them. So he laid over that day, his men lolling in what shade they could find and the horses gratefully drowsing on the picket line, switching flies and being groomed by troopers who thought more of their mounts than they did of themselves. Eight miles below, on Cave Creek, Rafferty also rested his men for the trial to come and waited for his superior officer. Tupper

4 Galeyville was a short-lived silver camp named for a Pennsylvania oil and mining figure, John H. Galey, and located in an oak grove about two miles north of present-day Paradise on the eastern slope of the Chiricahuas. Nothing remains now but a slag dump, and although it once boasted a population of three to four hundred, it was always more of a camp than a town. It became notorious after its silver days as a rustlers' retreat and reportedly served as headquarters for Curly Bill Brocius and his ilk.

had Lieutenant Francis Joseph Andrew Darr's[5] company of Apache scouts, with Sieber as chief of scouts and guide. With Rafferty was Lieutenant Mills, with Rohner as guide and Pat Keogh, who had dropped in from nowhere, anxious to go along as scout, guide, or anything else as long as a fight was promised.[6]

Late in the day, Tupper joined Rafferty and at six o'clock, although there was still some daylight, they risked it, threw out their trailers, and dropped down into the wide valley, a unit of 107 men. It was a tanned, bullhide-tough column, tireless and relentless; the chase they had embarked on would demand the most of these qualities.

Through the night they filed southeastward on the trail, which was as plainly defined as a railroad track. Sieber said the column marched "at a trot and gallop for about thirty miles. At this point the hostiles had scattered so the trail disappeared." They struck the Peloncillos at 3:00 A.M. at Skeleton Canyon and, it being impossible to continue working out the now faint trail until daylight, wrapped themselves in their overcoats and saddle blankets and shivered out the rest of a chilly night wishing that the pack train had kept up and that there was something to eat.

Within a few hours Sieber sent out the scouts once more to ferret out the trail, and they found it quickly enough. It led by a "very hard march over a new pass," according to Rafferty, avoiding the easier, better-known way. The column struggled up to five thousand feet to cross the Peloncillos. The trail was much broken: the Indians seemed to be hunting water. It more or less paralleled the old smuggler's route where Curly Bill Brocius was said to have ambushed and hijacked a Mexican pack train a few months before, killing the fourteen or fif-

[5] Darr, born in Ohio, went to West Point and was assigned to the Twelfth Infantry in 1880 as a second lieutenant. He was made a first lieutenant in 1886 and resigned September 1, 1887.

[6] Horn, 73–79, says that he, Sieber, and Mickey Free alone trailed these Indians south, being joined by Tupper at or near Cloverdale, but Sieber does not hint at any such arrangement, nor does anyone else who was known to have been there. However, Horn does indicate some personal knowledge of certain phases of the operation and may have been a packer with Tupper's command. Sieber says in a letter printed in Horn's book that "Tom went to work for me in the government pack train in 1882," and it could have been during this campaign.

teen *contrabandistas* accompanying it; their skulls would serve near-
by ranches as soap dishes for some years to come.[7] But the soldiers
had no thoughts for such romanticisms.

Although it was a trying day, Sieber was glad to note that the trail
was warming up, even if it remained difficult to follow. At 6:30 P.M.
they were obliged to go into camp a few miles north of Cloverdale.
What consoled them most was that their four pack trains, trembling
with weariness and caked with dried sweat, joined them here, having
covered fifty-two miles in twenty-four hours of continuous marching.
But there was still little time for rest. At 4:30 A.M. on April 27, the
column broke camp and set out once more on the hostiles' trail.

They passed within two miles of Cloverdale, as had the Indians,
and pushed on sixteen miles across the Animas Valley, working south
along the eastern slope of the Sierra de San Luis, for by this time they
had crossed the border and entered Old Mexico, although no international agreement permitted this. Hot on the trail, the troopers had
little patience with formalities, and besides, they didn't think they
would run into enough Mexican force to argue with. The Apaches had
forced their way through thick manzanita, which delayed them considerably, so the troopers were gaining fast, crunching along on the
pathway beaten down by the hostiles. Up through a sharp and fearsome canyon led the trail, then over the very highest peak of the San
Luis Mountains, perhaps seven thousand feet high, where the Indians
had broken out a fresh trail, never before used. "This proved a terrible hard pull for the boys," wrote Rafferty in his diary. By 6:00 P.M.
they had come thirty-five excruciatingly difficult miles over the spiny
ridge of a virtually unexplored range and dropped down to its base
on the eastern side. They rested two and one-half hours, then left their
pack trains in camp under guard, and the rest of the column, rein-
vigorated by the apparent closeness of the hostiles, set out once more,
thirty-nine troopers and forty-five Apache scouts, eager to take on
more than their number of the most vicious fighters the Southwest

---

[7] Barnes, *Place Names*, 410. Sources for this account of the campaign include Sieber's
letter, Horn, 311–14; George A. Forsyth, *Thrilling Days in Army Life*; Captain Rafferty,
whose diary was printed in the *Arizona Star*, May 17, 1882; Lieutenant Darr, who was
interviewed and whose story appeared in the *Star* on January 22, 1884; and Horn.

ever knew. "The trail at this point was very fresh," wrote Rafferty.

Sieber led the way, stepping out easily and surely, never looking back, intent only on catching up with the quarry. Ten scouts followed him. One and one-half miles behind them strode the rest of the Indians, also on foot, and in file. Three miles to their rear was the cavalry, held back to avoid routing the hostiles by the clatter of hoofs "or other noises made by the horses," according to Darr.

About 10:00 P.M., after a seven- or eight-mile march, Sieber rose up as if from the ground itself in the gloom surrounding the column and beckoned to Captain Tupper. "I told him I thought the Indians were camped about two or three miles ahead," wrote Sieber, "and that if he would halt the command I would go and investigate. I took three scouts and in half an hour discovered the camp. One of the scouts crawled up to the camp and discovered they were making medicine. As soon as I familiarized myself with the location, I went back and reported to Captain Tupper how the camp was situated and what could be safely done if proper care was taken." Al estimated the hostiles to number 115 warriors. Quite a matter-of-fact account of as daring a feat as you will find in the annals of Indian war: four men, one of them white, creeping through unfamiliar terrain around a camp of the wariest, most merciless mortals on earth, "familiarizing" themselves with the lay of the land despite the pitch blackness, and returning to bring up the fighting men! If a rock had clicked, a twig snapped, a rattlesnake buzzed—any of these things or countless others—disaster would have been unleashed on them and the chance for a surprise assault gone forever.

Tom Horn wrote that the impending action took place "at the Sierra Media . . . a very rough, small mountain in the middle of the Janos plains."[8] A detailed map of this part of Mexico[9] shows just such a mountain, called Sierra Enmedio, which perfectly agrees with Horn's translation: "Middle Mountain." It is also shaped right, and features just such a basin as the fighting men described. There is today a tiny inhabited place there called Los Huerigos, so there must

[8] Horn, 81.

[9] American Geographical Society map, "Sonora," scale 1:1,000,000, provisional edition, N. H-12, 1958.

be water present. Horn explained that "on the west side of this mountain was a fine, big spring. At that time of year there was bound to be lots of water there, and it took lots of water for that bunch of Indians when they were all together. There we felt sure the Indians would camp to rest up, for they were tired, and their stock was all tired, and the place was inside of the Mexican line, about twenty miles.[10] The Indians knew we dared not cross the line, so they would feel perfectly safe, but it was necessary to use a great deal of caution in attacking them, for if we made a mistake they would kill all of us."[11]

The site was a perfect one for defense, but, oddly, it afforded advantages to the assault parties, too, perhaps because the hostiles had not expected to be attacked now that they were in what they considered the Mexican sanctuary. They knew that American troops were not supposed to cross the line, and they never feared Mexican soldiers much.

Tupper ordered the two companies of scouts under Lieutenant Mills and Lieutenant Darr and Guides Rohner and Pat Keogh to move out to the east, gain the main range of mountains, about two miles distant, and follow it until they could emplace themselves on a rocky hillock adjacent to the mountains, giving them about a fifty-

[10] The site is almost seventeen airline miles south of the line, making it almost exactly twenty miles by trail. Since writing the above, I have found three other references which pinpoint the action at Sierra Enmedio. "With Crawford in Mexico," by Robert Hanna, first published in the *Clifton Clarion* on July 7 and 14, 1886, and reprinted in the *Arizona Historical Review*, Vol. VI, No. 2 (April, 1935), 56–65, says (p. 58): "We turned off to the east toward a rugged looking mountain that stood out into the plain, called the Sierra en Media or Middle Mountain. Here a very few years ago the troops had a fight with the hostiles. A rough, rocky hill, somewhat detached from the main mountain with an occasional skeleton of a horse or a man about it, and the rocks spattered with lead, told the story." The second account, "Experiences of an Indian Scout," by John Rope, as told to Grenville Goodwin, *Arizona Historical Review*, Vol. VII, No. 2 (April, 1936), 31–73, says (p. 52): "We . . . came out on the edge of the open country to cross over to Sierra de Media. . . . After a while we came to a rocky place with lots of holes in it, and Na-nod-di said that the Chiricahuas had a fight here once with the troops. There was an old cartridge belt, all dried up, lying on the ground." Finally, Henry W. Daly, chief packer for the Quartermaster Department, states (p. 71) in "The Geronimo Campaign," *Journal of the Cavalry Association*, Vol. XIX, No. 69 (July, 1908), 68–103: "We passed by the Sierra Medio, the scene of the Tupper and Rafferty fight of 1881 [*sic*]."

[11] Horn, 81.

foot elevation advantage over the hostile camp some four hundred yards away. With the two companies of troopers, Tupper and Rafferty would move down a broad valley to the basin in which the hostiles were bivouacked, coming out eight hundred to one thousand yards distant from the Indian camp.

The plans were to be carried out between midnight and daylight. At about 4:30 A.M., silent as shadows, the Apache scouts melted into the blackness, their moccasined feet making no more sound than the rustle of a lizard through the brush. To maintain the complete silence, Darr and Mills slipped off their shoes and padded along in their stocking feet through the cactus-choked, snake-infested wilderness. They had only a limited time to get into position, for the scouts' fire, as soon as it was light enough to take aim, would start the action.

Sieber guided the troopers and by the first hint of dawn had them in position. He was mounted now, with Rafferty's command, his carbine cocked and his horse alert, ready for action. It was cool and very clear, and from the far distance came the faint sounds of the enemy, still at their business of making medicine, celebrating their safe arrival in Mexico. They did not suspect that a deadly snare was being tightened about them.

Lieutenant Mills, who had farthest to go, was to fire the opening shot, but it didn't work out that way. Lieutenant Darr had his scouts at their appointed place, each aiming his weapon at some selected target in the unsuspecting hostile camp and the Lieutenant himself quivering just a little in a soldier's anticipation of the action to come. He was awaiting the signal that Mills was in position when, abruptly, an enemy head bobbed over the crest of his hill, to be followed by another—and another and another! They were within twenty-five yards of him: point-blank range. Even in the dim light he recognized one of them as Loco's son; the other three were women. All were chattering and giggling as they poked about among the rocks for mescal which had been hidden there.

Another step or two and the scouts would be discovered, the alarm given. Darr silently signaled, and the roar of rifle fire shattered the unearthly quiet of predawn. The four Indians were killed and the hostile camp jarred into action. A rattle of fire broke on the camp from the hilltop assailants, the scouts delivering eight hundred rounds in four minutes, while far across the basin the eager cries of charging cavalrymen told the enemy the sad news that the border was no longer the edge of a sanctuary for him.

The commands of Tupper and Rafferty separated, Tupper's company being deployed by Lieutenant Timothy A. Touey[12] around a rocky hill some four hundred yards from the main mountains and placed to prevent the hostiles from escaping toward the Janos Plains. Touey received a bullet through the lining of his coat, but held his post.[13] Tupper himself stayed with Rafferty, whose company was to form the main assault team.

"Forward you men of M Company!" cried Captain Rafferty. With Tupper and Lieutenant Bo Blake the dismounted troopers surged across the plain in a formidable attack, charging directly toward the hostile camp. The Indians, rolling out of their torpor like demons, lost six men killed at once, then took cover behind the rocks. They had presence of mind enough to kick their fires to death and a few dashed for the horses loose in the basin, but were beaten back by the deadly fire. Others were hastily returning the troopers' shots, volley for volley. Fortunately, Sieber recalled, they were excited. "In fact, if the hostiles had kept cool, there would have been no chance at all," he reported, "and every man would have been shot down. As it was they fired too high, and the bullets passed over our heads every time."

That sort of luck couldn't last. The bold whites had stormed to within rock-throwing distance of the hostiles, who had now sought secure cover in the jumble of rocks dead ahead. It was obvious that the handful of troopers would never be able to dislodge three times their number; in fact, they would be lucky to get away with whole skins. Sieber describes the situation:

> There was but one thing left for every one to do and that was for each man to get out the best way he could. They withdrew slowly and continued firing into the rocks where the Indians were hidden. About 150 yards to the rear there was a small sink in the ground in which five men and my-

---

[12] Touey, a New Yorker and West Point graduate, became a first lieutenant in 1880 and died September 28, 1887.
[13] Newspaper clipping, Los Angeles Public Library.

self concealed ourselves. There was not room for another man, and the rest of the company continued to move back.

We soon saw that we could do nothing, so we concluded to get out and as the safest way one man would get up and run about twenty or thirty yards and drop on the ground for a few seconds. In about five minutes another man would do the same thing. Bullets hailed about every man.

Captain Tupper's company, under Lieutenant Touey, and the Indian scouts kept up a storm of fire on the hostiles to cover the withdrawal of Rafferty's men, and only their gallant stubbornness saved the little command from annihilation. Private Goodrich[14] was killed running from Sieber's sink and Private Miller[15] badly wounded. A Chiricahua saw Miller fall and dashed out of the hostile stronghold full into the fire of the troopers' rifles to finish the wounded soldier off. "He got within forty yards of where the cavalryman lay, and all the time exposed to the fire of the scouts and soldiers," wrote Darr. "Finding the bullets coming too thick he started back, but fell dead within fifteen feet of his former shelter."

As soon as the troopers regained their horses and swung into the saddle, Tupper ordered Blake, "the most efficient type of Cavalryman,"[16] and twenty men to sweep between the hostiles and their ponies. "The danger of this foolhardy maneuver was realized," wrote Cruse, "but Tupper and Rafferty were willing to risk it.[17] Blake took his troopers at the pounding gallop along the hostile front, receiving their close-range fire at every step. With his men yelling like Comanches he gathered the pony herd and swept it off down a valley and onto the plain below." They captured seventy-four animals, leaving Loco almost completely afoot.

The whole action up to this point had lasted probably half an hour, but the wily Apache was not taking his licking lying down. "Loco tried to get the scouts to turn against us," Sieber reported, "but they

14 Sieber spells the name "Goldick."

15 Horn makes this man "Sergeant Murray" and says he was shot in the side and knocked off his horse and that he, Horn, then rescued him under heavy fire.

16 Thomas Cruse, *Apache Days and After*, 136.

17 Horn, 83, says that above all, Tupper wanted "to capture a pony for his little girl" and (p. 84) that Mickey Free "wanted to get a few ponies and bring back to Tupper, as he seemed to want ponies worse than anything else."

would abuse and curse him and fire into the rocks where he was."[18] Never was there an instance when Apache scouts deserted under fire to join the enemy.

Rafferty, his own horse, Old Jim, badly wounded, had extricated his company and formed a skirmish line on Tupper's right. The two companies were almost exactly opposite the scouts. With so few men, and they thirty-six hours without sleep and twenty-one without water, and with a dwindling ammunition supply, they now found it impossible to surround the hostiles and equally impossible to inflict much more damage unless a surround could be accomplished. Both sides kept up a desultory fire into the heat of the day, but without much effect. Several attempts to recover Goodrich's body failed.

At 11:30 A.M., Tupper held a conference with Rafferty, Sieber, and his own officers and concluded that "we could not get the savages out of the rocks and that no good could result from further firing, which would reduce our supply of ammunition." He added that "I suppose every man fired from 50 to 80 shots, some more. I used about 40 cartridges, shooting very deliberately at intervals." Darr estimated that the command was down to three rounds per man. As far as these brave fighters knew, there were no other troops within 150 miles, and they were on foreign soil. They concluded, reluctantly, that the thing to do was to withdraw. This was done slowly, Tupper reported, "one company holding the skirmish line at a time. The Indian scouts first filed out, close to the mountains, we trying to keep a heavy fire on the Indians to prevent them from giving their whole attention to the scouts whilst they were withdrawing. The Indians were mighty glad to suspend operations, and did not fire a shot after we began to retire."

Sieber, Keogh, and others estimated that Tupper's command had killed about seventeen warriors and seven women, along with fifteen ponies in addition to the seventy-four they had captured. Twenty Indian saddles were left on the field. Tupper had lost one man killed, one badly wounded, one slightly wounded, and three horses killed,

[18] Jason Betzinez, *I Fought with Geronimo*, 69, says that "Old Man Loco was wounded slightly in the leg while leaning against a rock right beside me." On pp. 68–70, Betzinez writes interestingly of the Indian side of this fight, saying that he didn't know of any casualties they suffered. In general, his account fits in well with the white versions.

among them Old Jim. "I had to have him shot," the Captain explained sadly. "I had ridden him for over seven years. But he could not travel, and to put him out of his misery I got ———— to put a carbine ball through his head. Poor old fellow, I felt sorry for him."

The command was withdrawn about nine miles, to where they had begun their stalk the night before, and went into camp about 8:00 P.M. The weary, powder-begrimed men were just completing a belated and tasteless meal when, with a great clatter of hoofs and equipment, what seemed to them an immense army rode into camp. It was Colonel Forsyth with seven companies of cavalry and two or three companies of scouts. They, wrote Tupper, "joined us—and gobbled us." Forsyth was chagrined to think he had missed the fight, and the tired veterans of that battle were even more chagrined to think that, if they had known relief was so near, they could have held the hostiles for a massive pummeling. Sieber and the men of the Sixth Cavalry later had some mighty caustic things to say about Forsyth's belated arrival, but for the moment they held their tongues.

The Colonel's command, augmented by Sixth Cavalry troopers picked up en route, had rapidly followed the well-defined hostile trail from Stein's toward the Chiricahuas until the Indians scattered, then pushed on to Turkey Creek, near Galeyville, where Forsyth contacted Captain Chaffee with another part of the Sixth and Lieutenant Frank West[19] with more Indian scouts. Forsyth picked up a couple of guides at Galeyville, relocated the Indian trail at daylight, and followed it down the wide San Simon Valley and up into the wild Peloncillos, making a dry camp on the crest within five miles of Tupper's camp beyond, although Forsyth didn't realize it. At dawn the command saddled up and rode on down the valley, still on the trail of the hostiles but losing it when the Indians again scattered. The Colonel then made for the Cloverdale *ciénagas*, or marshes, watering his command there and then locating Tupper's trail. Forsyth spent the night at the *ciénagas* while in Mexico, Tupper was moving up to the assault. The next day, Forsyth, "on one of the worst trails that I have ever seen

[19] A New Yorker, Frank West attended the United States Military Academy and was assigned to the Sixth Cavalry in 1872. For a long time he was in command of Indian scouts. Cullum.

or heard of," followed the trail blocked out by scores of Indians and their livestock plus eighty-odd soldiers and scouts and four pack trains. So it was that the large and ineffective column arrived at Tupper's camp after dark—and after the fight.

The Colonel was now all energy and enthusiasm, and, as Tupper said, he "gobbled" up the smaller command by virtue of his superior rank. "On learning of the fight," wrote Sieber, Forsyth "told Capt. Tupper that he wanted his command to go with him that night after Indians as they were only ten miles away. Tupper told him that he could not go as his command must have sleep and rest, but said that he would overtake him the next day." But the bold Colonel did not relish the notion of floundering around in the dark after the same resolute Indians who had whipped him back in Doubtful Canyon. "Being determined to have a large command that the Indians could see for fifty miles," continued Sieber sarcastically, "Col. Forsyth went into camp for the night with his small detachment of 400 soldiers and fifty scouts." Then he hit the nail squarely on the head:

> The truth of the matter is that Capt. Tupper with thirty-nine soldiers and forty-five scouts for fighting duty had attacked the Indians in one of the strongest places I ever saw (and I have seen a great many), while Col. Forsyth, then in command of 450 soldiers and scouts, did not pursue and attack the same Indians because he wished to display a larger command.
>
> A long column of troops makes a big show, but they don't catch Indians.

Sure enough, the delay was too long. When the command broke camp at six o'clock the following morning and retraced the way to the scene of the fight, they found it deserted, except for three dead hostiles and signs that the Indians had pulled out during the night.

Forsyth now faced a grave decision. He was already deep in Mexico, where he had no business being, and "had strict orders in my possession on no account to enter Mexican territory." He decided to follow the Indian trail anyway. "They had murdered and plundered our citizens, believing we dare not follow them into Mexico. Captain Tupper had taught them otherwise, and I had determined from the start to follow them as far as I could no matter where they went." Besides, Forsyth reasoned, it was a wild part of Mexico and his troops might catch and annihilate the band and return to the border without the knowledge of the Mexican government. So the column moved sinuously down the trail after Loco, this time with expert scouts and trailers to make sure the sign was not lost.

About ten miles farther on they captured a terrified, wounded old woman who surely expected to be put to death. She told them, or so Forsyth understood, that the band had lost six braves killed in the Tupper fight and thirteen at Doubtful Canyon, in addition to "many" wounded in both actions. The soldiers gave her some bread and water and left her on the trail.

In her estimate of casualties, the woman may have told Forsyth what she believed he wanted to hear, her statement may have been misinterpreted for his benefit, or perhaps the interpreter misunderstood. At any rate, Forsyth's report on the casualties inflicted on the Indians in these battles has been generally accepted, although it is almost certainly wrong. Logic would dictate that the figures should be reversed, with the heaviest Loco losses in the Tupper fight, and, in fact, that seems to have been the way it was. General Crook, in an official report submitted almost a year later, had this to say:

> From repeated conversations with their relations at the San Carlos reservation and from other reliable information I learned that when the Chiricahuas broke out from their agency last April they numbered all told 176 fighting men.[20] . . . Their losses have been as follows: Killed in fight with Capt. Tupper, 6" Cavy. 14 men. In fight with Lt. Col. Forsyth, 4" Cavy. one man. . . . To guard against any possibility of mistakes, intentional or unintentional in this story, I examined the relatives several times one by one, without shaking their testimony in the slightest. Their story was so circumstantial that they gave me the name of every male Indian who was killed and where and how.[21]

Crook's scrupulous honesty and his vast experience in Indian affairs, with Apaches in particular, added to his care always to employ only the most skilled and reliable interpreters and his meticulous precautions to assure their accuracy, all militate in favor of his estimate

[20] This would probably make the over-all number of hostiles, including women, the aged, and children, at least seven hundred.
[21] Crook to AAG, Division of the Pacific, March 28, 1883, Hayes Collection.

of the actual losses the Loco band sustained. It is notable that his total jibes well with the eyewitness estimates of Sieber and Pat Keogh, who made the total warrior kill in the Tupper attack seventeen. From a distance of hundreds of yards it would be difficult to tell a slain from a badly wounded adversary, but they came close to the true count. It should be pointed out that Forsyth himself, until the interview with the wounded woman, had claimed to have killed only two hostiles in Doubtful Canyon and that the Indian woman's purported testimony was to him a pleasant surprise.[22]

Meanwhile, the troops probed deeper into Mexico in pursuit of a cloud of dust far ahead of them across the plain to which they had now descended. Shortly they passed the body of a warrior, "the wicker stretcher that lay by his side showing that he was of sufficient importance in rank for his companions to try to get him off, notwithstanding they were so sorely pressed." By nightfall the command had reached the headwaters of a small tributary of the Janos and made camp, certain that with the coming day they would catch up to and have their fight with the dismounted hostiles. But it was not to be.

"At daylight," wrote Forsyth, "I heard the sound of reveille by Mexican buglers, and my command had not moved over a mile when Lieutenant [C. S.] Hall, who had the advance, reported a Mexican camp a few miles beyond. After marching about two miles I was met by Colonel Lorenzo Garcia,[23] of the Sixth Mexican Infantry, who with his adjutant came across a small ravine to meet our forces. He most courteously desired to know if I was aware that my command was upon Mexican soil. If so, what authority, if any, I had for crossing the line." Quite as courteously, and as decidedly, and at much greater length, Forsyth told García he had orders to capture or ex-

[22] Later Forsyth said that Mexican captives confirmed the figures given him by the wounded Indian woman, but Lieutenant Darr, who was present when the prisoners were questioned, asserted that "it was agreed that 17 bucks and 7 squaws were killed in Tupper's fight, and that 16 of those killed by Garcia had wounds received by Tupper's command." *Arizona Star*, May 26, 1882.

[23] García, one of the most famous and successful of Mexican army Indian fighters, was apparently as popular below the border as north of it. He moved in regimental strength and left the Indians to their mountains, but woe betide them when they rampaged through the lowlands—if he could catch them.

terminate the hostiles and was determined to do so. García observed that Mexico was strong enough to handle its own Indian problem. Forsyth proved as stubborn, and García as adamant, and the deadlocked conversation "continued for some time," neither side willing to give in. Then García dropped his bombshell. "If your sole object is the punishment of this band of marauders, it is already accomplished," he said. "My command fought, routed and scattered them yesterday."

Forsyth's chin must have dropped a foot at this, but he recovered quickly and asked García's permission to visit the battlefield, to which the Mexican readily assented. The officers, accompanied by their interpreters and Sieber, rode over the bloody field,[24] still strewn with the bodies of 78 Indians and 19 soldiers and 3 officers[25] of the 250-man Mexican force. The Mexicans also lost 3 officers and 13 men wounded, but had captured 33 women and children, among them a daughter of Loco.[26]

Cruse said that the Mexicans had camped at Paso Pulpito, on or near the Río Corralitos,[27] and were breaking camp when their scouts reported the approach of Loco's band. He believed that only Chihuahua, Nana, and three or four others escaped, but this is not correct, nor is his estimate of eighty Mexicans killed. "Rafferty and Blake [who came on the scene that night]," wrote Lieutenant Cruse, "said

[24] The fight was on, or very near, the Corralitos (Janos) River, also called the San Pedro, whose nearest point is twenty-nine miles southeast of where I believe the Tupper fight took place. Cruse, in a letter to Davis dated October 8, 1927, said it was thirty-four miles by trail, which would place it at this point.

[25] Mexican officers killed were the first captain of the Sixth Battalion, Antonio Rhoda; the lieutenant of the Bavispe National Guard, Serapio Lugo; and a second lieutenant from the Fourth Battalion of Sonora. Wounded were Major Luis Corón of the Fourth Battalion and a Lieutenant Jesús García. *Arizona Star*, May 19, 1882.

[26] Crook learned that the Apache loss in the Casas Grandes ambush included only eleven warriors. "The Apaches tell the story," he wrote, "that after their encounters with Tupper and Forsyth, they sent their women and children to the front, so as to be clear of incumbrance in any fight they might have with our troops, who were close in pursuit. Garcia's troops killed the greater no. of women and children before the male Apaches came to their rescue. The Agency Apaches claim that the hostiles killed more than twice as many Mexicans in what they call the fight, that is, the fight with their *men*, than they themselves lost." Crook to AAG, Division of the Pacific, March 28, 1883, Hayes Collection.

[27] Cruse to Britton Davis, October 8, 1927.

they never saw such shambles and ghastly scenes in their lives."[28] One old Indian took a heavy toll of Mexicans. Concealed behind cactus in a small depression, he killed eight soldiers before his ammunition gave out and they could dispose of him.[29] Sieber said that as soon as the first Mexican volley crashed into them, "all of Juh's bucks and the young bucks belonging to the Warm Spring band put spurs to their horses and made their escape. The old bucks stood and fought for their families and there they died with them. Young bucks look out for themselves—old bucks fight for their families." Among those who escaped, besides Juh, Nana, and Chihuahua, was Loco, and he would be heard from again.

Two years later a romanticized and exaggerated version of this fight, told from the Mexican viewpoint, was published in the San Francisco *Examiner*. The narrator claimed that 170 Indians were slain, along with 32 Mexicans.[30]

Forsyth offered García some rations after discovering that the Mexican troops were on half rations, almost destitute, and hungrier than the Indians. The way he found out, according to Horn, was when García invited Forsyth to "breakfast."

> Forsyth accepted the invitation. We all went further up the creek and made camp. Garcia and his command had not had breakfast. That regiment of Garcia's, which he said was one of the best in the Mexican Army, had twelve burros for their transportation. They had no grub and no clothes, and many of them did not have a cartridge after their fight with the Indians.
>
> Colonel Forsyth . . . soon saw that breakfast with Garcia was nothing at all, so he asked Garcia to have breakfast with him, which he did.[31]

Not only were the heroic Mexicans destitute of provisions, but they had no medical supplies or attendants for their wounded, so Forsyth assigned his command's surgeons to care for García's wounded, an action which must have saved many lives. The commands parted amicably.

28 *Ibid.*
29 Britton Davis, *Geronimo*, 8.
30 *Arizona Star*, January 22, 1884.
31 Horn, 90–91.

lian Agent John P. Clum, with Diablo (left) and Eskiminzin, at San Carlos in 1875.

Al Sieber (seated), an unidentified Washington official, and four Indian scouts in 1883.

"Colonel Garcia informed me," wrote Forsyth, "that so imperative were the orders of his government [against permitting American troops to penetrate Mexican territory] that he would have been compelled to oppose my further progress by force, though, as he admitted, with no reasonable hope of success against my larger command." García gave Forsyth a written protest against the "invasion" and Forsyth submitted a formal reply in writing, then headed north. The Sixth Cavalry units were directed to return to Arizona by the route they had followed against the hostiles, and Forsyth moved directly north into New Mexico.

No official report on the Forsyth-García meeting was ever filed in this country or, as far as is known, in Mexico.³² General Ranald S. Mackenzie, realizing the diplomatic furor that would surely follow revelation of the action, courteously returned Forsyth's official report to him, informing the Colonel that "it was not unlikely I might find myself in trouble for my action. However, if the Mexicans did not make a direct complaint to the State Department, he should not take action, as the result justified the end; but the less said about it the better." Rafferty, in his diary, which was published in the *Arizona Star* on May 17, 1882, frankly reported the operation in Old Mexico, but his account apparently went no farther than the borders of Arizona. The full story was not revealed until Forsyth told it in his book in 1900.

Southwesterners were most caustic in their comments on Forsyth's conduct of the campaign but generous in their praise of Tupper and García. The latter was formally presented with a handsome sword by the North American residents of Hermosillo, Mexico, on November 9, 1882,³³ in commemoration of his notable feat. Federal infantry and cavalry were drawn up in dress parade in the central plaza, and while the band played, a heavy gold box containing the Damascene blade was carried to the center of the plaza, where an appropriate ora-

³² Tupper had cautiously wired Willcox, via Perry, on April 28 that his fight with the hostiles was thirty-five miles *east* of Cloverdale instead of south, as it really was, to avoid revealing that he was illegally operating in Mexican territory. Newspaper clipping, Los Angeles Public Library.

³³ *Arizona Star*, November 10, 1882.

tion was delivered and the presentation ceremony performed. García, "overcome with emotion," presented the sword to his battalion.[34] Al Sieber's analysis of the campaign, warmly worded as it was, though undeniably authoritative, probably expressed accurately the feelings of many of the bold and fiery frontiersmen. He wrote in part:

Col. Forsythe [*sic*] had attacked the band [at Stein's Peak] in a place where he could have held them as long as he might wish. If he could not handle the band to any purpose, why did he not send for more troops, as plenty of them were near and he could have had as many as he wanted inside of twelve hours. If the hostiles had withdrawn they could have gone nowhere but into a valley, and in that case what better could he wish.

Capts. Tupper and Rafferty performed their duty well as United States officers, and infinitely better than could have possibly been expected and at a time when they did not know there were any troops nearer than 125 miles. Col. Forsythe's own guides say that they saw the dust of Tupper's command at different times for two days, and yet failed to overtake it. Be it remembered also that Col. Forsythe made a dry camp on the 26th only five miles in Tupper's rear, and on the 27th left Tupper's trail, went twelve miles to Miners creek, watered his stock, went back twelve miles, took the trail and then after following it a short distance, went into camp again. Col. Forsythe, it is said, got lost when he was only five miles in Tupper's rear. If a man cannot follow a fresh trail, well beaten by a large body of Indians, a command of cavalry and four pack trains, would it not be better for him to stay at home?

The band of Warm Spring Indians will be heard of no more since the old bucks and nearly all of the squaws have been killed. The young bucks will unite with Juh and form one of the strongest bands of Indians that has existed for years in this part of the Territory. The time will come when we will have to fight again. Many a poor man will fall at their hands before their final destruction. No small command of troops will ever be able to do anything with them and nothing but a small command will ever

34 The presentation was made despite a short-lived revolution and political commotion which left the North Americans in some doubt as regarded the propriety of their gesture. They wanted to pay tribute to García, but they didn't want to appear to be entering into Mexico's political complexities. Many Hermosillo North Americans, however, were railroad people, soon to leave Sonora for Chihuahua, and for that reason believed they ought to get the presentation over with and therefore arranged it very carefully so that nothing about it "could be construed as politics of any degree or shade." Political wariness may have influenced García in his action upon receiving the tribute.

be able to catch them. If Col. Forsythe had shown the same energy as Capts. Tupper and Rafferty he could have overtaken us before the fight, and the entire band of Indians would have been good, in other words dead, Indians. Major D. Perry so distributed his troops in small commands that it was actually impossible for the Indians to escape without striking one of them. His commands were necessarily small because he had but few troops, but, by placing them within supporting distance of each other, he saw that he could annihilate the entire band. But Col. Forsythe's Cavalry, on reaching Arizona, took possession of every command, or tried to, that Major Perry had started in pursuit of the band. He thus upset every arrangement that Maj. Perry had made. He is the sole cause of two commands of the 6th Cavalry . . . not overtaking us in time for the fight, and thus, instead of destroying the whole band, we were only able to cripple them. If Tupper had not fought them on the 28th, the Mexicans would never have seen them.

No one can truthfully deny anything I have said, because I have not deviated in the least from actual facts.

XV.   The Battle of Big Dry Wash

UPON HIS RETURN FROM MEXICO, Al Sieber was assigned to Camp
McDowell, where he remained for some weeks. A. R. Chaffee was
commander at McDowell, but having taken a troop as far south as
the border during the recent operations, he had gone all the way to
Whipple, presumably to refit and recondition his men.

It was from McDowell that Sieber wrote his analysis of the Loco
campaign and sent it to his friend John Marion, who had just started
the *Prescott Morning Courier*, his fourth Arizona newspaper enterprise and the one with which he would remain for the rest of his life.
Marion corrected Sieber's intriguing spelling but apparently printed
the document in the sense in which it was written.

Al probably continued his patrolling and scouting, seeking some
trace of the renegade Apaches who were still free, never having come
in after the Cibecue affair. Although they had stayed in hiding for
almost a year, their time had come. They were not the sort of people
who could remain quiescent indefinitely. So it was that on July 6,
1882, they set in motion events that were to have a profound effect
on the Apache Indian wars.

The renegades had found a leader in the person of Na-ti-o-tish,
who, by the standards of Mangas Coloradas, Cochise, or even Geronimo, was a nobody, but in the view of his band he probably deserved
the appellation "chief." He became convinced that if a sharp blow
could be struck against the whites, many disaffected Apaches from
the reservation would take the warpath.

Their opportunity finally came. Cibicu Charley Colvig,[1] who had

[1] J. L. Colvig, nicknamed "Cibicu Charley," had been a mail rider between Fort

succeeded Albert D. Sterling as San Carlos chief of police, and three of his men were ambushed and all were slain. Two buggies rolling toward San Carlos from Globe were halted short of the scene by a loyal Indian who shouted to the drivers to go back, that everyone had been killed at San Carlos. Those in the conveyances hurried to Globe and repeated what they had been told. The *Silver Belt* took it from there:

> The report of the murder of all the whites at the San Carlos agency and the sacking of the agency buildings by Indians caused the wildest excitement here and was carried by whip and spur to the uttermost parts of the country. Bells were rung and drums beat in Globe, and persons were seen carrying guns, buying cartridges and otherwise preparing for the supposed impending conflict. But happily neither a shot or a funeral note was heard, nor a surgeon called to dress a gaping wound. . . .
>
> The greatest damage done by the "outbreak" was freighting the wires with sensational dispatches which have already been read in the various states by at least 25,000,000 of people who swallow them as gospel truth and naturally conclude that hell's broke loose in Arizona. It is true that the killing of Colvig is to be regretted, as indeed it is to see human life take flight in any shape, but he and his Indians scouts who gave up the ghost at the same time have gone to join the myriad host that preceded them, and you, gentle reader, cannot dodge the issue, and, therefore, had better keep your eye on the editor of this paper, if you want to be an angel, and imitate his purity of character in order that when you cross the shining river you will find friends to welcome you to a seat at David's hip.[2]

Apache and Camp Thomas and knew every foot of the trail; later he became a civilian packer with the army. He had fought at Cibecue and was both fearless and respected. It was he who volunteered for the perilous task of running a message from besieged Fort Apache to the telegraph line at Thomas.

[2] Judge Aaron Harrison Hackney was editor of the *Silver Belt* at this time. There is reason to believe that some difference of opinion existed between Hackney and some of his readers regarding his qualifications as an angel, but none whatever concerning his boldness, ability, and influence as a frontier editor. Born in Pennsylvania in 1815, he gradually moved west, "keeping ahead of the railroads." In Missouri he became associated with the *Missouri Republican* and the *Post-Dispatch*, owned a fleet of river boats plying between St. Louis and New Orleans, and became a county judge, the title following him westward to Mesilla, on the Río Grande, where he arrived in 1857, and thence, by way of Silver City, to Globe. At Silver City, which he is said to have named, it then numbering but a single house, he established a newspaper and helped to organize—and suggested the name for—Grant County. Hackney and a nephew, Joseph Hamill, came

Na-ti-o-tish's warriors had paused barely long enough to strip four hundred feet of yellow wire from the telegraph poles and heave it down an arroyo. Gathering adherents until they numbered fifty-four fighting men, they slashed at McMillen, a small mining town, and wounded one man, swept over to the Salt and down it to Tonto Creek, then swung north up that well-remembered route into Tonto Basin. The uprising had curled the hair of the frontier communities as not even Loco had done, and civilians, soldiers, and even other Apaches swarmed out onto the main trails to intercept and destroy the renegades. Even faraway Washington was alarmed. It had had enough of what it believed to be incompetence in army management of Indian affairs, and besides speeding troop reinforcements, it determined to return the old master, General Crook, to Arizona to resolve what it considered to be developing chaos.[3]

---

to Globe in the spring of 1878, established the *Arizona Silver Belt*, and laboriously printed its first edition, dated May 2, 1878. The Judge couldn't find type large enough for the masthead, and so he whittled what he wanted from a seasoned ox yoke. Hackney, a leading promoter of Globe and its mineral wealth, urged construction of a railroad to the town, "where the iron horse finally caught up with him," and became the virtual father of the community, being remembered to this day for his kindliness and good deeds, as well as for his foresight and editorial ability. He is said never to have left Globe, except for a short trip to Tucson in 1882, from the time of his arrival until his death. Struck by paralysis late in life, Judge Hackney died on December 2, 1899, at eighty-four and was buried in Globe Cemetery. Information from McClintock, II, 507, and articles by Mrs. Clara T. Woody and Jess G. Hayes in the eightieth-anniversary edition of the *Arizona Silver Belt*, May 8, 1958.

3 Crook apparently received his orders July 13 but did not leave the Department of the Platte until August 30, arriving at Prescott on September 3, 1882. He had been in command of that important theater of operations since April 27, 1875, directing the Big Horn campaign, February 17 to April 2, 1876, and May 9, 1876, to June 13, 1877, during the course of which he helped to pick up the pieces from the disastrous Custer expedition and rounded up most of the Sioux and Cheyenne hostiles. Things were therefore very quiet on the Northern Plains in 1882, and he could readily be spared for the more active Arizona region. General Oliver O. Howard succeeded Crook as commander of the Department of the Platte, and Willcox was assigned, with his regiment, the Twelfth Infantry, to that department, but was sent almost immediately to command Madison Barracks, New York, until 1886. He was then promoted to brigadier general (he had won a brevet rank of major general much earlier) and assumed command of the Department of Missouri until his retirement in 1887. Willcox was a valuable officer and is not to be blamed for the conditions which led to his removal from the Arizona command, although his competence in dealing with the Apaches was decidedly less than Crook's.

The redoubtable Globe Rangers, a party of eleven civilians attempting to live up to the terrible threats they had made concerning what they would do to hostiles if they could get within range of them, took the trail, "well primed with the best brand of whiskey," and kept bravely on until the Apaches stole all their horses while the Rangers were taking a siesta at Middleton Ranch, up in Pleasant Valley. They were forced to trudge back to Globe, chagrined and afoot.

More to the point, troops were dispatched into the field from camps around the perimeter of the Tonto Basin—from Verde, Whipple, Mc-Dowell, Thomas, and Apache. They marched to perform "the most remarkable concentration of troops at a danger point ever known on the frontier."[4] Sieber and his scouts hurriedly left McDowell and pushed hard past Old Camp Reno, its remains by now barely visible, northeast to Wild Rye Creek, where they met Chaffee and a party of Indian scouts under Second Lieutenant George H. Morgan,[5] who had come from Verde and Whipple.[6] Sieber became chief of scouts for the whole outfit.

It was after dark when the junction was made. Camp was made and supper was cooking when a wounded man staggered into the firelight. His name was Sigsbee,[7] and he said the hostiles had attacked a horse ranch run by him and his brother on the headwaters of Tonto Creek. They had all but cut off the brothers as they fled for home, wounding him through the shoulder. His brother and Louis Houdon, a workman, sought to drive some stallions from a log corral into a stable but were killed and mutilated in approved Apache fashion, although the Indians didn't get away scot free, judging from the

---

[4] Carter, *Chaffee*, 84.

[5] A West Pointer, Canadian-born Morgan, who entered the army from Minneapolis, eventually made colonel before his retirement.

[6] This is according to Cruse. He described the engagement well in his *Apache Days and After*, 158–72, and also supplied information to Britton Davis; he has been widely rewritten, as he is here. Other sources I have used heavily include a summary by Morgan in a letter to Davis dated September 14, 1927; a second summary from then Second Lieutenant Converse in a letter to Davis of September 17, 1927; comments by Barnes in "The Apaches' Last Stand in Arizona," *loc. cit.*; correspondence between Cruse and Davis; and Horn, 103–13.

[7] Many sources spell the name "Sigsby," but Bob Riell of Globe, who knew the brothers, says it should be spelled "Sigsbee."

bloody shirts some of them left behind. The wounded Sigsbee, barricaded in the cabin, held the Indians off all day; at dusk he killed a brave who crept in too close. When it became quite dark, he fled, making his way through a cordon of hostiles to his meeting with the white command.

Waiting only to finish supper, Sieber, Chaffee, and the scouts set out at a swift pace toward the ranch, reaching it early the next morning. A brief news dispatch told the story:

> The troops under Major Chaffee and a company of scouts under Al Sieber arrived at the valley and encamped at Sigsby's. The bodies of the murdered men were found, horribly mutilated by the Indians, and were decently interred.[8]

It was an all too common incident in the long decades of Indian war in Arizona. Men had become hardened to such scenes and no one thought much about it. There was no particular desire for revenge, a luxury emotion for noncombatants in faraway Tucson and other safe places. The command was pleased that it had beaten all other troops to the hostile trail and was ahead of them; if it could remain ahead, it would have the first crack at the enemy. The column turned north up the trail, which was an open book to the scouts.

By this time other troop columns were converging on the Upper Tonto Basin from various directions. The ranking officer was Colonel A. W. Evans, a "famous old Indian fighter," as Cruse calls him, who was coming from Fort Apache and whose scouts had just cut Chaffee's trail in advance of his own column. He sent an officer's patrol forward, and it returned with Chaffee and Sieber after dark, the officer explaining the situation. Evans had been having trouble with his scouts, who apparently had no stomach for closing with the hostiles. They, wrote Lieutenant Morgan, "had made Colonel Evans believe that the renegades were too far ahead for our forces to overhaul them."[9]

But Sieber and Chaffee knew better. "I'm sure that the hostiles are just a little way ahead," Cruse overheard Chaffee tell the Colonel. "Sieber thinks they expect close pursuit and his idea is that they'll

[8] *Arizona Star*, July 26, 1882.
[9] Morgan to Davis, September 14, 1927.

stop at General Springs to fight. That's a steep cliff where the trail climbs out of Tonto Basin onto the Crook Road. Sieber feels that they'll expect to cut up even a superior number of troops, because of their position."

"Well," Colonel Evans replied, "you can go on tomorrow just as if you were acting alone. Your troop is mounted on white horses, and so is [Lieutenant George] Converse's[10] troop of the 3rd. I'll put Converse at the head of my column. So if the Indians do stop to fight, you'll have two 'white horse troops' to throw against them. It may confuse them."[11] Chaffee rode off through the darkness for his camp. At 3:30 A.M., Morgan left Evans' camp for Chaffee's, arriving at 6:30 just as the advance units were filing out.

All morning the column worked hard along the hostile trail, with scouts out right and left and at point to thwart any ambush attempt. They marched through country that "looks as though during the Creation it had been God's workshop, and the scraps had never been swept."[12]

"The chase pointed toward the pass over the Rim Rock below the General Springs,"[13] wrote Morgan. "Guarded by our scouts the troop just made the best time it could over the plain trail of the hostile horses. When my scouts, who were by this time joined by the Fort Apache scouts, gained the top of the Rim Rock, they sat down on a log and, influenced I think by the Fort Apache outfit, told me that the enemy was too far ahead, and it was useless to go farther and also that the country ahead was bad medicine and they did not care for it. As we had that day passed three fortified camps, which showed we were making three of the hostile day's journeys in one, this was nonsense of course." But the officer could do nothing with the scouts, al-

10 Converse was one of Morgan's West Point classmates.

11 Cruse, *op. cit.*, 160–61.

12 *Arizona Star*, April 13, 1883.

13 General's Springs, or Generals' Springs, as Bourke writes it, was named for General Crook. The water hole, which Crook himself discovered "and near which he had such a narrow escape from being killed by Apaches," according to Bourke, was indeed an oasis. Barnes, *Place Names*, 174, says it is a "fine large spring" not far from the Mogollon Rim east of Baker Butte.

though he was nominally in command,[14] and so he turned to Sieber, who could handle them. "Sieber, in his abrupt way, started them along pronto," wrote Morgan.

This was about noon. Three hours later, the scouts, with Al in the advance, crept up to the rim of a sharp gash from the south and somehow discerned the hostiles in ambush some seven hundred yards distant on the opposite side of the canyon,[15] thereby saving the command from a bloody trap. Meanwhile, Converse had come upon a note, which Chaffee had stuck in a forked stick at the side of the trail, urging him on because he was "close on the Indians & would strike them soon & needed help in a hurry."[16] Converse's troop was instantly detached by Evans and advanced at a gallop up the trail to Chaffee, arriving just as he was deploying along the rim.

Converse was ordered to deploy to the right and do what he could to keep the hostiles occupied until some way could be found to get at them with a substantial force. As soon as Colonel Evans arrived, he would cover the center with fire. Because he was junior to Evans, Chaffee prepared to turn over the command, but Evans would have none of it. "It's your fight," he courteously told Chaffee, to the latter's delight. "You found the Indians and they belong to you. I give you full control." This was all the more generous because Chaffee and Evans belonged to rival regiments.

The battle started too soon because "unfortunately a recruit in my troop got nervous & let his piece go before we got into position," Converse wrote. "Up to that time the Indians did not know we were so

14 This is an interesting—and authoritative—refutation, in Morgan's own words, of Colonel C. C. Smith's theory that the chiefs of scouts were guides and nothing else. Here, Morgan, nominally in command, could do nothing with the Apaches. It was Sieber, not Morgan, who issued orders which they could not mistake and which they promptly obeyed.

15 The site of the battle of July 17, 1882, has been identified and is marked, despite confusing accounts which place the battlefield at Chevelon's Fork, Big Dry Fork, or General's Springs Canyon. Cruse also calls it Canyon Diablo, but Barnes says it was actually on East Clear Creek west of where General's Springs Canyon enters that stream. In his official report, Evans called the fight the "Battle of Big Dry Wash," but there is no geographic feature of that name today, although one 1880 map, which Evans may have used, adopted that title, presumably for East Clear Creek.

16 Converse to Davis, September 17, 1927.

close."[17] Sporadic fire was exchanged, and Cruse soon heard that Converse had been shot in the head, despite the extreme range. As Cruse stopped to have a word with him, Converse said dazedly that something was wrong with his eyes, "but it will pass." It did not pass. A .44 slug had split on a rock and one piece penetrated Converse's eye. Skilled surgeons were never able to remove it, although Converse remained in service and, in spite of sometimes almost unbearable pain, advanced in rank until he retired as a full colonel.

Some of the Indian scouts under Cruse and Sieber were ordered to circle far to the right, or east, cross the canyon within a mile, and come up on the hostiles from the rear. They were to be accompanied by Troop E of the Sixth, under Captain Adam Kramer and Lieutenant West, and Troop I, Chaffee's own.

Lieutenant Morgan had asked Chaffee if he might take the rest of the scouts and try the same maneuver on the left, but Chaffee gruffly turned him down. "I'm sure those scouts won't fight, or if you do get into it, they'll abandon you in a pinch," he growled to Morgan.[18] But he needed someone to pressure the hostiles on that flank and finally told Morgan to take his scouts, along with the Sixth's K Troop, under Captain Lemuel A. Abbott and Second Lieutenant Frederick G. Hodgson, and Troop D of the Third, under Lieutenants F. H. Hardie and Franklin C. "Friday" Johnson, and deploy in that direction along the rim.

Tom Horn, who probably was not in the battle but who often passed along interesting gossip, reported that Chaffee urged his men on at every phase of the rim action. "Chaffee, in a fight, can beat any man swearing I ever heard," Horn wrote. "He swears by ear, and by note in a common way, and by everything else in a general way. He would swear when his men would miss a good shot, and he would swear when they made a good shot. He swore at himself for not bringing more ammunition, and he would swear at his men for wasting their ammunition or shooting too often. Then an Indian would expose himself, and he would swear and yell: 'Shoot, you damned idiots! What do you suppose I give you ammunition for—to eat?' "[19] And his men

[17] *Ibid.*
[18] Morgan to Davis, September 14, 1927.   [19] Horn, 108–109.

swore, too—they swore by Chaffee and loved him. Sieber and Chaffee had faith in and respect for each other, and they worked together in many actions.

Chaffee chewed on a twig and finally sent for Morgan again. "Lieutenant," he said, "when K and D are deployed, take some troopers and work across the canyon if you can, and circle to the rear of the Indians, trying to contact Kramer."[20] Morgan hurriedly carried out his orders. Finding a way down the almost impassable pitches and up the opposite precipice, he and his small command ran head on into a hostile force seeking to duplicate Chaffee's strategy and fall upon the whites' flank. A cascade of fire ensued.

Far down the canyon, Sieber and the other flankers had gained its floor. Bright sunlight had been on them when they started down, but so narrow was the defile at the bottom that someone gasped, pointed upward, and all peered at the unrivaled spectacle of stars shining in broad daylight. But there was little time to enjoy the sight; the hardbitten little party scrambled breathlessly up the other wall, arriving in a beautiful, parklike pine forest with little or no underbrush.

Sieber and his Tontos were on the right of the skirmish line, scouting that flank, when they reached the hostiles' pony herd. Fortunately, just then Morgan's group and the hostile right wing opened fire on each other and the horse guards cocked their heads to listen, trying to guess what it meant and ready to flee if it meant what they thought it did. With no warning, "Sieber and West opened up on them, wiping them out," Cruse recalled, then scooped up the horses and sent them with the scouts to safety. Pushing their advantage, Cruse and Sieber led an assault which swept around the hostiles and swung in upon them from the rear just as Abbott's and Morgan's element routed the raiders on the opposite side and drove them back upon the main hostile line, which was still firing across the canyon into Chaffee's men.

The panic affected all of the enemy at once. The whole of them milled backward toward where they had left the pony herd. "It seemed to us that our capture of the herd had roused the Indians to a rush," Cruse wrote, "bent on retaking the ponies. But actually they had no thought of our presence; they only wanted to get away."[21] By

[20] Morgan to Davis, September 14, 1927.   [21] Cruse, *op. cit.*, 165.

now the hostiles, not the whites, were in a trap, for the wings of Chaffee's flankers had joined at the Navaho Trail—behind the Indians. "We fired into them and saw some fall and others jump to hunt cover behind the pines," wrote Cruse. "Shadows were thickening in the forest, and it was not easy to see. I had the left flank of our E Troop, at the canyon rim, some two hundred yards in front of what had been the main camp of the hostiles. Al Sieber was at my side."

Early in the battle a scout, Private Pete, was killed. One account says that one of Sieber's scouts, during the thickest part of the fight, "saw two of his brothers and his father with the Indians. He threw his gun down and started to run to his folks. Sieber told him to halt. He did not heed him. Sieber raised his rifle and fired, shooting him in the back of the head."[22]

Lieutenant Morgan sought to get actively into the fight. It was his first major brush with the Apaches. A crack shot, winner of a gold medal for shooting that very month, he fired now and again, but so fleeting were the glimpses of the hostiles that he could not be sure of his luck. At last he dropped one everybody could see and yelled triumphantly: "Got him! I got him!" In his excitement, however, Morgan exposed himself and a bullet crashed through his arm and into his body. "We thought him sure to die," Cruse said, "but the slug had only gone around his ribs and lodged in the back muscles." Sieber later confided to Converse that he personally killed the Indian who had shot Morgan.[23]

Sergeant Daniel Conn of Troop E was "a whisp of a Boston Irishman" with a brogue you could cut with a knife and twenty years in the regiment, where, through one means or another, he had secured a relatively soft detail as ration sergeant: issuing the Apache scouts their rations. They nicknamed him *Coche Sergeant*, or "Hog Ser-

[22] Letter from C. P. Wingfield of Humboldt, *Arizona Historical Review*, Vol. III, No. 4 (January, 1931), 47. There is nothing to suggest that this executed scout—if the story is true—is Pete, and it may be that an injustice is done a brave and loyal scout by tying the two incidents together. Whatever the truth, Private Pete is the only Apache scout listed as killed in the battle; Barnes says he was shot through the head, and Wingfield's letter is the only reference in print to explain how any scout was killed in the action.

[23] Converse to Davis, September 17, 1927.

geant," since pork was a staple of the ration. Now, some of the renegades who had been scouts before the Cibecue fight heard Conn giving
orders to troopers and taunted him: "Aaaaiiah! Coche Sergeant!
Coche Sergeant!" One, versed in English, went further: "Coward!
Hog Sergeant! Come here and *I* will kill you!" Conn yelled something back and the Indian, firing at the sound of his voice, shot him
through the throat, opening a hole as big as a silver dollar through a
size-thirteen neck, according to Cruse. Conn dropped and heard Captain Kramer observe to First Sergeant Tony Hagerup: "I'm afraid
they got poor Conn."

Afterward, Conn joked about the incident. "Sure, I heard the Cap'n
say I was kilt," he affirmed. "But I knew I was not. I was only
spa-a-chless!"

There was more fighting to be done, and Cruse has described it in
some detail:

> Our men and Sieber wiped out that whole bunch of hostiles and we
> pushed on. Sieber was still beside me, and I saw him kill three of the rene
> gades in quick succession, as they crept toward the edge of the canyon to
> go over and away from the battle.
>
> "There he goes," he would grunt at me.
>
> With the report of his rifle an Indian I had not seen would suddenly
> appear, flinging up his arms as if to catch at some support. Then under
> the momentum of his rush he would plunge forward on his head and roll
> over and over. One man shot at the very rim plunged over, and it seemed
> to me that he continued to fall for many minutes.

It was 5:30 P.M. and shadows were gathering in the pine forest.
Cruse feared that soon the Indians might slip away in the darkness.
About seventy-five yards separated his men from the knot of hostiles
at the head of the trail.

> "I'm going into the camp," I told Sieber.
>
> "No! Don't you do it, Lieutenant! Don't you do it!" he objected, much
> to my surprise. "There's lots of Indians over there and they'll get you
> sure!"
>
> "Why, Al!" I said, "You've killed every one of them!"

Cruse yelled to his men to come along and the little line charged directly at the hostile position, covered by heavy fire from Sieber and Captain Kramer's troopers. "When we got into the open, I discovered that Sieber had been right," Cruse admitted. There were lots of Indians, but Cruse had such veterans as Corporal John T. Horan and others, well able to handle any situation as long as their ammunition held out.

Suddenly a hostile jumped up within two yards of the Lieutenant, leveled his rifle, and fired, but "he was so nervous and jerked just enough as he pulled the trigger to send the bullet past me. A young Scotchman named Joseph McLernon[24] was just to my left and slightly in the rear. The bullet hit him, and he dropped. I shot the Indian and threw myself to the ground—which caused Captain Kramer and Sieber to believe that I had been struck. McLernon was sprawling beside me and I asked if he were hurt. 'Yes sir,' he answered. 'Through the arm. I think it's broken.' "

McLernon was wounded more seriously than he knew: the bullet had passed through both lungs and he died within an hour. Cruse dragged him back to a position of comparative safety and when Kramer's men overran the hostile camp, secured a blanket from it to make the soldier comfortable. Cruse received a Medal of Honor for his one-man charge on the Indian camp.

It had been a day of fire and slaughter, and now a raging storm swept out of nowhere to put a stop to it. Tom Horn called it "the heaviest hail and rain storm that I ever saw in my life." He observed that "the storm came up suddenly, and it got so very dark that we could not see across the canyon. Then the hail and rain commenced. Wah! I feel cold and wet from it yet! It was over in twenty minutes, and the fight was over, also. All of us were so cold and wet we could neither see nor shoot."[25] Will Barnes agreed that this began as "a

[24] Cruse mistakenly remembered this name as "McLellan."

[25] Barnes, "The Apaches' Last Stand in Arizona," *loc. cit.*, said that "reliable Army officers have told me Horn was not in the fight, but was with the pack-trains back of the lines," even though Tom writes as if he had not only been in the thickest part of the battle, but practically won it singlehandedly. He had an accurate memory of the site, which is remarkable in view of the fact that he wrote his account thirty years before Cruse or others put their recollections down, and lists First Sergeant Zacariah T. Woodall of I Troop as performing yeoman sharpshooter service. Woodall, a Medal of Honor

terrible thunderstorm," and said that the rain soon turned to hail, covering the ground four or five inches deep, almost burying the dead in an icy shroud.[26] In the words of Lieutenant West, it was so paralyzing that "Major Chaffee got so cold and wet he had to stop swearing."[27]

Under cover of darkness and the storm, those hostiles who were still alive slipped away, most of them wounded, and made their way across the reservation line, some twenty miles to the south. But many never again went anywhere. With the clear, frosty dawn, patrols ransacked the battleground, searching out bodies and hunting for wounded. They counted either twenty-one or twenty-two enemy dead and presumed that many others lay concealed in crevices or loose rocks, future food for coyotes and vultures. The *Chronological List* places the hostile dead at sixteen, and it is interesting to note that Sieber apparently accounted for almost half of these by himself. Cruse saw him kill three Apaches, Sieber claimed he killed the Indian who shot Morgan, and the Sieber-led scouts wiped out the guards of the enemy pony herd, so of the sixteen officially reported slain, Al accounted for perhaps six or eight.

Lieutenant Hodgson had been left all night with a patrol on the north side of the chasm, and during the darkness he had heard groans. At daylight he set out to investigate when his men suddenly were fired upon—three times. Then there were no more shots. The men found a young Apache woman shielding her baby with her body; in her hands was a rifle and beside her lay three spent cartridges, all she had. She was desperately wounded yet endured without a murmur the amputation of her shattered leg and moved, aboard a mule, with the com-

---

winner and a survivor of a widely known buffalo-wallow fight fought near the Canadian River in Texas on September 12, 1874, had won medals with his marksmanship.

[26] Barnes, "The Apaches' Last Stand in Arizona," *loc. cit.*

[27] West, a first lieutenant by this time, was born at Mohawk, New York, and graduated from West Point in 1872. He arrived at Camp Verde in 1875 and had assumed command of Indian scouts there in 1878. He was cited for rallying his men at Big Dry Wash and leading them "in an advance against the enemy's fortified position," earning a Medal of Honor for it. Horn says that West was killed on San Juan Hill in the Spanish-American War, but Tom was mistaken. Horn, 110. Morgan also won a Medal of Honor for his part in the engagement.

mand back to Fort Apache, where she recovered. It was, Sieber may have thought, quite a sample of Apache stoicism and will to fight under the most adverse circumstances.

Little of note occurred immediately after the fight, save that some "self-styled local cowboys," as Cruse put it, showed up to claim the pony herd Al and his Indians had captured. They were driven off under a cloud of Chaffee profanity. A few white ghouls showed up to scalp the dead warriors, but Sieber was used to this and contemptuous of those who sought profit from his victories.

The Big Dry Wash affair was not without lasting significance, however. For one thing it marked the final major battle between Apaches and troops on Arizona soil. Of all the Apaches, only the Chiricahuas would henceforth challenge government control with violence. And the congressman-father of wounded George Converse secured passage of legislation authorizing additional army surgeons at frontier posts and prohibiting the future movement of sizable bodies of troops after hostiles unless accompanied by a surgeon.

The troops owed a lot to luck, too, in the success of their fight, but, Sieber may have shrugged, that was the way it was—the luck would never remain all on one side, for long. As far as he was concerned, it was simply another hard scout, shorter and more successful than most but otherwise indistinguishable from others he had guided.

XVI. A Man of Note

AL SIEBER had become a man of note in Arizona; in all of Apachería, for that matter. He was the only scout regularly on the government payroll, although others were hired from time to time, or for special tasks, and his conscientious work during the various campaigns and forays may often have made the difference between success and failure. A scout, or chief of scouts, did not bulk importantly in government regulations, but in the field he could, as often as not, spell the difference between missing the enemy and finding him, between defeat and a consuming victory.

Surely it is not all coincidence that when Sieber was present, success almost invariably attended punitive operations against the Apaches; when he was absent, a triumph was rare. Forsyth's fight with Loco, the affair at Cibecue, Nana's raid, and the later one by Chato, all were resounding Indian successes, in Al's absence. The Tupper fight with the hostiles, the battle at Big Dry Wash, and the campaign into Mexico were devastating white victories, with Sieber present. Why the abrupt difference?

This is not to claim for Al Sieber more than was his due. He was a chief of scouts and perhaps little more, but he was a most unusual chief of scouts—the most uniformly successful one in the long and sanguinary history of Arizona's Indian wars.

He had come anew to General Crook's attention, perhaps because of his careful analysis of the Loco campaign, a study which may well have been inspired by disgruntled officers who themselves could not afford to criticize Forsyth, superior to them in rank. Just as likely, however, it was because of enthusiastic mention of the scout by the growing circle of officers for whom he had worked.

Crook no doubt remembered Sieber well from his first Arizona offensive and for his work with Schuyler at Camp Verde thereafter. Chaffee may have mentioned Sieber's key role in the Big Dry Wash affair. At any rate, in Crook's plans Al began to take the place once occupied by Archie McIntosh, who now was on and off the government payroll, being as interested in his ranch at Black Mesquite Springs south of the Salt as in scouting. He had married an Apache woman and fathered a son.

Crook, who arrived at Fort Whipple on his new assignment early in September, reached Apache by the middle of the month, finding the Indians "sullen, distrustful" and mostly in hiding—a far cry from the situation he had left seven years before. Crook's was the direct way, and he wanted to ferret out the skulking Apaches, talk to them face to face, listen to their problems, and try to work out reasonable solutions before the whole of Arizona blew up in another, still bloodier Indian war. So at Apache he made up a tiny expedition composed of himself, Sieber, Corydon E. Cooley as interpreter, and Captain John Bourke, and set off into the wilderness. Perhaps Sieber had come to Apache after the Big Dry Wash fight, or maybe he had been ordered there from McDowell to meet Crook, but at any rate he was available.

Before leaving Apache, Crook had counciled with such of the Apaches as could be induced to come in, men like Alchise, Cut-Mouth Moses, Mosby, and half a hundred others. He heard them complain that the army men in whom they had confidence had been removed from positions over them, leaving the Indians prey to the ring of crooked agents and contractors, and that they were being literally starved as well as otherwise abused in other ways. They had had no remedy but war for this sad state of affairs. In a letter to a United States district attorney, Crook said that a policy of preventing outbreaks before they occur could "only be successful when the officers of justice fearlessly perform their duty in proceeding against the villains who fatten on the supplies intended for the use of Indians. . . . Bad as Indians often are, I have never yet seen one so demoralized that he was not an example of honor and nobility compared to the wretches who enrich themselves by plundering him of the little our Government appropriates for him."[1]

Crook, Sieber, Cooley, and Bourke dropped into the deep and gloomy canyon of the Black River above where it joins the White to become the Salt and at a secluded glade found more than one hundred Apaches ready and anxious to talk. Alchise, sent from Fort Apache to call his fellow tribesmen to this place, was there, along with Nagatah, A-ha-ni, Kan-tzi-chi, Tzi-di-ku, and many others, all reporting on "the general worthlessness and rascality of the agents who had been placed in charge of them; the constant robbery going on without an attempt at concealment; the selling of supplies and clothing intended for the Indians, to traders in the little towns of Globe, Maxey, and Solomonville; the destruction of the corn and melon fields of the Apache, who had been making their own living, and the compelling of all who could be forced to do so to depend upon the agent for meagre supplies; the arbitrary punishment inflicted without trial, or without testimony of any kind; the cutting down of the reservation limits without reference to the Apaches."[2] The miserable story was reiterated until its sordid nature became appalling by sheer weight of testimony.

Having heard the Apaches out, Crook and his companions headed for San Carlos, where they fully expected to be treated to more of the same. Yet even on this trip everything was not grim. Shortly after the party arrived at San Carlos, Crook good-humoredly told Bill Mc-Nelly how fine a hunter Sieber was:

> I hired a man to hunt on this expedition, and he was supposed to supply the mess with game. At the end of two weeks he had not brought in a single deer.
>
> Sieber came to me and said: "General, that fellow you employed as a hunter is no good. I see signs of deer right along. Not a day has passed that I couldn't have got a deer. Send me out tomorrow, and I'll prove it to you—just send out the pack mule when you hear the report of my rifle."
>
> He started out the next morning and had not been gone fifteen minutes

---

1 Bourke, *Border*, 445.
2 *Ibid.*, 441.

when I heard his shot. By the time the packer arrived with the mule, Sieber had the deer ready to bring into camp. I gave the useless hunter his marching orders and said, "Sieber, there must be some body odor about you that the deer can't get away from!"

The General chuckled at remembrance of his sally, and Sieber laughed aloud, as McNelly recalled the incident. Of such was humor on the frontier.[3]

Once more Crook was busy analyzing a difficult situation and plotting the course he must follow to solve it. He had heard the Indian side of the story; now he called in most of the officers in southern Arizona and one by one heard them explain their problems as they understood them. He was convinced that within a short time there would have been a general outbreak, but he promptly closed the sluices of graft and corruption, reassured the tame Apaches, and quieted them. The Indian problem would never be solved, he realized, until the pool of wild Chiricahuas in Mexico was brought under control. There lay the most difficult puzzle—and the one that would be hardest to crack. It was only a question of time until they could resume their raids across the border.

To solidify his gains and stabilize the situation on the giant reservations, Crook selected his officers with care. He called in Captain Emmet Crawford of the Third Cavalry, tall, slender, and described by Bourke as "a most intelligent and conscientious officer"; Lieutenant C. B. Gatewood of the Sixth Cavalry; Britton Davis,[4] a brand-new second lieutenant of the Third; and Second Lieutenant Hamilton Roach, also of the Third.

Crawford was given military control of the reservations, with orders to report directly to Crook. Gatewood was assigned control of

[3] Lockwood APHS.

[4] Britton Davis was born to a military family of note at Brownsville, Texas, on June 4, 1860, and graduated from West Point in 1881, joining the Third Cavalry and reaching Arizona in May; he was given a command of Indian scouts in September, 1882. Davis resigned his commission June 1, 1886, to become superintendent of the Corralitos Mining and Cattle Company in Mexico, amassing quite a fortune, which, however, was lost in the revolution that overthrew the Díaz regime. He lived for a time at Congers, New York, then moved to San Diego, where he died on January 23, 1930, at the age of sixty-nine. 1930 *Annual Report* of the Association of Graduates, U.S. Military Academy.

the White Mountain Apaches at Fort Apache, and Davis was to command Apache scouts at San Carlos. All were placed on "detached service as assistant chiefs of staff to the Commanding General of the Department."[5] Al Sieber was named chief of scouts, with Archie McIntosh and Sam Bowman as his assistants, and Mickey Free, enlisted as a scout but with the pay of a first sergeant, served as interpreter.

Britton Davis found Sieber "all bone and muscle" at this time. He also had other qualities:

> Capable and courageous, the Indians feared and respected him. A better selection for chief of scouts could not have been made. If there was ever a man who actually did not know physical fear, that man was Al Sieber! He was in no sense reckless, took all necessary precautions, but never hesitated when it became necessary to throw caution aside. He was in constant danger of assassination, as many of the Indians had personal grudges against him, but he went about his work as though all the world were his friends.[6]

One of Sieber's characteristics was his ability to get on well even with those of whom he disapproved. Archie and Sam Bowman were old acquaintances; they were of a kind who had shared enough hardships and adventure to become akin to one another, but the halfblood Mickey Free was something else again. Sieber once grunted to the Lieutenant that Mickey was "half Mexican, half Irish and whole son of a bitch,"[7] but perhaps he didn't quite mean it. For three and one-half years Mickey was Davis' faithful interpreter. "The Indians suspected him of coloring things to suit the whites," wrote Davis. "He may have fooled me on occasion, but if he did it was done so skilfully that I never found it out."[8]

[5] Britton Davis, *Geronimo*, 34–35. Lockwood, *The Apache Indians*, 261, says: "No braver, more honorable, more competent soldiers ever had dealings with American Indians than General Crook and these three young officers into whose hands he now committed the affairs of the reservation. All four of them have achieved lasting fame in the history of the Army and the literature of the Southwest for their resolute and just, yet gentle and humane, dealings with these fierce, misguided, mistreated Apaches."

[6] Britton Davis, *Geronimo*, 35–36.

[7] Britton Davis notes accompanying photographs he presented to the National Archives. Information from Mrs. J. F. Connor's collection of Britton Davis' correspondence (cited hereafter as Connor Collection).

[8] Britton Davis, *Geronimo*, 37.

Davis had some caustic things to say about books and magazine articles glorifying the deeds of alleged chiefs of scouts or other civilians, and in private correspondence he makes it clear that he was referring to Tom Horn's book, among others:

> Almost without exception these accounts are fakes, padded up to a semblance of truth by the introduction of incidents that actually occurred, but did not occur to the party glorified.
>
> During the three years from May, 1882, to May, 1885, Al Sieber alone was Chief of Scouts. Until May, 1885, there were no civilian employees in any way connected with the management of the Indians [at San Carlos] except Sieber, MacIntosh [sic], and Bowman. MacIntosh was dismissed in the fall of 1883. The reader can draw his own conclusions when he reads the historical romances of Tom, Bill, and Charley, if those romances refer to the period I have mentioned. After the outbreak in May, 1885, other civilians were employed in various capacities connected with the pursuit of the hostiles. Of these I have no knowledge.
>
> Micky Free I do not class as a civilian. He was with me as interpreter continuously during all my term of service except for a short time in the winter of 1882–3, when he was in the field with Crawford, and on the General's expedition into Mexico.

And, Davis added, "we used no civilians as scouts."[9]

Crook issued general orders stressing the demands he placed upon his officers and men in dealing with the Apaches and continued his conferences with the Indians through October and into November. He told them that the troops henceforth would not serve as a guard to protect those who would rob them, organized Indian police to maintain order, and promised that those who desired to farm would be given good land on which to do so. The Crook impress began to be felt everywhere.

Davis and Sieber had the actual running of San Carlos pretty much to themselves, and found they could always rely on Crawford for

---

[9] *Ibid.* It should be noted, however, that Sieber himself, in the letter which was reproduced as an appendix to Horn's book and which reads as if it had been written by Al, states that "Tom went to work for me in the government pack train in 1882; he was with me and worked steady with me for three years." Davis mentions the immediate organization of pack trains in 1882, and he must have excluded packers, who were always civilians, from his blanket statement.

authority for whatever action they deemed necessary. Crawford had a talk with the San Carlos trader, as a result of which the latter promptly cut his outrageous prices in half. The Indians complained —with reason—of the quality of issue beef, and Lieutenant Davis dropped around to watch the rationing. Beefs for the Indians were held on the hoof a few miles from the agency, and once a week the required number were cut out and driven into an adobe corral, where Indian policeman shot them down with a rifle. This was a favorite occupation, and the scout later known as the Apache Kid often assumed the welcome chore.[10] "The police saw to it that a more or less fair division was made of the meat among the families who sent for their share," wrote Davis. "The division, however, was not without the usual fighting and squabbling of the old women over choice bits of organs and entrails."[11]

The Lieutenant soon discovered that the agent had been up to his old tricks. The weights had been doctored so that the Indians received about fifteen hundred pounds less meat than was to be issued. In addition, the herd was kept south of the river, while the agency was north of it. The cattle were kept without water all the day before issue; naturally, when they came to the river, they drank heavily and "came on the scales looking like miniature Zeppelins. The Government was paying a pretty stiff price for half a barrel of Gila River water delivered with each beef."[12] A new contract was let with Colonel Henry Hooker, then running some twenty thousand head of cattle in the Sierra Bonitas on his fabulous Crooked H Ranch of a quarter-million acres, and there were no more complaints about the quality of issue beef. The Colonel was an honest man.

Davis and Sieber had many consultations and prescribed for each other's troubles over many a drink at the agency store, where whiskey was for whites only. The Lieutenant had been charged with purchasing hay from the Indians—a product to which they had ready access

10 Interview with Bud Ming of Ray, Arizona. Ming, son of a famous Arizona pioneer, Indian fighter, and cattleman, spent part of his boyhood at San Carlos and preserves a remarkably clear memory of many of the figures and scenes he was familiar with around the old post.

11 Britton Davis, *Geronimo*, 42.

12 *Ibid.*, 42–43.

and which the women could cut and pack in by themselves. The wily ladies soon learned every trick in the book for cheating on weights, and it became a game between them and the fledgling officer to see whether they could put anything over on him. It was a nuisance to Davis, but Crook laughed out loud at his tribulations, and Davis ruefully chuckled at them himself.

With just rationing, payment for their products, and friendly, honest treatment, the Apaches soon began to come out of the shell into which they had withdrawn for refuge from the tactics of the scoundrels who had been placed over them. Their native good humor took over and they were "children awakened from a nightmare!" as Davis put it.

Two young men had returned from Indian schools back east, and Crawford found them a room in a small building near the agency, curious to see what impact these men, one trained as a cobbler, the other as a carpenter, would have on their people. He even asked them what they were going to do now, and they said that at school they had been admonished to "tell the Indians 'bout Jesus," so that was what they were going to do. He kept his counsel for the moment. Then one night, Al Sieber, always prowling around keeping a weather eye on the turbulent charges, spied a light shining from their window. Curious, since it was quite late, he slipped over and peeked in—seeing a strange sight, indeed, for a couple of self-professed missionaries! "Through the window he was entertained with an Apache dance performed by the two young men and two young women, all hilariously drunk and garbed as nature garbed them," recalled Davis. In the morning Crawford booted them out, warning them that they would have to get to work and raise corn before they could drink it.

Other incidents ended less happily, but taught Davis more about Apache character. He said that one afternoon, he, Al Sieber, and Colonel S. B. Beaumont were sitting in the shade by the agency building, idly chatting. The prisoners had been brought out, as was customary, to meet their relatives on a ridge near the guardhouse, some two hundred yards from the trio; an armed guard accompanied them. Suddenly there was a commotion on the ridge and the guard raised his rifle as Sieber galloped over toward them crying in Apache: "Fire!

Fire!" The guard finally shot, and when the three whites panted up, they found the body of a young Indian prisoner lying across that of a young woman, who had been stabbed to death. The prisoner had been shot by the guard. No reason for the double tragedy was ever discovered. Other Indians merely shrugged: "Maybe mad."

And there were incidents not without humor. The Indians reported that two Americans had illegally entered the reservation and were prepared to work a coal vein two miles within its borders. They refused to leave, so Sieber and two or three scouts were sent to arrest them and bring them in, which they did with the greatest of pleasure, since it was by such unlawful acts that trouble forever was brewed. The pair laughed at Crawford when he threatened to put them off the reservation. It was not far to walk back to their coal camp, they boasted. The Captain's usually pleasant expression hardened. "Davis," he ordered, "have that light wagon hitched up. I think those mules need exercise." The men and their outfits were carted to a spot north of Fort Apache on the road to Holbrook, where they were dumped out to be faced with a 45-mile hike to the railroad, a 500-mile rail trip, and another hike of 100 miles back onto the reservation— if they cared to steal more coal. They didn't.

One of the Apache scouts was named Charlie, and like most of them, he looked up to Sieber.[13] Charlie, a San Carlos Indian, decided to get married about this time, his eye having fallen upon a comely woman of another band. He paid the price in horses and other things that her parents demanded, then took her for his own. But the woman wasn't having Charlie, and left him. The scout brooded about this, finally returned to his in-laws and demanded either the woman or her price, but was refused. So he killed her.

In accordance with General Crook's orders, this man now had to be tried—by the Indians themselves, although Captain Crawford sat in as assistant to the trial "judge." The jury's verdict was that Charlie must be turned over to his late wife's people, to be put to death. This the army officers did not want, since it might well lead to a feud.

13 This story is one of the better-known tales about Sieber, and the narrative here was compiled from that related in Williamson, "Sieber." Britton Davis, *Geronimo*, 48–49, gives an abbreviated account that differs in detail.

Charlie didn't want it, either. He appealed to Sieber, asserting he didn't mind being shot or hanged, but objected to torture.

Crawford, brave as a lion yet gentle as a girl, had meanwhile turned the matter over to Davis, conceding that the whites would have to take care of it but adding: "I so hate the thought of it that I wish you would have it done and not let me know anything about it." To complicate matters still more, the doomed man's relatives had demanded the prisoner, telling Sieber that they intended to punish him "in our own way," which he understood and refused to permit. They could shoot or hang, but not torture him, Sieber said. So they consulted, and compromised, leaving it up to Sieber. Davis had confessed to the veteran scout his distaste for the duty before him. "Now don't you worry, Lieutenant," Sieber told him in his curiously intent way. "Don't worry about it at all. I'll take care of it. You just leave it to me."

Al told Bill Duclin to hitch up a four-mule spring wagon, get a pick and shovel, and report to the guardhouse. He also ordered two scouts to report, armed and mounted, to escort in case of a break. At the guardhouse the prisoner was loaded in, and the cavalcade clattered off toward Camp Thomas, Sieber and Charlie gaily chatting of wild times in their adventure-strewn lives.

The road wound before them as the mules trotted along, the wheels crunching honestly on the clean, hard path, which swooped and dipped in graceful undulations until it dropped down into a dry, sandy creek bed. Charlie was grinning and talking and had turned to point up toward the skyline, where the moon stood over the ridge, when the air was split by a shattering report. Charlie pitched down upon the blankets in the wagon bed, a bullet through his skull. The sentence had been carried out.

Crook continued to be most concerned with the Chiricahuas in the mountains to the south. Their strength was nearly one hundred veteran warriors plus half as many boys and apprentice fighters old enough for combat. With a couple of staff officers, half a dozen Apache scouts "who had been in the camps of the hostile Chiricahuas," and probably Al Sieber, he rode to the extreme southeastern corner of Arizona and sent men deep into the mountains beyond, trying to get word of the hostiles.[14] Some of these were vaguely reported now and then slipping up through the wilderness to San Carlos, there to visit briefly with friends and collect what ammunition they could before leaving like wraiths on their perilous and arduous trek back into the Sierra Madre. The chance of intercepting one of these was about equal to that of catching a ghost, but Crook desperately needed a guide into the Mexican fastnesses, and he lost no opportunity to seek one.

The General hoped that his scouts could spy out the present location of the hostiles "and ascertain if they would be willing to come back and remain at peace upon the reservation." Otherwise he could enlist a number of scouts and send them, without soldiers but under Sieber or McIntosh or someone else, "over the line and clean them out," despite the lack of a treaty specifically authorizing this. He did send scouts into Mexico, but, although they searched the area where hostiles often were, they found no one. Unfortunately, the Mexicans "were having a revolution that week" and the spies, uneasy, hastened back. Later they were sent south again and this time found some of the enemy, but they "were so hostile that my messengers did not dare go further." He left Crawford with one hundred Apache scouts for a time to patrol the line near Cloverdale, the likeliest route for a raiding party to use coming north.[15]

Having tried all manner of schemes, Crook became convinced that only a full-fledged expedition into Mexico would clean out the hostiles. If he could get a guide, fine; if not, he would go south anyway. Toward the end of March, 1883, he sent Crawford and Gatewood, along with Sieber, McIntosh, and Mickey Free to Willcox, a station on the Southern Pacific in southeastern Arizona, to join other units in setting up such a foray. Crook was making these preparations mostly on faith. He wanted a guide into Mexico, and hoped he would catch one, but most of all he needed an excuse to drive south of the border. A treaty between Mexico and the United States provided for a limited "hot pursuit" crossing of the line and the hard-bitten Gen-

14 Horn, 128 et passim, tells of several times when scouts penetrated Mexico on "unofficial" missions against the hostiles. Whether he can be believed or not, his accounts suggest that some sorts of expeditions were occasionally indulged in.

15 Crook to AAG, Division of the Pacific, March 28, 1883, Hayes Collection.

eral no doubt was awaiting a raid that he felt in his bones was over-due. At last it came, and he got both of his wishes in one package.

On March 21 a raiding party under the brilliant Chato struck without warning at a charcoal burner's camp southwest of Tomb-stone, killing four men and losing one. San Carlos took on the appear-ance of an armed camp as the enemy was expected to attack there but didn't. The renegades swept northeast, murdering, robbing, pil-laging. Late in March they killed United States Judge and Mrs. H. C. McComas on the high road from Silver City to Lordsburg and kid-naped the McComas' six-year-old son, Charlie, who became the object of the most widespread and prolonged search in the annals of Apache warfare. He was never found.

Chato faded south across the border. In six whirlwind days, he and twenty-six warriors had traveled not less than four hundred miles, killed twenty-six whites, and stolen no one knew how many horses and how much war material. But Chato had provided Crook with an excuse to cross the border and in addition had lost two men: one by gunfire and the other to become a guide for the General. This indi-vidual, nicknamed "Peaches" by the whites, was captured by Britton Davis when he slipped onto San Carlos Reservation to visit relatives. He readily agreed to guide Crook south. The General made a quick trip into Mexico by train to prepare officials of that country for his expedition, then returned and was ready to embark on the most dar-ing campaign ever undertaken by an American officer during the various Indian wars.

XVII. Into Mexico

ON APRIL 23, 1883, a long, dust-stirring column moved south out of
Willcox and headed for San Bernardino Springs exactly one hundred
miles distant by winding road and directly on the border in the extreme southeastern corner of Arizona.[1] There it was joined by Captain Emmet Crawford with more Apache scouts and several pack
trains. For a few days the expedition remained at the springs, organizing, rearranging, and assigning duties to the white soldiers who
would be left to guard the border while the Apache-dominated main
column pushed south. Crook was depending on Indians and his white
chief of scouts for the success of this war against Indians; only a
handful of troopers would accompany him. Each officer and man was
allowed to carry the clothes he wore, one blanket, and forty rounds
of ammunition. Officers were to mess with the packers, a highly independent lot. One hundred and sixty rounds of extra ammunition for
each man and sixty days' rations of hard bread, coffee, and bacon
were loaded on the mules.

The composition of the assault force was settled here. Besides the
General and Captains John Bourke and G. J. Fieberger, those going
along included Captain A. R. Chaffee, Lieutenants Parker W. West
and William Woods Forsyth, 42 enlisted men of I Troop of the Sixth
Cavalry, Dr. George Andrews as surgeon, and Private A. F. Harmer

[1] Often this well-known old ranch was virtually the army's headquarters in its pursuit of Apaches. It was all that remained of a 73,240-acre land grant purchased early in
the nineteenth century for ninety dollars by Ignacio Pérez, although a ranch headquarters existed here earlier and it had been used as a base by Spanish soldiers. John H.
Slaughter bought it in 1884, acquiring title to only 2,366 acres of 8,688 claimed on the
American side of the line; the balance was in Mexico. Barnes, *Place Names*, 380.

of the General Service. In command of the 193 Chiricahua, White Mountain, Yuma, Mohave, and Tonto scouts were Captain Crawford, Lieutenant James O. Mackay of the Third Cavalry and Lieutenant Charles B. Gatewood of the Sixth. Al Sieber was chief of scouts, with Archie McIntosh and Sam Bowman as his assistants and Severiano and Mickey Free as interpreters. Five pack trains accompanied the force, and it is barely possible that Tom Horn was a packer with one of them, although he was not, as he alone claims, a principal scout or interpreter. His route agrees well with Crook's actual itinerary, but his ignorance of the General's purposes and decisions demonstrates that Horn was neither in Crook's confidence nor in a high echelon, while Sieber was in both.

On May 1, as "the first rays of the sun were beaming upon the eastern hills," Gatewood grunted *"Ugashe!"* and the scouts darted like jack rabbits into the advance, fanning out to cover the route and flanks of the point. "We swung into our saddles," wrote Bourke, "and, amid a chorus of good-byes and God-bless-yous from those left behind, pushed down the hot and sandy valley of the San Bernardino, past the mouth of Guadalupe Canyon, to near the confluence of Elias Creek."[2]

As far as the nation was aware, Crook and his men might have disappeared from the face of the earth at that point. It would be forty-two days before their adventures would become known; in the meantime, rumors of all sorts circulated, most of them utterly imaginary. However, there was plenty of action for imaginations to feed upon. The Apaches were keeping much of Sonora and Chihuahua in turmoil. Shortly before Crook's expedition there had been a major battle in the Moctezuma District, high in the Sierra Madre. Opinions on the outcome differed, depending upon whether one heard descriptions of it from Mexicans or from Apaches. Bourke, deep in Mexico, heard accounts of the "most bloodthirsty fight . . . in which, of course, the Apaches had been completely and ignominiously routed, each Mexican having performed prodigies of valor. . . . [But] they wouldn't go alone into their fields,—only a quarter of a mile off. . . .

[2] John G. Bourke, *An Apache Campaign in the Sierra Madre* (cited hereafter as Bourke, *Apache Campaign*), 57.

Peaches, our guide, smiled quietly, but said nothing, when told of this latest annihilation of the Chiricahuas."[3] Later a unit from Crook's command visited the site of the battle and, after a close examination, judged it "conclusive that the Indians had enticed the Mexicans into an ambuscade, killed a number with bullets and rocks, and put the rest to ignominious flight."[4]

But that was not all the activity in Mexico, not anything like it. Geronimo, with fewer than forty fighting men, had led a raid to the east in which six Mexican women were captured and taken along as hostages. The raiders started to return to their alpine lair, but scarcely had they done so when the warrior chief gave an illustration of what would seem to be his remarkable powers of clairvoyance. They were eating roasted beef before a campfire when Geronimo suddenly dropped his knife and blurted, "Men, our people whom we left at our base camp are now in the hands of U.S. troops!" Jason Betzinez, who describes this, wrote: "I cannot explain it to this day. But I was there and saw it. No, he didn't get word by some messenger. And no smoke signals had been made." Later the chieftain predicted exactly how the returning party would be informed of the astonishing capture of their camp by Crook and how it had come about; sure enough, this prophecy, too, was fulfilled. "I still cannot explain it," said Betzinez.[5]

Almost as difficult to explain was the sudden appearance of Crook and his potent task force in the heart of the Sierra Madre, for centuries the most secure of Apache retreats. Crook had marched hard to get there. His force, beyond the call of superior officers and commands, had left San Bernardino Springs on May 1 and moved about eighteen miles the first day, camping "on the banks of a pellucid

[3] *Ibid.*, 67.

[4] *Ibid.*, 86.

[5] As is true of all imaginative, primitive people, the Apaches were fascinated by individuals who pretended to tell fortunes or exercise clairvoyance of a substantial nature. Britton Davis, *Geronimo*, 83, tells how a medicine man predicted, correctly, the time of arrival of Geronimo from Mexico and the fact that he would be riding a white mule. In a letter written November 23, 1929, to Harry Carr of the *Los Angeles Times*, Davis expressed the opinion that the prediction was based simply on "a knowledge that the old devil when not on the warpath preferred a white mount; and a guess that it was about time for him to put in his appearance." Connor Collection. Nevertheless, Geronimo's precise forecast of the capture of the camp by Crook would seem difficult of explanation.

hato was described by Britton Davis as ne of the finest men, red or white, I ve ever known."

Peaches deserted Chato's raiding party in 1883 and later led General Crook to the Apache stronghold in Mexico's Sierra Madre.

Chief Loco, one of the wisest of Warm
Springs Apaches, gave the U.S. Army a
hard fight when it clashed with his
band, and that was quite often.

Incredible old Nana, who, at seventy—or ninety—led a tremendous raid across the
southwestern United States. Like the other renegade Apache chiefs, he, too, had a
hideout deep in Mexico.

stream [Elías Creek], under the shadow of graceful walnut and ash trees."[6] The busy scouts had brought in plenty of venison and turkeys, one of the latter seeking to escape through camp, only to be pursued by grinning Apaches, caught, and its head twisted off. Breakfast at 4:00 A.M. preceded a twenty-mile march to the Bavispe River, where a stop was made some thirty miles north of the town called Bavispe. "The country is beginning to grow rough," noted a diarist.[7]

Bourke messed with Monach's pack train, whose cook was a teamster named Martin, six feet, two inches in his socks, and built like Hercules. "A better man or a worse cook never thumped a mule or turned a flapjack," the officer wrote.

Captain Crawford and his scouts now took the lead and the column marched generally up the course of the river, that is, southeastward, toward the community of Bavispe, camping within five miles of it on May 4. "Still nothing to indicate the presence of the hostiles," the diarist noted. On May 5, Crook moved into the interior another twenty-five miles, past the town of Bavispe and Bacerac to Huachinera, being "greeted by the inhabitants with every demonstration of welcome. Every man, woman and child had gathered in the streets or squatted on flat roofs of the adobe houses to welcome our approach. They looked like a grand national convention of scarecrows"—aside from colorful serapes and gorgeous sombreros with silver bands. "The children were bright, dirty, and pretty; the women so closely enveloped in their rebozos that only one eye could be seen."

The whole country, wrote Bourke, was a desert. "On each hand were the ruins of depopulated and abandoned hamlets, destroyed by the Apaches. . . . The valley of the Bavispe had once been thickly populated; now all was wild and gloomy." *Conductas* of Mexican pack mules were known to come through occasionally, heavily guarded by companies of soldiers, but Crook's men didn't meet any.

Hemmed in by high and forbidding mountain ranges, the valley

[6] Bourke, *Apache Campaign*, 58.

[7] This diary of the expedition, printed in the *Arizona Star* on June 17, 1883, is used extensively here, along with Crook's *Annual Report* for 1883, Appendix E, which is a complete account of the expedition, and Bourke, *Apache Campaign*. The diarist is not identified in the newspaper, but was probably Forsyth; see McClintock, I, 246.

narrowed as the column worked downstream. Cactus was everywhere, as were greasewood and Spanish bayonet. The loose footing made hard going for pack mules and men alike, although the toughened scouts grinned, jested, and scrambled about as sure-footedly and tirelessly as bighorns. They never seemed to rest, even in camp, spending their time whittling bamboo pipes or flutes with which they regaled the songbirds in near-by shrubbery with melodic tunes of their own devising. A "Chinese sort of music," as Bourke described it.

Camp at Huachinera was on the banks of the Bavispe, under a bluff atop which perched the town, where the packers determined to have a party, first taking the precaution to buy out the hamlet's entire stock of liquor, paying $12.50 for the lot. The ladies of the town prudently declined to attend the grand *baile*, so the place was scoured for Mexican men, who were dragged in for the rousing affair, which might have gone on all night had not someone knocked the sax player through the head of the bass drum, making further music impossible.

The march resumed on May 6, the column making twenty miles to a place called Tesorababi, which does not show on modern maps but must have been southeast of Huachinera. Crook had decided, on the advice of Peaches, to plunge into the heart of the Sierra Madre east of the Bavispe River. The column must have gone southeast up the Bavispe tributary that heads out in the general direction of Cumbre, although on the west side of the divide from it. During the daylight hours of May 7 the expedition remained in camp, secluded from possible discovery by the sharp eyes of Apache lookouts, then moved on under cover of the pitch-black Sonora night. The foothills dripped with high grass and groves of oak, which gave way to cedar at higher elevations. The hills and ridges became steeper. Finally the command struck the trail made by Apaches driving cattle into the mountains, a trail already worked out by Sieber and the scouts well in advance, since, of course, it was impossible to follow it unaided in the darkness.

But the scouts were unhappy. At length they halted and refused to go forward. The trouble, they said, was the owl.

One of the party had caught an owl alive and had trussed it to his saddle horn. It would be manifestly impossible to whip the hostiles while this bird of ill omen was confined, the scouts patiently explained.

General Crook listened, acceded to their demand, ordered the owl freed, and the column scrambled on through the darkness once more. About midnight, after a ten-mile march, camp was made in a deep, thickly wooded canyon, but no fires were permitted and the men munched cold biscuit and bacon and shivered in the chill air until dawn while the laggard pack mules came in, were tallied by ghostly figures in the gloom, and clattered, by force of habit, into their accustomed places on the floating picket lines, eager to be fed and have their packs skinned off.

On May 8 the column, now well into the mountains and safely able to move by daylight, continued eastward for fifteen miles over a trail so rough that everyone, including General Crook, dismounted and hiked. Most of the way was up the steep and rocky canyon. The fresh trail had been pulverized by the hoofs of hundreds of stolen cattle and ponies, goaded into the mountains by the fierce and relentless hostiles. The expedition began to pass carcasses of butchered and mutilated livestock. Deep below them was the mangled body of a steer that had slipped on the precipitous slope and pinwheeled into the abyss. From this point on, the column never was out of sight of butchered or live animals looted by Apaches from the sorely suffering ranchos of the valleys. The command moved on, always upward. The landscape, Bourke reflected, was "fearfully corrugated into a perplexing alternation of ridges and chasms." Six mules slipped off the trail but were recovered after they had rolled down the slopes.

The command bivouacked on a plateau seven thousand feet above the sea, in a "country grand and gloomy, the whole face of nature being cut by immense gorges and mountains apparently piled one on top of the other," according to the diarist. The site was not far from the place where the Mexican troops had camped, "the farthest point of their penetration into the range," Bourke believed. Dense stands of pine covered the ridges near the crests, with scrub oak lower down, and everywhere was litter left by generations of dusky raiders: dress goods, saddles, bridles, letters, food, and other materials. The scouts had "become more vigilant, the 'medicine-men' more and more devotional," Bourke wrote.

May 9 saw the command break camp at 7:00 A.M. and climb still farther up the slopes to top out over a bony ridge and drop down into a narrow, rocky gorge, which was followed until it broadened into a small amphitheater. Here, Peaches said, the hostiles had camped, but, as Betzinez reported, the grass had been burned off, leaving no forage for the worn-out horses. A twelve-hour forced march of ten miles over incredibly rough country was necessary to find another good camping spot. Five mules were lost, tumbling from the mountain trails into the stony gorges, three broke their necks, and two had to be shot. On May 10 the diarist noted that "the country is almost impassable and looks as if the passage of men had been barred by the hand of the Almighty. But nine miles were made during the entire day's march of about ten hours." Because the command was now in the very heart of the hostile country, ambush could be expected anywhere. The troopers, packers, and main body had difficulty enough just passing over the country; Sieber and his scouts had to be everywhere—in front, on the flanks, in the rear—to scrutinize every track, every turned stone, every displaced or depressed mass of pine needles. They covered three miles to the command's one. In truth, they *were* everywhere, tireless, devoted, vigilant, as relentless as hounds. They were magnificent.

Ax and shovel crews worked ahead, chopping out a way for the mules and men, rolling loose rocks off the "trail," helping the column over the roughest spots. Five more mules were lost this day. The command climbed what seemed to be impossible ridges, slithered down almost perpendicular slopes into chasms where foaming torrents of icy water dashed furiously from one side to another, up more ridges and down and across other streams. In their confusion, two frightened white-tailed deer ran directely into a file of scouts, who flung stones at them, and grinned, but dared not shoot nor laugh aloud since they would then have to face the stern-visaged, bewhiskered "Gray Fox," who kept up with the best of them and stood ready to enforce personally his orders for silence.

Late that afternoon the scouts called on Crook, however, and, with Sieber as their spokesman, pointed out they were weary of nursing along the packs and suggested that they move out in advance, leaving the main command to camp where it was. Crook approved. Crawford was told that if he came on scattered parties he should attack boldly, kill as many as possible, and capture what he could. Should the Chiricahuas be too concentrated and too well positioned to be successfully smashed, he should engage them, but only to hold them until reinforcements could move up. He must be careful not to kill women or children or prisoners. The gleeful scouts busied themselves making ready, lighting small, smokeless fires in secluded nooks and baking bread, grinding coffee on flat rocks, cleaning weapons and ammunition, and patching footwear. Some of them even indulged in the semi-sacred sweat bath.[8]

At dawn on May 11, Captain Crawford, Lieutenants Gatewood and Mackay, Al Sieber, Archie, Mickey Free and Severiano, Peaches, and 150 scouts took four days' rations, canteens, and 100 rounds of ammunition and a blanket apiece and marched off, more swiftly now, the scouts lighthearted and cheerful that they were not slowed by the mules and white troopers. As for themselves, they could run up or down the slopes as swiftly as deer, and from time to time did so, out of sheer exuberance. Before the day was half over, a scout brought back word of a much better camping spot fifteen miles farther on, and the command moved up. Thereafter it trudged along, about a day behind the scouts, engaged mostly in sweeping up escaped Chiricahua livestock. On May 14, the command received another note from Crawford urging it to move up with supplies. He had found an abundance of fresh Indian sign, he said, and thought he was hard on the enemy's main camp, while there was nothing to indicate that the Apaches dreamed Crook was so close to them.

Crawford had pushed hard and was indeed nearing the goal. Early on the fifteenth, he received word from his advance scouts that he was closing in on a camp, which proved to be Chato's. He issued orders for the Indians to move up and try to surround the rancheria, which was, however, in such difficult country that a clean surround was all but impossible. Even while it was being prepared some hasty scouts fired on two men and a woman, killing the latter, at least, and thus

[8] Bourke, *Apache Campaign,* 85.

sealing the death sentence for little Charlie McComas, who had been a prisoner in this camp.[9] His fate, a mystery for three-quarters of a century, was revealed by Betzinez, who heard the details from an eyewitness, Ramona Chihuahua, daughter of the famous chief. She told him the story when they were students together at Carlisle. It seems that the slain woman was the mother of an Apache named Speedy, who was so enraged by her death that he turned and brained six-year-old Charlie with a rock, throwing the body into the brush. The Apaches told the soldiers that the boy had run off and become lost at the outset of the fight, and this was all that could be learned of his whereabouts at the time.[10]

The firing which killed the woman exploded the camp into confusion, whereupon it was charged from various sides. The surprise was complete. A few young people surrendered at once, while others took to the hills, many breaking through the troop cordon. One account said that the scouts could only be restrained from massacring the prisoners by officers with drawn revolvers. The statement is probably imaginary, although in the heat of the fight there may have been difficulty on that score. However, since the prisoners numbered only five, two boys and three girls, it seems doubtful that the crisis lasted very long.

At least nine hostiles were killed, with others wounded, and plunder falling into the hands of the attackers included four nickel-plated Winchester rifles, two revolvers, one of them a new-model Colt, "about 100 ponies and mules, an immense quantity of bridles, saddles, clothing of all kinds, gold and silver watches, American and Mexican silver and gold, in all amounting to eight or ten thousand dollars."[11] But Crawford and Sieber were less interested in killings or loot than in surrender of substantial numbers of hostiles, and the invaluable Peaches was sent alone into the mountains to persuade the fugitives to surrender. Crawford left strong forces at and near the captured

[9] General Crook, too, blamed this incident for his failure to rescue Charlie McComas but said that a scout slipped and fell down the steep mountainside, discharging his gun in the process. The shot alarmed the rancheria and put to flight some of the women, who took the little captive with them. *Arizona Star*, June 19, 1883.

[10] Betzinez, *op. cit.*, 119–20.

[11] *Arizona Star*, June 13, 1883.

rancheria and returned to Crook's command with his prisoners and loot, arriving on the evening of May 16. Crook moved up the next day and sent one of the captured girls to tell the hostiles that he would give them three days to surrender; if they did not do so, he would kill them all. Unfortunately, a heavy rain set in, making tracking impossible, as well as precluding the chances of ascertaining Charlie McComas' fate.

During the suspenseful days from the sixteenth to the twenty-third of May, small, deeply suspicious bands of Apache hostiles dribbled into camp to surrender. They "would not trust themselves in our hands all at once, but come dropping in from all sides in small fragments," wrote Crook. "They would say we give ourselves up do with us as you please. Had I seized upon the first who came in no others would have followed. 20 warriors out would have been as bad as the whole number. Chato in his raid thro' Arizona and New Mexico, had but 26 men and Hieronimo in his recent depredations in Chihuahua had less than 40."[12]

Scarcely had Crook's command moved up to the recently captured rancheria when the scouts heaped up pine cones and cedar branches to make a black smoke signal to the hostiles. Two women came in; two hours later, six other women arrived, one of them the sister of Chihuahua. On May 18, six new arrivals—four women, a man, and a boy—were in early; then came 16 others, including Chihuahua himself.[13] Before night, 45 Chiricahuas had come in, and by the next day the total had swollen to an even 100. There were 121 by May 21,

[12] Crook to General Schofield, June 19, 1883, Hayes Collection.

[13] Bourke called Chihuahua "a fine-looking man, whose countenance betokened great decision and courage," but Tommy Cruse said he was "the worst of all . . . the only Indian that ever gave me a creepy feeling." Cruse to Davis, September 14, 1927. In his book, Cruse unaccountably says that Chihuahua was executed for a role at Cibecue, but in the aforementioned letter he said he had seen him at Fort Sill, Oklahoma, in 1911. Chihuahua was an unreconstructed rebel in the 1880's and bolted the reservation with Geronimo and Nachez in May, 1885. Lockwood, *The Apache Indians*, 268, calls him "one of the ablest and most intelligent leaders among the renegades." He relates that Chihuahua became a Christian at Fort Marion, Florida, attended church regularly and refused to drink or gamble, later enlisted in the United States Army, and died at Fort Sill, leaving "two remarkable children," Ramona and Eugene, both fine examples of what education and religion could do for the Apaches.

including 60 women and girls, not counting Chihuahua and a couple of others who had taken to the mountains a few days before, promising to round up the rest of their people and bring them in.

About 8:00 p.m. on the twenty-first a "fearful hubbub" broke out in the cliffs above camp. Two aged Indian women limped in, wondering whether their men would be hurt if they came in. It was Geronimo's war party, returned from the Mexican state of Chihuahua, all armed to the hilt, wary as wolves, and skulking about the rocks on the precipice above the camp like so many vultures or hawks. Gradually they came in, by twos or threes, and lurked about the outskirts of the camp until Geronimo himself ventured up to Crook's campfire and said he wanted to talk.

Crook looked up without exhibiting much interest. "You can see," he said, through Mickey Free, his interpreter, "that we can search you out anywhere. You can see that your own people have turned against you. I don't want anything to do with you. I want no talk with you." He told Geronimo he had arranged at the city of Chihuahua for two thousand Mexican troops to support him there, and at Hermosillo for five hundred to one thousand more to cut off the hostiles in that direction. Their only hope was to surrender unconditionally or fight it out, he said. "You can choose peace or war as you please."

Disconcerted, Geronimo hung around for an hour, cooling off, seeking to resume the conversation. Crook ignored him, planning to make the renegade desire sanctuary more earnestly before listening to him. "He and his warriors were certainly as fine-looking a lot of pirates as ever cut a throat or scuttled a ship," Bourke admitted. "Not one among them who was not able to travel forty to fifty miles a day over these gloomy precipices and along these gloomy canyons. In muscular development, lung and heart power, they were, without exception, the finest body of human beings I had ever looked upon. Each was armed with a breech-loading Winchester; most had nickel-plated revolvers of the latest pattern, and a few had also bows and lances."[14]

Again Geronimo sidled up to Crook and came as close to pleading as that proud Indian had ever come. He said his story was not all one

[14] Bourke, *Apache Campaign*, 102.

sided, that the Indians had been abused by dishonest whites, as Crook well knew. He also stated that the Mexicans had always proved treacherous to him and his people. If the General would allow him to return to San Carlos and would guarantee him just treatment, he would gladly work for his own living and follow the path of peace. Just try him out, Geronimo said. If he couldn't make peace, however, he and his men would die in these forbidding mountains, fighting to the last. He was surely not afraid of the Mexicans—the Apaches killed Mexicans with rocks. At this point he smiled grimly, drawing attention to the most recent battle between the two. But, Geronimo added, sobering, he could not hope to fight forever against the Mexicans if the Americans and their Apache allies entered the picture, too.

Crook listened. He said little. Geronimo could make up his own mind about what he wanted, peace or war. That the General said, and nothing else.[15]

This was the tensest period for the most dangerous expedition ever undertaken by American forces during the frontier era. Geronimo was the key, though not by any means the most noted or notorious of Apache chieftains being sought. But he was easily the most intractable—and the most suspicious. If he came around, probably most of the others would. If he bolted for the fragmented and misshapen peaks, the expedition would be a failure, no matter how much or little else might be accomplished. Crook pretended unconcern over Geronimo's decision. In reality, however, he was keyed to a high pitch, was playing his considerable hand as cautiously and wisely as the most experienced gambler, and he guessed right.

May 22 was the crucial day for the expedition. At dawn Geronimo came to see Crook.

It was said that Al Sieber sat in on this talk, that he sat there with one hand inside his shirt, clutching a revolver, and that he intended

---

[15] *Ibid.*, 103. Tom Horn says in his autobiography that he was interpreter for Crook at these talks. In an oft-reprinted passage which is supposedly illustrative of the immense peril under which the conferences were conducted, he quotes Sieber as advising him, Horn, to take a knife and "stand while you are talking, forget that you may not live one more minute and think only of the talk." Horn, 152. As a matter of fact, Horn is betrayed by his own account, which demonstrates that he was not the interpreter and may not even have been with the pack train.

to blow Geronimo's brains out at the first suggestion of treachery.[16] But Geronimo had determined on peace.

Geronimo begged to be taken back to San Carlos.[17] He asked permission to collect his people, since they would not come in as requested by smoke signals, fearing that the Apache scouts had made these signs in order to betray them. So this talk, too, was inconclusive.

All morning the Chiricahuas of other bands came in, many sent by Chihuahua, all heavily armed. Among them was the band of Ka-ya-ten-nae, a prominent warrior who loomed large in the later history of his people. They rode fine ponies, which they had stolen from some luckless whites, and drove pack animals and beef steers, some of which had to be butchered to feed the growing throng. Later in the day, a most pitiful entrance upon this strange stage was made by a group of five "wretched, broken-down Mexican women, one of whom bore a nursing baby, who . . . stood in mute terror, wonder, joy, and hope, unable to realize that they were free."[18] These were the captives whom Geronimo wanted to swap to the Mexicans for those of his own people who had been captured but whom he had abandoned to their own resources when he saw that Crook controlled the country. All possible kindness was shown to them.

Geronimo had still another talk with Crook, again being read off by that immutable officer. "I am not taking your arms from you," said Crook, "because I am not afraid of you. You have been allowed to go about camp freely, merely to let you see that we have strength enough to exterminate you if we want to."

Turning to the renegade's request that he be permitted to surrender and given protection at some reservation, Crook told him he was asking much. He had no power to put him on a reservation, but if he and his people would pledge their word to keep good faith and remain there, he would do what he could for them. "You must remember," said Crook, "that I have been fighting you for our people, and if I

16 McClintock, I, 247. This passage is probably based on Horn's fictitious account, since Tom also described the meeting thus, but there is some reason to believe that the incident may have been factual. Certainly it is in keeping with the times and the principals.

17 Bourke, *Apache Campaign*, 104.

18 *Ibid.*, 107–108.

take you back and attempt to put you on the reservation the Americans and Mexicans will make a hard fight against it, for you have been murdering their people, stealing their stock and burning their houses. You have been acting in a most cruel manner, and the people will demand that you be punished." Crook patiently explained the situation. "You see," said the General to Geronimo, "you are asking me to fight my own people in order to defend your wrongs."[19] Yet he agreed to accept the Apache's surrender.

Geronimo expressed a desire to remain behind when Crook left in order to gather up his women and children, now widely scattered. At first he and Nachez insisted that Crook remain until they returned, as they were afraid to come in alone. This he refused to do, explaining that his rations were disappearing too fast. Crook was, as he himself said, greatly embarrassed. He was limited by treaty terms and admonitions from General W. T. Sherman to remain in Mexico only as long as actual military operations required, and with the capture of Chato's camp and the surrender of the Chiricahuas in general, that was accomplished. If he insisted that Geronimo return with him now, it would at best leave a nucleus of bad Indians in the Sierra Madre and at worst signal a bolt by Geronimo and perhaps the bulk of his wild Indians, the war to begin all over again. He chose the lesser evil and gave Geronimo permission to round up his stragglers and come in as soon as he could.[20]

Geronimo asked for written passes so that he could come directly through the valleys to San Carlos. Crook refused; he felt that the Indians might expose themselves and be killed as hostiles and that his passes found upon their bodies might complicate matters. They agreed, then, to take their chances.

With the surrender of Geronimo, a great dance of peace and good will was held. The following morning, May 23, the old woman who was sent after Loco returned with him and a long talk was held, this one on more friendly terms than those with Geronimo, since Crook was convinced that Loco had been sinned against more than he had sinned and that he had always wanted a sincere peace.

[19] *Arizona Star*, June 21, 1883.
[20] *Ibid.*, June 12, 1883.

That evening, more Apaches came in: old Nana, Bonito and Chato, a chief known only as the brother of one called Navaho Bill, and 264 others, mostly women and children. From this day until May 29, Crook remained in camp, giving other Indians who desired it a chance to come in and surrender, and many did, filtering in by two and threes. A roundup and tally was held on May 28 and the count showed 123 warriors and 251 women and children, a grand total of 374 Indians. Of the great chiefs of the Chiricahuas and related peoples, only Juh was missing. He had squabbled with others of the band in March and had retired deeper into the mountains with his family and one other warrior. He never again returned to raid in the United States.[21]

One day during this layover, on May 27 to be exact, one of the Apache scouts ran in and excitedly reported having been fired on by some Mexican soldiers. He was wearing the scarlet headband that distinguished the scouts from hostile Apaches. While hunting, he had discovered a large body of Mexican soldiers rounding up cattle stolen by Geronimo. The scout tried to make contact with the Mexicans, but they probably thought him an outlaw and fired three shots at him. Lieutenant Forsyth, Al Sieber, and a few white and Indian soldiers swung into their saddles and thundered out in pursuit of the Mexicans, hoping to set things right. Although they rode hard for fifteen miles, they could never overtake them.

On May 30, Crook broke camp and started for home, arriving June 10 at Colonel James Biddle's headquarters on Silver Creek[22] with 52 Apache warriors, 273 women and children, and the noted Chiefs Nana, Loco, and Bonito.

The movement must have resembled the exodus of the Israelites from Egypt. All the old folks, the children, and the ill were piled on mules, donkeys, or weak and docile nags, but most of the Indians walked. Wearing garlands of cottonwood to screen them from the sun,

[21] According to Cruse, in a letter to Davis written on October 8, 1927, Juh, a short time later, "went to Casas Grandes to get supplies—and got drunk on tequila and mounting his pony rode off to the mountains; on the rough trail he swayed too far, overbalanced the pony and both went over the precipice and Juh's neck was broken." Connor Collection.

[22] Silver Creek is about fourteen miles northeast of Douglas, heading in South College Peak and flowing southeast into Mexico. Barnes, *Place Names*, 407.

they streamed along the trail, spilling gratefully into the cool streams and springs along the way, busily dressing and curing the game shot by the hunters, for the rations soon gave out and the party had to live off the country. The Apache scouts spent every available moment gambling with the Chiricahuas, whom they "fleeced unmercifully" of their ill-gotten gains.

Bourke now had an opportunity to study the enemy. He found "all the chiefs of the Chiricahuas—Geronimo, Loco, Chato, Nana, Bonito, Chihuahua, Mangas, Zele and Ka-ya-ten-nae—men of noticeable brain power, physically perfect, and mentally acute—just the individuals to lead a forlorn hope in the face of every obstacle."[23]

The line of travel lay on the eastern slope of the high Sierra Madre, close to the summit. The country was extremely rough, canyons and ravines flowing water at this elevation, pine forests, oak, juniper, maple, willow, rose and blackberry bushes and strawberry vines, all giving of their largesse and impeding easy transit of the route. The days were clear and hot, the nights frigid, with thick ice forming on still water. Game was plentiful, and the scouts gleefully demonstrated their skill at hunting and marksmanship.

Down on the Janos Plains, a terrible prairie fire threatened the column, and everyone—scouts, soldiers, women, Chiricahua warriors, and even the children—turned out in desperation to fight it. Relentlessly the fire swept down upon them, and just as relentlessly they fought back. Somehow they won. That is, they managed to save their camp and a small area around it, but the countryside was blackened and seared and, for a season, ruined.

On Alisos Creek, near its confluence with the Janos, they passed the ghastly field where Colonel García had massacred the Chiricahua women and children, a field white with scattered Indian bones picked clean by coyotes and marked with the humped graves, adorned by teetering crosses, of the Mexican dead.

Geronimo had remained in the mountains—ostensibly to collect his stragglers but really to make one more sweep for livestock, plunder, and blood—and was not yet even on the horizon, although he had pledged himself to follow speedily on the path of the exodus. It

[23] Bourke, *Apache Campaign*, 119.

seemed doubtful to many whether he would ever come in. The territorial press was full of wild suggestions that the Chiricahua men all be hanged and the women and children parceled out among the tribes in Indian Territory. Such inflammatory proposals, reaching the Indians, soon filtered down into Mexico and possibly delayed the arrival of the last of the renegades.

Some of the former hostiles preceded the main body to San Carlos. About twenty, including seven leading warriors, left the Sierra Madre independently and marched swiftly to the north and across the border. They passed Stein's Peak and pressed on to the Gila, then followed its northern bank to the reservation, arriving there early in June. They cheerfully surrendered their firearms, only to discover that Agent P. P. Wilcox didn't want the responsibility of their care. He turned them over to the military, and they were held in close confinement pending Crawford's arrival from Silver Creek with the bulk of the captives.

On June 23 there was great excitement at San Carlos Agency. Toward the foothills, on a southerly slope, a vast streamer of dust was seen, at its base tiny figures that proved to be men on horseback, driven stock, and people trudging on foot. Captain Crawford and four companies of cavalry and nearly two hundred Indian scouts formed the escort for the long line of Indians headed by Loco and his family. Lieutenant Davis rode out two miles from the agency to greet them and bring them in.

The hostiles were temporarily located in the bottom lands along the Gila and San Carlos rivers, close to the agency, where Crawford, Davis, and Sieber could keep an eye on them. The other Indians hated and feared them, so many of them naturally turned to the whites for comfort and, eventually, companionship.

Others of the renegades continued to dribble in. On the twentieth of December, thirteen Chiricahuas, including eight warriors, arrived. On February 7, 1884, Chato and his band came in, and on February 25, Geronimo himself showed up at last, bringing with him 350 head of stolen livestock that posed a first-class problem, solved when they were taken from the old fox and sold, the proceeds, $1,762.50,[24] being turned over to the Mexican government for distribution to the original owners. One party of hostiles did not arrive at the reservation until May 15, but at last all were there and Crook had solved, for the moment, the problem of the enemy nest in the Sierra Madre.

[24] Britton Davis, *Geronimo*, 82–101.

XVIII. "If we could only get rid of Geronimo . . ."

AL SIEBER was reassigned to San Carlos upon his return from Mexico, still in his old job as chief of scouts. Archie McIntosh was there, too, in charge of rationing the Chiricahuas, since he was one of the few white men they would trust and because many were related to him through his wife. Britton Davis, with Sam Bowman, was assigned to move some of the wilder Indians to whatever part of the reservation they might select as the place where they would settle down and try to adopt the ways of white civilization. Ultimately they located on Turkey Creek, up near Fort Apache, and Davis and Bowman moved there with them. Sieber was left at San Carlos with Captain Crawford and McIntosh and some of the Chiricahuas, along with other Indians who were no problem for the scouts. Lieutenant Gatewood was at Fort Apache.

For the moment, the Indians were so quiet that Crook, in his 1884 *Annual Report*, could state that "for the first time in the history of that fierce people, every member of the Apache tribe is at peace." Anyway, *almost* every member. Juh had never come in, and there were a few others who still ran wild in the Sierra Madre; there always would be. But their great raiding potential was gone, at least for the time being.

Not all of the unruly Indians were in Mexico, however, not by any means. For example, there was Ka-ya-ten-nae, a surly, moody warrior who had never been on a reservation before and who didn't like this one. He stalked about, truculent, insolent, scowling, stirring up trouble, and yet, withal, openly remaining a man of influence and an Indian to cultivate. He was suspicious and unmanageable while

Geronimo was still out, and Crawford resignedly wrote Crook: "If we could only get rid of Geronimo, Chatto & this man Ka-e-ten-nae the rest of them would be all right & could easily be managed."[1]

At long last Geronimo arrived, and Crawford made Ka-ya-ten-nae a scout and put him on good behavior; for a time, he seemed pacified. He moved north with many of the other hostiles and thus came under Davis's watchful eyes—and ears. Before long the Lieutenant heard that Ka-ya-ten-nae planned to assassinate him and bolt the reservation, so, at the risk of losing his life, he arrested Ka-ya-ten-nae and sent him to San Carlos. Crook forwarded him to Alcatraz to be tamed down, a task which took two years. Ultimately, Ka-ya-ten-nae became a relatively co-operative Indian, although never a thoroughly peaceful one, and Crook made good use of him.

Emmet Crawford wanted, above all, to get his Apaches busy and keep them that way, and farming seemed to be the likeliest occupation. He sent Sieber to Tucson with what little money was available, and Al, if he remained true to form, had a fine time there, but saved enough of the Captain's money to buy $160 worth of seed and farming tools. The army had to scratch around for such materials, since the Indian Bureau, which had taken second place in control of the lately warlike Apaches, locked its supplies in the warehouse pending the day when it would regain control over the reservation.

Repeatedly, Crook pleaded—going as high as Washington with his requests—for help to put the Indians to work so that they could become self-supporting. "These Indians are absolutely destitute of seed and farming implements of all kinds and it is not probable that they will be able to get anything from the Interior Dep't," he wrote the Adjutant General. "It is of the first importance that now, while the Indians are in . . . the humor for planting, that they should be assisted in every possible way."[2] Several years later, while in command of the Division of the Missouri, Crook recalled that when he was trying to settle the Apaches and teach them civilized pursuits, "I could not, in spite of the most strenuous efforts, secure for them agricultural implements, except perhaps a few hoes and shovels. Even seed was

[1] Crawford to Crook, November 20, 1883, Hayes Collection.
[2] Crook to AGO, November 22, 1883, Hayes Collection.

denied, and to furnish this, I had to give them the grain saved in making issues to my pack trains and troop horses. The ground was cultivated with these few hoes and shovels, which did not average one to each family, and in many, perhaps most, instances, with pointed sticks hardened by fire. I saw long extent of irrigating ditches the entire labor on which had been performed with such implements, the loose earth being carried in baskets and flour sacks and deposited at needed points."[3]

As if Crook did not have enough on his mind, there now came the unkindest cut of all: Archie McIntosh, good old faithful Archie, slipped. What a shock it must have been to the General! He trusted Archie as he had no other scout, except perhaps Sieber. McIntosh had hunted his Indians in three nations and had saved Crook's life in the frozen Northwest. He had scouted for him and hunted Indians with him since immediately after the Civil War until now, a matter of twenty years. His bravery was as unquestioned as his capacity for whiskey or a good yarn. Archie had come to Arizona with Crook in the wild old days and had campaigned with him through those bitter, cruel years when the frontier seemed limitless and untamable. McIntosh had been a leading figure in the Battle of the Cave on Salt River and in uncounted other engagements and scouts. He had always been loyal, until now, when temptation struck him down.

Bush Crawford blew the whistle on Archie via a letter to Sieber which Al, presumably after considerable soul searching (although he, personally, had never liked Archie), had shown to Captain Crawford and which the Captain digested for Crook in a personal letter on March 28, 1884.[4] Shocked though he was, and knowing the impact the news would have on Crook, the Captain nevertheless told the sordid story in soldierly fashion, with no evasion:

Dear Genl.
I enclose you an extract from a private letter from a man on Salt River to Mr Sieber. The man lives in the vicinity of Archie's ranch. Mr. Sieber says he knows it is so. I am afraid also it is true. . . . I have been trusting

3 Crook to AGO, May 17, 1889, Hayes Collection.
4 This correspondence, along with an extract from Bushrod Crawford's letter, is in the Hayes Collection, dated March 28, 1884.

Archie with the issue of [the Chiricahuas'] rations & their management as they all think a good deal of him. . . . I have sent Lt [Parker W.] West to Salt River to examine into the report & when he returns, if the report be true, I think it will be best to discharge him. Sieber can manage their rations for them & I think they will be satisfied. . . . The people living on Salt River it seems know of this & if we allow Archie to stay they will probably say something about it & criticize us. . . . Archie . . . was one of the few men here who seemed to be attending strictly for what he was paid for & this report coming out against him has taken me back entirely.

What Archie had done followed a common pattern of corruption at various of the posts in pre-Crook days. The scout, charged with rationing the Indians, had held back some issue bacon, vinegar, and soap, thus establishing a credit at the commissary. This should have been used for the purchase of flour and sugar for the Indians "as the allowance is not sufficient," Crawford noted. Instead, McIntosh took some of the unissued bacon and used the money on account for the purchase of other provisions, loading the whole into wagons and freighting it to his ranch, near Salt River, where it could be sold, Mc-Intosh pocketing the proceeds.

Bush Crawford's letter said that on a single trip Archie brought to his ranch "one bl. vinegar, 500 lbs bacon, 2 cases yeast powder, 600 lbs flour, one bl sugar, tobacco &c." On another occasion, Archie got away with "700 lbs bacon, yeast powder, sugar, coffee, beans and in fact all that 4 animals could haul. They have brought at least calculation $500 worth of stuff in the 2 loads. Yeager [a man who lived on Archie's ranch in Archie's absence] told me he paid Archie over $250 for the 1st load."

Lieutenant West returned from Salt River with confirmation of the bad news, and on April 6, Captain Crawford reported to Crook:

Archie has been acting in bad faith with us ever since I gave him charge of the Chiricahua rations. When Lt West returned & made his report I sent for all the Chiefs & told them about it. They all said they wanted Archie kept. They said it made no difference if he took half of their rations he was a good man & could have them. I sent for Archie & he acknowledged before the Chiefs that Lt West's report was true & he had the impudence to tell me that it was done at every Military Post in the Dept.

The Chiefs tell me to telegraph you & say they wanted him kept but if you said discharge him all right. . . . After talking Ka-e-ten-nae Chihuahua & two or three others left. Geronimo Chatto & Mangas remained behind. They said that they thought what I had done was right, that their women & children ought to have that ration that they received enough themselves. Archie I think has been feeding up the Chiefs & principal men but cutting down the rest.[5]

Crawford told McIntosh he was fired, but gave him permission to send a telegram to Crook.

He then went to work & collected some of the Chiefs together in the Agency & then unbeknown to me, got the Agency Interpreter & had a telegram written out to send to you signed by the Chiefs. The operator would not send it without first seeing me, when I saw it I told him not to send it.

The wire to Crook read:

We the undersigned after a council yesterday—we all have said we want Archie McIntosh to stay with us. You put him over us and he is our friend. He gives us all we want to eat and he is good. Capt Crawford told us that Archie stole our provisions from us that some white man reported it to him. We all saw what was taken away in the wagon—We want you to come to us right away to straighten things for us. He brought us back with you and we want to talk to you.

It was signed with the names of Geronimo, Ka-ya-ten-nae, Bonito, Loco, Chihuahua, Chato, Mangas, Nachez, and Zele.

After reading the telegram, Crawford angrily ordered McIntosh off the reservation forthwith, telling him "that if he ever attempted to again call the Indians together for the purpose of breeding discontent I would put him in irons. . . . He is a bad man & has acted in direct violation of your policy in managing the Indians. I think he put Geronimo up to asking for a store near where they are going to live [on Turkey Creek] for the reason that he thought he could get it himself. I think he has thrown obstacles in the way of their farming. The Indians, with the exception probably of Chihuahua & two or three other relations of Mrs. McIntosh's are all satisfied. Even Chi-

5 Crawford to Crook, April 6, 1884, Hayes Collection.

huahua has told me that it is all right, in discharging Archie."[6] So brave, resourceful old Archie (he was now fifty) trundled his few belongings to Globe in a mule-drawn wagon and went from there to his ranch at Black Mesquite Springs, on Pinto Creek, where Domingo, his wife, had continued to live.

Archie couldn't remain for long away from San Carlos, the army, and the half-tame Apaches. He never again campaigned with Crook, nor did he take any part in the extensive Geronimo expeditions to come, but after Crook and Miles had left the department and his peculations had been forgotten, Archie briefly appeared again. He was hired in 1893 at Fort Bowie as scout for an expedition after the Apache Kid, but he got drunk before the party left and missed it. They didn't find the Kid, anyway.

Back in the mid-eighties, there was less and less for a scout to do to keep himself occupied, and that may have been the basic trouble with Archie. Sieber, too, was less than busy most of the time. Occasionally he accompanied John G. Bourke, now a captain, on some ethnological expedition or other. "I went out with Al. Seiber and a small party of Apache to examine three of their 'sacred caves' in the Sierra Pinal and Sierra Ancha," wrote Bourke, years later,[7] in describing such trips. Even these, though, were in the nature of a lark; there was no real work to them.

Al spent a lot of time in the sutler's store, drinking and yarning with the boys during the day and playing poker nights, laughing, funning, talking over the good old days when there were hostiles out and plenty for everyone to do. Crawford and Davis had been kept on the reservation when the Third Cavalry was rotated east, but at length the Captain had had enough and requested a transfer back to his own regiment in Texas.

Captain Francis C. Pierce of the First Infantry, brought in from duty with the Walapais, succeeded Crawford in what Davis called a "fatal" move.[8] Unfortunately, Pierce lacked Crawford's intimate

---

[6] *Ibid.*

[7] John G. Bourke, "Medicine-Men of the Apache," Bureau of American Ethnology, *Ninth Annual Report* (1892), 504.

[8] Britton Davis, *Geronimo*, 141.

knowledge of Apache character, and to make up for this, as far as possible, Pierce worked closely with Al Sieber. On the rolls, Sieber continued to be carried as merely "Superintendent of Pack Trains" at a salary of $133.33 a month,[9] but in fact he was guide, scout, sometimes interpreter, counselor, and foreman for Pierce.

One night, about the middle of May, 1885, Al and the boys had themselves a wild time, drinking and gambling until the first light of dawn shone down on San Carlos. Al then wandered back to his quarters, the first pangs of a hang-over spreading through him, and rolled onto his cot. Some time later, he couldn't be sure just when, Captain Pierce shook him awake and thrust a telegram form at him. "From Davis," he said. "What about it?" Sieber rubbed his eyes, turned the form to the light, and read:

Capt. Pierce,
Comd'g San Carlos, A.T.

There was an extensive tiswin drunk here last night, and this morning the following chiefs came up and said that they, with their bands, were all concerned in it: Geronimo, Chihuahua, Mangus, Natchez, Zele and Loco. The wh[ole] business is a put up job to save those who were drunk. In regard to the others, I request instructions. The guard house here is not large enough to hold them all, and the arrest of so many prominent men will probably cause trouble. Have told the Indians that I would lay the matter before the General. . . . I think they are endeavoring to screen Natchez and Chihuahua.[10]

DAVIS, LIEUT.

"Oh, it's nothing but a tiswin drunk," Al said as he handed the paper back to Pierce. "Davis will handle it."

And with that Al Sieber made the greatest mistake of his life. Pierce returned to his office, pigeonholed the message, and Crook didn't see it for months. Disaster resulted. It is impossible not to place the blame squarely upon Al Sieber's broad shoulders.

[9] Quartermaster Records, Old Records Section, National Archives.

[10] Appendix A, Report of Crook on Apache Operations, in the field, Fort Bowie, April 10, 1886, Hayes Collection.

XIX. Chasing Geronimo

BRITTON DAVIS had the thankless chore of keeping the lately hostile Chiricahuas under surveillance, settling them where they chose to be settled, leading them into the ways of agricultural tranquility and stability, listening to their complaints and explaining them away when he could, keeping up their spirits and morale, and enforcing Crook's edicts, such as those which forbade slicing off an errant wife's nose and the making and drinking of tiswin. Tiswin, a native beer made of fermented corn mash, led to no end of trouble with the Indians, whom it made cantankerous; hence Crook's proscription.

For many months Lieutenant Davis was successful in policing his turbulent charges, but then the monotony of civilized existence apparently got the better of them and several took to making tiswin surreptitiously and getting drunk on it. In order to protect the guilty parties, all of the important men came to Davis one May day and said they had been getting drunk and what was he going to do about it? That was when he decided to telegraph Crook; his charges acceded to this, and all eagerly awaited the General's decision. None realized that because of Sieber's faulty judgment the wire had been pigeonholed before its contents reached Crook.

As days passed with no reply, the Indians grew more and more uneasy. Fright completely possessed them as their imaginations conjured up all sorts of activities Crook might be up to, and at last they bolted—or thirty-four men, eight boys of fighting age, and ninety-two others did.

Davis found it difficult to be too harsh on Sieber for the tragedy. "True he made a disastrous mistake," Davis wrote. "But we should remember him by the many critical situations he handled successfully over a period of nearly fifteen years, risking his life repeatedly that others might be saved."[1]

The bust-out caused an uproar throughout the Southwest. Davis and Gatewood futilely chased the flying enemy over into New Mexico, up into the Mogollon Mountains, and southward, toward the line, never finding more positive trace of them than the white corpses with which their course was littered. Captain Pierce's pack train, under Sieber, was sent to Fort Bayard, near Silver City, New Mexico. Then, as it became evident that the hostiles had gained temporary sanctuary in Mexico, Sieber was hurried south to the mouth of Guadalupe Canyon, there to join Crawford and Davis in a plunge below the line.

While Crawford was en route to Guadalupe Canyon, Crook wired him: "You had best take your own and Davis' scouts and follow Indians into the Sierra Madre. If you feel strong enough, leave Cavalry at Boundary."[2] Crook didn't want his officer encumbered with heavy-footed whites; he wanted Indians to chase Indians. Only thus would he have a chance of catching up with them and fighting it out. Yet Crawford decided to take a single troop of cavalrymen with him.

Al Sieber trotted his dusty pack train into Crawford's camp at Guadalupe Canyon early in June, and as soon as Britton Davis arrived, the Captain took the whole column, now including 130 scouts[3] and Captain Henry F. Kendall's Troop A of the Sixth Cavalry, and pointed them south. Sieber was chief of scouts once more.

Everyone was in high spirits, with the possible exception of Crawford, upon whom most of the responsibility must fall. The scouts, the forty cavalrymen, and the two pack trains strung out on the long and sinuous trail "made quite an impressive sight," Davis noted, but the orderly and neat arrangement was too much for Sieber. "Just as we crossed the Mexican-American border the scouts killed two bears," recalled Davis. What happened after that was hilarious.

> Sieber was riding at the head of the leading pack train. In his train was a mule we called Leppy, the largest mule in the train, who had made good

[1] Britton Davis, *Geronimo*, 36.

[2] Crook to Crawford, June 5, 1885, Hayes Collection.

[3] Lockwood, *The Apache Indians*, 282, says ninety-two scouts.

her right to the place next to old Tom, the white bell horse. Any mule attempting to take that place next to Tom was in for a bad few minutes. Sieber took Leppy out of the train, had some of the packers skin the bears, put the fresh skins on Leppy, and turned her loose.

If there is anything that will frighten a mule it is the smell of blood, and the smell of a bear will set him wild. By the time Leppy was loaded both trains had passed. Crawford with the troop of cavalry was far in advance. With a snort and a bawl, Leppy started to regain her place at the head of the leading pack train, the bearskins flopping and splashing blood and bear smell on the packs of the other mules as she brushed them out of her way. The plain was full of bawling, crazed mules, running in every direction, frantically trying, and many succeeding, to get rid of their packs and that awful smell.

Fortunately, the column was in flat, treeless country with lots of room or Sieber's joke might have been a disaster.

Thirty or more mules scattered their packs all over the plain, and swearing, sweating packers were employed for hours recovering them and their cargoes. For two or three days afterward a mule would suddenly start bawling and running, demoralizing half the train.

What Crawford said to Sieber cured him of any more pack-train jokes.[4]

But it's odds-on that Crawford grinned inwardly as he said it. You had to put up a front when handling half-wild men in pursuit of completely wild ones, but Crawford had been on the frontier for a long time, and he certainly wouldn't have lasted through it all if he didn't appreciate such heavy-handed jokes.

Crawford's party was ordered south June 11. One month later, on July 13, Captain Wirt Davis, with a troop of the Fourth Cavalry and one hundred Indian scouts, plus supporting pack trains, was also ordered into Mexico.[5] Between them the columns worked the Sierra

[4] Britton Davis, *Geronimo*, 154–55.

[5] Lockwood, *The Apache Indians*, 282. Britton Davis, *Geronimo*, 172, writes that this column included only about thirty scouts, commanded by Lieutenant Matthias W. Day, one troop of cavalry, and a single pack train. Wirt Davis, a Virginian, enlisted during the Civil War, won a field commission, and emerged a first lieutenant. He was promoted regularly and attained the rank of colonel, at which time he commanded the Third Cavalry; he retired in 1901 and died in 1914. Davis won several brevet ranks, including brevets for gallantry against Texas and Wyoming Indians.

Madre and its stony-skirted recesses as thoroughly as cowboys riding a roundup. Their trails met and crossed and unwound again as they penetrated to the beclouded summit of the great range, pushed through its tightly woven chaparral defenses, and strained up some of its cliffs or skidded down others.

The officers rode mules—when they could ride anything at all. No one had more than a semblance of a uniform. Davis carried his blouse, with its insignia, tightly rolled and tied to his saddle lest he should come to some hidden Mexican village and have to make "an impression," but most of the time he wore only toil-shiny canvas pants and a small sheet of canvas with a hole punched in it for his head, draped across his shoulders like a serape, with a southwestern sombrero to top the costume off. What clothes they had were full of holes and mostly in shreds; their footwear was little better. They washed when they had time and water, ate what they could, some of them carried a canteen filled with mescal instead of water, and all hoped for a fight. Sun-browned, whiskered, and dirty, the whites were in as superb physical condition as the Indians, bursting with health and vigor.

Moving south, the Crawford column scouted along the crest of the Sierra Madre, following more or less the trail Crook had come out on in 1883 but finding no trace of hostiles. On June 20 they camped near Bavispe. Some Mexicans visited the bivouac, were overjoyed to see *los americanos* once more in their country to punish *los indios*, and invited the whites to their camp for *un traguito de vino*, which turned out to be *vino del país*, or mescal. It was Davis' introduction to the stuff. When the gourd was passed, he took a healthy swallow of the fiery liquid, then, with his throat aflame, his eyes watering, and his lungs bursting for air, groped blindly for water to chase the potent liquor. Sieber, all sympathy, handed him a canteen, which Davis gratefully clutched, put to his mouth, and upended—only to find that it was full of mescal, too. "I got two big gulps of the liquor down before I realized what he had done," chuckled Davis years later. "Subsequent proceedings interested me no more and I made a bee-line for camp and my roll of bedding."

Again the column worked south, passing through the towns of Bacerac, Estancia, and Huachinera, which Sieber remembered well, then cut west, over the mountains, toward Oputo. On the twenty-first it was making camp "in a heat that our surgeon pronounced 128° in the shade, and the rest pronounced at least a hundred degrees hotter" when a commotion in the scout camp caused Crawford, Davis, and Sieber to run and investigate. The scouts were just coming in, one badly shot up and weak from loss of blood. They reported that another scout had been killed when someone fired at them from ambush, mounted a mule, and fled. "Hell, or at least the threat of it, broke loose in the scout camp," wrote Davis. Thirty or forty scouts stripped and started for the nearest town to kill all the Mexicans they could. Only with the greatest difficulty could the whites persuade the Indians to parley. "All night long we argued the matter with them. Nine-tenths were for returning to the United States at once, killing any Mexicans they might meet enroute." At last the scouts agreed to let Davis and Sieber look into the matter, which the two did as soon as it was daylight. Unknown to them, however, they were trailed by some of the dead man's friends, no doubt seeking some hapless Mexican upon whom to wreak vengeance.

The pair's investigation showed that an American named Woodward had done the shooting, thinking the Indians were hostiles. Davis couldn't blame him: "I could but admire his courage in tackling three well-armed Apache, not knowing how many more there might be in the vicinity." Fortunately, it was discovered that hostiles had run off some horses in the vicinity the night before, and the scouts could be persuaded that it might have been them who killed their comrade. But they shot up a herd of Mexican cattle anyway, just for an emotional outlet, and the officers let them do it. "A hundred dollars would cover the damage," commented Davis. "Cheap at the price for what might have happened."

Sieber and the Lieutenant rode on into Oputo in the course of their investigation, and arrived just as *el presidente* was lining up his "militia" on the plaza before trailing the hostile horse thieves. "All the able-bodied men of the town, some thirty-five or forty, were lined up in front of the principal *cantina* ready to take the warpath," wrote Davis. "They were armed with every conceivable type of antiquated firearm, aged cap and ball horse pistols, muzzle-loading, single-barreled shotguns," and so on. "One thing, however, was not lacking—abundant provision for Dutch courage. The *cantina* was doing a land-office business." The townspeople hadn't known the column was in the vicinity, but when Davis donned his uniform blouse and rode into the plaza, the "militia" broke up in the wildest cheers for the *soldados americanos*—cheers of relief more than anything, since it meant that they would not, after all, have to go hunting the ferocious and better-armed Apaches. *Los americanos* would do it.[6]

Now and then the column visited similar villages, occasionally running across some refugee from the United States, such as a one-time Confederate guerrilla whom Davis found to have become an influential man in one forgotten settlement. Most Americans were looked upon with suspicion, however, since they were apt to be rustlers, as worthless and merciless as the Apaches.

From Oputo the scouts struck a fresh trail made by the hostiles, who had swept off the town's horses, and Crawford sent thirty scouts under Chato and a White Mountain Indian, Big Dave, to follow them, taking two days' rations. Sieber and Davis wanted to go along, but Crawford gruffly told them they would only be "an encumbrance." But, Davis recalled, "we had the satisfaction, if it was satisfaction, of having him regret that he did not let us go."

It was raining when the scouts took up the trail, but not enough to wipe out all sign. The trail went up a sharp-nosed ridge which fell off the west face of the Sierra Madre. The scouts had been blundering along, which was careless for Apaches, because of the rain, covering

6 Britton Davis, *Geronimo*, 155–66. For my description of this scout into Mexico, I have depended equally on Davis' *Geronimo* and his "The Difficulties of Indian Warfare" (cited hereafter as Britton Davis, *Journal*), a report which he filed from Fort Bowie on September 15, 1885, with the Adjutant General, Department of Arizona, and which was reprinted textually in the *Army-Navy Journal*, October 24, 1885. In some respects the latter account is superior to the version in *Geronimo*, mainly because it was written while the campaign was fresh in his mind, whereas *Geronimo* was written from memory forty years after the events, although it was checked against the recollections of surviving acquaintances of those days. Daly, "The Geronimo Campaign," *loc. cit.*, says (p. 70) that about June 22, a detachment under Davis, Lieutenant Charles P. Elliott, Sieber, Chato, and fifty scouts struck a camp of the hostiles in the Sierra Madre foothills east of Oputo, killing one and capturing fifteen, among them old Nana. Yet later (p. 95) he says Nana surrendered with Geronimo. The latter version is probably correct. Nana was also falsely reported killed in August.

their heads with blankets. Suddenly the clouds parted; some five or six hundred yards away and spotlighted above them in the golden sunshine was a hostile camp. The renegades and the scouts saw each other at the same time. The Indian men and most of the women fled up the ridge into some timber, firing back at the scouts as they did so and wounding Big Dave in the elbow. "Both Sieber and I felt, and Crawford now agreed with us, that had either of us been with the scouts we would have bagged the entire camp," wrote Davis.[7] Coming from different bands, they acknowledged no over-all leader save a white man, and the young men got out of control "and became careless when they should have been most careful."

Fifteen women and children were captured, but the tragedy was the escape of Chihuahua—for it was his camp—and most of his people. The scouts recaptured five Fourth Cavalry horses and one white mule, three saddles, revolvers, belts, and some of the ammunition taken from soldiers killed at Guadalupe Canyon some time before. The women arrived at the border by early July.[8]

Crawford continued his scout to the south. He followed the mountain range east of where the Bavispe joins the Haros to become the Yaqui. The country grew poorer and wilder and more remote from anything that might be called civilization—long since removed from that status by the incessant depredations of the fierce mountain tribes. In Nacori Chico, near the headwaters of the Río Nacori, Davis found a town of 313 souls, only 15 of whom were adult males, the remainder having been killed off by the Apaches. With no sign of the enemy, Crawford turned north along the valley of the Bavispe, but soon swung east again toward the main range of the Sierra Madre.

Meanwhile, Wirt Davis and his men were also working through the main range. Late in July a band of ten or twelve Indians who had been hiding somewhere in the New Mexico mountains swooped down on the border from the north, driving at a run some forty head of stolen horses. The affair seemed to be designed to keep the border troops on the alert more than anything else. A command chased the

[7] Britton Davis, *Geronimo*, 167–68.

[8] Crook to AAG, Division of the Pacific, June 28, 1885, Hayes Collection; Crook to General John Pope, Presidio, July 3, 1885, *ibid.*

raiders sixty miles or so to the south, forcing them to drop the stolen stock, much of it worn out and ruined, but failed to catch the hostiles.

Crawford's command clambered on up the rolling crest of the Sierra Madre, losing a few mules that rolled down the mountainsides or plunged into rocky abysses, killing themselves or becoming so crippled they had to be destroyed. Most of this happened to the big northern mules; the little southwestern mules were more sure-footed, more nimble in mountain work.

A week on the crest of the range brought no results, and the command slipped down off the mountains again and went into camp near good grass on the Bavispe, sending pack trains north for more rations. During the two-week interval, Sieber and Davis with a dozen scouts went south of the river and up the Haros "as far . . . as they would go in fear of meeting Mexican troops, but no trail of the hostiles was found."[9] Trouble was, they didn't go south quite far enough—Mangus and his small band were in that country, but east and south of where Sieber and Davis scouted.

While this pair was out, Crawford had been energetically scouting all the country within fifty miles of his base camp, but he didn't have any luck, either. When rations arrived and the big mules were exchanged for small ones, he determined to penetrate the Sierra Madre once more. The hostiles *must* be there, since they were nowhere else. Sure enough, once atop the range he struck a hostile trail, and shortly there came alongside it the trail of a scouting party, which turned out to be from Wirt Davis' command. Britton Davis rode up to two Americans seated on the ground, their feet on a log before them.

> They were in their undershirts and torn overalls; hatless, dirty, unshaven for weeks, their feet swathed in bandages made from their flannel shirts.
> "Hi, there!" called one of the scarecrows. "Are you Davis?"
> "Yes," I replied, "but who the hell are you?"
> "I'm Day. Got anything to smoke and eat?"

With Lieutenant Matthias W. Day was Charlie Roberts, one of his chiefs of scouts. While they were eating Davis' lunch, they told "of the nerviest piece of work of which I have ever had personal knowledge." Three days earlier, they had set out with about thirty scouts on Geronimo's trail, thinking it fresher than it was and taking along only one day's lunch. To travel better, they soon discarded shoes for moccasins. The rains came and soaked their footgear, which became useless. For three days they had scrambled barefoot over sharp rocks and cactus, while their feet swelled to almost twice the normal size, although bandaged in strips from their shirts. "When our surgeon removed the bandages," wrote Davis, "their toes were hardly distinguishable. A good example of 'elephantitus of the feet,' he pronounced it." But their expedition had not been without results: late on the third day they had jumped Geronimo and his band. Davis was under the impression that Day and Roberts and their scouts had killed only a woman and a boy of fifteen,[10] but Crook's official report to headquarters and the *Chronological List* tell it differently.[11]

Despite the unusual and very heavy rains that continued to plague the country, Buckskin Frank Leslie,[12] another of the chiefs of scouts of Wirt Davis, brought in a message that said:

> Lieutenant Day and Mr. Roberts with seventy-eight scouts of his command, struck Geronimo's camp in the mountains a little north of east of Nakari [Nacori], on the seventh of August, and killed Chief Nana,[13] three other bucks and one squaw—one of the bucks the son of Geronimo. They captured fifteen women and children, among them three wives and five children of Geronimo's family, and Huera, the wife of Mangus. Geronimo was wounded and escaped, though trailed some distance by the

---

[9] Britton Davis, *Geronimo*, 173.

[10] *Ibid.*, 174–76.

[11] Lockwood, *The Apache Indians*, 282, says three noncombatants were killed.

[12] Leslie was a noted frontiersman of the time. It was he who killed William Clayborne, alias Billy the Kid (not to be confused with William Bonney of the same nickname), at Tombstone's Oriental Saloon on November 14, 1882, in what a jury called "justifiable homicide." He had also been in at least one Apache fight, in 1883.

[13] This was an error. Some aged Apache may have been killed, but it wasn't almost-indestructible old Nana, who lived through the Apache peregrinations as far as Oklahoma, where he died "at a great age—unreconstructed," according to Lockwood, *The Apache Indians*, 324. Betzinez, *op. cit.*, 196, says merely that Nana died at Fort Sill, indicating it was sometime before 1911. Britton Davis, in a notation on a memo sent him February 4, 1928, by Charles B. Gatewood, Jr., said that this report was in error and that "no bucks [were] killed in this fight."

blood.[14] Two other bucks and one squaw got away. On the twenty-ninth of July the scouts ambushed a party of four Chiricahuas in [the Sierra de] Joya Mountains and killed two of the bucks. In Geronimo's camp were captured thirteen horses and mules, beside saddles, blankets, dried meat, etc.[15]

The following day, Crook called his headquarters' attention to "the excessive hardships and difficulties which both commands in the Sierra Madre have endured," and explained:

In the first place the whole country is of indescribable roughness. The Indians act differently than ever before, are split up in small bands and are constantly on the watch. Their trails are so scattered that it is almost impossible to follow them, particularly over rocks, which often delays the party following trails for several hours, even if the trail isn't entirely lost, while the party being pursued loses no time. . . .

Owing to the rains which reports show to have been of more than usual severity, the troops have been almost continually drenched to the skin for the last month. . . . Mr. Leslie, who brought in Captain Davis's report, states that he swam the Bavispe River eleven times in one day, a stream that is usually easily forded. It should be understood that the Indians are so split up in small parties and are so constantly on the watch that our scouts are practically compelled to cover the entire region, and cannot even venture to follow trails where they pass over prominent points for fear of their pursuit being discovered. . . . In daylight they frequently have been obliged to conceal themselves in canyons where not only no rest was to be obtained, but where the extremely heavy mountain rains made their position one of great danger. At these times they have of course been separated from the pack trains for a period of from three to fifteen days . . . have been compelled to live for several days at a time on a half allowance of bacon, supplemented by acorns and roots.[16]

Crawford was now convinced, if he didn't already know it, that pursuit of the hostiles by troops was useless, and he had also learned,

14 This, too, was in error. As far as is known, Geronimo was not wounded in this encounter.

15 Crook to AAG, Division of the Pacific, August 17, 1885, Hayes Collection. Sieber reported that the hostiles had been caught by surprise by Day's scouts and many were forced to jump over a steep bluff in order to escape being captured. Daly, "The Geronimo Campaign," *loc. cit.*, 72.

16 Crook to AAG, Division of the Pacific, August 18, 1885, Hayes Collection.

to his sorrow, that their pursuit by scouts alone was unfruitful. Accordingly, he detailed Davis and Al Sieber to follow Geronimo's trail, wherever it might lead, and to stick to it like leeches until they dropped in their tracks or achieved results. The pair took Mickey Free, Chato, and forty picked scouts, five pack mules loaded with rations and ammunition, two packers, and a night herder. Davis didn't realize it, as he turned to wave at Crawford before plunging into the wilds, but he would never rejoin the command, nor would he ever see Crawford again.

By this time the small band of hostiles possessed only one shod mule and four or five shoeless Mexican ponies, and had they been wise, they would have knifed and eaten the mule. The incessant rains all but obliterated the trail, and Davis's scouts could keep to it mainly by the sharp-cut track of the muleshoes. The Indians kept killing the ponies for food—although they preferred mule meat to horseflesh— and finally only the mule was left, and it had lost three of its shoes. Davis' scouts lived off the pony flesh the hostiles left.

The rains fell almost daily. Crawford had expected Geronimo to come down off the mountain somewhere in Sonora, but instead the trail led due east, over the roof of the Mother Range. "On one lucky occasion we caught several young turkeys," Davis remembered. He does not say so, but the Indians may have run them down, a favorite Apache trick, although they would rarely eat the huge birds unless starving.

Trailing was not easy. The Indians suspected they would be followed. They did everything they could to obscure the trail, switching direction, doubling back, altering their course when on bald rocks where even the shod mule's tracks would not show. Frequently the scouts had to circle for hours before they could again find a lost trail, but they doggedly kept on. It was necessary to keep scouts eight or ten miles in advance each day, lest the main body be spotted by the hostiles, who might be closer than was thought. That meant extra traveling for the hardy Indian trackers.

Gradually the man hunters descended toward the Valley of San Buenaventura in Chihuahua, southeast of Galeana, finding the eastern slope of the Sierra Madre infinitely easier and more gradual than the precipitous Sonora wall. But their task became no easier. Now they were in the land of ranches, and the hostiles stole fresh horses, moving more swiftly now, killing their mounts as they tired and catching up fresh ones to renew their flight.

Short of food and weary with long marches, Davis began to suffer anew. He was, as he wrote, an inveterate cigarette smoker and had long since run out of tobacco. On the trail one day he espied Sieber pull out a part of a plug of chewing tobacco, bite off a chunk, and stuff what was left of the plug back into his pocket. Davis' imagination set to work and he figured that chewing tobacco would be better than nothing. He said as much to Sieber. "With no show of enthusiasm he passed the plug over," Davis wrote.

The Lieutenant managed to get some satisfaction from his experiment, and later in the day he suggested another helping. Al's reaction was scarcely ecstatic.

> Taking his knife from his pocket, he cut off a piece you could put in a thimble, passed it to me, and securely retrenched the plug in a back pocket, which he ostentatiously buttoned up. For a little distance we rode in silence, but Sieber was thinking. Presently he spurred his mule up beside mine and unburdened his mind.
>
> "Lieutenant," he said, "I don't want you to think that I begrudge you anything. You're welcome to most any thing I've got; but I must say, Lieutenant, that this is a damned poor time for an amateur to learn to chew."[17]

Progress of the scouts continued to be slowed by rain and soft terrain. "The country through which we passed was so soft that our mules with even their light loads sank to their knees in the mud, and riding at times was out of the question," Davis reported.[18] Meanwhile, with no word back from his tracking expedition, Crawford had sent Lieutenant Charles Pinckney Elliott to overtake it if possible. The officer's little company included five scouts, two packers, and mules with rations. Following a plain trail, Elliott was able to make two days' marches to Davis' one.

On August 25, Davis slipped down off the main Sierra Madre,

17 Britton Davis, *Geronimo*, 183.
18 Britton Davis, *Journal*.

crossed either the Sierra del Arco (Bow Mountains) or the Sierra de la Culebra (Range of the Snake) and camped on the Upper Santa María, a dozen miles above San Buenaventura and about fifty miles southeast of Casas Grandes. The hostiles had killed a beef, and Davis' party enjoyed a feast on the ill-gotten remains. Unfortunately, a *vaquero* had discovered the butchered carcass and the tracks, not only of the hostiles, but of Davis' scouts. He raced to town as fast as his dumpy little pony could carry him and reported his discovery to the soldiers. About 150 troops were at San Buenaventura and 100 civilians joined them in a rush to seek out and destroy the enemy.

Elliott, meanwhile, not sure how far ahead Davis was, camped only four miles distant, after he and his group also had helped themselves to what was left of the steer, which had now fed successively three hungry bands of fighting men. The stage clearly was arranged for some lively action. Davis describes it:

> The sun was just setting when my scouts suddenly began yelling and stripping for action. Two Indians had appeared on a small knoll a quarter of a mile back on our trail and were calling to our scouts, who were now streaming over the trail back to them, shedding their clothing and loading their guns as they went. I called to Sieber asking what was the matter. He did not answer but ran to his mule and jumping on it bareback took out after the scouts, calling to them to stop. I followed suit.
>
> Half a mile from camp we caught up with the leading scouts and succeeded in halting them. With them were the two Indians we had seen on the knoll, who turned out to be scouts we had left with Crawford. They told us that . . . Elliott . . . had been attacked by an overwhelming force of Mexicans.

The scouts, who had been hunting, believed that Elliott and everyone else in their camp had been killed and had come upon Davis' bivouac quite by accident.

Davis, fearing that Elliott had indeed been killed, was too busy to think about it at once, for his scouts wanted to tackle the Mexicans, kill all they could, and light out for the United States. Sieber and Davis talked them out of that, then, with the scouts, pushed on to Elliott's campsite. They found no trace of him or his Indians. Davis sent Sieber and the scouts back to his own camp and determined to go alone into San Buenaventura to see if he could find out what had happened to Elliott. It was now dark and the venture was a most hazardous thing for him to do, but there was no help for it. He dared not take any Apaches with him, for they would only complicate the issue, nor could he take Sieber, for he was depending on Al to hold and control the Indians.

It had begun to rain hard. Lightning flashed all around and the thunder growled and exploded in typical plains fashion. Halfway to town, in a flash of lightning, Davis saw four mounted men approaching him. They challenged him, and Davis identified himself. They were two Mexican officers and two soldiers, who told him that Elliott and his packers were unharmed but "detained" in San Buenaventura until they could be identified. Elliott couldn't speak any Spanish, and the Mexicans had not yet found any of their number who could speak English. "We had all halted and were quietly sitting our animals," Davis wrote, when in "a flash of lightning, the snort of a horse and an exclamation of fright from one of the soldiers caused me to glance around." What he saw was enough to scare anyone:

> We were surrounded by ten or a dozen naked men, their black eyes flashing in their set, determined faces, upturned inquiringly. Dark bands about their heads to keep the hair from their eyes, the inevitable breech cloths and double belts of cartridges—beyond these they were as nature had sent them into the world. In an instant all was black again. One could not see ten feet away. . . .
>
> Then came another flash of lightning, and I recognized Chatto and some of my scouts. Chatto afterward explained that they were determined that I should not go alone to the Mexican town for fear that I might be killed by Mexicans on the way. If I were killed they were going to take toll of those who killed me, then make their way back to Sieber and the command. They had slipped away from our camp in the darkness without Sieber's knowledge, and had followed a few yards behind me.

This was a sample of the Apaches' loyalty and courage, in view of their traditional reluctance to fight at night, aside from their willingness to take on, at their own initiative, some 250 Mexicans, if necessary, to protect their officer.

Chato insisted on accompanying the whites to the edge of town.

Davis went on in and learned that the Mexicans had located a couple of Americans who ran a wagon shop in the community. Elliott's innocence was promptly established. What might have been a catastrophe turned out all right, with the Mexican colonel providing a midnight feast for his unannounced visitors. But Elliott could not see the humor of the situation. The Mexicans had fired more than one hundred shots into his camp, and only atrocious marksmanship had prevented a disaster. He growled: "All I want now is to live to see the day when I will come down here with a saber in my hand and a troop of cavalry!" Davis just grinned at him.[19]

Three days southeast of San Buenaventura, Davis' column, refreshed by the rations Elliott had brought but still moving slowly, actually saw, in the distance, Geronimo's raiders disappearing toward the horizon on fresh mounts they had stolen from General Luis Terrazas' Santa Clara Ranch. "We took the trail again, although the chase was now practically hopeless," Davis wrote. "Our only hope was to continue to push them on the possibility of giving them so little rest they might run into another command."[20]

The hostiles now turned north, and a new difficulty threatened the Davis-Sieber party. Once the Indians had fresh mounts, they doubled their marches, while the seven weary pack mules of the punitive expedition were wearing out.

In addition to a distance of more than a thousand miles marched by these mules in the earlier part of the campaign, we had called upon them during the last two weeks to make a march of three hundred and fifty miles through a mountainous country where their food was, as a rule, coarse pine grass, with very little strength in it. To attempt to double our marches under such circumstances was likely to prove fatal to our success, but, as it subsequently appeared, we had no choice in the matter. The day we turned north we marched forty-five miles to obtain water, the follow-

[19] Britton Davis, *Geronimo*, 183–88. Daly, "The Geronimo Campaign," *loc. cit.*, 74–76, tells this story very differently. He says that Davis wanted to lose no time in his pursuit of the hostiles and, knowing that Crawford would take care of Elliott, pushed ahead, Daly and Crawford then effecting the release of Elliott. This is the only report indicating that Crawford had crossed the mountains to the eastern side, and in view of Davis' categorically opposed story, Daly's account must be disallowed.

[20] Britton Davis, *Geronimo*, 189.

ing day thirty miles, and the day after this we were obliged to go fifty miles before we camped. At the end of this last march the water, when obtained, was so strongly alkaline that the following morning three mules gave out and two others grew weak. It was impossible to take them further.

We would have proceeded on foot and trusted to the country for food had we not been met by a Mexican force under Col. Messilla, who informed me that two other Mexican forces—one infantry and one cavalry —had cut the trail twenty-four hours in advance of us and would push the Indians across the [Sonora-Chihuahua] line into the Sierra Madre. However, they went northwest, toward the international boundary.

At this time we were without food; the country through which we would have to pass was an alkali desert, destitute of game; our shoes were worn out and the Indians partly barefooted, several were sick, and in order to proceed further we would have to abandon our mules.

The Lieutenant, "knowing that it would be impossible to effect anything in that condition, and that I would endanger the lives of my party by attempting to cross the desert north of us afoot, without food and no facilities for carrying water," thought it best to head for some communication point.

The Davis-Sieber party staggered into an English-owned ranch, the Santa Domingo Cattle Company, operated by Lord Delaval Heresford, obtaining there sufficient supplies but, of course, no money. When they finally reached a telegraph station on the railroad, the agent would not send a collect wire to Crook. This meant a delay in getting to Crook the vital news that the hostiles were making for the border, so that he might put into operation his elaborate plans for trapping them. Davis sent couriers, however, to Crawford and to Fort Bliss, Texas, reporting that this hostile party seemed to consist of twenty-five Indians, nine of them warriors, and that they were heading north for the line. The Fort Bliss message finally reached Crook, who telegraphed the commandant at Fort Bayard to "clean out this party" if he could.[21]

Davis and his group reached Bliss on September 5. Since August 14 they had traveled more than five hundred miles, but, as the Lieutenant said, "the actual distance scouted over was largely in excess of

21 Crook to AAG, Division of the Pacific, September 6, 1885, Hayes Collection.

this" figure. "When we started on the trail we knew nothing of the country through which we would have to pass. There are no maps of it, and the information obtained from the Indians was necessarily meagre." He digressed at length on the difficulties of tracking such wary and intelligent Indians as the Apaches, then continued:

At one time during the campaign a band of Indians whom I was following caught sight of the scouts, and with their women and children in twenty-four hours marched more than ninety miles without rest. Had it been necessary I believe they could have gone a hundred further with equal ease.

It is little trouble for them to obtain all the fresh stock they need, the bucks going eight or ten miles to either side to raid while the women and children travel rapidly toward whatever point they desire to reach, the bucks joining them on the road with fresh horses. While being pursued they have guards to the front, to the rear, and on either flank, who keep the main body advised of any force seen in the vicinity. When they camp they choose the most inaccessible points they can find, preferably the rocky extremity of some mountain spur, along which they can retreat into the mountains proper in case they are attacked. These camps are often several miles from wood and water, which will be carried up to the camp by the squaws.

Guards are put in such positions that they can watch the country for miles around, and upon the first indication of the approach of danger the camp is alarmed and the race begins again. Even when not pursued they seldom stop for more than three or four days in any one place. When necessary they abandon all their property, and getting into the mountains afoot they scatter in every direction, making it . . . at times impossible to trail them. Some of the Indians, when they left the reservation, had excellent field glasses, and with these their lookouts can watch a large extent of country. . . . Dust or smoke is sufficient to set them running again for two or three hundred miles.

It is not so much a question of fighting these Indians as it is of our catching them. . . . On one occasion I marched the scouts fifteen and a half hours at an average speed of about three and a half miles per hour. But it is impossible to keep this up for any length of time without breaking the scouts down completely. . . . At one place it became necessary to cross a shallow alkali pond, some four or five miles in width, and as we could not ride through the mud we were obliged to wade, leading the mules. The alkali was so strong in the water that it blistered our feet and legs, some of the Indians becoming so footsore that it was only with great pain that they could travel at all. The hostiles had crossed this flat before the rain.[22]

The tribulations of Lieutenant Davis' party, however severe, were probably no worse than those endured by other columns; it was typical Indian fighting for that time and place, and soldiers and scouts expected nothing less trying. But for thirteen dollars a month it was a lot of work.

At El Paso, Davis met a family acquaintance with large cattle holdings near Corralitos, on the Río Casas Grandes about twenty-five miles northwest of the city of that name. It was Apache country, the ranch manager had just quit, and Davis was persuaded—rather easily—to resign from the army and take over the job, even though Crook tried to dissuade him. Sieber was apparently sent back to San Carlos, where he remained as chief of scouts for what enlisted Indians still were there. Late in November he went out with a party which trailed Josanie's hurrying raiders through Aravaipa Canyon, but the trail was cold by the time he struck it and he couldn't catch the enemy.

Crawford had come out of Mexico long enough to refit, and in late fall or early winter, Sieber again accompanied him southward as chief of scouts, but he didn't go far. While Al was gone, "the balance of the Apaches on the reservation became very unruly, which caused General Crook to call me from Mexico back to the Indian Reservation,"[23]

[22] Britton Davis, *Journal.*

[23] Horn, 312. Williamson, "Sieber," 65, says Al was recalled because "the Indians remaining at San Carlos were getting restless," Sieber having "a calming effect on the dissatisfied ones." Lockwood, "Sieber," 29, writes that "the Indians on the reservation had again grown restless and difficult to control. There was no one who had greater power over them than Sieber, so Crook soon recalled him in order that he might exert his quieting influence." Horn, 197, says he returned because he was bothered with rheumatism. The *Prescott Weekly Courier* for October 2, 1885, had this to say: "Al. Sieber, a noted scout, has been sent back to San Carlos. Mickey Free, a friendly Sierra Blanca Apache, went with Al. This move looks as if Capt. Pierce, the new agent, was desirous of having men in whom he can rely to assist him in standing off Indian Ring fellows on the big reservation." Daly, "The Geronimo Campaign," *loc. cit.*, 78–79, implies that Crook relieved both Davis and Sieber after they returned to the United States because he abruptly discovered through an interview with them the real causes of the outbreak.

and thus ended his last real expedition, although not nearly all of his frontier experiences. Tom Horn was named chief of scouts by Crawford on Sieber's recommendation, and remained with the command through its coming vicissitudes.

So it was that Sieber did not attend the campaign's more sensational moments. He was not present when Crawford was slain, probably by design, by a Mexican irregular unit; he was absent from the three-day conference at Cañon de Los Embudos, near San Bernardino, when Geronimo surrendered to Crook, nor was he present at the subsequent breakout. He was not in Mexico for General Nelson A. Miles's long-winded campaign to track down and destroy the hostiles, nor for Gatewood's heroic visit with the enemy which resulted in their final surrender.

The question may naturally be asked—would the outcome of any of these events have been different had Sieber been there? The answer is that they *might* have been. Perhaps a scout with more experience than Horn could have prevented the shooting imbroglio in which Crawford lost his life; maybe not. Sieber, with his immense personal influence over even the hostile Chiricahuas, could more likely have prevented their getting drunk and unruly after the Los Embudos conference, or at least he would probably have taken a page from Crook's notebook and attended to the whiskey seller who sent them back on the warpath. And had Sieber been along, it is certain that Miles's columns would not have wandered off into the Sierra Madre hunting Geronimo when that wily Indian was in fact on the Middle Bavispe River not far from Fronteras, which was near the border. Months of fruitless campaigning would therefore have been saved. There is no way of knowing how much, or whether, events would have been modified had Al Sieber still been chief of scouts in Mexico, though they would, in all probability, have been tempered to some degree. But this was not to be.

Yet this cannot be, because the *émeute* was in no way Davis' fault, as Crook would have discovered, and Sieber was retained as chief of scouts in the field for several more months. Regarding Sieber, Daly adds: "A better scout, one who understood the Indian in all his numerous phases, I never met. He was utterly fearless, but still had sense enough to know when numbers were too many for him. His services to the government ever since the close of the Civil War had been invaluable."

XX. Keeping the Peace

THERE WASN'T MUCH TO DO around old San Carlos with the Chiricahuas gone and only a scattering of broncos in the hills. Sometimes they raided up from Mexico, but it wasn't like the old days, Sieber found. As a matter of fact, Captain Pierce had things pretty well under control. Most of the Apaches were industrious and serious about learning the white man's inscrutable ways. A good many had followed this path for so long that they were more civilized than certain turbulent border elements of whites who were still keeping the Southwest in turmoil.

Under Pierce's direction, Sieber occasionally took a party of scouts out on one mission or another. He spent a lot of time in the sutler's store, playing poker or sitting back in the dark, cool interior, swapping yarns with men who had shared his wild life. Sometimes someone brought up an outrageous tale he had heard and all had a good laugh. For instance, there was the big lie Charley Meadows was supposed to be circulating about an imaginary fight with Geronimo. Charley was one of the most popular men in southeastern Arizona at this time—six feet, four inches tall, a really top hand, one of the finest ropers and bronc riders in the Southwest—and with an imagination few could equal, much less top.

Charley's favorite yarn concerned a fight in a place he called, probably on the spur of the moment, Battle Creek Canyon, where nine cowboys were camped at Bear Springs, deep in the gorge. "Them Indians," Charley would say, "lowered themselves down the cliffs on riatas, mistook our saddles for sleeping cowboys and fired on them.

314

That woke us up, you can bet. Old Geronimo, he was up on the cliff and tried to get down to the fight, but in slipping down the slope he spooked the horses, driving them up past us." By this time it was about 10:00 A.M. and the alert cowboys, still under fire, roped some of the horses, saddled up, and streaked down the canyon after the Indians. Charley (as he told it) was in the lead, his face blackened by a powder burn, so close did he get to the hostiles, and his hand dripping blood from a lance wound. With the last cartridge in his pistol, heroic Charley fired at Geronimo, breaking his thigh, then roped his horse, captured the warrior, and turned him in for trial.

Some openmouthed reporter heard the tale, and it was printed in the newspaper, being described as relating "the hardest fought Indian scrape ever known in the Territory of Arizona." It might have been, at that, had it really taken place,[1] but it was alleged to have occurred September 3, 1886, the day Geronimo was talking surrender to General Miles in Skeleton Canyon. Besides, Geronimo was never wounded in any fight with cowboys, was not captured, and never stood trial. But the story was a sample of the sort that would ultimately be circulated as gospel truth about the Apache days. Sieber and the other old-timers generally chuckled at them and said nothing; it didn't make any difference anyway, for those days were all but over.

Once in a while there was a scout to be made, and it was good to get out again, follow a trail, hunt down the errant red men, and maybe take a shot or two at them—or get shot at. Reminded a man of old times. Typical of such missions was a scout from March 3 to 15. A copy of Al Sieber's report on it survives in the Arizona Pioneers' Historical Society Archives:

[1] The story was printed January 6, 1895, in a newspaper which, unfortunately, is not identified in the clipping in Gertrude Hill's possession. "Arizona Charley" Meadows was said to have been born in California about 1863 and brought to Arizona as a child. He literally grew up as a cowboy and thought so highly of the skills he acquired thereby that when his sister was married, Charley handed a lariat to the groom and promised him as a wedding present all the wild cattle he could rope in a day. Charley lost thirty-two head that way. He once roped against Tom Horn in a speed contest at Phoenix, in 1891, and lost. Charley organized a wild West show and took it to many places, including Australia. En route he was exercising a bucking horse on deck and the mount plunged into the Pacific—with Charley. Both were rescued by lariat.

San Carlos, Arizona,
March 16, 1887.

Post Adjutant,
San Carlos, A.T.

Sir:

In compliance with verbal orders from Captain P. L. Lee, 10th Cav'y., Commanding, I was ordered to take ten days rations along with six scouts to go to Dripping Springs close to the western line of the reservation, to see about the report of the stealing of twenty head of horses, the killing of one horse and of one steer.

On my arrival, March 3rd, about seven miles west of Dripping Springs, I was told by Mr. Bernard, the man who is taking care of Mr. Griffith's stock, that he had seen five Indians, in camp about two miles from there; on my way up with him to the place indicated I found the signs of five Indians and two horses, they having left before about four or five hours, going in a westerly direction. I also found one horse and one steer killed, both in my opinion having been done by Indians; I also found two small bands of horses on their ranch which were supposed stolen; I found no signs whatever of horses driven off by Indians from their ranch.

On the morning of the 4th, I took up the trail of these five Indians leading in a westerly direction towards the Picket Post and the Silver King Mine; about noon this day I saw by their trail that they picked up another horse somewhere along the road; I followed them up until dark going towards the Superstitious Mountain crossing the road between Picket Post and the King Mine.

On the 5th, about 10 o'clock A.M., I met a man who had seen four of the five Indians the day before, still traveling in the direction of the Super-stitious Mountain, having four horses in their possession. About three o'clock in the afternoon I found where they had killed a steer the day before taking considerable of the beef and quite a lot of raw-hide with them. A few miles beyond this place they left one of their ponies and by the footprints I saw that they caught another horse in its place, having then five horses with them. I followed them until dark, camping that night in the heart of the Superstitious Mountain, the Indians having so far travelled between 60 and 70 miles without camping.

On the morning of the 6th, I took up the trail which was now leading towards the Four Peaks of the Mazatzal Mountains, just north of Salt River; this day about nine o'clock in the morning I came across to where the hostiles had killed one cow, taking very little of the beef and raw-hide

316

with them. When I met the man who is taking care of these cattle I learned from him that he had seen them where they killed the cow in the morning, and at the moment the Indians perceived him, all took to their horses and ran off. About six miles farther, in following up the trail I found where they had killed another beef, taking very nearly half of the beef and all of the rawhide with them, striking north towards Walnut Creek, due south of the Four Peaks. Between sundown and dark, one of my scouts who was ahead on foot about half a mile, came back and told me that the Indians were camped on Walnut Creek. Leaving my pack animals in charge of my two packers, I went ahead with my scouts and found that the Indians were camped there; from my point of observation I could hear them talk and laugh, but could not locate them exactly; I split up my scouts sending three off to the right, telling them to get on a rocky bench overlooking the creek; with the other three scouts I went around to the left trying to get between the hostiles and their horses. At the moment the three first scouts were getting upon this rocky bench they saw three of the Indians moving out from behind a big mass of rocks one of the three scouts acting bewildered and anxious of an attack commenced at once firing before I got anywhere near *where* I intended to; when I heard the shooting I went at once to the place where I supposed they had camped and saw three Indians running towards the mountain four hundred yards away the scouts following them up and firing at them. As the night was then coming on it was impracticable to follow them any further. I came back to the place where they had camped and found that they had left behind them two carbines, four belts and one-hundred and forty rounds of Government cartridges, also four horses, several blankets, clothing and provisions of all kinds. As night was pretty far advanced I camped in the same place. As two of the Indians were absent at the time I attacked their camp I concluded for the next morning to try and hunt them up.

On the morning of the 7th, about sunrise, as I was getting up from breakfast, there were two shots fired at us from a high bluff of rocks, about four hundred yards off; one of these shots wounding one of my scouts through the right hand. I took four of the scouts and ran up towards where the shots were fired from; I found one cartridge shell but no other sign of the Indians, the ground being so rocky it was impossible to see a moccasin track. I hunted around with the scouts for fully an hour over the hills, but could not find any sign whatever as to the direction these two Indians had taken; all my animals being bare-footed and not having rations enough to continue the scouting I went back to camp, packed up and moved towards Fort McDowell, thinking under the circumstances it was the best I could do in order to follow up these Indians and either capture or run them back on the reservation.

On the morning of the 9th I left Camp McDowell, with Lieutenant [Herbert S.] Whipple in command of twelve men. I circled all around the Four Peaks, not being able to find any sign of the Indians for four days.

On the morning of the 13th, I found their trail leading towards the Sierra Ancha Mountains; they hunted for horses in crossing the valley of Tonto Creek. When I reached Mr. Kline's ranch I learned that these Indians had passed there four days before, having on their way shot at a white man named Bouguet about six miles east of this ranch, running him away from his house, which they went through, taking with them flour, sugar, coffee, etc., such things as they wanted, then striking for the reservation, where they could have reached by the 14th. Lieut. Whipple came with me as far as Globe City, and then went home, Camp McDowell, by the way of Riverside and Florence. Myself and Scouts started home arriving on the 15th. On the trip I had to abandon one mule entirely played out, and some aparejo, and also was compelled to leave two mules behind me at Camp McDowell, being furnished transportation there by Lt. Whipple to bring me home.

> Very respectfully,
> Your obedient servant
> Al Sieber,
> Chief of Scouts.

On some similar occasion Al Sieber was benighted near Globe while on a scout. It was a rainy, blustering night, and Al led his party toward the warm, dry oasis of Bill McNelly's saloon. Everyone was soaked, including Lieutenant James W. Watson, who was in command. While Al sampled a double whiskey, the Lieutenant asked McNelly if his scouts might sleep there that wet night, and the genial proprietor said, "Certainly!" They turned their stock out in Tom Pascoe's corral, returned to the saloon, and bedded down on the floor on their wet saddle blankets. Watson got a bottle of whiskey and a glass from McNelly and made the rounds, giving each man a good stiff drink—to "avert the chills,"[2] which it apparently did.

Police activity on the reservation was rarely thrilling, although you

2 Lockwood APHS.

never knew when you were in for an exciting few hours or days. Early in March, 1887, a young Indian named Nah-deiz-az was quietly working his farm on the Gila. Having recently returned from Carlisle Indian School, he was known to some of the whites as "the Carlisle Kid." At the agency, Lieutenant Seward Mott, twenty-five years old and scarcely eight months out of West Point, was temporarily in charge, and he evidently decided that Nah-deiz-az's tract should be used for some other purpose. The Indian refused to move off the land, and the officer himself rode out to the place with a couple of scouts and ordered them to make an arrest. Nah-deiz-az promptly shot Mott, who, mortally wounded, died on March 12. His slayer readily surrendered[3] after the shooting and was given a life sentence in Yuma Territorial Prison; he was later moved to the federal penitentiary at Menard, Illinois, since he was a federal, not a territorial, prisoner. The United States had contracted at this time to place its prisoners either at Menard or at the Ohio State Prison at Columbus. Sieber apparently had nothing to do with this case.

Al was gradually becoming civilized. He spent more and more time working his Delshay property, a gold mine east of Four Peaks in the Sierra Ancha, within twenty-five miles of Payson. To get there, you went thirty miles up Tonto Creek and turned right on a trail between two peaks to a basin seven or eight miles long. A trail led up to the rim, short of Pleasant Valley, and the mine was just below the rim on the west side of the basin. In 1878, Al had made a location there with some old-time packers: Long Jim Cook, Sam Hill, Charley Dupont, and Frank Story.[4] A lot of work was done on the mine and it looked good for a time, but you never could tell about gold properties. Anyway, it was something to occupy a man's time.

---

[3] Hayes, 11–18, in discussing this case, says that Nah-deiz-az was arrested by Sieber and the Apache Kid (then a noncommissioned officer of the scouts), but Sieber, by his own account, was on his extended scout toward McDowell and could not have made the arrest. I think it likely that the Kid was with Sieber. William Sparks, *The Apache Kid, a Bear Fight and Other True Stories of the Old West* (cited hereafter as Sparks), 20–21, has a detailed and more credible account of the shooting of Mott. However, Hayes correctly says that Nah-deiz-az was sent to Yuma under a life sentence and then returned to Globe for a second trial, a detail which Sparks omits.

[4] Lockwood APHS; see also Lockwood, "Sieber," 33.

XXI. The Tragedy of the Apache Kid

THE BEGINNINGS AND END of the Apache Kid are shrouded in mystery. Only in the prime of his spectacular life does he stand highlighted on the horizon of southwestern history. The Kid was Al Sieber's creation—for good and for evil, and he was a strange mixture of both.[1] It is next to impossible to study his life objectively and not conclude that here was a frontier tragedy on the grand scale. He had greatness within him, and the tragedy of the Kid is that of lost greatness. If the course of events had shifted ever so slightly at one or another of the crisis points of his career, his monument today might be to a notable and good man.

There are many such tales of the southwestern border country, differing only in degree. In a sense, the Kid epitomizes them all, but

[1] In working out the story of the Apache Kid, and particularly of his early career, which ends with his plunge into full-fledged outlawry, I have used a number of accounts, but three in particular: Sparks, who was acquainted with many of the principals and wrote the first and most detailed account; Dan Williamson, "The Apache Kid: Red Renegade of the West," *Arizona Highways*, Vol. XV, No. 5 (May, 1939), 14–15, 30–31, who tells much that is not told elsewhere; and Hayes, who has made most use of still-extant civil court records. Unfortunately, Hayes is confused about dates and in some other details and his attempt to dramatize further the already dramatic incidents does not come off well, but he has collected a great deal of new material and some of his reconstructions are well done. B. Ira Judd's "The Apache Kid," *Arizona Highways*, Vol. XXIX, No. 9 (September, 1955), is of little value; the first part is a rewrite of Sparks and where that ends the mistakes begin. Joseph Miller's narrative of the Kid in his book *The Arizona Story*, 78–88, is, as he says, "a composite of stories of the period" and adds little that is new. Tom Horn doesn't have much more to add to other accounts, either. The manuscript by Edward Arhelger in the APHS Archives is important, however, since he was an eyewitness at significant points in the Kid's story.

he also outdistances them all, for his is a saga on the heroic scale. It is customary to refer to him as a "fiend," or "evil incarnate," or as a "devil marauder," or by some other of the clichés with which some writers paint their word canvases in bold, primary colors, but a study of his record fails to reveal much supporting evidence for such epithets. He killed men, but many others tried to kill him; he was blamed for much killing that was not his. This, of course, was, and is, not uncommon. Many a police department, having caught some adept thief, has cleared its dusty files of unsolved cases by hanging them on him. And in the border country of the late nineteenth century, one may surmise that many a slaying was made to look like the work of the Apache Kid when he was, in fact, half a thousand miles away.

A perusal of his career shows that he was intelligent, manly to an unusual degree, and that he had clear scruples and something approaching an ethical code which many a frontier white might have used to advantage. Often the Kid could have killed, but did not. He could easily have ambushed Al Sieber, who, to some extent, was responsible for his outlawry, but he wouldn't do it. There is no case on record where he ever harmed a white woman or child. He kidnaped Indian women when he needed them, but from clans he regarded as his enemies, and his final recorded act is of mercy toward one of them. Nor was he given to depredation for the sheer exultation of devilment. He and his followers sometimes rode through range country for days and molested no livestock, stole nothing but fresh horses and an occasional beef. There is no doubt that he killed for the sake of robbery in Mexico, but relations between the Apaches and the Mexicans were of special complexity, the outgrowth of generations of treachery, deceit, murder, pillage, and rapine on both sides; the Kid couldn't have changed that even if he had wanted to.

This is not to condone the Kid's actions. I would merely point out what has been stressed: that violence begets violence, treachery breeds treachery, evil generates evil. It was so in the bloody relations between Mexican and Apache, and had always been so, or at least for a very long time. On at least two occasions, and perhaps on others, the Kid tried honestly to settle the score Arizona whites had against him. He failed each time, but there is nothing to show that he felt rancor or bitterness. These are some of the reasons why this brief story must be chronicled as the tragedy of the Apache Kid.

There are those who say the Kid was orphaned in an Apache-cowboy fight, rescued by the whites, sent to Carlisle, and then returned to take up the threads of reservation life,[2] but most writers believe that tale a mixture of fiction and mistaken identity. One-time Arizona State Historian Dan Williamson wrote that the Kid "was born in Aravaipa Canyon, a member of Capitan Chiquito's band, around 1860."[3] Jess G. Hayes, who has researched the Kid's career, says that he was the eldest of seven children and was born in a wickiup near the site of Globe in 1868.[4] He may have been a White Mountain Apache,[5] for he missed the grand exodus of the Chiricahuas to Florida, although as a loyal scout he may have attended the departure of some of them from Bowie Station.[6] By this time he was already a veteran of several enlistments, trusted and hardened by Al Sieber and others. He was dark-complexioned, even for an Indian, handsome, tall, with piercing black eyes and a knife-slash mouth. Smooth-faced and lean, he wore a black sombrero and, when he could get them, boots.

The Apache Kid's father, Togo-de-Chuz, legend says, won out over a rival, Rip, for the affections of a girl and thus engendered a feud that was to smolder twenty years. Whether the Kid, at first named Ski-be-nan-ted,[7] was born at the site of Globe or somewhere else, his

2 This version no doubt results from confusion with the capture of the "Doubtful Kid" in a Doubtful Canyon skirmish. The two Indians were not the same man.

3 Williamson, "The Apache Kid: Red Renegade of the West," loc. cit.

4 Hayes, 4.

5 McClintock, I, 267, says as much.

6 Hayes, 1–5.

7 Sparks, 10. Hayes says he was named Haskay-bay-nay-ntayl, which he translates as "the tall brave man destined to come to a mysterious end." Williamson says he was named Oska-ben-nan-telz, translating it as "terrible tempered." And on a well-known picture of ten Apache scouts, the Kid's name is given as Es-ki-bi-nadel. These obviously may be variant spellings of the same name, even though translations differ. Hayes, however, had the assistance of the Reverend F. F. Uplegger, now beyond his ninetieth year, who has devoted some forty years at San Carlos to compiling an Apache vocabulary and whose knowledge of the language is unrivaled. His version must therefore assume weight, even though the translation suggests an after-the-fact interpretation. Williamson also lists Oh-yes-sonna, translated as "hears something in the night," and Gon-te-e-e, "four fingers," while C. L. Sonnichsen in "The Apache Kid," Around Here, the South-

father had moved the family there by 1875 and the boy made himself useful around the saloons and shops of the growing community. So it was that he came to Sieber's attention. Al made him "a sort of orderly for himself. Wherever Sieber went, the Kid went,"[8] and Al even taught the boy his version of cooking. Eventually the Kid enlisted in the scouts, where he soon rose to the rank of sergeant and in that grade took part in the Big Dry Wash fight with Lieutenant Morgan's Troop E. Within two years he had made first sergeant and in that capacity went to Mexico with Crook, in 1883,[9] when Sieber was chief of scouts.

"Kid's eyesight is amazingly keen," wrote one newspaperman who had a personal acquaintanceship with many who later chased the Indian. "An Army officer once commanding Kid as a scout tells [this] correspondent that one day, while attended by Kid on a bluff overlooking a vast plain, the scout reported a band of mounted men fully fifteen miles distant. With the aid of powerful field glasses the officer could barely discern moving specks on the plain. With the naked eye the Kid discerned not only the number of mounted men in the distant party, but could also tell the number of white men, the number of Indians, and the number of horses and mules in the outfit. The officer met the party later and found that Kid's report was exactly correct. Such keenness of vision seems almost phenomenal."[10] Phenomenal it was indeed! Allowing for a bit of exaggeration, the incident still reveals a remarkable quality, not only of vision, but of intelligence. At that distance the Indian could not actually *see* the difference between white and Indian, and how many of each were in the party, but he could *deduce* it from his experience and from the dust raised and other

---

west in Picture and Story, Vol. X, No. 1 (1952), 61, says the Kid's name was Zenogolache, "the crazy one." All of these names may have been applied to him at various times during his life.

[8] Sparks, 11.

[9] *Ibid.* Sparks is a little ambiguous on this point. I have not seen a roster of that operation, but Sparks says that "when General George A. Crook [*sic*] went down into Mexico after the Chiricahua Apaches under Juh, and Geronimo, Sieber was with him, and the Kid was among his scouts." In the next breath he says that when Sieber returned to the reservation in mid-campaign, the Kid also returned, but the expedition to capture Juh was in 1883 and Sieber returned to San Carlos late in the 1885–86 campaign. It is probable that the Kid was on both.

[10] M. Y. Beach, writing in the *Los Angeles Times*, November 11, 1894.

signs. An experienced stockman can differentiate between a horse and a mule almost as far as he can see anything. A pack mule and a saddle animal move differently and can readily be distinguished by the seasoned eye. White men and red men do not sit their mounts in an identical way, so that distinguishing the elements of a party at that distance in the luminous clarity of the southwestern deserts becomes a matter of observation *plus* deduction *plus* what might be called intuition. The Kid's feat on this occasion was a tribute not only to his phenomenal eyesight, but to his imagination and intelligence as well.

The Kid returned to Mexico during the Geronimo campaign early in 1885 and again in the fall, but when Sieber was recalled, the Kid returned to San Carlos with him. He went briefly to the White Mountains until Crawford arrived to enlist one hundred scouts for Mexican duty, then signed on again. He went south late in 1885. William Sparks describes an incident which occurred on that trip:

> On one occasion several American soldiers, packers, and scouts, got drunk in the Mexican town of Huasavas. There was a Mexican Major there with a battalion of Mexican infantry. Some of the Mexican soldiers were called out to stop a small riot, that was said to have been precipitated by an attack three Apache scouts had made on a Mexican woman.
>
> When the soldiers appeared on the scene, the scouts tried to run away. The Mexicans fired on them, killing one, and wounding another. The third man was captured. It was the Kid. The Mexican Major wanted to take him out and execute him, according to Mexican custom; but the Alcalde of the town said he was afraid it would cause trouble between the two governments; so he fined the Kid Twenty Dollars which was paid, and the Kid was sent back to Sieber at San Carlos.[11]

The Kid had become a family man, taking as his wife a daughter of old Chief Eskiminzin; he never took another wife until he became

---

11 Sparks, 11–12. Huásabas, which is the town meant here, is on the ·Bavispe River scarcely a dozen miles northwest of Bacadéhuachi, where, Wood reported, some of the scouts had a fine drunk in the summer of 1886; it was quelled by the first sergeant. It is possible that Sparks and Wood are writing of the same incident, which would put the Kid with Lawton's column after Crawford's murder. It is also possible that the incident Sparks records is that referred to by General Crook in his letter of January 11, 1886, to Governor Torres of Sonora, or it may be a third and different affair.

an outlaw. During the summer of 1887,[12] Captain Pierce, who was still agent at San Carlos, and Al Sieber went up to Fort Apache and beyond to White River Subagency, leaving the Kid in charge of the scouts and guardhouse. What then ensued is pretty much a matter for conjecture, but the course of events was probably as follows.[13]

A band of Apaches about ten miles above San Carlos decided that with both Pierce and Sieber away, this was the time to brew tiswin, and word of their frolic reached the Kid. Complicating the picture was the fact that his father was living in the camp, but before the scouts could arrive, Togo-de-Chuz was dead, shot in the back by one Gon-zizzie,[14] who, in turn, was pursued by friends of the Kid's father and himself slain. This, however, did not appease the young Sergeant. Gon-zizzie was a brother of Rip, the Apache who had nursed a grudge against Togo-de-Chuz for more than twenty years, and the Kid may have felt that somehow Rip was behind the killing of his father. He took his scouts to Rip's place, killed him, and returned to Togo-de-Chuz's stormy camp to drink tiswin and brood over the death of his father. Remorse over failing Sieber's trust may have afflicted him, although he might then have taken to the mountains and joined the broncos, but at length, for whatever reason, he gathered his scouts and rode back to San Carlos to face the music. "Sitting in front of the agency I saw a row of Indians coming on horse-back single file," recalled Edward Arhelger. It was June 1, 1887. "I said to Frank Porter,[15] 'Frank, that looks like old times. I believe we're going to have some fun here tonight!'"[16]

[12] Both Hayes and Sparks mistakenly date the ensuing events in 1888.

[13] You can find as many versions as there are written accounts. There was no one to give the complete details, save the Indian participants, who were not available for questioning, and no one to set them down immediately after the émeute. The published accounts are all based on scraps of evidence, much speculation, and interviews with individuals long after the affair was over. In this version I have followed most closely Dan Williamson, who seriously tried to get the truth and who was acquainted with the surviving principals, being one of Sieber's close friends and having once received, and considered, an offer to ambush the Kid personally.

[14] Whose name meant "shirt sleeve."

[15] Porter was called "Boss Farmer" at the agency, which meant that he was general instructor of agriculture for the Indians. Sparks, 17.

[16] Arhelger manuscript, APHS Files. Arhelger arrived in Arizona, by way of Lordsburg and Shakespeare, about March 1, 1882, and two years later signed on as pack-train

Al was at the agency, seventy-five yards from his tent, which faced it, and the Kid sent Sergeant Toney to tell his chief that he wanted a talk. Sieber replied that he would come down at once with Captain Pierce. The Kid's six or seven companions stood about uneasily, holding their horses and keeping arms ready, alert and no doubt with still-throbbing heads. Pierce, Sieber, and two interpreters soon hurried up. None was armed.

By this time a crowd of curious Apaches, many with weapons, had gathered to watch—and complicate matters. Sieber gruffly told the Kid to hand over his rifle and ammunition, which the Indian did, and then to disarm the other scouts, which he also accomplished. Captain Pierce then ordered the Kid to go to the guardhouse and tell the sergeant there to lock up the other scouts and himself as well. This was about to be done, and the entire incident might have passed, when some hothead in the crowd took action.

Al Sieber had laid the scouts' firearms on a table just behind the entrance of his tent when someone started shooting, for what reason is not known. It was the spark that touched off a fight. Firing became general. An Indian jumped for his carbine and snatched it off the table, but Al kicked it out of his hands and leaped into the tent to arm himself. The Kid fled without a weapon. As Sieber ran out of his tent through a hail of bullets, a scout named Curley jumped into a hole, from which clay to make adobe bricks had been taken and fired at him.[17] A .45-70 slug, heavy enough to drop a buffalo, smashed into Al's left foot, felling him instantly, and his tent was riddled with bullets. The scouts fled.

"Quicker than I ever saw them before," Arhelger recalled, the troops were ready to take the field. Two troops of the Fourth Cavalry,

---

blacksmith at San Carlos. He went into Mexico with Crawford's column late in 1885 and was an "industrial instructor," i.e., taught blacksmithing, at the agency at this time.

17 Williamson said it was Pas-lau-tau who fired this memorable shot. "It has always been thought that Curley fired this shot," he wrote, "but Paul Patton—ex-scout and full brother of Pas-lau-tau—told me this on February 22, 1939." Nevertheless, Arhelger, who was there, says it was Curley, and Sparks and others agree. Probably, in the melee, several Indians were firing in the general direction of Sieber and no one knew whose bullet struck him, but it is worthy of note that no one ever blamed the Kid for it, since he was unarmed at the time.

under Lieutenant Charles Elliott,[18] galloped off along the plain trail for ten or fifteen miles up the San Carlos River before darkness overtook them. Next morning, they found that their quarry had doubled back, heading for Aravaipa Canyon and the San Pedro River Valley. The troops doggedly continued the pursuit.

During the night, an Indian courier had been dispatched to Globe for Dr. T. B. Davis, close friend of Sieber and a veteran of the Mexican campaigns. Davis and Bill McNelly hurried to the agency to do what they could for the scout, who was reported mortally wounded.[19] Many newspapers commented on the incident, one of them opining that "an Indian cannot be trusted in any capacity" and others editorializing similarly. From McDowell, Major E. J. Spaulding of the Fourth Cavalry wired appropriate law officers to "notify the settlers to be careful of their stock and not to go about single until the Indians are back on the reservation." Higher officers were concerned. General Miles made hurried preparations to go to San Carlos from his Los Angeles headquarters, and a press statement was issued from there blaming the trouble on a "drunken row" and a feud between two bands in which Rip was slain because he was "believed the cause" of the killing of Togo-de-Chuz. "The Indians have been well treated," said Miles, "and the affair is the result of the innate deviltry of the Indian character, excited by very bad liquor."[20]

Miles left Los Angeles on June 13, accompanied by Lieutenant Gatewood, his new aide. When he arrived at San Carlos, he went immediately to see Sieber, declaring that Al "was the most self-contained and most fearless Indian scout in the service."[21] The General looked around, saw that everything which could be done to catch the outlaws was being done, and had prepared to return to his headquarters when he was amazed to receive an offer to settle the whole business.

---

[18] Arhelger says this was Lieutenant James B. Hughes. It may be that both Elliott and Hughes were on the expedition, but if so, Elliott would have been in command, since he was senior in rank to Hughes by two years.

[19] *Arizona Star*, June 7, 1887.

[20] *Ibid.*

[21] From the biographical statement Sieber dictated to Ben G. Fox for James H. McClintock in 1903. *Arizona Republican*, April 18, 1925.

After doubling back to the south, stealing a horse from Tom Horn[22] on the way, the mutineers followed the San Pedro, passing Benson and the familiar Whetstones, still heading toward the border. Perhaps they intended to drop down into Mexico, where broncos still lurked, but if so they changed their minds, although it would have been easy enough to slip across the border. It seems evident that the Kid didn't yet consider himself an outlaw, was still troubled over the question of mutiny, and desired to return to Sieber and duty. The band turned north again. They had committed no important depredations, although in some quarters they were charged with the slaying of Bill Diehl, a prospector-partner of Walapai Ed Clark, and Mike Grace, who was killed near Crittenden on Sonoita Creek. Miles wrote that the Indians "stole but very little" on this hard ride, often passing through herds of cattle without molesting them. He said it was believed that a Yaqui Indian named Miguel instigated the whole "uprising," if it may be called that, fired the first shot, and personally killed the two whites, and this all mitigated for the mutineers.

Hard on the Indians' trail was Lieutenant Carter Johnson with scouts from Camp Thomas. He met Lieutenant James B. Hughes at the mouth of Aravaipa Canyon, and the two officers chased the Kid's band south, then doubled back, and were now pushing the Kid hard. In the Rincon Mountains, seven thousand feet up, the Kid's party made camp. They were idling in the sun when their reverie was shattered by the uproar of gunfire as the two lieutenants' troopers swept in upon them. There was no kill,[23] although camp equipage and loose horses were captured, including Horn's "pretty badly used up" mount. Then Johnson was abruptly ordered by the General to quit the trail.

The Kid had sent couriers to Miles saying that he wanted to come in, but couldn't do it with Johnson crowding him so hard. The General took a chance and called off the Lieutenant; the Kid, a man of his word, surrendered as he had promised. On June 22, eight of those

22 Horn, 250–54, has a surprisingly accurate version of the Apache Kid's first breakout, although, understandably, it contains a few errors, since Horn makes it clear that he got the facts secondhand. He adds details not available elsewhere.
23 Horn, 253, says Johnson "killed a couple of them," but in this he was mistaken.

who had been out gave themselves up and three days later the Kid and seven companions did so. Miles wrote that although he realized the scouts didn't fully comprehend the charges against them, he ordered a general court-martial, "as if they had been white soldiers."[24]

There can be little question that it was a drumhead court[25] and that its proceedings were merely a formality. Its original six members, including such officers as Johnson and Hughes, who had chased the Kid so hard, were each challenged by the defense. Several admitted "bias and prejudice" but assured the court, that is, themselves, that they could set these feelings aside and "arrive at a judgment on the basis of the evidence presented." Captain A. H. Bowman later decided he did not want to sit on the court and amended his testimony, asserting that he could not control his "bias and prejudice." He was excused. Miles assigned three other officers, headed by Major Anson Mills, to the court, and Mills, by reason of rank, became its president.

The witnesses, almost without exception, said that they did not see the Kid armed, or shoot at anyone, or do anything but try to get away once the firing began. Captain Pierce, first witness for the prosecution, testified that about sundown on June 1 he had been told that Kid had returned

and was at Mr. Sieber's quarters. I went there with Mr. Sieber and also with Antonio Diaz and Fred Knipple [issue clerk] as interpreters. Four other scouts who absented themselves at the same time that "Kid" did were at Mr. Sieber's tent with him. When I reached them I said, where are the five scouts who have been absent. They all stepped to the front in line. I said to "Kid" give me your rifle. He handed it to me and I said give me your belt. He handed it to me and I put it on a chair that was standing there. The same conversation and occurrences took place with the other four scouts. I then said "Calaboose." Two or three stepped to the chair picked up their belts and commenced removing their knife scabbards and knives from their belts, they being their personal property. Just then I

[24] Nelson A. Miles, *Personal Recollections*, 536.

[25] This account is based on Transcript, Court Martial of 1st Sergeant Kid, Company A, Indian Scouts, Judge Advocate General, Records Received, 4475, January 17, 1888, National Archives. The 148-page document, assembled day by day as the trial proceeded, reveals clearly the formality with which the court went through the motions of a trial.

heard a little noise that attracted my attention in front of the tent and I saw a few men on horseback who were bringing down their firearms and getting cartridges from their belts. I said look out Sieber they are going to fire. Immediately there was a shot fired by some one in the party in front of the tent. I turned round walked into the front door of the tent and through the tent. The tent had two doors, one front and one rear, both open. Sieber got down and crawled into his tent, also Knipple. I did not see what became of Antonio Diaz. There were about fifteen to twenty-five shots fired by persons in front of the tent, quite a number of them passing through the back of the tent, all entering the front door. I came back through the back door of the tent and through the front door. Sieber was in his tent wounded through the left leg below the knee. The belts that I had left in the chair had all disappeared and also two of the firearms that I had taken from the scouts. Those rifles were lying on the ground near where I had stood them after I had taken them from the scouts. I picked them up, carried them into Mr. Sieber's tent and put them on his bed. The five scouts and some Indians who were in front of the tent besides them had disappeared and the firing had nearly ceased when I came to the front of the tent again. I can not identify any particular one as having fired a shot. After they disappeared from the front of the tent on the evening of the 1st of June they were not seen by me again until the 24th of June.

On July 3 the court met in Sieber's room, where the wounded scout lay in misery, too ill to attend the regular sessions. Sieber was sworn in and identified himself and the Kid, whom he said he had known for about eight years. "On June 1st Kid the 1st Sergeant of Scouts who had been absent for five days without permission returned along in the evening about 5 o'clock I should judge, and I saw him coming up to my tent," Sieber testified.

I happened to be up here at the agency and went down and reported it to Captain Pierce that they were at my tent. The Captain then walked down with myself to my tent; on arriving there he asked me to point out the five Indians who had been absent without leave and returned. As I did so he disarmed them, took their guns from them, belts, and after receiving their arms and belts he ordered them to the calaboose. He gave the order two or three times to the 1st Sergeant Kid and the other four scouts. Kid gave a look which signified— [Al was interrupted at this

330

point by an objection, which was not sustained.] —to me for them all to rush for their arms which they did all five of them. Captain Pierce jumped in between two of the scouts and their arms and shoved their arms away from them, and I jumped between the three others and their guns. Kid being the nearest to me made a grab for his carbine which I grabbed with my right hand and shoved Kid back with my left, and about this time Captain Pierce hollowed [sic] to me, "look out, Sieber, they are going to shoot," and he broke for my tent, that is the Captain. I throwed and kicked the guns that were within my reach towards my tent as far as I could. At this time there were two shots fired one right after the other. Kid jumped away from me and ran around the shade of my tent, and I then ran into my tent, throwed myself down to get my gun. At this time there were scattering shots being fired that I could hear going through my tent, some of them. I by this time got my gun and went out doors and took a shot at the first Indian I saw who was on horse-back, evidently had just fired. At the same time that I fired I was shot in the leg, my leg broken and I was knocked down. I fell back into my tent and found Fred Knipple there and he commenced bringing water for my leg.

In response to questioning, Sieber said that he thought the appearance and attitude of the scouts on that day was "warlike." "I thought so by their looks, and by them having arms in their hands which is against orders here." He added that "they looked cross as I came up and went by them. I spoke to Kid and he answered me gruffly." He said he interpreted the "look" that Kid gave the other four as they sought to regain their arms as indicating "they had an understanding before they came in here, that if a certain thing transpired, which was ordering them to the guardhouse . . . that by a look from the Kid, each man knew what to do, which they did, in each man jumping for their arms." Dr. Davis reported that Sieber was too ill from his wound to testify further, and the court adjourned for the day.

At a subsequent session, Antonio Díaz testified in part that he had arrived at the scene before either Pierce or Sieber. He shook hands with the Kid, he said, and asked him, "How is it you have been out so long?" The Kid replied, "We have been off and have killed a man at the Aravaipa."

Then I said to him I am sorry for it. Then he replied to me, It is no matter of yours nor of the agents. It is our affair and no one elses. Then

I said to him that it is all right, it does not matter to me whether you kill ten or a dozen Indians a day, and I suppose it does not matter to the Captain either. . . . I says to him how is it that you have gone forty miles from here, killed a man in cold blood and returned here? It is not our custom to kill people thus. Yes, said "Kid," but we did it. It is nobody's business.

When Sieber arrived, Díaz testified, he said, "Hello Kid," and the Kid replied, "Hello."

Several days later, the court reconvened in Sieber's room for cross-examination, during which Al admitted that the Kid did not get re-possession of a gun during the melee. But he insisted that the look he saw the Kid give his fellows was "certainly not accidental."

Say-es, one of the accused, told how word to come in was brought from Sieber by Gon-shay-ee, the band leader, to the five scouts up on the Gila; the Kid said they would. "We will obey orders, whatever Sieber says. If he gave them an order to go to the guard house they would go, because they went away without permission."

The Kid himself, in a formal statement, admitted drinking tiswin, shooting Rip, and then returning to Sieber's tent, where he gave up his arms. Then, the Kid said, Antonio Díaz "spoke in Apache, and said, all the Indians that don't obey the orders, will be sent to Florida. At the same time all the Indians outside made a noise and were much excited about what Antonio spoke. I thought those outside thought then that we scouts would be sent to Florida." The shooting started, and the Kid fled. He ended his testimony with this statement:

God sent bad spirit in my heart, I think. You all know all the people can't get along very well in the world. There are some good people and some bad people amongst them all. I am not afraid to tell all these things because I have not done very much harm. I killed only one man whose name is "Rip" because he killed my grandfather. I am not educated like you and therefore can't say very much. If I had made any arrangement before I came in, I would not have given up my arms at Mr. Sieber's tent. That is all I have to say.

The case was concluded. The predetermined sentence was clear. The Kid was found guilty and sentenced to death by shooting. So were the other four.

Miles objected to this finding, largely on the basis that Díaz's purported statement about the scouts' being sent to Florida might well have excited other Indians within hearing. Then, too, the General had his doubts that there was anything premeditated about the "mutiny." He therefore ordered the court to reconsider its verdict. It met August 3 at Camp Thomas and resentenced the five to life imprisonment, which Miles reduced to ten years. Under heavy guard, they were sent to Alcatraz for confinement.

Sieber, bedridden as he was, could not have been lonesome for long. A Globe committee saw to that. Its members went to San Carlos to investigate things in general and dropped in on Al several times. They were "pleased to find him cheerful and looking so well—better than was expected. Dr. Davis is encouraged over the favorable condition of his patient [and] it is hoped the limb will rapidly mend."[26] It never mended. Not until the spring of 1888 did Sieber begin to get around once more—now on crutches—but soon he was handling Indians again and doing such duty as his condition permitted.[27]

"Sieber was very bitter against the Kid," wrote William Sparks, "whom he held responsible for the whole trouble. He had been crippled for life . . . [and] Sieber blamed him for the whole mutiny."[28] It is not clear from any other source that Al was quite as angry with his former protégé as Sparks makes out or that he remained bitter very long. There is evidence from Dan Williamson and others that he never bore a grudge for the affair or, if he did, that he soon put it aside. "Sieber had a good word for everyone—even for the Indian Kid who shot him," according to Bud Ming.[29]

There was in Arizona, however, a continued and scarcely suppressed fury with the Indians that would not subside, and it is possible that Sieber lent himself to those who saw in the Kid's case an outlet for their emotions. At any rate, legal minds went to work and ulti-

[26] *Arizona Silver Belt*, June 30, 1887.

[27] The *Arizona Republican* for May 14, 1928, reported in its "Forty Years Ago" column (which would date the item May 14, 1888): "The trusty Al Seiber, chief of scouts for Arizona, is visiting Phoenix for the first time since his recovery from his wounds. He brings six Apache Indians who are to be tried at this term of court."

[28] Sparks, 17–18.

[29] Bud Ming in correspondence with the author, January 30, 1958.

333

mately convinced the courts that the military had no jurisdiction in this case because Congress had decided that civil courts had jurisdiction in cases where Indians were charged with such crimes as murder, rape, assault with intent to kill, arson, or burglary.[30] Thus the Indians could be returned to the Territory and perhaps tried again— if it were feasible to charge them once more. The Kid and his companions were ordered back to San Carlos, although they were not apprised of the legal reasoning behind their newly won but temporary freedom.

New charges of assault with intent to commit murder were filed against the former scouts; Sieber, the target of their attack, was to be chief witness. Jess Hayes gives a circumstantial version of events preceding the trial, indicating that Sieber was chief instigator, but his account is not convincing.[31] For example, if Al had wished to press charges, he would have called upon the district attorney with his evidence for their implementation, not the sheriff, as Hayes alleges, who was merely an executive officer. At any rate, a list of Apaches to be arrested was drawn up and Sheriff Glenn Reynolds[32] wired General Miles for military assistance in picking them up. Miles telegraphed Reynolds the same day,[33] stating he had instructed Sieber and Captain John L. Bullis,[34] who had succeeded Captain Pierce[35] as agent at

[30] Hayes, 14–15.

[31] *Ibid.*, 43–44. The circumstances leading to the U.S. Supreme Court decision which returned the Indians to San Carlos from federal incarceration and paved the way for their second trial are explained briefly in *ibid.*, 37–42.

[32] A cattleman, Reynolds came from Albany, Texas, where he was born in 1853, arriving in Arizona in 1885 with his wife and four children and settling in the Sierra Ancha. He had been a sheriff of Throckmorton County, Texas. His Arizona ranch was not far from Pleasant Valley, where the feud soon broke out, indirectly causing the death of one of Reynolds' children. Earle R. Forrest, in *Arizona's Dark and Bloody Ground*, says (p. 174) that Reynolds took some part in the feud killing. He reports one of the faction leaders as having said that Reynolds ambushed Al Rose, killing him with a shotgun. Reynolds moved to Globe, where he was elected sheriff of Gila County in November, 1888. He was well liked and apparently an honest and efficient law officer. In addition to his other accomplishments, he was reputed to be the best pistol shot in the Territory. Hayes, 31–34.

[33] Hayes, 46.

[34] Bullis is an enigmatic figure of significance in the Al Sieber story. He was born in New York State on April 17, 1841, and on August 8, 1862, he enlisted in the One Hundred Twenty-sixth New York Volunteer Infantry. In 1864 he was promoted to captain of the

San Carlos, to assist in their arrest. On October 14, Reynolds secured warrants and within two days all but the Kid were taken; the latter, unarmed, was arrested by Deputy Sheriff Jerry Ryan without incident.[36] The Globe Courthouse jail was now crowded with some of the toughest individuals in Arizona. Among them were the Kid, charged with assault with intent to murder; Say-es, Hale, and Pas-lau-tau (or Pash-tere-tah), charged with being accomplices; and many more accused of various unrelated offenses: Nah-deiz-az, on trial again for murder in connection with the shooting of Lieutenant Mott; Hascal-te; Bi-the-ja-be-tish-to-ce-an, El-cahn, and Te-te-che-le, murder; Bob McIntosh,[37] horse stealing; and others, some of whom never came to trial.

The four charged with the assault on Sieber were first to be tried,

One Hundred Eighteenth New York Infantry, served on the Texas-Mexico border during 1865 and 1866, and entered the Regular Army in 1867. Bullis gained recognition through his work with mixed Negro and Seminole scouts along the Río Grande. The *Chronological List* shows that, among other fights, he was in actions on April 25, 1875, on the Pecos River; near Saragossa, Mexico, on July 30, 1876; on the Río Grande near Devil's River on April 1, 1877; near Saragossa again and at the Big Bend of Texas on September 26 and November 1, 1877, respectively; and in the Sierra Burros of Mexico on May 3, 1881. Bullis was cited for gallantry in engagements against Indians at Remolino, Mexico, on May 18, 1873; at the Pecos River, Texas, on April 25, 1875; the Saragossa engagement of July 30, 1876; and the Burro Mountains fight of 1881. In 1882 the Texas Legislature adopted a resolution thanking him for his service against Comanches and "other frontier enemies." Information from Tom McGowan, city editor of the San Antonio *Express*. Bullis had obviously had wide experience with Indians, both hostile and scouts, by 1889, although the composition of his units would indicate that his attitude toward them might have differed from that required of those who would command Apaches, a fact which would have a bearing on his future relationship with Sieber and the San Carlos tribesmen. Grave charges against Bullis were to be whispered about San Carlos and to break into the open within a year or two, but to my knowledge, these were never proved.

[35] Pierce, who had become "one of the best 'Indian men' we ever had," according to Cruse (*op. cit.*, 205), was not through with Indians, however. He was to be named agent for the Sioux at Pine Ridge, South Dakota, shortly after the Battle of Wounded Knee. *Arizona Silver Belt*, January 10, 1891. He died at the Presidio, San Francisco, in November of 1896 from blood poisoning and internal injuries suffered in a fall from the balcony of his home on October 22. *Arizona Silver Belt*, November 19, 1896.

[36] Although by an interesting stratagem; see Hayes, 48–50.

[37] Bob was apparently one of Archie's kinsman, but their exact relationship is not clear. San Carlos Superintendent Thomas Dodge, in a letter to me dated September 28, 1958, said Bob was related to Archie McIntosh.

appearing in court on October 23, 1889. Joseph H. Kibbey, later governor of the Territory, was judge; J. D. McCabe, district attorney, was prosecutor; Ben Fox was clerk; and E. H. Cook and Mills Van Wegenen were the court-appointed defense attorneys.[38] Witnesses for the prosecution included Curley, who many say actually fired the shot which struck Sieber, and Al himself.[39] Old Merijilda Grijalba was court interpreter, a role which he often fulfilled.

Out of the relatively brief testimony came a picture of a long-standing dispute or feud between Curley and the Apache Kid, which leads to the suspicion that Curley's testimony was not altogether disinterested.[40] Nor was Al Sieber's testimony what might be called

[38] Hayes (p. 54n) says that public defenders in such Indian trials were paid fifty dollars for each case and that "scores of attorneys flocked to Globe to get this practice."

[39] Hayes, 44, 67, says that Sieber told Reynolds, "I will have my naturalization papers and be a handy witness at the trials," but the implication is unclear. He cannot mean that Sieber secured his naturalization papers only to testify, for that would not have been necessary, since Justice Department records show that there was no requirement of citizenship for witnesses in the territorial courts of this period. I think the explanation is more innocuous and that Sieber really said, "I will be getting my naturalization papers at that time, and thus will be handy as a witness." He was naturalized at Globe on Wednesday, October 30, 1889, with testimony by Charles F. Martin and Dr. Davis to support his claim to Civil War service as a soldier of the Republic. Minutes of the Second Judicial District Court, Globe, Arizona, Book 2, p. 39. Even before that Sieber had voted: in the Gila County election of 1882 he gave his country of nativity as the United States and subsequently stated that he was a native of Pennsylvania. Hayes, 67n. This was not unprecedented; Schurz, *Reminiscences*, II, 47, says: "In Wisconsin the immigrant became a voter after one year's residence, no matter whether he had acquired his citizenship of the United States or not. . . . And of such early voters there were a good many." The *Arizona Star* of January 29, 1879, commenting on a legislative proposal to disenfranchise aliens who had merely indicated their intention to become citizens, observed that the existing federal statute said: "The right of suffrage . . . shall be exercised only by citizens of the United States . . . and by those . . . who have declared on oath . . . their intention to become such, and have taken an oath to support the constitution and government of the United States." The paper commented approvingly: "It has been one of the principles of the national government from its earliest history to encourage immigration. . . . To this end, it says to the foreigner, 'go with your friends and families into our great wilderness . . . and assist in building up new states, we will allow you to exercise the rights of citizens, vote, hold office and make laws.'" Sieber had no business stating that his nativity was American—if he understood the question properly—but a man's actions should be judged in the framework of the morality of his times. In the Arizona of the 1880's, such voting was probably the least heinous of daily crimes.

[40] Hayes, 54–58, has the most complete summary of the trial.

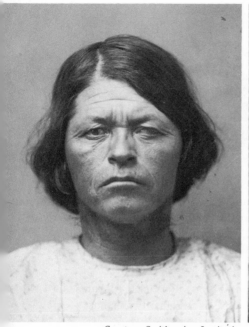

Courtesy Smithsonian Institution
Bureau of American Ethnology

Courtesy National Archives

ickey Free, called by some "an Irish
»aniard," served Crook as interpreter
ring the expedition into Mexico.

Convicted of assaulting and attempting to
kill Al Sieber, the Apache Kid later
escaped and was never apprehended.
Ironically, he was Sieber's best scout
and was said to possess almost
unbelievable vision.

Courtesy George S. Scha

(Above) General George Crook (center) and some of his officers and scouts about 1886. Al Sieber (standing, wearing a dark shirt, suspenders, and a large hat) is the fourth man to the General's left. Tom Horn (wearing a white shirt) is the fourth seated man on Crook's right. Standing behind Horn and to Horn's left, with arms folded, is Lieutenant Marion Maus.

(Below) In this photograph taken at Mount Vernon Barracks, Alabama, in 1893 are some of the Apaches' foremost leaders. From left to right: Chihuahua, unidentified, Loco, Nana, and Geronimo.

Courtesy National Arc

objective. The Kid himself took the stand in his own defense. He said that Curley was his enemy, jealous of the close relationship between Sieber and himself and, in particular, of his, the Kid's, good fortune with certain Apache girls. The Kid denied that he or any of his co-defendants had shot Sieber, but said he believed Curley had done so in order to get him into trouble. A surprise witness for the Kid was Na-shay-shay, an Apache girl the whites called "Beauty," who testified to the Kid's good behavior.

In rebuttal, Sieber charged that the Kid had made up the story merely to clear himself. The old scout's statement was good enough for the jury, which found the defendants guilty as charged; in the Arizona of that day, any other verdict was unthinkable. Edward Arhelger, who was there at the time, put it succinctly: "All were promptly found guilty, which I think myself was wrong, but the sentiment was such that a good Indian was a dead Indian."[41]

The sentences were not unduly severe, it would seem. Each of the four charged with assault on Sieber was sentenced to seven years in Yuma Territorial Prison. Nah-deiz-az, against whom Sieber also testified from personal knowledge of the case, was found guilty of murder and sentenced to be hanged.[42] El-cahn got eight years; Has-cal-te, twelve; Bi-the-ja-be-tish-to-ce-an and Te-te-che-le, life. Bob McIntosh was acquitted. A Mexican prisoner, Jesús Avott, got a year for horse stealing.

Glenn Reynolds now had the problem of transporting the prisoners from Globe to Casa Grande, en route to Yuma. Sieber offered him an escort of Indian scouts but Glenn shrugged, "I don't need your scouts. I can take those Indians alone with a corn-cob and a lightning-bug." He selected a single deputy, W. A. "Hunkydory" Holmes,[43] as guard

[41] Arhelger manuscript, APHS Files.

[42] The public hanging was a particularly clumsy and brutal affair according to Hayes, 124–30, who incorporates a description from the *Silver Belt* of December 28, 1889.

[43] W. A. Holmes, also a Texan, came to Arizona as a hawker of religious tracts, but adventure called and he became a prospector, staking out the Daisy Dean, a rich silver claim which netted him a small fortune, but lost it defending himself for killing Banjack Marco, a claim jumper. After that, he directed his talents in various directions, tried politics, and wrote poetry of a sort, reciting it in saloons for what he could get. His best-known poem was "Hunkydory," from which he won his nickname. Hayes, 31n, who reprints the poem in the appendix.

and chartered a new green and yellow stagecoach driven by Gene Middleton for the trip to the railroad. Middleton carried a pistol, Holmes a lever-action Winchester and a pistol, and Reynolds a Colt .45 and a double-barreled shotgun. The first night, the cavalcade reached Riverside, forty miles south of Globe, leaving about 5:00 A.M. the next day in order to meet the 4:00 P.M. train for Yuma at Casa Grande.

The Mexican, Jesús Avott, rode inside the coach that morning. The Kid and Say-es were handcuffed separately and the others in pairs, so that each would have a free hand. At the start Reynolds rode atop the stage with Middleton and Holmes because "it's too dark to ride inside beside those fellows." Both Reynolds and Holmes were bundled up in long overcoats because of the cold, and the horses were unaccountably fractious[44] until the coach got under way. It was barely dawn when they reached the foot of a high, cactus-covered ridge where the road turned up a steep, sandy wash. Up it the horses could pull the coach, but not much of a load. Reynolds and Holmes got out with Avott and the prisoners who were shackled in pairs, leaving the Kid and his companion on the front seat of the coach. The stage then rocked on up the difficult climb. After it trudged Reynolds in the lead, then the prisoners, and finally Holmes. The stage soon forged quite a distance ahead of the prisoners. Just before it turned a rocky point, Middleton glanced back and saw the column straggling behind him. After he turned the point, Gene stopped to blow the horses, bent over to look into the coach, where he found the prisoners secure, and straightened up in time to hear a shot from back down the road. Since both Reynolds and Holmes had been target shooting from time to time, he thought little of it. What had happened was told later by the Mexican.

As the column approached the rock point, the foremost Indians got as close as they could to Reynolds and the others dropped back toward Holmes. The latter seized Holmes with their shackled hands while Pas-lau-tau snatched the guard's rifle away. At the same instant, the forward Indians seized the sheriff and in a furious struggle

44 Hayes, 88, quotes Middleton as later writing to Mrs. Reynolds: "I never saw horses act in such an unaccountable way."

338

took his shotgun away, he being unable to get at the revolver under his overcoat. Pas-lau-tau ran up with the rifle and shot Reynolds, killing him instantly. It was this shot that Middleton had heard. Holmes's body showed no wounds, he having died of fright.[45] The Mexican was unharmed.

The outlaws swiftly stripped Reynolds' body of weapons and the keys to their manacles and hurried to catch up to the stage. The Mexican, however, was ahead of them and warned Middleton, who pulled his pistol and forced the Kid, about to leap from the vehicle, back inside. Then, hearing the click of a weapon being cocked on the other side of the stage, Gene turned. A bullet from Holmes's rifle ripped through his mouth and neck, missing his teeth and spinal cord but toppling him from his high seat onto the ground, where he crumpled and lay still, although not quite unconscious. Into the coach leaped the Apaches to free the Kid and Say-es, who sprawled to safety just as the restless horses ran away with the empty vehicle.

Middleton lay in a widening pool of his own blood, sure, as he later put it, that "his last moments had come."[46] His eyes were open a bit, and he could not close them. The Kid may have noticed, but the other Indians did not. El-cahn stood over him a moment, then raised a jagged rock high above him, prepared to hurl it at the wounded man's head. The Kid spoke to El-cahn, grabbed his arm, and caused him to cast it aside. The Indians then ripped off Gene's overcoat, emptied the pockets, and disappeared in the brush.

This is the version given by Sparks, and since it came from Gene Middleton himself, it seems most worthy of acceptance. Williamson adopts it, but adds that another Indian planned to shoot Middleton as he lay on the ground but was forestalled by the Kid, who said,

[45] "Heart failure" was the way the coroner described it, according to Sparks, 25–26. Williamson, "The Apache Kid: Red Renegade of the West," *loc. cit.*, agrees. Hayes has a gory version in which Holmes is shot and his head crushed by "vicious stomping"; his authority is not revealed. Hayes also has Reynolds shot once with the rifle, once with his own .45, and twice in the face with the shotgun. It seems incredible that all this shooting, plus the whooping and yelling he reports, could have taken place without alarming Middleton, but Hayes insists that Middleton was not yet aware of anything amiss.

[46] Sparks, 24–25.

"Don't shoot, the man is dead. You may need the cartridge." The Indian then stopped over the driver, explored his wound with a dirty finger and agreed, "Yes, he is dead." This exchange, often printed, is difficult to accept. Middleton understood no Apache except perhaps a few odd words and it is illogical to suppose that the Kid would address another Indian in English—unless, of course, he wanted Middleton to know that he had saved his life. Lee Middleton, younger brother of Gene, told me that his brother had specifically denied to him that the Apache Kid had made this remark. "He thought I *was* dead," Gene believed.

Jesús Avott hurried to where the coach had overturned, slashed one of the horses loose, and climbed on it; the animal threw him three times before he managed to stay aboard. He galloped into Florence and recited the news. Dizzy and staggering, the weakened Middleton recovered sufficiently to make his way back down the road until he met Shorty Saylor, another stagecoach driver, who carried the word to Globe. It was wired to San Carlos, where Dan Williamson took the message to Sieber, abed with a recurrence of weakness from his wounded leg. Al grimly read the telegram. "I was afraid of that," he muttered to Williamson, "and that was why I offered a scout escort to Casa Grande." From his bed he helped organize a twenty-man scouting party, under Lieutenant Watson, to take the trail. Troops and scouts were rushed into the field from all southeastern Arizona posts, but without much hope of success.

Up to this point, as can be seen from the above, the Kid had almost no record as an outlaw. He admitted killing Rip, believing him responsible for the slaying of his father, but otherwise he had shot no one except in line of duty, had committed no recorded crime, except possibly desertion. He had even rejected the possibility of fleeing into Mexico and certain sanctuary and returned to surrender voluntarily. He had been sentenced to death and then put in jail for something he did not do. He had been returned to the reservation, rearrested, and again sentenced to prison. While en route to the penitentiary, his companions overpowered the guards, killed one of them, frightened another to death, and wounded a third, whose life the Kid saved, for he would have had no reason to stay the executioner's hand had he not known Middleton was alive. The Kid was driven into outlawry with a record that was extraordinarily clean.

But now the deed was done. The Kid, Pas-lau-tau, and the others stuffed their pockets with cartridges, belted on the revolvers, and with the other weapons melted into the brushy wilderness, traveling fast. Even as they left the scene of death and violence they felt the sting of snow: hard, driving flakes that presaged a long fall, one that the wind would whip and drift across the frozen countryside, bleaching the brown earth, sifting against the sage and scrub, filling in the gullies and swirling into the washes and arroyos. In moments their tracks would be covered over, blotted out forever, making futile the work of the man hunters.

Those disappearing tracks, at first so fresh and hot and now so cold and faint, were the last solid clues that the forces of law and order would ever have to the Apache Kid. To this day they have come no closer to arresting him than they were on that frozen desert in southern Arizona, with arctic drifts erasing his last certain sign.

XXII. The Kid Loses His Band

AL SIEBER, it has been reported, was given a "secret service" fund and men were assigned to him to track down and kill the Apache Kid and his band when and as they could be found.[1] Whether this was effective or not, the Kid and those associated with him, either at the outset or later, occupied much of Sieber's thoughts during the next few years, and for a time the renegades were much in the news.

In March of 1890 a Mormon freighter was shot by Apaches on the high road between San Carlos and Camp Thomas. By the following sunrise, troop detachments led by Lieutenants James Waterman Watson and Powhatan H. Clarke had assembled at the site. Guided by 28-year-old Sergeant Rowdy,[2] "old in Indian war, [who] loved campaigning and fighting and killing even better than he loved whiskey,"[3] the combined command relentlessly dogged the trail. By sunset they were fifty miles out along a trail heading northwest. The next day, the task was resumed, the trail apparently heading for the Sierra Ancha. They found where the hostiles had slain the horses stolen from the teamster, then the trail was lost at times for several hours.

The next day, the scouts followed the trail, on foot and alone, into difficult country, while the troops worked their horses carefully along the bed of the stream below. "We were watering our horses in the

1 Williamson, "Sieber," 69, for example.

2 Rowdy was killed several years later in a drunken brawl in a saloon near Camp Grant. *Arizona Silver Belt*, April 1, 1893.

3 James Waterman Watson, "Scouting in Arizona, 1890," *Journal of the Cavalry Association*, Vol. X, No. 37 (June, 1897), 128–35. I have used this article as the basis for the description of this 1890 fight. See also "A Hot Trail," by Powhatan Clarke, in *Cosmopolitan Magazine*, Vol. XXII, No. 6 (October, 1894), 706–16.

river, when suddenly the distant echoes of a rifle shot were heard in the mountains behind us, then another, then another," wrote Watson. "It meant the scouts had come up with the hostiles. Next was seen the dim outline of a human figure on top of a high ridge a mile or so distant waving his arms. It did not take long to get to the top of the ridge. After a short dash over brush and boulders the horses were left at the foot of the ridge, and everyone clambered on foot up the steep and rocky sides." The waving figure was Rowdy, "already in fighting costume, that is, entirely naked except his breech-clout. The other scouts hurriedly got themselves in the same savage but warlike dress, taking off even their moccasins, so their feet would have firmer hold on the rocks, and tieing their long hair back behind their heads to keep their eyesight always clear."

The hostiles were pinned by a triangle of fighting men, but, hidden in a clump of rocks and bushes, they resolutely returned bullet for bullet. "The hot fire of the three groups [of attackers] was raising a cloud of dust, leaves and broken fragments of rock about the hostile position; the mountains and hills around reverberated with the rapid reports of the carbines; and the whole valley became filled with smoke and every variety of 'whiz' from the flying bullets," wrote Watson. The two groups worked in closer—to within fifty yards. Then "a small party of about ten scouts and soldiers, including Clarke and Rowdy . . . made a rush which took them right among the rocks of the hostile position. Here was a large rock . . . approximately the size of a freight car. . . . We were on one side of this rock and the hostiles were on the other and not more than forty feet distant."

Clarke clambered atop the rock, glimpsed some red skin, and put two shots into it before realizing the hostile was dead. Rowdy, also on top of the boulder, spotted an arm and fired at it, three bullets striking back at him. He fired again and was the target for three more shots, but squirted a mouthful of tobacco juice over the rock and remarked, "I guess I got that feller that time." The wounded Apache called out that he could not fight any more and had told the others to surrender.

The command tried to carry the wounded Indian back to camp, Rowdy grumbling, "I don't think we'll ever get that feller up that hill; I think we better kill him," but he died of his own accord. He was Pas-lau-tau, and another dead Indian was Hale. Bi-the-ja-be-tish-to-ce-an, Te-te-che-le, and a boy were captured. At their trial for murder of the freighter, Rowdy was a prize prosecution witness and left no doubt about who commanded the punitive expedition: "I told Lieutenant Watson he go there and Lieutenant Watson he go there. . . . I told Lieutenant Watson he stay here and Lieutenant Watson he stay here," the irrepressible scout testified as judge and court tittered and the young officer became more embarrassed.[4] As a result of the trial, one of those captured was sentenced to hang, another got life, and the boy a minimum sentence.

Say-es, El-cahn, and Has-cal-te had hidden in the rough country of Mescal Creek, a tributary to the Gila, and on September 20 the former slew, with Reynolds' pistol, Has-cal-te's father-in-law because he was refused food. Has-cal-te hurried to San Carlos and gave himself up, reporting to Sieber the whereabouts of the other two. Troops dispatched to the village killed El-cahn and captured Say-es, who was tried at Florence and sentenced, on October 18, 1890, to life imprisonment at Yuma for slaying Reynolds, which he had not done. Has-cal-te was also sent to Yuma to complete his seven-year term.[5]

These rapid actions left the Kid running alone. Or did it? Not quite. He now had a more formidable ally. The white civilians found out about it from the soldiers, and the soldiers from the scouts.[6] One day a small body of troops and a few scouts were following the supposed trail of the Kid, picked up after a family had been slain in the Chiricahua Mountains. The scouts had been strung out along the trail; now they gathered in a tight little knot, pointing down and chattering excitedly. As the troops came up, one of them indicated a track and said: "Massai!" The officer thought it was impossible—the last he had heard of Massai he was with the bulk of the Chiricahuas sent from Holbrook to Florida. There had been rumors that he had jumped the train somewhere in Missouri, but this was Arizona. The scouts must be wrong. But they were correct.

[4] Richard E. Sloan, *Memories of an Arizona Judge*, 145.
[5] Hayes, 147.
[6] Bud Ming in correspondence with the author, August 13, 1958.

Not a great deal was known of Massai[7] by the whites, and he was considered just another warrior, although he was to prove no ordinary Indian. A Warm Springs Apache, he had enlisted as a scout for the 1880 Victorio campaign. Two years later he jumped from a moving train in Texas to rejoin those of his people who had fled San Carlos with Loco and made his way to the Sierra Madre.[8] But he soon got restless there, stole Jason Betzinez's horse, and made his way back to the reservation. He broke out with Geronimo in May of 1885 but tired of the flight and secretly made his way back to Fort Apache. He may have enlisted with the scouts once more, for he was said to have been in Mexico with Crawford when that officer was slain.[9] He was back at Fort Apache when his people were rounded up for shipment to Florida, but jumped the train in Missouri and headed west once more.[10]

"For weeks no human being ever saw Massai," Betzinez reported. "Traveling on foot at night, stealing food and water, and hiding by day, he succeeded in getting back to his native country in the Black Mountains of western New Mexico. . . . To appreciate this amazing feat you should remember that this Indian could not read printed road signs, did not dare ask questions, had no map, and had never been in this country before except while on the train. Like a coyote or a wolf he lived off the country, remaining completely out of sight even while passing through a thickly settled part of the country in

[7] This remarkable Indian, whose name has also been spelled "Massa," "Massi," "Masai," "Wasse," and "Massey," has become widely known through Paul I. Wellman's novel *Broncho Apache* and the motion picture made from it. The book catches the spirit of the Apaches—and especially the broncos—more vividly than could a factual account. Much of my version is based on Betzinez, *op. cit.*, 143–45, who knew Massai well.

[8] Horn, 248, in his customary garbled fashion, reports an escape by this Indian which he confused with the 1886 flight but which may describe this one in 1882. In part, Horn says: "He turned up in the Sierra Madres later, having made all the distance on foot, through settlements of Texas, and the Texas marshals were after him all the time. He spoke Mexican like a native, and could pass for one anywhere in Texas."

[9] Morris E. Opler, "A Chiricahua Apache's Account of the Geronimo Campaign of 1886," *New Mexico Historical Review*, Vol. XIII, No. 4 (October, 1938), 383. This account is from Samuel E. Kenoi, who was a child at the time of the Geronimo affair and did not take part in it but who gives a sort of Chiricahua consensus of the matter.

[10] Hayes, 9, says that this is the story told by present-day Apaches, who may or may not be correct. At least it is a possible explanation.

Missouri and Kansas." He had demonstrated, as Jason pointed out, "the almost superhuman power of the Apache to find his way through unknown country and to survive great hardships." Yet, he added, "we never considered him to be outstanding as a fighter. He was just an average Apache."

Massai must have arrived back in Arizona almost three years before Sheriff Reynolds was slain,[11] and from that time forward lived like a wolf. He first appeared out of the brush near a camp of White Mountain Apaches to accost a mother and daughter chopping grass with rough-handled hoes near a horse and colt they had tethered.[12] Massai caught the young woman, Natastale, crushed the skull of the older one with her hoe, flung his captive on the pony, and fled. When the colt gave out, he killed it, taking some of its meat for food. The mare wore out and he killed her, making the woman carry what had been on the horse.[13] And so they reached the deep Sierra Madre, where there was sanctuary for Massai and other broncos of his kind.

The Kid far surpassed Massai in notoriety, and perhaps in ability, and soon his reported depredations were so widespread that the territorial legislature offered a five-thousand-dollar reward on him, dead or alive. Several army officers, among them Lieutenant Clarke, were given roving assignments to catch him. They were freed of garrison duties, allowed to select the personnel of their commands, and could go when and where they desired, in line of duty.[14] Occasionally they caught fleeting glimpses of Massai, but never of the Apache Kid: he was elusive as a ghost.

Once the Tontos threw a dance down on the Gila River, about where Coolidge Dam was later built. Dan Williamson, his brother, Al, and Morris Belknap rode down after dark to take it in. About

[11] Miles, *op. cit.*, 529, says it took Massai a year to get back to the reservation; so does Frederic Remington, *Crooked Trails*, 87. This account ("Massai's Crooked Trail") is generally accurate and gives a secondhand contemporary version of the Indian's feats. Sparks, 29, figures it took Massai about two months to reach Turkey Creek from Missouri; some other writers put it at six weeks. It would seem that less than three months would be time enough.

[12] Sparks, 29–31.

[13] This information was obtained from the woman whom Massai released later.

[14] Williamson, "The Apache Kid: Red Renegade of the West," *loc. cit.*, and "Sieber," 70.

midnight they sought to leave, but the Indians dissuaded them. At two o'clock they repeated the performance, but at three the visitors stubbornly insisted on going home. The next day they learned that the Kid had also attended the dance and the Indians sought to keep the whites with them for moral support. Kid stole a woman that afternoon, sending her son and daughter to the rancheria with the message that their mother had gone to Mexico, that it would be no use to try to catch up, that on the previous day when scouts of a roving command were hunting him a scout passed so close to the Kid that he could have reached out and touched him, and that he recognized the three whites at the previous night's party.

On another occasion a woman, Joe Ashey, who had been stolen and lived for a time with the Kid, suddenly appeared at a trading post at the little town of Mammoth, making minor purchases with twenty-dollar gold pieces. Questioned, she revealed that Kid was lurking near by. The cavalry was called, but in the ensuing darkness the outlaw escaped once more.

While the Kid and Massai were blamed for many murders which they probably did not commit, they also performed killings for which others received the "credit," no doubt. Early in July, 1890, a young man named Ed Baker, who lived at a lonely ranch, was shooting at a stump, trying out a new rifle, when he was murdered. Captain Lewis Johnson at San Carlos ordered out two detachments of troops and scouts under Sieber and Lieutenant Watson, and they proceeded to the Sierra Ancha site, where, it was reported, the tracks of three Indians were found. Nevertheless, Sieber was convinced that Massai had done the deed, although he never could persuade anyone else to accept this. "Mr. Seiber is entitled to his opinion," said the *Silver Belt* on July 26, "but there is nothing in the circumstances that warrants such a belief. . . . The facts . . . point strongly to Cibicu Indians." Subsequently, three Indians were convicted for the slaying, but even the *Silver Belt* conceded that the evidence against them was flimsy.

Meanwhile, the reputations of Massai and, particularly, the Kid grew. Wrote William Sparks: "Soon a killing on some lonely ranch, or of some traveling cowboy, or prospector, became such a common occurrence that it hardly excited comment outside of the neighborhood where it occurred. Many ranchmen moved their families into the towns. . . . While they had no dread of the Apache Kid if they could have met him face to face, there was always fear of finding their families slaughtered when they returned. . . . And yet there was no authentic known instance where the Kid took the life of a white woman or child."[15]

An old government guide and packer named Nat Whitman was found shot through the heart; behind a boulder near the house were found moccasin tracks of an Indian and his woman. A settler in the Mogollons was digging potatoes in his field; his body was found, shot through the heart, and near by were moccasin tracks. At a rancheria eight miles from San Carlos the Kid shot a man and sought to steal his daughter. Again he stole a woman from another rancheria, evaded a Tenth Cavalry detachment, shot two ranchers and stole their horses, and made his way safely into Mexico. Not far from Willcox, three cowboys approached a dead cow in a field; two Indians rose from behind it, fired twice, killed two of the cowboys, and chased the other away. Old Eskiminzin, suspected of giving aid to the Kid, his son-in-law, was exiled from Arizona, but it did no good: the Kid lived and flourished anyway. Cowmen Bellmeyer and Gardner were slain near Eagle Creek and their bodies left where they fell, their saddles and several horses gone.[16]

In Sonora a battalion of rurales, commanded by one Emilio Kosterlitzky, was charged with patrolling the wild country. Kosterlitzky was something of a man of mystery. He was born on November 16, 1853, in Moscow, the son of a Russian father and German mother. On December 3, 1872, as a midshipman aboard a Russian warship, he deserted in Venezuela, found his way to the United States, and is said to have enlisted in the Third, Sixth, or Eighth Cavalry, rising to noncommissioned rank.[17] He is reported to have deserted[18] and fled to Mexico, where, somehow, he became a colonel of rurales within a few

15 Sparks, 28.   16 *Ibid.*, 28–40.

17 Thomas H. Rynning, *Gun Notches*, 307, says he deserted from D Troop of the Third; Dane Coolidge, *Fighting Men of the West*, 224, says he deserted the Sixth Cavalry at Fort Apache after being "ill treated" by Captain Adna Chaffee; Britton Davis, in a letter to Harry Carr of the *Los Angeles Times* dated November 23, 1929, wrote that Kosterlitzky "was a deserter from (I think 8th) cavalry, where he had at-

years. The earliest mention of him from Mexico that I have found is a dispatch which appeared in the *Arizona Star* on July 4, 1882: "A force of fifty men was organized and placed under the command of Captain Emuelio Kosterlyden" to chase the Apaches. The bulk of his force, it was said, "was comprised of bandits, former outlaws often chosen by [President] Porfirio Diaz, himself." Yet out of these men Kosterlitzky, a harsh disciplinarian, forged "the finest body of mounted men in all Mexico."[19]

A flamboyant dresser in the bizarre uniforms permitted in the Mexican armed forces of that day, Kosterlitzky saw to it that his men were also well dressed. He organized and maintained an excellent spy and intelligence system and ruled his portion of the border with an iron fist. "His methods were sharp and decisive and a known criminal rarely ever was left to the delay and doubtful justice of the courts. The rurales . . . resorted to 'la ley fuga' and the criminal was left in a shallow grave."[20]

Kosterlitzky retained his command through a number of vicissitudes following the overthrow of President Díaz, but in 1913 he was pushed across the border into the United States and interned. For some unexplained reason, his earlier desertion, if such it was, from the United States forces was forgotten and Kosterlitzky was admitted to residence as a refugee. He became affiliated with the Department of Justice from March 26, 1917, to September 4, 1926, rendering "invaluable service" according to J. Edgar Hoover. He died at Los Angeles on March 2, 1928.[21] He spoke Russian, French, German, Italian, Spanish, and English and his experiences were many, but for all of that, he remains a man of mystery.

Anyway, back in 1890, Kosterlitzky and his rurales were following

---

tained the rank of sergeant." I have tried diligently to get confirmation from the National Archives of Kosterlitzky's American military service, but have not uncovered any such data.

[18] McClintock, II, 605.

[19] Quoted from Clark A. Cubley and Joseph A. Steiner, "Emilio Kosterlitzky," *Arizoniana*, Vol. I, No. 4 (Winter, 1960), 12–14. The article is a good summary of his career.

[20] McClintock, II, 605.

[21] Cubley and Steiner, "Emilio Kosterlitzky," *loc. cit.*

a band of smugglers who had come out of the United States when they suddenly ran across their dead bodies—slain by the Apaches. The next day, the rurales, following the Indian trail, came to a wide flat beyond which was a point of rocks and brush. A man-hunting dog owned by the detachment had gone ahead, around the point. Just as the dog began barking, the rurales charged across the flat under fire from Apaches concealed among the rocks. Three Apaches and two rurales were killed and several wounded. On one of the dead Indians, Kosterlitzky found Glenn Reynolds' watch and pistol, both of which were ultimately returned to his widow at Globe.[22] The fight probably occurred in late May or early June, 1890, which no doubt would preclude any of the victims' having been the Apache Kid or Massai, both believed to have been active long afterward. In a letter to a Globe attorney, the Colonel described the Indian who carried Reynolds' watch as being "an old man, having gray streaks in his hair." He did not describe the others killed.

Early in 1894, Walapai Ed Clark, who lived in the Galiuro Mountains fifteen miles from Mammoth, saw moccasin tracks near his cabin and all day slunk around from one hiding place to another. About dusk, checking on his horses, he was fired at and took a quick shot at the flash, then fired again and heard a woman scream. Clark hiked to Mammoth. A posse was formed, and when the men returned to the ranch, they found a dead Indian woman, who, shot through both legs, had bled to death. The trail which they followed, now and then spotting a drop of blood, led to the head of Copper Creek, thence to the head of Four Mile Creek. There it faded out,[23] and with it went the last really good clue to the Apache Kid. He was never definitely heard from again in Arizona.

Later that year an Apache woman returned from the Sierra Madre, reporting that she had left the Kid sick unto death of what from her description may have been tuberculosis. Whether her story was true, one can only guess, but the reward for his capture or death was withdrawn by the territorial legislature.[24]

22 Sparks, 44; Hayes, 160–64, 173–75.
23 Bud Ming in correspondence with the author, November 5, 1958.
24 Sparks, 46–49; Hayes, 169–70.

XXIII. Fired

ALTHOUGH HIS RUGGED CONSTITUTION would not let him succumb to a shattering wound that might have done in a lesser man, Al Sieber found that the battle to regain his physical independence was to be one of the toughest of his strife-torn career. For weeks and dreary months he lay on his back on a cot in the stifling room at San Carlos, where summertime temperatures often go above 110°F. and there is no shade. Of course he had visitors, but while they helped pass the time they must also have added to his melancholy as he reviewed the wild old days, when he could foot it sixty miles a day or more and leave even the steel-spring Apaches unable to keep up. Those days were gone forever. He was lucky, and he knew it. For a long time it was touch and go whether he would lose his leg, but somehow Doc Davis saved it for him.

Old cronies kept dropping in on Al to gossip, yarn, and chuckle about such things as General Miles and his gold sword. The city of Tucson wanted to do something to celebrate what everyone knew was the end of the Indian wars in the Southwest, and someone came up with the notion of presenting a gold sword to Miles for his role, however insignificant, in bringing about a lasting peace. No one thought better of the idea than Miles. It was even whispered in some quarters that, public subscriptions having failed to raise enough cash for the trophy, the vain-glorious General reached into his own pocket and "pungled" up the difference,[1] although, naturally, such tales were

---

[1] E. A. Brininstool wrote of this on October 27, 1929, in a letter to Major C. B. Gatewood, the son of Lieutenant Charles B. Gatewood. A copy of the letter is in the Connor Collection.

hard to prove. Still, that was a day to read about, the day that Miles got his sword. Unfortunately, it had to be delayed because the General had the bad luck to break his ankle when his coach upset at Santa Monica, California, shortly before he was to leave for Arizona, but as soon as they could, the General and Mrs. Miles sent word they were ready and, he outfitted with a crutch and a cane, came to Tucson, putting up at the San Xavier, his favorite stopping place.

Many were the military and other dignitaries who were in town for the occasion—and many who should have been there were not. General Eugene Asa Carr, distinguished veteran of a score of Indian battles, was on hand, and so was Major Anson Mills. Captain William Stanton of the Cibecue expedition and Leonard Wood, who had chased Geronimo so stubbornly, if fruitlessly, had come from Los Angeles in Miles's party, as had Major and Mrs. A. S. Kimball, Lieutenant J. A. Dapray, and others, including the wife of Captain G. E. Overton, who had fought in the Loco and early Geronimo campaigns.

The presentation was to be made on November 8, 1887. Long before that day the hotels were overflowing and optimists predicted that a full ten thousand—the largest crowd in the history of the Territory—would be on hand. If anything, they underestimated. Delegates arrived from every section of Arizona and New Mexico. The town was streaming with bunting and fragrant with evergreens brought in from the higher reaches of near-by mountains. "The day," gushed a reporter, "was one of great beauty."

A triumphal arch had been erected at the corner of Pennington and Main streets and was considered "a work of art and a credit to the committee and the designer." The L. Zeckendorf & Co. store was ablaze with flags, bunting, and boughs of pine, for William Zeckendorf was to be grand marshal. "To stand at the intersection of Main and Congress Streets and look up toward the depot one can see only a mass of evergreens and a bright array of flags and bunting," proudly reported the *Arizona Star*. "Truly Tucson does honor to the hero and itself."

Nothing as elaborate as the parade had ever been witnessed in the Southwest—nor would it soon be again. Police Chief William Roche was parade marshal. His was the task of organizing the mammoth demonstration, which included the Fourth Cavalry Band, led by J. K. Kreyer; a unit of the Grand Army of the Republic, Thomas Hughes, commander; the Junior and Senior Pioneers of Arizona, A. B. Samson, marshal; the Pioneer Hose Company of firemen, as well as part of the present Hook and Ladder Company, under D. J. Bolyn; members of the Mexican Society, all in colorful attire and with Carlos I. Velasco, its president, acting as marshal; plus hundreds of citizens on foot, school children, carriages, and four hundred mounted Papagos in war paint and fighting regalia, led by Chief Ascension Ruis. "The Papagos, the hereditary enemy of the Apache, presented a wild, barbaric scene," commented the *Arizona Citizen*. "Mounted on their compact and sinewy ponies, bedaubed with paint in its many barbaric hues, and bedecked with feathers and armed with every species of weapon imaginable, from the primitive war club and bow to the latest and most improved models of warfare, they presented a strange, wild sight common only to Indian countries." They didn't frighten anyone, of course, since the Papagos were never known to have killed a white American, but, what the hell, they added color. No one, apparently, could bring himself to suggesting Apaches for the parade.

You could hardly envision anything grander than this procession, a mile and a half long. Hours before it was to begin, citizens and organized units began to assemble. At 1:00 P.M., Grand Marshal Zeckendorf gave the signal, and it swayed into motion from its point of origin at Main and Congress streets. It moved up Congress to Stone Avenue, thence to Pennington and up Pennington to the San Xavier, where it was reviewed by General Miles from the west porch. He then laboriously clambered into his carriage and was moved into line between the Grand Army of the Republic and the Pioneers, while a cannon east of the railroad tracks boomed a salute appropriate to his rank. The procession reached Levin's Park in time for the two o'clock ceremony. There, Judge W. H. Barnes, one of the more colorful luminaries of the Territory, presented the splendid trophy to the General. The blade and grip of the sword were of Tiffany steel; the other parts and the scabbard were of glittering gold. No man could have received a more handsome—or less deserved—tribute.

The General's remarks were eloquent, even for that day of the flowery phrase, and singular in the meticulous editing by which he managed to convey the impression that in a four-month chase after a couple of dozen ragged renegades he personally had climaxed the Indian wars of the continent. "If there is a difficult problem in military science, it is the subjugation of a mountain race, and few, if any, have been trained to war for a greater number of years than the Apache Indians who, for generations past, had roamed over this Territory like a fearful scourge," said Miles. "To give the largest degree of protection to the scattered settlements of Arizona and New Mexico, and at the same time to so organize and distribute the available military forces as to fight, harrass and pursue a body of ruthless warriors over two thousand miles of the most rugged mountain country upon the face of the globe, and force them to surrender, was, indeed, a difficult task; and there never was more laborious or faithful service rendered by any body of troops than that of the officers and soldiers who in those four weary months of the summer of 1886, by their spirit and fortitude alone, secured permanent peace for your territory." The General then cast all modesty aside:

It was in April, 1886, that I was assigned to the command of this military department—a trust unexpected and unsolicited—yet I fully realized the degree of responsibility and the obstacles that were to be encountered. . . . It is true that savage cunning may devise means to deceive and mislead, but that savages possess one element of strength which the fortitude and skill of our civilized race cannot circumvent and overcome is an unjust reflection upon our intelligence and a libel on truth. . . . I never had but one opinion and one faith, from first to last, regarding the result, which was finally fulfilled in the absolute surrender of Geronimo and Nachez and their followers.

I also became convinced that there could be no permanent peace and security in this part of our country except in one way, namely, the capture and complete disarmament of the hostiles, and the removal far beyond the limits of your Territory of the entire body of those Indians—not only those on the warpath, but also those who were giving the hostiles aid and support, and who were living in a state of semi-hostility on the Indian reservation. . . .[2]

[2] The text of Miles's address, no doubt thoughtfully provided by his aide–press agent, was printed in the *Los Angeles Times* on November 9, 1887.

There are few instances in our military history of an officer so callously taking upon himself credit for great feats to which he contributed so slightly, nor did anyone else so unabashedly assume the responsibility for what can only be considered the treachery which accompanied the removal of not only the hostiles, for which no excuse was needed, but also the loyal Chiricahuas, who alone had made possible the subjugation of their errant brethren.

As Sieber lay on his back in his hot room at San Carlos and read the glowing tributes to Miles, he could scarcely have failed to speculate on the absence from the scene of virtually all those who had made peace possible in Apachería. Of course Crook was not there. Nor was Bourke, nor any officers of Crook's staff, nor any who had served with distinction under him, except Carr. None of the valiant old guides who had done so much to make possible the military victories of the bloody sixties and seventies was on hand, or if some of them were, they occupied no prominent place. No newspaper account mentions Dan O'Leary, Ed Peck, Willard Rice, Archie McIntosh, Sam Bowman, Mickey Free, Tom Jeffords, or any of the others. Nor was Gatewood, the real hero of the Geronimo surrender, on hand. Miles had taken care of that. Gatewood now was on his staff, and Miles had seen to it that he was assigned to Los Angeles headquarters duty during the General's absence, so that no ray of glory might be deflected from the General himself. Sieber must have wondered at that.

Lieutenant Gatewood seemed destined for the hardest duty, the most complete devotion to army and country—and the least reward for his heroism. It is true that in 1891 *General Order No. 39* of the department belatedly paid him tribute for "bravery in boldly and alone riding into Geronimo's camp of hostile Apache Indians in Arizona [*sic*] and demanding their surrender," but he received none of the four Medals of Honor bestowed for lesser feats during the long campaign. Wood got one for hiking one hundred miles in two days,[3]

[3] *American Decorations: A List of Awards of the Congressional Medal of Honor, the Distinguished-Service Cross and the Distinguished-Service Medal, Awarded Under Authority of the Congress of the United States: 1862–1926.* This government publication says Wood's medal was awarded because he "voluntarily carried dispatches through a region infested with hostile Indians, making a journey of 70 miles in one night and walking 30 miles the next day. Also for several weeks, while in close pursuit of Geroni-

but what officer chasing Geronimo deep into Mexico had not done that much?

After Geronimo's surrender, Gatewood applied for a staff appointment, but this was denied. He was detailed instead as an aide to Miles, possibly as a reward, but more likely to advise the General in the event of recurring Apache difficulties. After four years he rejoined his regiment at Fort Wingate, New Mexico.[4] Gatewood went with his outfit to the Dakotas to take part in the Sioux War of 1890–91; his health, never robust, broke down, and he was practically an invalid for a year.

The Lieutenant then rejoined his regiment at Fort McKinney, Wyoming, where his squadron became involved in the so-called "Rustlers' War." Under Colonel J. J. Van Horn, three troops were hurriedly dispatched to the scene of a fight, from which they rescued a party and escorted it back to the fort, confining its members as prisoners under guard. Some of the opposing faction indignantly sought to burn the prisoners out, and soon the sweeping flames threatened the entire post. Officers decided to blow up a building or two to save the remainder. Gatewood volunteered for this dangerous task and dashed into a flaming structure to place gunpowder in position, but glowing rafters fell on him, setting off the explosive prematurely and blowing the intrepid Lieutenant against the side of the building. He barely escaped with his life, but was so badly maimed that he was forced to retire permanently from active duty.[5]

---

mo's band and constantly expecting an encounter, [he] commanded a detachment of Infantry, which was then without an officer, and to the command of which he was assigned upon his own request."

[4] C. D. Rhodes, later a major general, said that Gatewood served with him at Fort Wingate in 1889. "We could rarely get him to talk about Geronimo, and the part he played—he was so diffident and modest, as you know. But we were all very sure that it was Gatewood who . . . secured Geronimo's surrender. And we of the old Sixth Cavalry, were always indignant that Lawton, fine soldier though he may have been, reaped all the reward from Miles, and Gatewood got little or nothing out of it. . . . It was not a generous or magnanimous attitude on Miles' part." C. D. Rhodes to John P. Clum, January 26, 1930, Connor Collection.

[5] William Harding Carter, *From Yorktown to Santiago with the Sixth Cavalry*, 268–69; A. S. Mercer, *The Banditti of the Plains; or, the Cattlemen's Invasion of Wyoming in 1892*, 68–82.

Crippled, his health gone, Gatewood died in May, 1896. "His reward, for services that have often been described as unusual, was like that of many another soldier who has given his all that his country might grow and prosper; for himself a free plot of ground in Arlington Cemetery, and to his widow a tardy seventeen dollars a month."[6] For Gatewood, no speeches, no honors, no medals; just oblivion. Thus America disposed of one of her bravest and most devoted sons.

Wood deserved recognition for his heroic and selfless conduct in that Indian affair, but his role was insignificant compared with that of Gatewood, Crawford, Maus, or any of a dozen others, and one cannot help but wonder whether his medal came for what he did—or for whom he knew.

Crook was generous in his praise of Gatewood. In a "To Whom It May Concern" letter dated October 14, 1889, he wrote: "1st Lieutenant C. B. Gatewood, 6th Cavalry, served with me for several years in Arizona—in command of Apache Scouts. In the performance of this service, often one of great danger, especially in campaigns against hostile Indians, he displayed personal intrepidity, efficiency, intelligence and untiring energy—which merited and received the encomium of his superiors and reflected great credit upon himself."[7] But the rugged old General never commented publicly, as far as I know, upon the golden sword presented to Miles. Feelings between the two were strained, to put it mildly.[8] Added to Crook's natural resentment at being replaced on the point of winding up satisfactorily his eight years of Apache Indian service, there was his suspicion that Miles was deliberately attempting to color the record in order to tarnish

[6] Charles B. Gatewood, "The Surrender of Geronimo," *Proceedings of the Annual Meeting and Dinner of the Order of Indian Wars of the United States*, 6. The introduction to the article was written by Gatewood's son, Major C. B. Gatewood.

[7] The letter is in the Hayes Collection.

[8] Britton Davis, in a letter to E. A. Brininstool dated November 5, 1929, says: "You may not know that General Crook preferred charges against Miles and I was to have been a witness before a court martial. But the charges were suppressed through Miles's political influence and the influence of [General Philip H.] Sheridan, who for some inexplicable reason was 'sold on' Miles and hated Crook." Connor Collection. I have seen no other reference to this detail, but have no reason to doubt its accuracy.

his, Crook's, distinguished service and add to his own mediocre accomplishments.[9]

Nor did Al Sieber ever have anything that was quoted in print to say about the glittering Tucson tribute to the end of the Indian wars. What he did say must have been pungent, but, unfortunately, it was not made permanent. He was able to get around a little by this time, though laboriously, with crutches. There was no place he wanted to go but Ezra Kingsbury's store, where he could sit on a wooden chair and prop his ailing leg on a nail keg while he drank whiskey and played poker with the boys.

The long period of enforced idleness had given Al time, perhaps the first occasion in years, for reflection. Curiously, he found his thoughts wandering back to Minnesota and the family he had left there almost a quarter-century earlier. Although he apparently had heard from his mother or John or some other member of the family at long intervals and thus, in a way, had kept in touch, even that sporadic correspondence had fallen off. Distances were too great, too much had happened in the long years since the youngster, fresh out of the Civil War, had taken his bundle and set out toward the vast and mysterious West, too many adventures had intervened for him to have maintained the close ties he would have enjoyed.

Early in October of 1888, however, he received a letter from John E. Wall, the son of his sister Magdalena and John Wall,[10] who were

[9] In a long exchange of letters which evolved into outright demands before satisfaction was given, Crook insisted that Miles return to him his personal records, which, he said, he had left with Miles at the latter's request to enable him to familiarize himself with the background and conditions in his new command but which Miles refused to return, presumably while copies were being made. Curiously, these copies, or extracts, drawn out of context and otherwise perverted, turned up from time to time in the public press, and Crook suspected Miles of being responsible for this rather underhanded method of building one's reputation at the expense of one's predecessor. Crook Papers, Hayes Collection.

[10] John Wall and Magdalena were married at Lancaster, Pennsylvania. The Walls had come there from Frankfurt, Germany, where John's father had been burgomaster. John was a Civil War veteran, having served with the Seventy-seventh Pennsylvania Infantry, organized at Pittsburgh on October 15, 1861, and was mustered out December 6, 1865, after service with the Army of Ohio, in the Cumberlands, and in Texas. Among their children were John E. Wall, apparently born just before the Civil War; Lilly; and another daughter, Louise, born in 1870, who married a man named Taylor.

living at Minneapolis and whom Al must have known as a youngster before he went west in 1866. In his confident hand but shaky spelling, he answered the letter on October 7, writing from San Carlos:

> You take my by serprice. I sapose you are litlse Johnny Wall I remember of when I left hom you were quite small. I am clade to hear from you and your mouther. I thought you had left Minneapolis, at lest I hirt so, but by your letter I se that Minneapolis is your home again. Johny I cant tell you when I will be able to cum home. I have not quite god over my shatt yet. My left leg is not held up yet. So I cant traval so far but as soon as my leg hels up I will cum home. But I dond think it will be this winter for I could not stant the cold wether in Minnesota in the winter time. So Il hafto [wait] till spring. A nather thing I have a grade dele of work to do here this fall that I cant git at for a Month or two.
>
> Give my kindest regards to all my folks,
> I am your truly,
> Albert Sieber.

The notion was planted, although that "grade dele of work" remained to be done first.

Early in February, 1889, a freighter, Freeman T. Cosper, was shot and killed four miles west of Gilson's Wells because a couple of Indians wanted his fancily decorated rifle. An army detachment futilely took up the trail, and it was several weeks before the guilty parties were identified. By April they had left their own band and were living with one under Chil-chu-a-na, who resented them as troublemakers and willingly co-operated toward a white plan for their capture. Sieber, with a scout detachment, was assigned the task of arresting them, and surprised them in the camp. A brief melee resulted, with one of the suspected murderers being killed and the other captured, although not before Chil-chu-a-na was knifed in the back. Fortunately, his wound was not serious.[11]

The winter storms had now passed, and a refreshing green swept briefly over the Arizona deserts. Things were quiet at last, and Al

---

Of their four children, Mrs. Lillian Taylor Bennett, now of Minneapolis, was the eldest, and to her I am indebted for the letters Al Sieber wrote late in life, which she has kindly permitted to be deposited with the APHS collections.

[11] *Arizona Silver Belt*, April 13, 1889; Hayes, 27–31.

journeyed down to the Southern Pacific station and entrained for Minneapolis. Apparently, it was his first trip back to Minnesota since he left there in 1866,[12] and he may have financed it with the sale of his one-fifth interst in the Delshay mine (which he had obtained from Frank Story) to Dan Williamson.

Al probably went to Minneapolis by way of some hot springs near Camp Thomas, where he remained several weeks, hoping that the medicinal waters would be beneficial to his injured leg.[13] While passing through Chicago, Sieber took the opportunity to call on General Crook, receiving as a memento of his visit an autographed photo of the General. It was signed, "As ever, your friend."[14] And at Minneapolis he met his niece, Louise Wall Taylor, with whom he corresponded from time to time during the balance of his life.

Late in the summer, whether because of "unrest" on San Carlos Reservation, or at the insistence of whites at Globe that he sign complaints for the second trial of the Apache Kid and others, or for some other reason, Sieber hurriedly broke off his visit to Minneapolis and returned to Arizona. On September 24 he was at Tucson to be a witness before a federal grand jury. A reporter from the *Arizona Citizen* used the occasion to interview him on rumors of ominous developments at the reservation and secured a disquieting report. This, of course, was just a month before the trial and three weeks before complaints would be issued against the Kid and his companions.

In view of charges which suggest that Sieber laid full blame for the San Carlos unrest on the Kid—and for that reason signed the complaints against him and his band—it is noteworthy that he did not mention the Kid as the cause of the San Carlos trouble in this interview.[15] "The Indians," he told the reporter, "are just now showing

[12] In a letter to Frank C. Lockwood dated September 3, 1933, Louise Taylor wrote that "I think it was in 1885" that Sieber visited Minneapolis, but this is apparently in error. Internal evidence in his own correspondence and elsewhere clearly shows this visit to have been in the spring or summer of 1889. Mrs. Taylor adds that Al's visit was "abruptly terminated" upon his receiving word of trouble at San Carlos Reservation.

[13] *Arizona Citizen*, September 25, 1889.

[14] This photograph was still in Sieber's possession when he died. The autograph on the back of the picture bears the date May 7, 1888, but this must be a misprint for 1889.

[15] Hayes says the complaints against the Kid were issued October 15, 1889, but the

unmistakable signs of uneasiness and restlessness, which is considered a very bad sign. . . . They are a dissatisfied people, and will always be as long as the present conditions surround them." Asked to specify, Sieber replied:

> First, and worst of all, is the Negro soldiers that are stationed at the post. They are a disturbing element, and beyond control, or rather are not controlled. Their presence is a menace to the peace of the reservation, and a disgrace to the Government that keeps them there. They put in their time hanging around the Indian squaws and bucks. They will procure any thing that an Indian wants and has the money to pay for, whiskey, ammunition, and other things which the reservation rules forbid them having. . . .
>
> Another element that is bad on the reservation is a number of full blooded Mexicans are allowed to live and mix with the Indians. They are generally renegades from Sonora, and . . . they are used by the Indians in procuring arms, whiskey, and ammunition. These Mexicans are treated about the same as the Indians, some of them drawing ration tickets from the Government. This I know to be a fact, as I have had them present their tickets to me for meat, which is distributed under my supervision.[16]

Naturally, this interview and these statements did not sit well with Captain John L. Bullis, the agent.[17]

Al wrote Louise Taylor on October 1 that he had "just come Home from Tucson, where I had to go on corte bisness in fact I will Be Besy all Next Month as well as this with Indian Murter cases." He was sorry to hear that Magdalena had not been feeling well and had gone to "the Springs" (probably Hot Springs, Arkansas) and that she hadn't stayed there longer, but realized "She Knowes Best what is good for hir." He wondered what the effect of an Arizona winter would be on her—he thought beneficial—and suggested that Louise's brother-in-law, Jacob C. Klein, who ran a barbershop in the Nicollet

Citizen story, which had appeared on September 25, said that by this date the Indians were already being held at San Carlos for their second trial.

[16] Arizona Citizen, September 25, 1889.

[17] Bullis assumed his duties as agent on June 1, 1888, succeeding Captain Pierce, and served until November 24, 1891, when he was succeeded by Lewis Johnson, another army officer. Jane F. Smith, archivist in charge, Interior Branch, National Archives, in correspondence with the author.

Hotel at Minneapolis, buy one at Phoenix so that Magdalena could move to Arizona's warm, dry climate. He pointed out that "this country Beets Minnesota to My Notion althow Phoenix is Very warm for about 4 month in the year But Folks git yoused to it" and added that one hundred dollars would pay all of Klein's expenses out to Arizona to look around and back to Minnesota again. But Jake evidently never made the trip, although he later renewed his interest in it.

On November 4, before he yet had heard of the Apache Kid's escape, Sieber wrote Louise: "I have just Returned from Globe where I have Bin at corte. . . . For the Last two Month I have Bin off Most all the time and it will Be about the Same for the Next two Month to come." He was sorry to hear that Klein had decided not to move to Phoenix, but noted that times were hard in the barber business anyway, since "Shaveing is Down to 15 Snts. in place of .25." He then answered a question Louise had posed:

> You ask me about work in this country for you I dond think thad you wood Like this country for work as it is very harde for young Ladis to git work out here there are No large Cityes yet in this country and Small Towns are pure places for Girls to git work if I was Living in Some Town I might help you to a good job But as I am here among the Indians it wood Be a harde Matter for Me to Loock you up a good Job of work. if I could Onley Sell one of my Mines I could help your Mother and wood Do So Verey quick. But Selling Mines is Slow work just now No Matter how good the Mine May Be. thinks have takin a change here and I dond Like the way thinks Loock amoung the Indians Just at presand we are Likely to have truble with them this winter if So I will Be out Most all the time So you Must Nott Loock for to Maney Letters from Me.

That same day, Sieber must have heard of the Apache Kid's escape.

There was grave danger of a major breakout, or would have been had the Kid been interested in creating trouble. He sought rather to minimize his offense, however, and the flurry of excitement soon passed, for all but the scouts and army patrols.

Al wrote Louise on December 8, sending her one hundred dollars, half for herself and the other half for Lena for Christmas, explaining that he was quite busy:

I am cept Verey harte at work Just at present and when you was Etting your turkey I was Ritting for all thad was out after some Indians. I wond have Mutch Rest this winter till I catch the 8 Indian Murdters thad Kild Sheriff Raynolts and Garde about a Month ago. But for them I wood have a good time this winter.

In addition, things at San Carlos had taken a turn for the worse.

Most ominous for the old scout's future was the growing tension between himself and Captain Bullis. Instead of slacking off, this feeling intensified, week by week and as the months and seasons passed. Its precise origin is uncertain. Both Sieber and Bullis were strong-willed men, both highly recommended by their partisans. Perhaps Sieber's outspoken criticism of the military in his interview with the reporter from the *Citizen* had something to do with it, but more likely it was but a symptom. Bud Ming, who as a boy knew both Sieber and Bullis and liked them, said "they were both *some men* around San Carlos in the 1880s."[18] Wrote Ming:

> The last time I saw Captain Bullis was October, 1889. I was with my father and other ranchers delivering a bunch of steers to butcher for the Indians. We corraled the steers at sundown in the big adobe corrals, camped there for the night. Next morning at daybreak Bullis was there. They went to weighing out the steers on the Government scales. . . . Bullis was turning gray at this time, rather short, not tall, his face inclined to be full, not sharp, nice features, pleasant and friendly, well liked by all— Indians, whites, civilians, a friend of the Ranchers adjoining the reservation. He had all kinds and classes of people to deal with. San Carlos was on the main and only wagon road from south to north in the eastern part of the Territory. Military personnel from Fort Huachuca, Fort Bowie, Fort Grant, Fort Thomas came that route moving to other posts to the north. San Carlos was the junction of the wagon road to Fort Apache on White River, going east and north to Utah and Colorado. Bullis was prominent and known by all. He operated mining claims at Tully Springs, 20 miles south from San Carlos and 3 miles from the old Aravaipa Post Office. He did not put in any time there, but kept men at work.

This last reference may be significant.

Dan Williamson, who knew Sieber well enough to have obtained

[18] Correspondence with the author, September 16, 1958.

the scout's version at first hand, and Frank C. Lockwood, who followed Williamson in this account, both blame the falling out between Bullis and Sieber to the former's highhanded treatment of the Indians. "Sieber worried a lot over what he considered the unjust way in which the Apaches were being treated," wrote Williamson, "and he hated to order his scouts to round up Indians on charges he thought were trumped up, and a coolness sprung up between him and Bullis and finally an open break, in which Sieber told the captain just what he thought of him. The result was that Sieber, after having given twenty years of his life, and in which service he had been crippled for life, was compelled to leave the reservation with only a few hours' notice."[19] Lockwood added that "Captain Bullis entered upon an ambitious scheme of road building. All work was done, without compensation, by Indian prisoners. A system of espionage and tattling was encouraged; so, in case there were no prisoners, various Indians were arrested on the unsupported word of fellow Apaches and sentenced without the formality of a trial and without permitting the prisoner to know who his accusers were. This system kept the guardhouse full and the road gangs working. . . . All this was very distasteful to Sieber."[20] In an earlier account, Williamson had charged that "Captain Bullis was understood to be a millionaire due to the thousands of acres of excellent valley land owned in Texas, and his method of procuring this land was said to be by his having been in command of a troop of semi-civilized Seminole Indian Scouts on the Texas frontier, with whose aid he would drive out the Mexican settlers, and buy up the land from the state at a few cents per acre."[21] This charge, or a version of it, also appears in official documents cited below, but, to my knowledge, it was never proved—or disproved.

In an article published shortly after Sieber was fired, the *Tombstone Prospector*, attempting to be objective, said that "Captain Bullis is a man of means and is considered to be worth a half million dollars made by fortunate investments in Texas lands." The article, nearly contemporary, went on to say that "Bullis had on more than

19 Williamson, "Sieber," 73.
20 Lockwood, "Sieber," 31. Lockwood enlarges slightly on Williamson's version.
21 *Arizona Silver Belt*, September 18, 1928.

one occasion sat down on Sieber, and the animosity of the latter was a natural result," but it did not specify the officer's charges against the scout.[22] Their dispute may well have originated because of the abuse of Indians, as alleged by Williamson. However, the actual firing came about as the climax to a chain of quite different events, perhaps engineered by Bullis, or at least eagerly taken advantage of by that officer.[23]

On November 8, 1890, Bullis wired the Indian Commissioner that he had closed the store of Ezra W. Kingsbury,[24] a sixty-year-old Civil War veteran and Indian trader, and in an explanatory letter said it was done because the trader had received a shipment of liquor and had frustrated Bullis' efforts to apprehend the soldier to whom it was consigned.[25] This launched a chain of events that led to two formal investigations at San Carlos, the leveling of vicious charges, the revelation of despicable crimes, and the firing of Sieber, who, from the record, was a fairly innocent bystander but was made the scapegoat.

In his letter, Bullis said that on November 6 a box was received by Kingsbury in his capacity as agent for the stage company. The box, Bullis knew, contained liquor and had been shipped by a saloon-keeper in notorious Maxey to a Private M. Bird, A Troop, Tenth Cavalry. Bullis explained that he had gone to Kingsbury, directed him to hold the box until Bird called for it, then told him to arrest Bird with the box in his possession. A scout was stationed in or near the store to make the actual arrest.[26] Someone had warned Bird, however, Bullis suspected, and although Bird called at the store, he didn't pick up the package. Instead, he had another soldier stop by and

[22] Reprinted September 19, 1891, in the *Florence-Tucson Enterprise.*

[23] The account which follows is taken from Indian Service, Documents Received, National Archives (cited hereafter as IS, followed by the serial number and year).

[24] There was a Captain E. W. Kingsbury, who quite probably was the same Ezra W. Kingsbury who was said to have been instrumental in spreading the exaggerated story of Wild Bill Hickok's bloody battle with the so-called "McCanles Gang" at the Rock Creek stage station in Nebraska in 1861. By 1881, Kingsbury was reported to be chief storekeeper for the western district of Missouri. Richard O'Connor, *Wild Bill Hickok: A Biography of James Butler Hickok, the West's Greatest Gunfighter,* 27–29.

[25] IS 34507–1890, 35512–1890.

[26] This scout was not Sieber, although he is identified as Al in the Tombstone *Prospector* story cited earlier.

have the box shipped on to a Smith Johnson at Globe, beyond reach of the military.

The gist of the whole thing is this that Mr. Kingsbury, and his clerk, Mr. [Charles W.] Pfeiffer, instead of assisting me in my efforts to bring the offence home to the guilty party, directly opposed me, and disobeyed my instructions, by shipping the liquor.

It is for this reason that I closed the store.

Bullis's case was weakened by the fact that Kingsbury hadn't permitted the package to be forwarded. The old man was away from San Carlos at the time, and his assistant made the mistake. Bullis, however, used Kingsbury's absence to add another charge: that the trader was away from his place of business more than Indian Bureau regulations permitted.

It now was Kingsbury's turn. He frantically wired the Commissioner that his store had been "arbitrarily closed" and reported that he was writing Washington "the absolute facts." He formally demanded that Bullis explain to him why he had closed "my store and post office," to which the officer replied curtly that Kingsbury had "no right to demand my reasons" and, anyway, the post office was not closed.[27]

In his letter, Kingsbury told the Commissioner that "I, prior to leaving San Carlos . . . notified Mr. A. Sieber, Chief of Scouts, of the presence of the package and a scout was placed on duty to view the disposition of the package referred to. Both the Scout and Mr. Sieber saw the package loaded on the mail coach and Mr. Sieber declined to seize it stating that he had no orders to do so from Capt. Bullis."[28] For good measure, Kingsbury added his suspicion that Bullis "has always been inimicable to me" and promised that in the near future he would "lay before the Department a statement which I think will satisfy it that the administration of Indian affairs here, is conducted in an improper manner and an investigation will develop a laxity of morality such as is seldom met with." By thus bringing Sieber into it and no doubt correctly describing him as reluctant to interfere with

27 IS 35891–1890.
28 IS 35832–1890.

a shipment of whiskey safely outside the reservation, Kingsbury added fuel to the fire of Bullis' apparent dislike for the veteran scout and placed Sieber squarely in the middle. Al seems to have had no other connection with the affair, although he was no doubt one of Kingsbury's poker-playing cronies—another reason why the fiery-tempered Bullis would dislike him.

Through the flurry of telegrams, letters, and affidavits which followed comes the impression of Kingsbury as a cantankerous old man, leaping to often erroneous conclusions, and of a vindictive Bullis, unrelenting and unwilling to compromise a legalistic feud which he had evidently begun on insufficient grounds. The storekeeper now tried a demand to Captain Lewis Johnson, Twenty-fourth Infantry, that the sentinel be withdrawn and his store reopened. Johnson passed the buck to Bullis, who insisted that the situation remain static pending instructions from the Indian Bureau.[29]

An investigation seemingly indicated, George W. Parker, special Indian agent, was directed by the Commissioner to visit San Carlos and report back. On December 6, 1890, he sent in his findings, stating that he had interviewed most of the principals, as well as others, and had found the facts to be approximately as previous communications described them. "I do not believe," he wrote, "that the clerk reshipped the box for the purpose of serving the parties interested in the transaction, but done it heedlessly & without thought of what the consequences would be, & was severely reprimanded by Mr. Kingsbury on his return & had he been at home it would not have occurred." Parker added that no one suspected Mr. Kingsbury of ever introducing liquor onto the reservation. No one but Bullis, but Parker didn't realize that.

Parker understood and appreciated Bullis' diligent efforts to do "all in his power to suppress the introduction of an article, that causes so much trouble" and his irritation at being "foiled . . . by the stupidity of the clerk and the cupidity of the Chief of Scouts, Seaver, who was discharged,"[30] but didn't think the case sufficiently strong to warrant

29 IS 36541–1890.

30 In all of the correspondence and other documents relating to the affair, this is the only reference that Sieber planned to gain anything by the transaction. In view of the lack of supporting evidence—plus its being illogical on the surface—this charge must be disallowed.

putting Kingsbury out of business. Parker mentioned that Bullis had told him of a $2.50 payment to Kingsbury on one occasion by a butcher on the reservation, Charles A. Gropp, but explained that this was included in a large account settled in a single payment and not necessarily damning.[31]

Upon receipt of Parker's report, the Commissioner wired Bullis to let Kingsbury reopen his store. The officer exploded. In a lengthy letter dated December 31, he ripped into Parker's report, alleging that it "excuses more than the actual state of the case warrants." Bullis charged that politics had also entered the case, Kingsbury being a Republican, and asserted that this should not be a factor.[32] He said of the trader: "In reference to his general character as it has become known to me here I would say that he is an industrious card player." Among Kingsbury's friends, Bullis charged, "and who was also his agent in the delivery, at the post, of hay and wood, *by Indians*, under his contract for same, I have succeeded in ridding the reservation of. This man, whose name is Al Sieber, was an employe in the Quartermaster's Department, U.S.A., here and was in immediate charge, under the direction of an officer, of the Indian Scouts. He was a drunkard, vulgar, profane and brutal in his treatment of the Indians, and from his position had ample opportunity to exercise his evil propensities. As soon as I requested his discharge he was paid off, and ordered to leave the reservation within three days, by the commanding officer here, Col. Johnson, whose action was promptly ratified by the Department Commander, Gen. McCook; and although efforts were made from certain quarters to whitewash this moral sepulchre, it did not avail."[33] Bullis further charged that Kingsbury was a "hail

31 IS 38747–1890.

32 The Tombstone *Prospector* said that "Kingsbury had a pull with McKinley and it would be a breach of political etiquette to fire him. His devotion to the interests of the party was also too great to be overlooked. These facts were shown to Captain Bullis and a compromise made whereby Sieber went but Kingsbury was allowed to ·stay." This statement is only a guess at the situation, but a close one.

33 Documents in support of these charges were forwarded to the Adjutant General in Washington on November 25, 1891, by Brigadier General Alexander McDowell McCook, then in command of the Department of Arizona, who sent them along in protest to an AGO letter authorizing the re-employment of Sieber. His five enclosures included: two statements by Corporal Oliver Eaton to the effect that Sieber "cursed the Indians on

bove) Al Sieber (standing in doorway) and his mining partner Con Crowley at a
untain cabin in the Sierra Anchas about 1900.

low) This picture of Al Sieber (center), Colonel Jesse W. Ellison (left), and cow-
 Tink Owens was probably made in the Sierra Anchas just after the turn
he century.

Ed Peck, one of Al Sieber's best friends and a superb scout himself, is shown here in his wedding clothes.

This photograph of Al Sieber is the las known to have been taken of the scout and was probably made in late 1906, only a few months before his tragic death.

fellow well met with all the rum sellers that infest this reservation, and who have been . . . my bitter enemies ever since I took charge of the Agency. . . . Anonymous threats against my life are not infrequent occurrences . . . [but] I pay little attention to such cowardly attempts at intimidation."[34]

Ezra learned that same day that Bullis had sent in his tirade. He hastily readied his own charges, even more grave, against the officer, advising the Commissioner by telegram that they were on the way lest that official be swayed by Bullis' document. Kingsbury's charges had been prepared a month earlier, in mid-December, and they were all-encompassing. "It is the general impression that Capt Bullis cohabits with his housekeeper," Kingsbury began, mildly, adding that the Indians, other officers, and even the white woman's daughter thought so. He then heaped charge upon charge for two closely typed pages. Kingsbury charged that Bullis winked at immorality and drunkenness on the part of Jack Benton, who was supposed to teach

occasion," that he "got . . . drunk," and that he struck "squaws with his cane" on issue days; a charge from Bullis, unsupported, against Sieber's "general uncouthness, insolent bearing, vulgarity, profanity and coarseness, and tyrannical behavior toward the Indians"; a statement from H. John Windmiller, who ran a store at San Carlos in tight competition with Kingsbury, that "Al Sieber made me a proposition to buy barley from him at the rate of one dollar per sack, said barley belonging to the United States . . . the proceeds of such a sale should go towards liquidation of the rent for two rooms, which said Al Sieber then occupied"; and a statement by William F. Muller, a Windmiller employee, to the effect that Al Sieber sold government barley, saying as he did so, "I'll make the sons of bitches pay my house rent anyhow." Record Group 94, National Archives. These statements do not amount to serious charges in substance and were prejudiced in particular, as is self-evident. In all of his long career, both in handling Apaches and at other pursuits, there are on record no other charges against Sieber comparable to those lodged by Bullis; there are, however, innumerable evaluations of Al's character which are directly at variance with them. That Sieber was a drinking man there is no doubt; that he was a drunkard was never before nor afterward alleged. All of his associates, those now living and others, insist that he was rarely profane and never vulgar, as that word is commonly used. Sieber was firm, perhaps to the point of brutality at times, with the Indians, but he could not have been cruel or vindictive toward them and lived as long as he did in intimate association with them. Sometimes he was out for weeks at a time with scores of vicious fighting men, the Apache scouts, and yet he came through twenty years of this hazardous sort of life without important incident —scarcely the record of a "moral sepulchre," as charged by Bullis. This statement, more than anything else on the record, attests to the basic lack of validity of Bullis' charges.

[34] IS 1507–1891. This blast is seven handwritten pages long.

the Indians farming, and named him Chief of Scouts to succeed Sieber; that an Indian named Nelley, jailed for drunkenness, claimed he got the whiskey from Bullis' house; that Bullis interfered with a federal grand jury to thwart the indictment of one Frederick Dalton, who was charged with thefts from the agency flour mill; that Bullis refused to prosecute Dalton for molesting the daughter of his house-keeper until Dr. E. W. Mann, acting post surgeon, swore out a war-rant, causing Dalton's arrest; that Bullis abused the Indians by arresting them for trivial offenses in order to get laborers for "his wild schemes"; and that under Bullis' management, affairs on the reserva-tion were going to pot, with not as much grain being raised as there had been seven years earlier and the irrigation works largely in dis-repair. These and a number of other charges were specified in Kings-bury's statement.

"Bullis's lack of experience in Indian affairs is thoroughly known here," the old trader continued. "For a number of years he com-manded a few scouts, Negroes; they were called Indian Seminole Negro scouts. He captured a few ponies . . . and killed a few, very few, Indians in Texas . . . he spent a good deal of his time in locating lands for his own use and benefit, while presumably scouting, and as a matter of fact he located some 90 thousand acres of land together with mining property, during the time he was supposed to be hunting Indians. One of the mining properties he recently sold for $25,000.00, cash." Kingsbury made further charges that Bullis knew of whiskey and beer being delivered onto the reservation—but not through his store—and concluded: "I can and do charge Capt Bullis with permit-ting immorality and crime among his employees and himself with such immorality as presents a bad example to Indians and employees."[35]

Clearly, all of these charges and countercharges were enough to worry Washington officials, and Commissioner T. J. Morgan urged the Secretary of the Interior to investigate them, along with other matters. Consequently, late in the spring of 1891, Indian Inspector Robert S. Gardener conducted such a study and exonerated Bullis. But he did so on some curious testimony, and he apparently did not

[35] IS 2617–1891.

investigate many of Kingsbury's charges at all, or if he did, he failed to include them in his report, which was dated June 15.[36]

Bullis' general good character was attested to by Carl Hyldahl, whom he had appointed clerk at the agency about a year before Kingsbury's store was closed; by Captain Johnson, a brother officer of Bullis in the Twenty-fourth Infantry who had been acquainted with him "about 25 years"; and First Lieutenant Arthur C. Ducat, Jr., also of the Twenty-fourth, who testified he had known Captain Bullis about four years, in Indian Territory and in Arizona, had been a guest in his home, and had known his housekeeper, Mrs. M. Emerson, both at Fort Sill and at San Carlos. None of these men said he noted any undue familiarity between Bullis and Mrs. Emerson, but then none could have been called an impartial witness, either. Hyldahl, although no longer in the Indian Service, owed his employment to the Captain. Johnson and Bullis were cronies of a quarter-century's standing, and Ducat would scarcely have testified against a senior officer under any circumstances, for reasons any army veteran can understand.

Charles A. Fisk, a Globe banker and member of the grand jury,[37] denied that Bullis had sought to avert an indictment of Fred Dalton on theft charges but admitted that as soon as the jury had decided not to act he had hastened to Bullis with the news. He explained his singular action: "My reason for this was that Captain Bullis, was, the agent at San Carlos, and a witness in the case, and he being sick with La Grippe, was anxious to return to the Agency, as soon as the case was disposed of."

The more serious charge against Dalton, that involving Mrs. Emerson's six-year-old daughter, Olivett, was dismissed after he had been in the Globe jail for a year, Gardener found, because "of no prosecut-

[36] IS 22948–1891.

[37] Seven years earlier, Fisk had been charged by San Carlos Agent P. P. Wilcox with being a member of "a corrupt cabal" having ulterior motives in its interest in things on the reservation. Fisk was alleged to have been "the financial manager of the syndicate that pretended to purchase the coal lands on the reservation for the payment of forty dollars per head to fourteen ignorant and deceived Indian chiefs." *Arizona Star*, March 13, 1883. At that time, Wilcox was strongly supported by Crook in a letter to Secretary of the Interior H. M. Teller.

ing witnesses appearing against him." Dr. S. G. Pangborn, one such witness, had died in December, 1890; Dr. Mann was absent from Arizona; Mrs. C. W. Feiss was out of the Territory; and Mrs. Emerson had taken her daughter to parts unknown on the evening of April 7, 1891. Gardener said: "I am of the opinion that Captain Bullis did not shield or attempt to shield Frederick Dalton from being prosecuted." But someone had stalled the case for an unprecedented period, or at least until all prosecution witnesses had eliminated themselves.

Hyldahl was not asked for his evaluation of Sieber, but other witnesses were. Captain Johnson, who had known him only a little over a year (Johnson arrived at San Carlos only in May, 1889), agreed with Bullis' description of him. He testified that Sieber "was discharged by my order, as Post Commander, the immediate cause being the request of the Acting Indian Agent Captain Bullis, on account of suspected implication of the introduction of whiskey upon this reservation."

"What were the habits of Al Sieber for sobriety?" asked the investigator.

"They were bad," replied Captain Johnson, "very irregular. I have repeatedly seen him drunk, at this post, and his irregular habits in part caused me to order his discharge. He was an exceedingly rough man, frequently brutal to the Indians and others, and upon the whole was very objectionable man to live among Indians, or to be upon an Indian reservation."

Charles Fisk, however, who had known Sieber for "10 or 11 years," asked whether he knew Sieber's "general character for truth and veracity," tersely replied that he had "never heard it questioned."

Johnson conceded that he had hired Benton "at the request of no one," explaining, "I simply had the Quartermaster hire him as he was available and suitable for the place on account of his knowledge of the country, the Indians, and the Apache language." Asked whether Benton was a "drinking man," Johnson admitted that "I have heard he has been, but I never saw him drink or drunk," adding that he could only remain in government employ if temperate.

It may be that Gardener's opinion was based on other testimony which he did not include in his report, but the chances are it was not. The testimony he includes is not persuasive. On the basis of it, one must conclude that the grave charges leveled by Kingsbury were, for the most part, unanswered and that only in minor details could Bullis consider himself cleared of suspicion.

There was no dress parade when the aged veteran of unrivaled service in the Apache wars saddled up. No troops were aligned for him to inspect. There was no ceremony, no farewell. Al climbed stiffly aboard his big, strong saddle horse, whistled an authoritative "Let's go!" to his other horses and mules, and eased out of San Carlos and up the long grade on the road to Globe, thirty-five miles away. It is doubtful that he looked back.

Though fired, Sieber was not without friends. The *Prescott Morning Courier* noted at the time that "a southern Arizona paper says that Al Sieber has left San Carlos. Hope not. Al knows more about managing Indians than a hundred agents and the Government had best keep him."[38] It spoke for the Territory. Probably, it spoke for Al, for Sieber is not known ever to have alluded in detail to the incident. In a letter to Louise Taylor dated February 2, 1891, he wrote that "I have nothing more to do with the Indians and am clade of it," and that was all he had to say.

[38] December 5, 1890.

373

XXIV. Autumn

AL SIEBER was faced with a problem. He could look around, loaf a bit, and become settled in his town surroundings, or he could pick up his shovel and set to work on one or another of his mining claims. He chose to look, first.

He wrote Louise on February 2, 1891, from Alexander Graydon's smithy, carriage shop, and livery stable that he thought he might take over the layout in the spring, but he didn't sound too convinced. His guess about its availability, however, was more accurate than he could know: Alex died the twenty-eighth of that month. Graydon's last few weeks had been somewhat tempestuous. In October of 1890 he had shot and killed a man named D. A. Reynolds in the Broad Street office after Reynolds, who was drunk, had become abusive. Graydon pumped four bullets into him. Although the coroner's jury found the shooting to be justifiable homicide and a grand jury refused to return a true bill against him, Graydon brooded about it, and this may have hastened his demise.[1]

Scarcely waiting for Graydon's funeral, Al and a man named John Purritt volunteered to hunt for the body of John Kennedy, who had drowned in the Verde River the same day Graydon died. They rode up there, but before they arrived, Kennedy was found by searchers from Phoenix and buried in the military cemetery at Camp McDowell. Sieber rode on into the northern part of the Territory, secured a band of sheep, and moved them slowly south.[2] This must have been a contract job, for Al was an unlikely sheep herder, and he returned to

[1] *Arizona Silver Belt*, October 25, 1890, March 7, 1891.
[2] *Ibid.*, March 7, 1881; Sieber to Louise Taylor, April 26, 1891.

Globe late in April, finding there a letter from Louise with the news that Al's sister, Magdalena, Louise's mother, had died.[3] "I lost two of my Partteners Both died[4] and then god your Letter about your Mother all three in one week I tell you Louise it gave Me a harte hit all cuming together and it Sett me Back in Every thing wich it will take Me all Sumer to Straten out," Sieber replied. "You must kepe up your Pluck and Not give up to Dispare. Thad will not do. Everything will cum out all Right in the End. I have had meny ups and Downs But Still hold up and fight it through."

Al must have been over in Florence late in May, because the *Enterprise* noted that passengers on the Riverside stage had mistaken a container of his "poisonous preparation for his troublesome wounds" for a bottle of whiskey and had taken it along when the vehicle pulled out. A horseman hurried after it and overtook the stage seven miles out, fortunately before the contents of the "fatal bottle" had been sampled.[5] Sieber brought it back to Globe and, eventually turned his thoughts to mining once more. He made his way up Tonto Creek to his claims in the Del Shay Basin of the Sierra Ancha, which he had found in 1878 while Indian hunting, according to one report.[6]

To get to his properties, you went up Tonto Creek about thirty miles above its junction with the Salt, then turned to the right on a trail between two peaks and entered the mountains. At last you came to a basin seven or eight miles long and in it took a trail leading up toward the west rim. The principal claim was centered about three hundred feet below the crest on the west side of the basin and was located twenty-five miles southeast of Payson, the nearest settlement.

Others interested initially in the claims included Long Jim Cook, a noted packmaster; Sam Hill, another widely known army packer Al had known for many years;[7] Charley Dupont, a civilian guide and

---

[3] The death certificate from the City of Minneapolis shows this to have been on February 5; Magdalena was fifty-three years old and died of consumption.

[4] Besides Graydon, Frank Story, or Storey, who taught the Indians farming at San Carlos, died February 15, 1891, of complications following a severe cold. He had been associated with Sieber in a Tonto Basin mine. *Arizona Silver Belt*, February 21, 1891.

[5] Reprinted by the *Arizona Silver Belt*, May 23, 1891.

[6] Barnes, *Place Names*, 2nd ed., 100–101.

[7] English-born Sam Hill had come to Arizona from California in the 1870's via

scout; and Frank Story, who had just died. None of the old-timers except Sieber apparently stuck with the claim, and Dan Williamson and Bush Crawford bought into the operation, although Dupont and Hill retained an interest for a couple of years. Al set up his camp on the site and, with those of his partners who could devote the time, set about becoming a miner. Dan Williamson often visited the place, finding there some of the happiest days of his life amid hard work and good companionship.[8]

Sieber was a superlative camper, in the days when that involved an art and consummate skill. He rarely used a tent, preferring to sleep under a wagon fly stretched across a rope between two trees, one end abutting a huge rock, the other open to sky and wind. He was a fine, imaginative cook, and he liked to eat, so he was left to that sort of work which most campers despised. Sieber never went prospecting without bringing in a load of wood for use after dark and in the morning. Whether on the trail or in quarters, he cleaned up the camp each morning. As soon as a meal was over, the dishes were washed and put away, the camp swept, and everything placed in order. When on the trail he would pick up leaves and cedar boughs for a bed, packing them along until a camp was made. Al always took splendid care of his horses and mules, and "was as good to them as he was to himself." They were turned loose to graze, never hobbled, and when they came up each day, he would give them a little salt and barley, rub and pet them, to make them good camp stock.

One of his particular pets was a white or gray jennet, which had the disconcerting habit of bucking viciously if mounted before being led about one hundred yards. Al once lent her to Charles M. Clark, president of the Arizona Pioneers' Historical Society, who wanted to ride

---

Hardyville, and became chief packer for the army at Fort Whipple. He was one of the packers accompanying the transfer of the Indians from Verde to San Carlos in 1876, and when the two Indian factions got into their fight, Hill and the others ducked flying bullets. He was a miner well into the 1920's, working in Tonto Basin. Reminiscences of Frederick W. Croxon, Sr., APHS Files.

8 Williamson, "Sieber," 62; Lockwood, "Sieber," 33. Most of the description which immediately follows (of Al in the Del Shay Basin area) comes from these two sources unless cited otherwise.

from Del Shay to Payson, but, by whimsical design or otherwise, neglected to tell Clark about this peculiar trait of the animal. Clark later confessed: "I positively did not ride that jennet to Payson."[9] Al's favorite horse was big Sancho, born the day Sieber was shot in the Apache Kid imbroglio.

Al had a couple of pockets made to fit over his saddle, and in them he carried all sorts of odds and ends, mostly food. Sometimes on the trail with Williamson, he'd rein up about noon and say, "Well, Dan, we'd better have a little lunch." Williamson would reply, "Why, we haven't got anything to eat!" "Oh, I guess we'll dig up something," Al would say. He would dive into the saddle pockets and bring out a can of sardines, onions, a small bottle of vinegar, and a package of soda crackers. He'd peel the onions, cut them up fine, mix in the sardines, pour vinegar over it all, and make a cracker sandwich. Al insisted on always having vinegar on hand, but with that, a little jerky, rice, beans, and coffee, he could concoct a "glorious feast," and if he had anything else, he would use it, too.

He was a great hunter and usually there were two or three deer hanging about camp for a meat supply. One day they were about out of venison and Williamson said, "Al, you knock off a little early and get a deer." Sieber prowled about the mountainside, spotted a herd, and, in order to get close enough for a good shot, took off his shoes and crawled up through a wind that was blowing a near-hurricane, luckily coming from the deer toward him. He shot several of the animals, dressed them out, and then, taking a few choice parts for supper, set out to find his shoes. He couldn't locate them and trudged on through the dark, barefooted, for camp, arriving with his feet "in terrible condition," but with the meat, just the same.

Always eager for a joke, Al once shot a deer and propped it up beside the trail, going on into camp. A partner, coming along, saw the animal and fired three or four shots into it before realizing that it was already dead. On another occasion, Williamson saw a lone sheep ranging with a bunch of cattle, shot it, dressed it out, and, saying nothing about its origin, brought the meat into camp. Eventually,

[9] *Arizona Republican*, April 18, 1925.

after the mutton was about gone, he brought in the sheep's head to show the others. "Sieber was adroit, and immediately exclaimed: 'Hell, I knew it was a sheep as soon as I looked at it.' "

Once in several months Al would come to Globe, for that was where he made his headquarters for most of the balance of his life. In October of 1891 he dropped in—at the same time Jack Benton, Captain and the new Mrs. Bullis, and E. W. Kingsbury were there. The little settlement must have been crowded, but if these erstwhile opponents met, what they said was not recorded.[10]

Sieber didn't spend all of his time at his mine or on assessment work there. He often visited his many friends in the Tonto Basin, being as welcome at one ranch as at another. People were glad to have a visitor, especially one so distinguished as Sieber, and he was just as happy to do chores and help about the place when he had time or was asked to do so.

One of his favorite stops was with the Armers, Bud and Maggie, who lived a mile west of Payson.[11] "I was about 14 or 15 when I first knew him," Maggie recalled. "Later he would often come to our house. I remember I'd always fix up the spring bed for him and he would wait until I retired, then ask my husband to help him put the spring bed on the floor, where he would sleep. The next morning they would replace it before I got up. And I'd fix it so good for him!" Another strong impression she had was that Sieber was a hearty eater and "would eat everything I put on the table."

Among close friends Sieber was always good at telling tales, some of them a mite tall, such as the one about how he and the scouts crept up on an Indian rancheria where everyone was asleep, feet to the fire and heads out in the darkness. "We grabbed rocks and just knocked them in the head as we came to them," Al would say. "He told that to us lots of times," said Mrs. Armer. You never could be sure when he was being serious and when he was slyly playing on the credulity of his audience.

10 *Arizona Silver Belt*, October 31, 1891.

11 The information which follows originated in an interview with Mrs. Maggie Armer on December 10, 1958, at her Phoenix home. She was born in 1874, the daughter of Emer L. Chilson, who died when she was sixteen. Bud Armer died in 1928.

Sieber and Armer were always laughing about some prank they had pulled, and the old scout was ever surrounded by children, whom he loved and for whom he whittled toys of soft wood and told yarns to which they raptly listened. Often the Armers would go to town and leave their place in Al's care, sure that he would care for everything properly. "Sieber was the best-known Indian fighter of my time," recalled Mrs. Armer. "I never heard anything against his character. He was said to be cruel, a little cold-blooded, but we found him kind and considerate. Often, it is said, he would take no prisoners, but cruelty was something that had to be, in those days."

Al would help his friends' children with their school lessons (let us hope it was not with spelling!), and the Armers named their first child Sieber James in honor of Al and the boy's father. Sieber James Armer, born in 1900, joined the army in 1917 and died in a training camp from spinal meningitis. Bush Crawford also named a son after the scout, Oran Sieber Crawford, and Al once gave the boy a big yellow mare named Nelly. He often presented things to his friends and their children. To one of the Crawford girls he gave a silver-mounted bridle and to Cordelia Adams Crawford, her mother, a fine Apache basket and other things. Sieber had been a witness to the Crawfords' wedding back in 1880 and seemed to have a proprietary interest in the family, Bush remaining a close friend until Sieber died. To both of the Crawford girls, still living, at this writing, in Globe, Al seemed well educated and an intelligent, quiet man. He was saddened when Oran Sieber Crawford died at the age of eleven in 1895, and sympathized deeply with the family. And his friendship was not shaken later, in 1897, when Bush Crawford shot down a neighbor in a dispute and was put away for a while.[12]

For amusement, Al, "like everyone else," would go to camp meetings run by Parson Calfry or some other itinerant preacher of whatever faith. "He never missed a one," Maggie Armer said. "I think Al Sieber had more or less religion, and he was not a wicked man. I never heard him use a curse word in my life, and he was every inch a gentleman."

All during these years Sieber had trouble with his wounded leg, and

[12] *Arizona Silver Belt*, June 29, 1895; July 29 and August 5, 1897.

although he never complained about it, close acquaintances knew that sometimes he was in considerable pain. Some of them knew him to use a cane; others did not, and it is likely that he did not always employ one. Nona Crawford has said that he used to sit on the porch and doctor it up with a concoction he made up, mostly of water and wood ashes, and Dan Williamson recalled that Al had a hole as big as a black walnut in his instep, where the bullet had smashed home. The wound got progressively worse in his later years, and probably because it limited his physical activity, he took on weight, although he always carried it well.

W. C. "Pecos" McFadden, as a boy of ten or twelve, used to go camping with Sieber in the Sierra Ancha on occasion. McFadden's father ranched over much of the range, and Al would come around every couple of months or so and talk Pecos' parents into letting him take the boy out prospecting or hunting. "He was a great meat eater," McFadden recalled. "When he'd cook a steak he would pull out a bottle of vinegar and pour it over the meat, then hand the bottle to me and say, 'Use lots of it, and you'll be as healthy and live as long as I have.' To please him I'd take a little but never liked the taste of it."[13]

Robert Riell, now of Globe, recalls that as boys he and Ed Anderson were once working a brushy canyon, trying to kill a fat beef, and they put Sieber on a bluff, planning to drive the cattle past him so that he could shoot one. Said Riell:

> We had some dogs with us, and instead of running the cattle, they treed a little old bear. I fired two shots at him, but seemed to miss, and went to get Al. When we returned, we saw where the bear had toppled out of the tree, and we decided to eat bear meat, instead of beef. We took the hide with us, and when we got to the ranch, threw it across a fence.
>
> The next morning Al came limping up and said, "You kids got a bear story?" We both shook our heads. "Well," said Al, "I got one. You tell it this way . . . ." He gave us a long winded story about how the bear came down the tree and chased me up another one, and Ed had to rope him, and how he got tangled up with the rope, and finally how the bear was killed. "Anyone questions your story," said Sieber, "don't say nothing—

[13] Interview with Pecos McFadden at Phoenix on December 10, 1958.

just point to the bear hide. The bear must have been killed, and that's your evidence. Just say, 'Well, there's his hide, ain't it?' "

The boys got a ten-dollar bounty from the county for the skin, payable with or without a yarn.[14]

Most of those who remember Al clearly aver that he had no accent, or, at best, only a slight one, yet Will Barnes, who knew him, wrote that he "spoke with a strong German accent."[15] Several writers who knew him in the early days spelled his name "Zeiber," or some such variation, indicating that he must have had something of an accent.[16] Most of those who knew him also exaggerated his height, thinking him to be six feet or more, but this was probably due to his enormous strength, so great that, as Tom Horn wrote, quartermaster's men in charge of pack trains often "told how he, one time, lifted a pack mule up and set it on a ledge from which it had fallen."[17] An apocryphal tale, no doubt, but illustrative.

Now Al was using his strength mainly on his mine, and that undoubtedly for lack of something more interesting to do. In the middle of July, 1893, Crawford brought to Globe and Phoenix some Del Shay ore which was said to average seventy dollars a ton, and Bush claimed that two thousand tons had been brought out of the shafts.[18] Three years later, Williamson brought to town some ore from the same mine

14 Told by Ed Anderson of Globe to Jess G. Hayes, April 15, 1959.

15 Barnes, *Place Names*, 403. On the other hand, the Corbusiers were convinced that Al retained a strong German accent. "He had a German accent, quite marked at times, when he got excited," said William T. Corbusier, in an interview. "My mother [Fanny Corbusier, wife of the Camp Verde doctor] was always chiding him about his 'inverted sentences.' She said his 'English was atrocious.' Sieber would explain that all he knew was 'Injun, Mexican and hoss talk,' but he knew a lot more than that. No man did so much for the Indians, the Army and Arizona."

16 See, for instance, the *Arizona Miner*, August 23, 1873, and Bourke, *Apache Campaign*, 57 *et passim*. Charles King, in some of his early novels, also refers to Al as "Zeiber," although the name is later spelled correctly. Other writers have also toyed with Sieber's supposed accent. In *Broncho Apache*, Paul I. Wellman gives him a distinct manner of speech, which, he confessed in a letter to me, was simply a fictional device. E. E. Halleran, *Crimson Desert*, gives him a heavy German accent, also, no doubt, a fictional maneuver, and many other writers have taken a turn at Sieber's supposed way of talking.

17 Horn, 167.

18 *Arizona Silver Belt*, July 15, 1893.

running one hundred dollars a ton in gold and sixteen in silver, claiming that it represented a "new strike" the partners had made on the property.[19] One would think that with that sort of material, a sale of the mine—if that is what the owners wanted—would have been easy, but they never did sell it. For one thing, there was little ready cash in the Arizona of those years. As Al wrote Louise, "It is hard to git Money anough to pay Living Expences here. I Never Saw the times So hard in this country Before as they are at Presand. A Man can hartly git 20 Dollars to Save his Life. But I hobe it will take a change Befour Long."[20]

Late in the summer of 1894, Al, Bill McNelly (whose saloon had just burned down in a Globe fire that destroyed much of the business district of the town), and Charlie Hopkins went up into the White Mountains for a hunting trip, finding the grass good, fish plentiful, and lots of turkeys, but no larger game to amount to anything—not much like it had been twenty years earlier, when the tips of the Whites were tramped by herds of elk and visited by other big game.[21] Sieber, no doubt happy with his hunting, was little concerned about such mundane things as, for example, the Apache Kid.

The *Arizona Gazette* of September 25, 1894, reported that a mountaineer had met the renegade Indian and said the Kid had asked for Sieber, saying he wanted to kill him. "The Gazette also states that Al. is on the Kid's trail, which is no less a romance than the residue of the Gazette's reference," growled the *Silver Belt*. Such fictioneering was common in the territorial newspapers of the day, but in some part it was due to the fact that no one knew anything definite about the Kid—except that he was alleged to be doing a lot of killing. The *Silver Belt* of June 18, 1892, had reported that the Indian "has committed murders in six counties: Pinal, Maricopa, Cochise, Graham, Apache and Gila," and that no one seemed able to catch him. Much of his alleged depredation must have been imaginary, or committed by someone else, and not necessarily by Indians. Sieber, for instance,

19 *Ibid.*, July 30, 1896.
20 Sieber to Louise Taylor, December 25, 1894.
21 *Arizona Silver Belt*, August 25 and September 22, 1894; Colonel William Baird to Britton Davis, November 25, 1929, Connor Collection.

always thought it was white men who were responsible for the celebrated killing of a lawyer named Hardie in Rucker Canyon in the early nineties, although the Kid was generally blamed.

One time an Indian, an experienced scout, approached Dan Williamson and told him that if he would supply an outfit for about ten days, the pair would get the Apache Kid, who at the time had a five-thousand-dollar price on his head. Williamson decided to go, but felt he must first tell Sieber. Al was astonished. "Did ——— tell you this?" he demanded, using the name of the scout. Williamson said he had. "Well, if he told you that, he will do it; he is the bravest Indian I ever saw, but why should you do this?" demanded Al. "Did the Kid ever harm you? Are you an officer? Are you employed to run down criminals? Do you want blood on your hands? Do you wish to kill a man for money? Take my advice and leave it alone." Sieber's earnestness and the stress he placed on the blood-money angle made the proposition look different to Dan, and he told the Indian scout he would not go. The trip was never made.[22]

Al's heated objections to the project would seem to point up the notion that he never held a grudge against the Apache Kid for the incident in which he was crippled and that he always nursed some affection for him. It also implies that in his more reflective moments, Al Sieber, too, tended to be thoughtful and somewhat morose over the sanguinary course of his own career, but of that there is no other evidence, and we can never be sure.

Williamson wrote that he joined Sieber several times, just the two of them, when "he went out to meet the Kid and induce him to surrender, with the understanding that the $5,000 reward would all be used in procuring him a pardon. We sat out under the stars a number of nights expecting him, and although he hovered near, he never met us. This was near the camp of an Indian, a mutual friend, who was our go-between."[23] Finally, about 1894, the Kid made his last recorded raid into Arizona, and after that no more was definitely heard of him in the Territory.

One winter, about Christmastime, Williamson got to thinking

22 Williamson, "Sieber," 71–72.
23 *Ibid.*, 73.

about the pleasures of Globe and mentioned to Al that they were almost out of grain for the horses anyway, so Sieber agreed that he ought to go to town. "Get the latest papers and, by the way, tell Bill McNelly to send me a gallon of whiskey for Christmas," Al said. Williamson went to town, loaded the grain and supplies, bought what papers he could find, and stopped in at the new Champion, where Bill was polishing the bar. "How's Sieber?" he asked. "Fine," said Williamson. "I want to send him a gallon of whiskey for Christmas," said McNelly, and Dan laughed. "You just saved me from asking," he said.

They had a celebration when Williamson returned to the mine. Al was lying on his bunk reading the San Francisco *Chronicle* when he suddenly began to laugh in his rich, infectious way. Asked why, he explained:

Here is an item that reads: "Major Simpson was married at the Occidental Hotel in San Francisco." Now that is the third time he has been married and he is over 70 years old. And it reminds me of a trip I made and we encountered one old buck and one sore-eyed squaw. We were coming back toward Fort McDowell, 30 miles out. Major Simpson heard we were coming in and came out with 10 soldiers for an escort and camped with us all night. Next morning when we got ready to start he came to me and said: "Mr. Sieber, how are you going to get those Indians to Fort McDowell? They can't walk that distance." I said, "I have no transportation, and I see no other way for them to get there." The Major walked over to the chief packer, a tall, young Missourian [who was probably Long Jim Cook] and asked him if he could furnish transportation. "Certainly, Major, certainly," said the packer. When we got ready to start this packer took out a shaved-tail mule from Missouri, then took a piece of canvas and wrapped it around the squaw and another piece around the buck. Then he picked up the squaw and threw her up on one side of the mule and put the buck on the other side. Then he lashed them on. The packer took the blind off of the mule and hit him with his hat. The mule gave a big jump and the buck Indian said, "Whoo!" That scared the mule worse. He started to run up a trail into the mountains. Every jump he would make that Indian would say, "Whoo!" The mule probably thought he had a bear on his back. They followed them up the mountains about three miles, and then lost all track of the mule and never saw it or the Indians again.[24]

One day in late March of 1896, a young man dropped around to the camp and made himself at home, being asked by no one who he was and volunteering no information, at first. He looked about, chatted with the partners, became acquainted with them, and finally admitted his identity; he was John Sieber, the son of Al's older brother, down from Grand Forks, North Dakota, where, it was said, he had been sheriff for a time, and now was looking for greener—and warmer—pastures. He thought he might settle in California, or maybe Arizona, but decided to visit Texas first, and he ultimately established himself at Houston, becoming quite comfortably fixed before his death on November 30, 1947. "I have had one letter from him Since he is in Texas. I Beleve that country up there was to cold for him," Al wrote to Louise.[25]

That Al, too, was getting restless is indicated by the various directions his thoughts took. Summer came and with it ideas for getting out of the drudgery of opening and working a mine. Starting with the first July issue and running all that month in the pages of the *Silver Belt* was a short announcement: once again Al Sieber was going to run for sheriff. This bid came to the same end as that in Yavapai County in 1878. On July 30 the newspaper announced that "we are authorized by Al Sieber to withdraw his announcement. . . . Al is engaged in mining at Delshay basin, and writes that he will have too much work to do this summer to give any time to politics. . . . Al has a host of friends in the county who will regret to learn of his determination." In the same issue was an announcement by Dan Williamson that he would run as a Republican candidate for sheriff. Obviously it was a deal, but what Al got out of it, if anything, was not reported. Williamson was elected and made a reasonably satisfactory sheriff for one term.

Al's attention continued to wander from the Del Shay property, and he turned to some copper claims that he had on Pinto Creek, six-

[24] Lockwood APHS. The "Major Simpson" referred to was probably James Ferdinand Simpson, born in Massachusetts, who was commissioned a second lieutenant in the Fourteenth Connecticut Infantry on August 20, 1862. He served in the Third Cavalry from March 15, 1871, made captain in 1884, and retired three years later, in 1887. Simpson died June 29, 1899. Heitman.

[25] *Arizona Silver Belt*, April 2, 1896; Sieber to Louise Taylor, January 5, 1897.

teen miles west of Globe, named the Hal and Al, Lost Coon, Dan and Mack, Monroe Doctrine, and so on. These, like Del Shay, were promising properties, and, as he wrote Louise, he would at least get his mail every week and not once each month or two as formerly.[26] Not only did these properties look good, but he and the other owners, Bill McNelly, his brother, Hal McNelly, and Dan Williamson, contracted with one Con Crowley for their development. Con would do much of the work, and Al as little or as much as he desired. Digging began at once; tunnels were driven, and the ore looked good.

About half a mile down the creek was the Yo Tambien and other mines owned by the Pinto Creek Mining and Smelting Company, and working there for a time was Lee Middleton, brother of Gene Middleton, who had driven the stage from which the Apache Kid and his companions escaped. Whether for this reason or some other, Sieber took a liking to Lee, and often they would sit and yarn before a fire, especially if there was a bottle in camp. Al was often reserved with strangers and usually quiet even with acquaintances, but with his close friends he could be loquacious and often proved a fine storyteller and amiable companion. Middleton said of him:

> Sieber always seemed to me serious and melancholy, but sometimes he would come out of it.
>
> Once we were riding in from Pinto Creek and he reined up and said, "Lee, see that spring down there?" and he pointed several miles below. He said:
>
> "I was scouting one time and a scout told me there were two others figuring on killing me before we got back to the reservation. So that night we made our beds at that spring. I made my bed facing those two. Way in the middle of the night I saw one of them raise up and look around and then lie down. Then the other one raised up. Pretty soon the first one started crawling toward my bed. I was laying with my gun in my hand and when he got within a few feet of me, I shot him in the head.
>
> "The other Indian started to run and I killed him. The camp was in an uproar by that time, and I made them all lay down until morning. Next morning I had the two bodies pulled under a high bank by the creek, and caved the bank in on them, and if the coyotes didn't get them then they are there yet."[27]

[26] Sieber to Louise Taylor, December 28, 1897.

The months passed, and Sieber and Crowley labored away at their mine, at some times elated by the turn of the ore, discouraged at others. Once things were so promising, the *Silver Belt* reported, that before returning to camp Sieber "ordered a barrel of sauer kraut."[28] Or something.

By way of variety, later that month (January, 1898) Al secured the services of an Indian trailer, picked up the tracks of three sheep thieves north of Globe, trailed them all the way to the Jerome area, and nabbed them, turning the prisoners over to Sheriff R. H. Cameron of Coconino County, who had chased them fruitlessly many a weary mile. "Cameron is doubtless an efficient officer, but in this instance did not distinguish himself" as the local boys did, the *Silver Belt* pointed out.[29]

Al continued to base himself at the Pinto Creek mines and, with Con Crowley, do a lot of assessment and development work on them, but he found time for extracurricular activities, too. For one thing, he helped engineers laying out a practicable route into Mineral Creek for the Gila Valley, Globe & Northern Railroad, utilizing his vast knowledge of the country, as did countless other scouts and backwoodsmen for most of the nation's westbound railroad-construction teams.[30] This one had the novelty, it might be pointed out, of being among the last of the railroads laid down in the West, but Sieber never did much for it, working at it in his spare time, one might say.

He must have been getting bored with the Pinto Creek claims by this time. Prospecting down the Salt with Frank Westbrook, he located a couple of claims, two and one-half miles below the mouth of Tonto Creek, featuring copper ore. They had been located "years ago," but little work was done on them and the locations were allowed to lapse.[31] He and Dan Williamson did some assessment work on copper claims on the Gila River, at the mouth of Dripping Springs Wash, to be exact, and again he reported that prospects were just

27 Interview with the author, July 13, 1958; correspondence with the author, February 16, 1958.

28 January 13, 1898.

29 February 3, 1898.

30 *Arizona Silver Belt*, September 28, 1899.

31 *Ibid.*, November 2, 1899.

fine.[32] He wrote Louise on January 4, 1900, that someone from Minneapolis was interested in the Del Shay property, but didn't know whether he could make a deal. Nothing came of it.

While Al was pecking away at the hills of Arizona in the twilight of his life, he was not forgotten for his good work in former years. For one thing, he was commissioned as aide-de-camp to General Eli Torrance, national commander of the Grand Army of the Republic and a fellow Minnesotan.[33] Then Colonel Welford Chapman Bridwell, in a newspaper interview, stated that Sieber was one of three white men who did more than anyone else to subdue the Apaches. Such a tribute from such a source must have been satisfying to the old scout, who by this time must often have felt something like an anachronism.[34] Newspaper correspondents and magazine writers increasingly sought him out, but Sieber rejected their offers, saying that if he were interviewed, he would have to say things about the army and military mistakes of the past better left unsaid.

Sometime during these years, Sieber gave up on the Pinto Creek mine, selling out for a few dollars, McNelly and Crowley retaining their interests. It was unfortunate that Al did this. In January, 1906, the mines were sold by the two remaining partners to the Arizona National Copper Company for a very good price—enough so that Bill could retire from the saloon business and take things easy for the rest of his life—and once more Sieber had brushed mineral wealth, come within a hair of it, and lost out. But if he ever complained, it was not reported in the press.

32 *Ibid.*, January 17, 1901.

33 Louise Taylor had the commission after Sieber died, and wrote Frank Lockwood that she would find it and send it to him, but apparently never did.

34 Bridwell, or Clay Beauford (or Buford), as he was known during his early years in the Territory, was born at Washington City, Maryland, in 1848. At fifteen he fought with Pickett at Gettysburg and after the Civil War enlisted in the Fifth Cavalry, winning a Medal of Honor for heroism during the Apache campaigns in the winter of 1872–73, by which time he was first sergeant of Company B. John Clum appointed him chief of San Carlos police after failing to get Al Sieber, whom he preferred, for the job, and Bridwell performed the duty well from 1874 to 1880. He subsequently married and established a ranch in the Aravaipa Valley and was a member of the Arizona Territorial Legislature in 1885. He died at Los Angeles on February 1, 1905. Barnes, *Place Names*, 66–67; Clum, *op. cit.*, 163; *Fifth Cavalry*, 673, 674, 680; *Arizona Star*, February 19 and 22, 1882; *Arizona Silver Belt*, November 28, 1901, and February 9, 1905.

Al was tired of mining, of grubbing like a mole for wages and little more, and although he retained an interest in several claims, he saddled up old Sancho about this time and headed north into Tonto Basin once more. He called on Colonel Jesse W. Ellison,[35] who owned the Q Ranch east of Payson in Pleasant Valley, and the Bud Armers and McFaddens and others of his friends, and eventually drifted over to the new town of Roosevelt, located about where Tonto Creek joined the Salt, and for the remainder of his life more or less made that his headquarters. But he didn't spend all his time there.

The great Roosevelt Dam, known in those days as the Tonto Dam, was authorized in late 1903, to be built just below the confluence of Tonto Creek and the Salt at the mouth of the first of a series of spectacular gorges that Sieber had often coursed afoot and on horseback in his Indian-fighting days. Louis Clarence Hill was the Reclamation Service's project engineer on this mammoth undertaking, and he came to know Sieber fairly well.[36] One of the jobs coincident with construction of the dam was the building of roads, including improvement of the trace to Globe and the laying out of what is now the Apache Trail from the damsite to Apache Junction, on the road to Phoenix. About midway to Apache Junction is Tortilla Flats, settled by Spanish-speaking people in 1865. All of its original buildings have been washed away by floods that occasionally come down Tortilla Creek. For a time, while the road was under construction, Al apparently ran a commissary there. "When I came driving the first rig that ever went over that road," wrote Hill, "Sieber stood there, jumped up and down, and waved his arms in the air as if he were wild. Being the first team of any kind that had ever been over the road, he was exceedingly glad

[35] One of the most colorful of Arizona cattlemen, Ellison was a Texan, a veteran of Kiowa and Comanche wars, a trail driver to the Kansas cow towns, and, from 1885, an Arizona stockman. His daughter, Duette, married George W. P. Hunt, who served many terms as governor of Arizona. Ellison, born in 1842, died in 1934 at the age of ninety-two and is buried at Phoenix. Willson, *Cattlemen*, I, 21.

[36] Hill, born at Ann Arbor, Michigan, on February 22, 1865, was educated at the University of Michigan and taught at the Colorado School of Mines. He worked for the Reclamation Service from 1903 to 1914, then entered private practice. In 1937 he was president of the American Society of Civil Engineers. He died at Hollywood, California, on November 5, 1938, and his ashes were moved to Roosevelt Dam, where he wanted them to rest.

to see us!" Hill added that his impression of Al was that "he was the kind of man for whom one would have a good deal of respect, and one with whom it would be better to have only mild arguments."[37]

Al worked for the project off and on for the rest of his life, but he also found time to engage in other activities. Bud Armer had secured a contract to supply some of the enormous quantities of cordwood consumed by the steam-producing engines on the Tonto Dam affair, and for several months Sieber helped out—with Indians and Mexicans to do most of the chopping, of course. "We camped out at the wood-cutting sites," recalled Maggie Armer. "Sieber and my husband would sit up late every night talking, but Al was always up at daylight to get the bean pot on and coffee ready. I was nominally the cook, but it was under Sieber's supervision. He was very particular, and insistent that we have beans every day. He always ate a great plate of them for breakfast."[38]

Sieber also ran a corral for a time at Roosevelt. Ed Anderson describes an incident which occurred there:

> One Christmas time, in 1905 or 1906, we decided to spend the Yuletide at the dam and arriving there we took our horses to the Al Sieber corral, located behind the Newman-Sultan store and told Sieber to feed them grain and hay. His native good spirits were at their genial best, and he treated us to a couple of drinks. While we visited with him, peace officers R. M. (Bob) Anderson and Jim Holmes rode up and joined us in merrymaking.
>
> Shortly a drunk Indian rode his horse up and asked Sieber for 25 cents worth of hay, paying for it with a one-dollar bill. Sieber delivered the hay and handed the Indian 75 cents in change, but he claimed he had given Sieber a $5 bill and insisted on $4.75 in change. Sieber refused the Apache's demand.

The Indian then made his mistake: he struck at Al, who was then in his sixties. Sieber hit him in the mouth and knocked him out, although his fingers were cut to the bone on the Indian's teeth and required a doctor's attention. Bob Anderson grabbed the Apache and took him to the bank of the Salt River, chaining him to a tree to sober up, since

37 Hill to Frank Lockwood, April 12, 1937, APHS Files.
38 Interview with Maggie Armer.

there was no jail. About midnight the Indian's wife came to Sieber and begged him to release her now sobered husband. Al sent word to Holmes and Anderson. The prisoner was liberated.[39]

Early in 1906, Sieber went to San Carlos to apply for a pension, which, the *Silver Belt* noted, "his great service to the government as soldier and scout certainly entitle him to."[40] Al had asked to be examined by a doctor at Roosevelt, but the War Department directed him to report to Fort Bayard, New Mexico, three hundred miles away. There is nothing to indicate that he ever went,[41] although he would surely have qualified for a pension if he had. As he wrote Louise, "I am gitting along in years my Self. This is a hard Winter here in Arizona and it kind of Nocks Me Out. But I grin and Bear it." He thanked her for sending him a bottle of whiskey for Christmas. "Some what Better then I can gitt here," he said, adding that "I hobe Some Day to Be able to Return your kind Presond But I will not sent you Eny Whiskey for I am afraid Taylor Might kick."[42]

Running a camp of several thousand laborers, far from home and anxious for excitement, was an exacting job, but Holmes and Anderson were the men for it, even though it sometimes required some shooting. Holmes killed Rinaldo Arvisa on the last day of September, 1905, when Arvisa resisted arrest on an illegal-liquor count, and in February of the following year he shot and killed an Indian, perhaps the same one Sieber had knocked out, who had engaged in a drunken brawl and fired once at Holmes.[43] Liquor was forbidden in the camp, but bootleggers kept bringing it in, and unrest among Apaches brought from San Carlos to work on the dam increased. One riot followed another. It may have been for this reason that Sieber was given a job managing a gang of Apaches starting construction on the "high road" going north from the damsite along Tonto Creek into the basin. At any rate, he was so employed as 1906 wore itself out and 1907 began.

[39] Ed Anderson in an interview with Jess G. Hayes, April 15, 1959.
[40] February 8, 1906.
[41] Record Group 94, National Archives.
[42] Sieber to Louise Taylor, January 1, 1906.
[43] *Arizona Silver Belt*, November 2, 1905, and February 22, 1906.

XXV. The Last Adventure

THE WINTER SUN rises late over Rockinstraw Mountain. It dyes the southern face of Black Mesa a bright orange and brings life and warmth to the womanly contours of Dutchwoman Butte, named, some say, by Al Sieber because it reminded him of a housewife stooped over her scrubbing board. In the days when the mighty Tonto Dam[1] was building, it would take the sun hours to climb high enough to touch Camp Roosevelt, frosted dead white in the shadows below the swollen hills enclosing the Salt River Basin.

Day after day, Sieber's Apaches moved into the sun's early light as they climbed the boulder-strewn slope to their job along the high-line route of the new Tonto Road, probing northward from the dam-site. Tuesday, January 1, New Year's Day, was just like any other and the calendar moved on into 1907. The foundation for the giant dam had been laid last September, and while it was too early for it to take shape as yet, engineers could envision its mammoth bulk across the Salt.

Order was maintained at Roosevelt and among the thousands of workingmen by James T. Holmes, a tough, single-minded former Arizona Ranger who had served in that rugged force for two years under Captain Tom H. Rynning,[2] and a local boy, Bob Anderson, also, it is said, a former Ranger. Thad Frazier,[3] who managed a work team of

1 Later called Roosevelt Dam.

2 James T. Holmes was enlisted as a member of the Arizona Rangers from September 2, 1902, to November 30, 1904, serving under Rynning. Mrs. Alice B. Good, director, Department of Library and Archives, Phoenix, in correspondence with the author.

3 T. T. Frazier, an octogenarian at this writing, still operates a combination filling station–snack bar–post office–boat landing at Roosevelt, Arizona, about a mile toward

Apaches, as did Sieber, and saw Holmes shoot down Rinaldo Arvisa, described Holmes as quiet of speech, wearing his badge under his jacket and a pistol in his pants pocket, and a man who tolerated no foolishness unless he chose to.

Three miles east of Roosevelt lived the Morrises, a happy, prosperous family. Laura Gordon Morris, about thirty-eight, and her husband, Harvey, were parents of a large and growing family, including Logan, twenty, working at Tonto; Eunice, sixteen, who attended a high school at Globe; another daughter of eleven and a boy nine, who were packed off to school at Roosevelt each morning; and Aminta Ann, a pretty little girl of four and a half. As a sideline, Laura baked bread, which her husband took to Roosevelt several times a week, and on Thursday, the last day of January, Laura baked enough for the week-end trade and she and Aminta Ann accompanied Harvey a short distance toward the camp. They parted just before 11:00 A.M.

Charley Hill's dairy lay in a bottom along the stage road, about a mile from Harvey's on the way to Roosevelt. On this morning, about noon, he heard his wife scream and ran up to the house, encountering there a tall, thin Negro with a gashed throat, crudely bandaged, and a tale of assault on a woman near the Morris home. He said his name was William Baldwin, that he had come upon the scene as the woman was being attacked by two Mexicans, and that he had been wounded when he tried to save her life and was beaten off. Hill told him to find Holmes and tell the story to the law officer. Baldwin ran off toward the camp, found Holmes, repeated the story, and led a group of men, including Holmes, storekeeper Edgar Sultan, and others, back to the glade where the bodies of Laura and Aminta Ann Morris lay. Obviously, there had been a desperate struggle there, but, Holmes noted, there were no tracks in the vicinity except those of the victims—and Baldwin's. He placed the Negro under arrest.

So far, this has been a recital of a double slaying, a sordid tale.

Globe from the dam. It is well up from the lake and has no connection, save proximity, with the camp called Roosevelt, the site of which lies under waters impounded by Roosevelt Dam. Frazier was at the camp during the construction period, knew Sieber and Holmes well, and retains a clear memory of the period and of these men. He was the last white man to see Sieber alive.

From this point, however, it attains a semblance of nobility as hardened frontiersmen, whose training had been in survival rather than the niceties of civilized life, now risked life, friendship, and even their reputations to uphold the integrity of a law which had not even existed when they entered the Territory.

Holmes guided the party back toward Roosevelt, which seethed with unrest as news of the murders preceded them. Baldwin pleaded with the officer not to be turned over to any mob, but Holmes said nothing. He must first check out the killings and find the murder weapon, if possible; meanwhile, he had to find a place to hold the prisoner, for the camp had no jail. The hospital, Holmes figured, would do as well as anything. He needed expert trackers, and for them he went to Louis Hill, the engineer in charge of the project. Hill, in turn, went to Sieber, and Al called in a pair of dark-faced Apaches, one named "Rabbit" and the other "Yesterday." "They understand a little English," Sieber explained. "Just tell them what you want and let them do the rest."

Thad Frazier watched the pair work when they reached the glade:

> We'd had lots of rain and the ground was soft. All the ravines were running water. They tracked the killer easily through mud, and with more difficulty over the rocks, and came at last to a pool where he'd knelt to wash his hands. A little way beyond the Indians stopped and said he'd thrown the knife away.
>
> You know, if you're a right-handed man, you drag your right foot just a little when you throw something. The Indians showed us a track where the right foot had dragged a little. They said the man there had thrown something. So the one Indian picked up a rock and threw it, followed to its landing, went all over and found nothing. Then the other Indian threw a rock, a couple of rocks, from that place. Again they went to where the rocks lit. They hunted for about a minute and goddam if they didn't come up with the knife![4]

The only other suspects besides Baldwin, a pair of Mexicans, easily established alibis, and suspicion narrowed to the Negro, whom the camp had already convicted by acclamation. When Holmes deposited

[4] Interview with T. T. Frazier, January 15, 1959.

him in the hospital, he felt that extra precautions would be necessary, pending the arrival of Sheriff Henry "Rimrock" Thompson, who had been called from Globe by telephone. Holmes got Al Sieber to agree to stay with the suspect during the night as Thompson was hurrying the forty-three horseback miles to the construction camp. Sieber followed Holmes into the room, now become a temporary cell. As he turned to leave, Holmes held out his hand to the old scout. "Al," he said, "I'll just take your gun."

Sieber, one may assume, was startled, for there is no record that anyone, in Al's sixty-four rather violent years, had ever taken away his gun before. "Why?" he demanded.

"Well, Al," Holmes is said to have explained, quietly, "if I leave you here with it, and a crowd shows up, you might decide to make a stand. If they come and you can't talk them out of it, they can have Baldwin, but I don't want you to maybe kill some of them or get killed for him." Sieber grunted and handed over his pistol. He never used a gun again.[5]

Holmes left, and Sieber was alone with Baldwin. The 25-year-old Negro had arrived at Roosevelt with seventy-seven others from Galveston six months before the crime. The group had been signed by contractor J. J. O'Rourke, for whom Willie had once worked during the construction of the Galveston sea wall. Baldwin had left his wife and child at Globe when he went up to the damsite. They quietly left Globe for Texas after his arrest, and were heard from no more.

Shortly after midnight, Sheriff Thompson and Deputies Bud Armer, Bob McMurray, and Charley Henderson clattered up to the hospital, somewhat surprised to find Baldwin still alive. The inquest would not get under way until dawn, but the Sheriff thought he had better get his prisoner out of town right away and at half-past three they started, barely in time. "The strangling grip of Judge Lynch was perilously near the colored man's throat," reported the *Silver Belt*. "Had Sheriff Thompson not left for Globe before the inquest had begun and before the excited residents of the government camp and surrounding country finally secured a leader, the limp and lifeless

[5] Interview with Bud Ming, July 12, 1958.

395

body of Baldwin, riddled with bullets, might now be swinging from a tree on the banks of the Salt River."[6] Nevertheless, Rimrock Henry was having his troubles.

The Negro was manacled to Henderson, who sat on the front seat of a borrowed buggy; Thompson and Armer, with Winchesters in their saddle boots, rode on either side. Hardly had the little cavalcade started when a menacing crowd swept up in its wake. Among them was an Indian dragging a rope with a big-as-life hangman's noose neatly tied. The crowd grew as the sheriff's party trotted on. Then, about a mile and a half out of Roosevelt, the lawmen were headed off by some fifteen cowboys and others on horseback and twice as many on foot. Among them Thompson recognized many of his friends, all local people who had known the Morrises well. The posse pulled up. Henry and Bud drew their carbines. Never in Thompson's unprecedented career as sheriff of huge and rambunctious Gila County, or even on the Arctic frontier, had he faced a more delicate situation. But for such he was made. "Me and Bud threw down on that crowd," he said later, according to an eyewitness. "They told me they was going to take him. I laughed at them."

"Why," he told the dangerous mob, "you couldn't take this prisoner from poor, crippled old Al Sieber when he didn't even have a gun! How in hell you think you're going to take him from me and Bud? I don't personally give a damn what happens to Baldwin, but it's my duty to get him to jail and I'm going to do just that. Now get along home, all of you. We're going through you with this man."

And through the throng they went. All but leaderless, it hesitated, and in that moment lost its opportunity. The would-be lynchers fell back and allowed the Sheriff's party to pass.[7]

At the county seat, Baldwin was lodged in the stone and iron jail, in the cold, damp basement of the brand-new courthouse. The results of the inquest followed Thompson to Globe, and friends of the Morrises were stirring up lynch talk anew. Both the inquest and the formal arraignment revealed that it was all but impossible for anyone but Baldwin to have committed the crime, and the community

[6] *Arizona Silver Belt*, February 1, 1907.

[7] Interview with T. T. Frazier; *Arizona Silver Belt*, February 1, 1907.

seethed with lust for vengeance. Never had Globe been so close to anarchy. Anger rippled through the mining camp; scores, then hundreds, milled the streets. It was reported that Negroes were buying arms and ammunition from a store at the lower edge of town, but the gravest danger was between mob and prisoner. On the evening of February 2, more than one thousand irate, shouting, grimly murderous-looking men grouped before the courthouse, demanding the slayer.[8] Rimrock Henry, all the deputies he could muster, and even District Judge Frederick S. Nave grouped on the high, stone steps, resisting the demands.

It was a singular thing, this stand by a judge sworn to uphold legal processes, braced on the granite steps of the huge copper-trimmed building that was the pride of Gila County. The Judge had a Winchester across his arm and a look of defiance on his finely chiseled face. "No matter what the cost in life and property," he warned the mob, "there will be no lynching here!"

His statement did little to quell the rising threat of the mob. A hurried conference took place on the steps. Bloodshed seemed inevitable. Many might be killed or wounded. Thompson turned to face the crowd. He seemed to surrender: *he threw the cell keys into the jeering mass of men.* "All right, boys," he said. "I guess you win. Go get him—if you can."

Someone clutched the keys, and the mighty assemblage surged forward with a yell. It swept into the courthouse, brushing aside the Judge, the deputies, and the Sheriff. Then the cry of the mob changed tone as from the basement came word that they couldn't find Baldwin. Rimrock Henry went quietly to his office; when the mob demanded he produce the prisoner, he answered quietly: "Find him yourselves." Like monkeys, almost, members of the throng surged through every room of the multistoried structure—even up onto its coppered roof, over adjoining roofs, and through adjacent buildings— but they could find no trace of the prisoner. Baldwin had disappeared. Thompson, too, vanished without a trace, and didn't return to his office for days; when he did, he was even more closemouthed than he usually was.

[8] *Arizona Gazette*, February 4, 1907.

Sieber may have chuckled when he read the accounts in the *Silver Belt*. The lawman in him would be satisfied that the prisoner had not been lynched, and the old Indian fighter would have relished Rimrock Henry's feat in outwitting his antagonists and escaping unharmed. And Sieber the prankster would have been delighted at the joke Thompson had pulled on half of Globe. It was a long time before the details of the Negro's escape became known, and they have never been printed until now.

Thompson had told a deputy, Jack Knight, to slip the prisoner out by way of a back entrance, a sheet-iron basement door of the jail, while the Sheriff was standing off the mob in front. Knight took Willie to an old-fashioned outhouse behind the Baptist Church, a block away. He was held there until things quieted down. Thompson had arranged for a handcar to be put at the trestle over the creek, behind some store buildings three blocks north of the courthouse. The little group made its way, by a devious route, of course, to the trestle, where Baldwin was told to lie flat on the handcar and gunny sacks were heaped over him. While the frustrated mob swirled through the main street of Globe, the handcar was pumped east a dozen miles to an overpass on the Safford Road. There the officers and their prisoner slipped from the vehicle, rolled it off the main track, and lay quietly in the shadows. The sheriff had arranged for the night passenger train to stop here at Knight's signal. Baldwin was bundled aboard and taken safely to the Graham County Jail at Solomonsville. He was held there, and at Tucson, beyond reach of his immediate enemies.

Willie Baldwin was tried in March. It took the jury all of ten minutes to find him guilty. On Friday, July 12, 1907, he went to the gallows on the grassless yard of the courthouse at Solomonsville. But he hadn't been lynched, Henry Thompson noted with satisfaction.

For Sieber and his Apaches, the Baldwin affair was a mere incident, interrupting momentarily the monotony of their days. Foot by foot, yard by yard, they and other Indian work gangs pushed the Tonto Road northward from the camp. Brush had to be cleared, rocks, some of them as big as a cookshack, moved out of the way, and there was always dirt to be shoveled. Work with the road gang was not arduous for Al; his job simply was to be there with a word of guidance now and then, for the Apaches were good workmen and needed little prodding. Each day they filed silently out of camp and swiftly climbed the mountainside path to the lengthening road as Sieber limped along behind. His leg probably was bothering him more now than it had been; there also was a twinge of arthritis at times. He hadn't written to Louise for more than a year, and he corresponded with no one else at all. If he did, there is no record of it.

Perhaps because of a strange loneliness, Al apparently turned toward the bottle anew. He purchased a bottle of "barel whiskey" from John D. Cline for $1.25 on November 15,[9] a two-dollar bottle of Green River on December 1, and two-dollar bottles of Old Crow on December 11 and 15. Then, after the first of the year, he bought more of it: two bottles of Old Crow on January 2, two more on the seventh and a couple on the fifteenth. If he purchased any after that, he paid cash for it.

Al's housekeeping bills didn't suffer meanwhile. He boarded with R. E. Frashier for about $14.25 a month, but must have done considerable cooking at his own A tent. He bought two pounds of peaches for forty cents and a quarter's worth of sugar on January 28; two hundred pounds of flour for $7.75, two dollars' worth of coffee, three dollars' worth of sugar, fifteen cents' worth of salt, and sixty cents' worth of tobacco early in February. From John Belser he bought forty-five pounds of meat for $4.50. He also purchased a two-dollar hat, an eight-dollar suitcase, a quilt for $2.50, and a complete outfit of work clothing for $5.00.

This doesn't add up to much, but Al's medical bills were very high for that time and place. The probate record shows that Dr. F. C. Pennell treated Sieber daily from November 17, 1906, to January 11, 1907, and four times a week from then until February 19, with the total bill coming to $178.25, on which Al paid $25.00 on January 30. It is not surprising that he sought a pension and government medical assistance.

Sieber must occasionally have thought of the old Indian fighters he had known and campaigned with. Their day was gone forever. It would never return—not in Arizona, not in Apachería, not in the

[9] Probate File 270, 1907, Globe Courthouse Records.

whole limitless Southwest. There wasn't a hostile this side of the Sierra Madre now, and not an outlaw, either, worthy of the name. The country was settled and, for old Indian fighters, finished. So were most of them. Ed Peck was living out his time in Nogales, down on the border, almost broke despite the million-dollar mine he had located and lost through litigation. C. E. Cooley and Mickey Free were over around Fort Apache someplace, but on the winter side of life. Archie McIntosh had died of cancer March 6, 1902, near San Carlos and had been buried right there. Dan O'Leary was dead, too. He died at Needles on January 20, 1900, of "exhaustion," it was said. An odd thing, that—who had ever heard of lively Dan O'Leary being exhausted? Willard Rice died in 1899 and Charley Spencer had been killed and General Crook and John Bourke were gone. Sam Bowman was shot from ambush, whispers had it, over near Fort Apache as he left the army with his accumulated pay in his pocket. Others were gone, too. There never would be any more men like them because there never would be any more work with which to train such men and which only they could do. A man just kept on doing what he could, and when his time came, he wouldn't have to try any more.

February 19, 1907, dawned like most winter days in central Arizona: bright and chilly. The Indian work gangs soon were strung out along the route of the high road, busying themselves at their various tasks. Frazier's band was the next beyond Sieber's. Al's Indians were worrying at one of the monstrous rocks athwart the route: it had to be moved. It was a rounded boulder of considerable size and must have weighed five or six tons. For more than a day the Apaches had been undercutting it on the downhill side and prying at it from above, but they couldn't get it to roll down the mountainside. Sieber idly watched them most of the morning and into the afternoon. It was getting late. Soon it would be time to knock off for the day, and that would mean leaving this job to be completed tomorrow. Sieber didn't like to leave a job unfinished. Once more his Indians pried at it from above, but the rock wouldn't budge. "Wait a minute," Al told his crew. "I'll see what's the trouble."

The old scout painfully hobbled down the slope, peering into the excavation, probing it with a stick, and then crawled out of sight under the great monolith. Suddenly it seemed to shudder, eased forward almost imperceptibly, then, with irresistible momentum, crashed down the slope, flattening everything in its path. The thirty Indians on the upper edge stared, horror stricken. The rock had apparently rolled of its own volition.[10] They rushed forward to cluster about the crushed body of the old man, setting up a moan that carried to Frazier's gang up the slope. Thad came running; so did his Indians. But they were too late.

The indomitable spirit of the ancient fighter had finally been crushed out of him. Al had made no sound. He had died as he had lived, with no fears, no lingering, no complaints. Al Sieber, immigrant, soldier, lawman, prospector, Indian fighter—a man—was off on his last adventure.

[10] There is some scattered dissent to this picture of the scout's last moments. I have been told, by a border adventurer, that the Apaches *pushed* the rock down on Sieber. The informant said he was told this by the Indians themselves during a drinking bout at a later date. "Indians will tell you things when they are drunk that they wouldn't say otherwise," he said. In view of the general lack of supporting evidence, I have not used this in my textual account, however, but include it here for what it may be worth. W. H. Napier, who served in the Arizona Cavalry after the Indian troubles were over, wrote to a comrade: "Al Sieber was killed. . . . Was it an accident? Some of the old timers shake their heads. He had some enemies among the Apaches." The letter to Marvin C. Hepler is dated August 1, 1956, and is in the possession of William T. Corbusier. Both Napier and Hepler were enlisted men in the Fourteenth Cavalry.

XXVI. Afterward

UNDERTAKER FRED JONES AND AL WILLIAMSON, Sieber's long-time friend, made the sorrowful journey from Globe to bring back the scout's broken body. The report of his death had been flashed to every part of the Territory and carried by wire services across the nation. Veteran Indian fighters, soldiers who had served with him, men of low and high position, all were saddened at the news. The Indians, Lee Middleton said, "carried on something awful." "The Apache Indians all over Arizona mourned his loss sincerely," wrote Dan Williamson. "There was weeping among the older Indians from San Carlos to Fort Apache, and to this day if you show any of the older Indians a picture of Al Sieber they look on it with awe and reverence."[1]

George W. P. Hunt, who was to serve an unequaled number of terms as governor of Arizona, was then a member of the Arizona Territorial Legislature. He submitted a resolution[2] which that body adopted by a unanimous rising vote as it adjourned for the day in respect of Sieber:

It has been learned that the slip of a cliff of rock on the road now building at the Tonto Storage Reservoir, resulted yesterday in the death of Al Sieber, late Chief of Scouts under General Crook, and for thirty years one of the bravest and most efficient servants of Arizona in her Apache wars. He was one of the ablest scouts ever enlisted and his counsel and advice did much to settle the long war with the Indians. He held to the day of his death the respect and confidence of every Indian who had ever

1 Williamson, "Sieber," 74.
2 Said to have been written by Sharlot Hall. Lockwood, "Sieber," 38–39.

fought with him or against him, and the respect and regard of every man and woman to whom he was known.

The full measure of his service to Arizona is a story that will never be told, for it is known to no one person, but his name will live as long as we have a history, and as long as brave deeds are cherished in the memory of men.

I, therefore, move you, that when we now adjourn, we do so with expressions of respect for this brave man now at rest and out of respect to his memory, and that such expressions of respect be embodied in the minutes of this council.[3]

Meanwhile, an inquest was held, with Judge Evans as ex officio coroner. Edgar Sultan, Thad Frazier and his brother, L. L. Frazier, Jay Louche, who was a driller, cattleman Henry Cooper, and one other man[4] served on the jury. Dr. Pennell testified that Sieber had apparently wrenched over on his side as the rock began to move but that death must have been almost instantaneous. His right side was smashed. The inquest report says that the thorax on that side and the right leg below the knee were "completely crushed," and both bones were broken in his right forearm. The verdict, as was to be expected, was accidental death.

The remains reached the F. L. Jones & Co. Mortuary at Globe late on February 20, and the funeral was set for two o'clock on the afternoon of Friday, February 22, with members of the Grand Army of the Republic and veterans of Indian wars especially invited. The *Silver Belt* printed an unsigned poem in warm and neighborly tribute to Sieber:

> Go, bring the grand old warrior in
> He who helped forge this glorious West
> And make it so that you and I
> Might live and see it at its best.

> God knows what he had suffered
> What dangers he had braved
> That we might go in safety
> Upon our special ways.

[3] *Journals of the 24th Legislative Assembly of the Territory of Arizona*, 121.

[4] His name, signed to the report, is not clearly decipherable, but may have been "Derrihecton." He cannot now be identified.

O Thou, who guides our every thought
Strange Thou would let him live
Through battle's smoke and desert's glare
To die so tame a death.

Be merciful to him, Oh God,
The calm, great child who's gone,
Whose life's long work availed him not
But those who live reap from.

County Treasurer Dan Williamson heard of the tragedy while at work in the Wells Fargo Express office, where he was also agent for that company. He immediately passed the hat among old associates to collect funds for a suitable memorial. "Do you know," he related afterwards, "there were not two men that would give anything?"[5]

This contrasted curiously with the "largely attended" funeral, one of the big turnouts in Globe's early history. Services were conducted by the G.A.R. in the small mortuary chapel, which measured only twenty-five by one hundred feet, at the corner of Sycamore and Broad streets just south of the Dominion Hotel. The chapel was packed, and still more people, unable to squeeze inside, exchanged Sieber anecdotes with acquaintances while awaiting the procession to the cemetery's G.A.R. plot.

The reason for Williamson's failure to collect from Al's friends does not suggest community-wide disapproval. Old-timers agree that Sieber was better liked and as highly respected as almost anyone else in Globe at this time. He had very few close friends but innumerable warm acquaintances; men and women alike enjoyed his company. The most logical explanation would seem to be that the notion of a memorial seemed out of place to those who remembered Al's distaste for publicity.

Within the mortuary, Sieber lay in state, a silken, gold-tasseled American flag, nine by twelve feet in size, folded across his breast as "a fitting tribute to a man who had given twenty-four years of the best part of his life in active service beneath its starry folds."[6] It was buried with him in the stony hillside grave.

[5] Lockwood APHS.
[6] Williamson, "Sieber," 74.

Although Al was raised a Catholic and was not without devout moments during his later life, even if he is not known to have attended a Mass or entered a Catholic church during all his years in Arizona, the funeral oration was delivered by the Reverend R. W. Durham of the Globe Baptist Church. Perhaps it was because no one knew what his faith had been; even his close associates could not recall that he ever mentioned religion. He, along with many others, had taken in the occasional camp meetings up in Tonto Basin and seemed to enjoy them, but religion did not appear ever to have occupied much of a place in his life, aside, perhaps, from his private thoughts.

Scarcely had the body of the veteran scout been laid to rest before Hunt introduced in the legislature a bill to appropriate one hundred dollars for a monument over Sieber's grave. In a letter he described the stone, which may be seen in the Globe cemetery to this day. "The work was completed on the 25th day of July," he wrote. "The monument is in two sections (one being the base) and the weight is 2,350 pounds. It is five feet six inches high, with only the face polished; it in a manner represents the rugged qualities of the gallant old Indian scout."[7] It was inscribed:

In Memoriam
Erected
by the
Territory
of Arizona
1907
to
Al Sieber
Born 1844
Died 1907

But Sieber, if he could have known of it, would probably have been even more pleased by the second monument raised to his memory—fashioned out of native stone by Apache laborers under direction of Construction Engineer Smith of the Reclamation Service and raised on the spot where Al met his death. Of the tawny color of the sun-

7 Unidentified clipping in Sieber Collection, Sharlot Hall Museum, Prescott.

blasted hills, it has since been moved to the other side of the road, but still is within twenty feet of the site, a mile toward Payson from the dam on the high road above the lake. Its faded inscription, still readable, says:

AL SIEBER
A Veteran of the Civil
War and for twenty
years a leader of
scouts for the U.S.
Army in Arizona Ind
ian troubles. Was
killed on this spot
February 19th 1907
by a falling rock dur
ing construction of
the Tonto Road.

His body is buried
in the cemetery at
Globe

Nor are these cold stone markers all that remain to his memory. Sieber Creek was named for him at least as early as 1879, when it first appears on a map. It is a pleasant little stream, at that time grass edged and shaded, flowing south from Green Valley in Gila County. It enters Wild Rye Creek at Gibson's Ranch, about twenty-five miles south of old Mazatzal City on the East Fork of the Verde. Sieber Creek is not, however, shown on any but the most detailed maps today.

To perpetuate his name further, Will Barnes suggested to the U.S. Board of Geographic Names that some promontory in Grand Canyon be named for Al, and in 1932 this was done.[8] Unfortunately, the name for the point was spelled "Seiber," and the paragraph of explanation in the record notes that it was "named for Al. Seiber, noted chief of scouts under General Crook for many years during the Apache Indian wars, 1868–1873," which is about as fat a collection of misstate-

[8] *Decisions of the U.S. Geographic Board*, No. 19, p. 10.

406

ments as can be readily compressed into a single official sentence. The errors were pointed out to Frank Bond, who served as chairman of the Board from 1926 to 1934, but with no discernible result.

Seiber Point, situated at latitude 36° 18′N., longitude 111° 57′W., is in the northeast corner of Grand Canyon National Park one and one-quarter miles south, by crow's flight, of Saddle Mountain, a peak directly on the northern boundary. At the same distance south of 6,400-foot Seiber Point is Bourke Point; southeast an equal distance is Marion Point, named for the Prescott editor; and southwest of Seiber Point, also a mile and one-fourth from it, is another promontory, this one named for King Woolsey, misspelled "Woosley" on the Geological Survey's 1:48,000 map of the park. Farther south are many other points and buttes named for such worthy Arizona characters as Jack Swilling; Oscar Hutton, who, Thomas E. Farish said, had the reputation of having personally killed more Indians than anyone else in the Territory; Darrell Duppa, the mysterious Englishman; A. F. Banta; Tom Jeffords; Cochise; Navaho trader Lorenzo Hubbell; Charles Poston; and many others. It is a laudable idea, this commemoration in nature's grandeur, but the pioneers' names ought to be spelled right. At least the custom is more praiseworthy than the fad which splattered masterpieces of the great gorge with such monstrous titles as Shiva Temple, Cheops Pyramid, Hindu Amphitheater, Zoroaster Temple, Tower of Set, and so on. Barnes doesn't dignify any of these cartographic aberrations with even a mention in his *Arizona Place Names*, attesting to his inherent good taste.

As might be supposed, Al Sieber left no estate of any consequence, although there were a number of mining claims in which he had some interest. He had a one-fifth interest in the Hal and Al, Dan and Mack, Monroe Doctrine, Arbitration, Lost Coon, Fraction, Wedge, Sure Thing, Iron Cap, and the Monroe Doctrine Wellsight claims in Gila County, and from these his estate ultimately received a total of one thousand dollars. His half-interest in three Salt River claims, the Sulphide No. 1, Sulphide No. 2, and Sulphide No. 3, never amounted to anything, although they had been appraised at five hundred dollars each. They "were not worth doing the [assessment] work on," as Al Williamson, the administrator, said. In addition, Al had an interest in both the Last Chance and the Blackbird claims in Del Shay Basin.

Al's personal property was also negligble. His two tents and appurtenances were valued at thirty-seven dollars, his riding saddle and bridle at ten dollars, and a Winchester rifle at five dollars. His bay saddle horse, Al's most treasured possession, was valued at seventy-five dollars, and he also had a roan worth twenty-five dollars. The silver-cased watch he carried at his death and which was dented by the boulder that crushed out his life was estimated to be worth three dollars. Bud Armer got it, and his wife, Maggie, has kept it through the years.[9] And that was about the sum total of the earthly possessions of this empire builder.

Al Williamson thought Al's estate should receive thirty dollars, which sum the government allowed at that time for the funeral expenses of veterans, but was informed that it was not applicable in this case, since it was granted only to a widow or minor child or if the deceased had not left sufficient funds to cover such expenses. So this veteran of twenty-five years of unmatched service was granted nothing for burial expenses. It made no real difference, of course, since he had paid his bills and there was no needy person to leave it to.

Of debts there were enough to match his holdings. With his bills all paid, there remained only a very small balance. So Al Sieber went out of this world as he came into it: broke, but owing not a dime to anyone, while leaving scarcely more in cash. What he had left, however, could scarcely be measured in dollars anyway. His legacy—in fact, that of the whole unmatchable agglomeration of which he was but an example—was an empire, snatched from the tigers of the human race, defended against the most murderous onslaughts any frontier had to face, and made secure so that prosperity and peace and gentleness could come to those who followed.

The savage, hard-bitten Indian fighters of Al Sieber's ilk had come to Apachería when its whites could be numbered in hundreds and its women in scores, the whites huddled in their mud and pole settlements, fearful of every shadow, themselves on reservations, and the Indians in control of the country. These white warriors went boldly into the haunts of the enemy, matched him wile for wile, cruelty

[9] Probate File 270, 1907, Globe Courthouse Records.

for cruelty, ambuscade for ambuscade, and death for death until he was whipped from the valleys, hurled from the peaks, smashed in his caves, battered, bloodied, and utterly defeated and herded onto reservations so that the white settlers, in their turn, could have the country. Right was not always on the side of the whites, but might ultimately was, and, right or wrong, might or weakness, they accomplished the inevitable.

I realize that it is fashionable in this day to blame all of the Indian troubles upon the whites, in contrast to an earlier time when the whites could do no wrong and the Indian was responsible for all frontier turmoil. At that time, even to suggest that the Indian had a case or that the whites were partly to blame or that a measure of reason and justice might make the use of force less necessary was dismissed with charges of "silly sentimentalism" and "interference with the manifest destiny of the superior race."

It is true, I suppose, that both sides were pushed by inexorable forces. White expansion into the largely vacant lands over which the Indian had roamed was more or less inevitable, but the means by which the white man made his advance were not foreordained, and it is with those means that I have my quarrel. Because the white was the aggressor, because he was usually motivated by the less attractive impulses, his case is weakened. At least in retrospect it seems thus.

Much of the brutality, much of the ruthlessness, much of the killing was unnecessary and evil. Everything that was done could have been done another way, as has been demonstrated elsewhere. There can be no excuse for treachery, whether white or Indian, for murder, double-dealing, corruption and dishonesty, merciless exploitation, hypocrisy, deliberate starvation, mercenary motives outweighing common morality, the slaughter of noncombatants, killing for sport or in order to acquire a reputation, unwillingness to judge another race by standards set for one's own. Each of these charges could be supported with evidence against the whites. Many of them could against the Indians. If the background of each people is carefully weighed, however, the moral advantage was perhaps on the side of the Indian. What he did was done because he was taught to do it through his cultural background or was goaded into it by evil white men. What the white man

409

did was done for vengeance, from fear, or because of less worthy motives.

Some of these matters must have been in the minds of those who "largely attended" Sieber's burial on that bleak and narrow ridge near Globe. And on the whole, they must have been satisfied with what they knew of his career. For, on the whole, it was good.

Bibliography

MANUSCRIPT MATERIALS, UNPUBLISHED DOCUMENTS, PHOTOGRAPHS

Arizona Pioneers' Historical Society Archives, Tucson. Files of or pertaining to Edward Arhelger, Albert F. Banta, Will C. Barnes, Charles F. Bennett, Mike Burns, Ed Clark, Corydon E. Cooley, William H. Corbusier, George Crook, Mickey Free, J. C. Hancock, Frank C. Lockwood, Nelson A. Miles, Carlos Montezuma, Dan O'Leary, Al Sieber, and Dan Williamson. George Crook, "The Apache Problem," typescript in Arizona Pioneers' Historical Museum. Joseph F. Fish, *History of Arizona*, unpublished manuscript.

Arizona State Department of Library and Archives, Phoenix. Newspapers, including a microfilm file of the *Arizona Silver Belt*, and some documents.

Bancroft Library, Berkeley, California. Vast newspaper file and many Arizona manuscripts, none relating directly to Sieber.

Bennett, Mrs. Lillian Taylor, Minneapolis, Minnesota. Collection of Sieber letters and related papers, many photographs.

Connor, Mrs. J. F., Englewood, New Jersey. Collection of Britton Davis' correspondence, including material from Thomas Cruse, George Morgan, George Converse, and other Arizona Indian fighters.

Corbusier, W. T., Long Beach, California. Many papers, including documents relative to Dr. William H. Corbusier, George O. Eaton, and Charles King.

Davis, Mrs. Sydney K., Atlanta, Georgia. Photographs and some recollections of Sieber.

French, Albert Francis, Los Angeles, California. Documents and photographs relating to John Townsend.

Gila County Courthouse, Globe, Arizona. Minutes of the Second Judicial District Court, Book 2, 1889, concerning Sieber's naturalization. District Court, Second Judicial District, October Term, 1889, concerning the trial of the Apache Kid on October 25, 26, and 29, 1889. Probate File 270, 1907, pertaining to the Sieber estate.

Huntington Library, San Marino, California. Papers of Walter Schuyler, including letters from Crook, a log and other documents relating to Schuyler's scouting days in Arizona, letters to his father describing his adventures, military orders, and other papers. A. H. Nickerson, *Major General George Crook and the Indians*, an unpublished manuscript.

Library of Congress, Washington, D.C. August V. Kautz Diary, 1876 to 1878. Leonard Wood Diary, 1886. Wood's handwritten narrative of the 1886 Apache campaign into Mexico.

Los Angeles Public Library. Two books of clippings from newspapers of the 1860's, 1870's, and 1880's relating to Indian affairs in Arizona.

McNelly, Mrs. Ben, Redwood City, California. Photographs and recollections of Sieber and early Globe days.

Middleton, Leroy, Phoenix, Arizona. Photographs and recollections relating to Pleasant Valley and the Apache Kid affair.

Oswald, Austin H., Palo Alto, California. Photographs and some clippings and recollections of Sieber.

Phoenix Public Library. Some of James H. McClintock's papers, including one or two documents and photographs relating to Sieber.

Rutherford B. Hayes Memorial Library, Fremont, Ohio. Collection of hundreds of Crook documents, including *Annual Reports*, official reports, letters, and other papers covering his service in Arizona in 1871–76 and 1882–86.

Sharlot Hall Historical Museum, Prescott, Arizona. Collections of documents and clippings, as well as photographs, relating to C. C. Bean, Dan O'Leary, Ed Peck, Willard Rice, Al Sieber, Charley Spencer, and others.

Southwest Museum Library, Los Angeles, California. Munk Collection of Arizoniana, including more than one thousand articles, books, pamphlets, and other documents.

United States Government. National Archives and Records Service, Civil War Branch. Department of Arizona, Letters Received, 1868–1893; Letters Sent, 1868–1893; Quartermaster Payrolls, Department of Arizona, 1871–1890; Record Group 94. Department of Interior, Bureau of Pensions, military records of veterans applying for pensions. Department of Interior, Bureau of Indian Affairs, Camp Verde, Letters Received, 1872–1876; San Carlos, Letters Received, 1876–1891; John P. Clum, *Annual Reports*, 1874–1877; Record Group 75. Judge Advocate General, Records Received, 4475, January 17, 1888, Court Martial of 1st Sergeant

Kid, transcript. United States Senate, 51st Cong., 1st sess., Sen. Exec. Doc. 88, "Letter from Secretary of War transmitting correspondence regarding Apache Indians"; House Report 1084, 1914, "Indian War History of the Army during the years 1865–1886, compiled from War Department Records."

University of Oregon Library, Eugene. Collection of about seventy-five Crook letters and related documents.

Woody, Mrs. Clara T., Miami, Arizona. Wealth of documents on central Arizona history, including, particularly, matters relating to King S. Woolsey and the Pleasant Valley War.

Government Publications

American Decorations: A List of Awards of the Congressional Medal of Honor, the Distinguished-Service Cross and the Distinguished-Service Medal, Awarded Under Authority of the Congress of the United States: 1862–1926. Washington, Government Printing Office, 1927.

Bourke, John G. "Medicine-Men of the Apache," Bureau of American Ethnology, *Ninth Annual Report.* Washington, 1892.

Chronological List of Actions, &c., with Indians, from January 1, 1866, to January, 1891. Washington, Adjutant General's Office, 1891.

Crook, George. *Resume of Operations Against Apache Indians, 1882–1886.* Washington, 1886.

Decisions of the U.S. Geographic Board, No. 19. "Decisions Rendered May 4, 1932, Grand Canyon National Park, Arizona." Washington, Government Printing Office, 1932.

Heitman, Francis Bernard. *Historical Register and Dictionary of the United States Army, from its Organization, September 29, 1789, to March 2, 1903.* 2 vols. Washington, Government Printing Office, 1903.

Hodge, Frederick Webb. *Handbook of American Indians North of Mexico.* 2 vols. Washington, Government Printing Office, 1907.

Journals of the 24th Legislative Assembly of the Territory of Arizona. Phoenix, 1907.

Palmer, William Jackson. *Report of Surveys Across the Continent in 1867–'68.* Washington, Government Printing Office, 1869.

Record of Engagements with Hostile Indians Within the Military Division of the Missouri, from 1868 to 1882, Compiled from Official Records. Washington, Government Printing Office, 1882.

U.S. Board of Indian Commissioners. Peace with the Apaches of New Mex-

ico and Arizona. Report of Vincent Colyer, Member of Board—1871. Washington, Government Printing Office, 1872.

NEWSPAPERS

Barnesville, Minnesota, *Record-Review.*
Florence-Tucson, Arizona, *Enterprise.*
Globe, Arizona, *Arizona Silver Belt.*
Holbrook, Arizona, *Holbrook Argus.*
Los Angeles, California, *Los Angeles Times.*
Los Angeles, California, *Star.*
Minneapolis, Minnesota, *Tribune.*
Phoenix, Arizona, *Arizona Gazette.*
Phoenix, Arizona, *Arizona Republican.*
Prescott, Arizona, *Arizona Miner.*
Prescott, Arizona, *Prescott Evening Courier.*
Prescott, Arizona, *Prescott Morning Courier.*
Prescott, Arizona, *Prescott Weekly Courier.*
Tombstone, Arizona, *Epitaph.*
Tombstone, Arizona, *Prospector.*
Treasure City, Nevada, *White Pine News.*
Tucson, Arizona, *Arizona Citizen.*
Tucson, Arizona, *Arizona Star.*

PRIMARY SOURCES

Betzinez, Jason. *I Fought With Geronimo.* Harrisburg, The Stackpole Company, 1959.

Bourke, John G. *An Apache Campaign in the Sierra Madre.* New York, Charles Scribner's Sons, 1886. New ed., 1958.

———. *On the Border With Crook.* New York, Charles Scribner's Sons, 1891. Reprinted by Long's College Book Company, Columbus, Ohio, 1958.

Clum, Woodworth. *Apache Agent.* Boston, Houghton Mifflin Company, 1936.

Conner, Daniel Ellis. *Joseph Reddeford Walker and the Arizona Adventure.* Ed. by Donald J. Berthrong and Odessa Davenport. Norman, University of Oklahoma Press, 1956.

Crook, George. *General George Crook: His Autobiography.* Ed. by Martin F. Schmitt. Norman, University of Oklahoma Press, 1946. New ed., 1960.

Cruse, Thomas. *Apache Days and After*. Caldwell, Idaho, The Caxton Press, 1941.

Davis, Britton. *The Truth About Geronimo*. New Haven, Yale University Press, 1929.

Forsyth, George A. *Thrilling Days in Army Life*. New York, Harper & Brothers, 1900.

Gatewood, Charles B. "The Surrender of Geronimo," *Proceedings of the Annual Meeting and Dinner of the Order of Indian Wars of the United States*. Washington, 1929.

Horn, Tom. *Life of Tom Horn: A Vindication*. Denver, The Louthan Company, 1904. Privately printed.

Price, George F. *Across the Continent with the Fifth Cavalry*. New York, Antiquarian Press, Ltd., 1959.

Rogers, Robert. *Journals of Major Robert Rogers*. New York, Corinth Books, 1961.

Schurz, Carl. *The Reminiscences of Carl Schurz*. 3 vols. New York, Doubleday, Page & Company, 1913.

Summerhayes, Martha. *Vanished Arizona*. Chicago, The Lakeside Press, 1939.

SECONDARY SOURCES

Angel, Myron (ed.). *History of Nevada*. Oakland, Thompson and West, 1881.

Bancroft, Hubert Howe. *History of Arizona and New Mexico*. San Francisco, The History Company, 1889.

———. *History of California*. 7 vols. San Francisco, The History Company, 1884–90.

Banning, Captain William, and George Hugh Banning. *Six Horses*. New York, The Century Company, 1930.

Barnes, Will Croft. *Apaches and Longhorns*. Los Angeles, Ward Ritchie Press, 1941.

———. *Arizona Place Names*. Tucson, University of Arizona, 1935. 2nd ed., revised and enlarged by Byrd H. Granger, University of Arizona Press, 1960.

Brandes, Ray. *Frontier Military Posts of Arizona*. Globe, Dale Stuart King, Publisher, 1960.

Burns, Walter Noble. *Tombstone: An Iliad of the Southwest*. New York, Penguin Books, Inc., 1942.

Carter, William Harding. *From Yorktown to Santiago with the Sixth Cavalry*. Baltimore, The Lord Baltimore Press, 1900.

———. *The Life of Lieutenant General Chaffee*. Chicago, University of Chicago Press, 1917.

Coolidge, Dane. *Fighting Men of the West*. New York, E. P. Dutton and Company, 1932.

Cullum, George W. *Biographical Register of the Officers and Graduates of the U.S. Military Academy at West Point, N.Y.* 8 vols. Boston, Houghton, Mifflin and Company, 1891–1910.

Davis, Samuel Post (ed.) *The History of Nevada*. 2 vols. Los Angeles, The Elms Publishing Company, 1913.

Dictionary of American Biography. 22 vols. New York, Charles Scribner's Sons, 1958.

Dunn, J. P., Jr. *Massacres of the Mountains*. New York, Archer House, Inc., n.d.

Farish, Thomas Edwin. *History of Arizona*. 8 vols. San Francisco, The Filmer Brothers Electrotype Company, 1915–18.

Folsom, W. H. C. *Fifty Years in the Northwest*. St. Paul, Pioneer Press Company, 1888.

Fowler, Gene. *Timberline*. New York, Blue Ribbon Books, 1940.

Forbes, Jack D. *Apache, Navaho, and Spaniard*. Norman, University of Oklahoma Press, 1960.

Forrest, Earle R. *Arizona's Dark and Bloody Ground*. Caldwell, The Caxton Printers, 1936.

Haight, Theron Wilber. *Three Wisconsin Cushings*. Madison, Wisconsin History Commission, 1910.

Halleran, E. E. *Crimson Desert*. New York, Ballantine Books, 1962.

Hamilton, Patrick. *The Resources of Arizona*. 3rd ed. San Francisco, A. L. Bancroft & Company, 1884.

Hanna, Phil Townsend. *The Dictionary of California Land Names*. Los Angeles, Automobile Club of Southern California, 1946.

Hayes, Jess G. *Apache Vengeance*. Albuquerque, University of New Mexico Press, 1954.

Hinton, Richard G. *The Handbook to Arizona*. San Francisco, Payot, Upham & Company, 1878. Reprinted by Arizona Silhouettes, Tucson, 1954.

Hunt, Aurora. *The Army of the Pacific*. Glendale, The Arthur H. Clark Company, 1951.

Jackson, Orick. *The White Conquest of Arizona*. Los Angeles, The Grafton Company, 1908.

King, Charles. *The Colonel's Daughter; or, Winning His Spurs.* Philadelphia, J. B. Lippincott Company, 1890.

——. *Sunset Pass; or, Running the Gauntlet Through Apache Land.* New York, John W. Lovell Company, 1890.

——. *Tonio, Son of the Sierras.* New York, G. W. Dillingham Company, 1906.

Klein, H. M. J. (ed.). *Lancaster County, Pennsylvania: A History.* 2 vols. New York and Chicago, Lewis Historical Publishing Company, Inc., 1924.

Lockwood, Frank C. *The Apache Indians.* New York, The Macmillan Company, 1938.

——. *More Arizona Characters.* Tucson, University of Arizona, 1943.

Lutrell, Estelle. *Newspapers and Periodicals of Arizona 1859–1911.* Tucson, University of Arizona, 1950.

McClintock, James H. *Arizona: Prehistoric, Aboriginal, Pioneer, Modern.* 3 vols. Chicago, S. J. Clarke Publishing Company, 1916.

Mercer, A. S. *The Banditti of the Plains; or, the Cattlemen's Invasion of Wyoming in 1892.* Norman, University of Oklahoma Press, 1954.

Miles, Nelson A. *Personal Recollections.* New York and Chicago, The Werner Company, 1897.

Miller, Joseph. *The Arizona Story.* New York, Hastings House, 1952.

Minnesota in the Civil and Indian Wars 1861–1865. 2 vols. St. Paul, Pioneer Press Company, 1891 and 1899.

National Cyclopædia of American Biography. 20 vols. New York, James T. White & Company, 1898–1926.

Neill, Edward Duffield. *The History of Minnesota from the Earliest French Explorations to the Present Time.* 4th ed. Minneapolis, Minnesota Historical Company, 1882.

O'Connor, Richard. *Wild Bill Hickok: A Biography of James Butler Hickok, the West's Greatest Gunfighter.* New York, Doubleday & Company, Inc., 1959.

Ogle, Ralph Hedrick. *Federal Control of the Western Apaches: 1848–1886.* Albuquerque, University of New Mexico Press, 1940.

Peplow, Edward Hadduck. *History of Arizona.* 3 vols. New York, Lewis Historical Publishing Company, 1958.

Remington, Frederic. *Crooked Trails.* New York, Harper & Brothers, 1899.

Rice, William B. *The Los Angeles Star 1851–1864.* Berkeley, University of California Press, 1947.

Robinson, W. W. *The Story of San Bernardino County.* San Bernardino, Pioneer Title Insurance Company, 1958.

Roddis, Louis H. *The Indian Wars of Minnesota*. Cedar Rapids, The Torch Press, 1956.

Russell, Don. *The Lives and Legends of Buffalo Bill*. Norman, University of Oklahoma Press, 1960.

Rynning, Thomas H. *Gun Notches*. New York, Stokes, 1931.

Santee, Ross. *Apache Land*. New York, Bantam Books, 1956.

Shay, Emma Freeland. *Mariet Hardy Freeland: A Faithful Witness*. Chicago, The Free Methodist Publishing House, 1913.

Sloan, Richard E. *Memories of an Arizona Judge*. Stanford, Stanford University Press, 1932.

Sparks, William. *The Apache Kid, a Bear Fight and Other True Stories of the Old West*. Los Angeles, Skelton Publishing Company, 1926.

Stackpole, General Edward J., and Colonel Wilbur S. Nye. *The Battle of Gettysburg: A Guided Tour*. Harrisburg, The Stackpole Company, 1960.

Waters, Frank. *The Earp Brothers of Tombstone*. New York, Clarkson N. Potter, Inc., 1960.

Wellman, Paul I. *Broncho Apache*. New York, The Macmillan Company, 1936.

Wells, Edmund. *Argonaut Tales*. New York, Frederick H. Hitchcock, The Grafton Press, 1927.

Who Was Who. Chicago, The A. N. Marquis Company, 1943.

Willson, Roscoe G. *No Room for Angels*. Phoenix, *Arizona Republic*, 1958.

———. *Pioneer and Well Known Cattlemen of Arizona*. 2 vols. Phoenix, Valley National Bank, 1951 and 1956.

Wilson, Neill C., and Frank J. Taylor. *Southern Pacific: The Roaring Story of a Fighting Railroad*. New York, McGraw Hill Book Company, 1952.

Wyllys, Rufus Kay. *Arizona, the History of a Frontier State*. Phoenix, Hobson & Herr, 1950.

ARTICLES AND ESSAYS

Barnes, Will Croft. "The Apaches' Last Stand in Arizona," *Arizona Historical Review*, Vol. III, No. 4 (January, 1931), 36–59.

Barney, James M. "The Townsend Expedition," *Arizona Highways*, Vol. XIII, No. 3 (March, 1937), 12 *et seq.*

Bourke, John G. "General Crook in the Indian Country," *Century*, Vol. XLI, No. 5 (March, 1891), 643–60.

Clarke, Powhatan. "A Hot Trail," *Cosmopolitan Magazine*, Vol. XVII, No. 6 (October, 1894), 706–16.

Clum, John P. "Apache Misrule," *New Mexico Historical Review*, Vol. V, Nos. 2 and 3 (April and July, 1930).

————. "Eskiminzin," *New Mexico Historical Review*, Vol. III, No. 4 (October, 1928), and Vol. IV, No. 1 (January, 1929).

————. "Geronimo," *New Mexico Historical Review*, Vol. III, Nos. 1, 2, and 3 (January, April, and July, 1928).

————. "The San Carlos Police," *New Mexico Historical Review*, Vol. IV, No. 3 (July, 1929), and Vol. V, No. 1 (January, 1930).

————. "Victorio," *New Mexico Historical Review*, Vol. IV, No. 4 (October, 1929).

Corbusier, Dr. William F. "The Apache-Yumas and Apache-Mojaves," *The American Antiquarian*, Vol. VIII, No. 5 (September, 1886), 276–84.

Cubley, Clark A., and Joseph A. Steiner. "Emilio Kosterlitzky," *Arizoniana*, Vol. I, No. 4 (Winter, 1960), 12–14.

Daly, Henry W. "The Geronimo Campaign," *Journal of the United States Cavalry Association*, Vol. XIX, No. 69 (July, 1908), 68–103.

————. "Scouts Good and Bad," *American Legion Monthly*, Vol. V, No. 2 (August, 1928), 24–25, 66–70.

Davis, Britton. "The Difficulties of Indian Warfare," *Army-Navy Journal*, October 24, 1885.

Eaton, George O. "Stopping an Apache Battle," ed. by Don Russell, *Journal of the United States Cavalry Association*, Vol. XLII, No. 178 (July–August, 1933), 12–18.

Gatewood, Charles B., U.S.A. "Campaigning Against Victorio in 1879," *The Great Divide* (April, 1894), 102–104.

Hall, Sharlot. "The Making of a Great Mine," *Out West*, Vol. XXV, No. 1 (July, 1906), 3–26.

Hanna, Robert. "With Crawford in Mexico," *Clifton Clarion*, July 7 and 14, 1886. Reprinted in *Arizona Historical Review*, Vol. VI, No. 2 (April, 1935), 56–65.

Hoyt, Franklyn. "The Bradshaw Road," *Pacific Historical Review*, Vol. XXI, No. 3 (August, 1952), 243–54.

Johnson, Carl P. "A War Chief of the Tontos," *Overland Monthly*, Vol. XXVIII (Second Series), No. 167 (November, 1896), 528–32.

Judd, B. Ira. "The Apache Kid," *Arizona Highways*, Vol. XXIX, No. 9 (September, 1955).

McClintock, James H. "Fighting Apaches—A Narrative of the Fifth Cavalry's Deadly Conflict in the Superstition Mountains of Arizona," *Sunset* (February, 1907), 340–43.

Neill, Edward Duffield. "St. Paul and Its Environs," *Graham's Magazine*, Vol. XLVI (January, 1855), 3–17. Reprinted in *Minnesota History*, Vol. XXX, No. 3 (September, 1949), 203–19.

Opler, Morris E. "A Chiricahua Apache's Account of the Geronimo Campaign of 1886," *New Mexico Historical Review*, Vol. XIII, No. 4 (October, 1938).

Rope, John (as told to Grenville Goodwin). "Experiences of an Indian Scout," *Arizona Historical Review*, Vol. VII, No. 2 (April, 1936), 31–73.

Sonnichsen, C. L. "The Apache Kid," *Around Here, the Southwest in Picture and Story.* Vol. X, No. 1 (1952), 61–62.

Watson, James Waterman. "Scouting in Arizona, 1890," *Journal of the United States Cavalry Association*, Vol. X, No. 37 (June, 1897), 128–35.

Williamson, Dan R. "Al Sieber, Famous Scout of the Southwest," *Arizona Historical Review*, Vol. III, No. 4 (January, 1931), 60–76.

———. "The Apache Kid: Red Renegade of the West," *Arizona Highways*, Vol. XV, No. 5 (May, 1939), 14–15, 30–31.

Index